Pioneers
of Psychology

Pioneers
of Psychology

Second Edition

Raymond E. Fancher

YORK UNIVERSITY

W · W · NORTON & COMPANY

New York · London

The text of this book is composed in Baskerville.
Composition by JGH Composition, Inc.
Manufacturing by The Murray Printing Company.
Book design by Marjorie J. Flock.

Cover illustration: Descartes, René, in
"De Homine" from *Philosophical Works*,
Cambridge University Press, 1911.

Second Edition

Library of Congress Cataloging-in-Publication Data

Fancher, Raymond E.
    Pioneers of psychology / Raymond E. Fancher. — 2nd ed.
        p.   cm.
    Includes bibliographical references.
    1. Psychology — History.   2. Psychologists — History.   I. Title.
BF95.F3   1990
150′.92′2 — dc20   89-39158

ISBN 0-393-95648-2

W. W. Norton & Company, Inc., 500 Fifth Avenue, New York, N.Y. 10110
W. W. Norton & Company Ltd., 37 Great Russell Street, London WC1B 3NU

1 2 3 4 5 6 7 8 9 0

Still for Joëlle and Seth

Contents

Contents

Preface

This revised edition of *Pioneers of Psychology* has two main purposes: to bring the stories of the original edition's pioneers up to date in terms of burgeoning historical scholarship, and to expand coverage to include a larger number of historically significant individuals.

The first goal requires little explanation. The past decade has seen impressive growth in the study of psychology's history, encouraged by organizations such as Cheiron (The International Society for the History of the Behavioral and Social Sciences), the American Psychological Association's Division 26 (devoted to the history of psychology), and recently formed historical divisions in both the British Psychological Society and the Canadian Psychological Association. The *Journal of the History of the Behavioral Sciences* publishes a steady stream of quality articles and reviews in the field, and nonspecialty journals such as *American Psychologist*, *Canadian Psychology*, and the *British Journal of Psychology* welcome historical papers of general psychological interest. *Isis*, the official journal of the History of Science Society, and *The British Journal for the History of Science* both carry occasional articles on the history of psychology, along with reviews of the numerous important new textbooks and monographs in the field. The present volume attempts to share some of the new knowledge generated by these and other sources.

My second aim has been to expand coverage and more adequately sample the varied topics that constitute psychology, without losing the personalized focus on individual figures that won many readers' approval for the first edition. In the preface to that edition, I correctly predicted that while few psychologists would object to the choices of pioneers I had included, many would regret the *omission* of one or more of their favorites. Shortly after the book's publication, for example, I overheard an experimental psychologist friend quietly complain that he didn't see how *anyone* could write a book on the history of psychology and leave out Ebbinghaus. Some readers lamented the absence of obvious giants such as Darwin, Fechner, or Binet; and still others complained about my failure to mention important predecessors for some of the ideas I attributed to my original pioneers, or about the almost exclusively masculine makeup of that cast.

Upon reflection, and with added experience in teaching both introductory psychology and the history of psychology, I concluded that many of these comments not only had merit, but could be accommodated in an expanded and more tightly written edition that would retain the personal flavor of the original. My ever-tactful editors at Norton have taught me over the years that virtually *anything* can be rewritten to say just as much in fewer words. Thus this revision retains almost all of the substantive material from its predecessor, although expressed more succinctly so that the completely new sections do not excessively inflate the book's overall size.

The book's coverage is now sufficiently broad that it can comfortably stand by itself as a basic history of psychology text for one-term courses in which the instructor wishes to present a relatively in-depth treatment of selected and representative figures, as opposed to encyclopedic coverage of the field. The new sections deal with several topics of continuing importance in contemporary psychology, including psychophysics, verbal learning, evolutionary theory, intelligence, and cognitive processes. Thus the book's usefulness as a supplement to a full course in introductory psychology should also be enhanced.

In this revised edition, the opening chapter on "René Descartes and the Foundations of Modern Psychology" largely parallels its predecessor. A completely new Chapter 2 focuses on John Locke and Gottfried Leibniz, two seventeenth-century philosophers of mind who each reacted strongly to Descartes, but in highly contrasting ways that established enduring "empiricist" and "nativist" traditions in psychology. Many of their basic ideas also persist in modern cognitive psychology. Chapter 3 updates the old one on "Physiologists of Mind," a series of major brain investigators from Franz Josef Gall to Wilder Penfield. Chapter 4, "The Sensing and Perceiving Mind," complements the previous coverage of Hermann Helmholtz and his predecessors with a major new section on Gustav Fechner and psychophysics.

Wilhelm Wundt and William James, previously paired in a single chapter, have here been separated. Chapter 5 presents a new account of Wundt, completely rewritten to reflect recent scholarship, followed by shorter sections on his successors E. B. Titchener, Oswald Külpe, the Gestalt psychologists, and (I hope to the satisfaction of my experimentalist friend) Hermann Ebbinghaus. Before introducing James and the more "functionalist" American psychology, I now interpose a completely new Chapter 6 on Charles Darwin and the theory of evolution by natural selection, and a slightly reworked version of the old Chapter 7 on Francis Galton and the origins of differential psychology. Then Chapter 8 takes up James, and concludes with new sections on his students G. Stanley Hall, Mary Calkins, and E. L. Thorndike. I hope and trust that the account of Calkins, and the outrageous obstacles she and other women had to overcome to obtain advanced training in psychology, will demonstrate that the dearth of women among psychology's early pioneers was caused by lack of opportunity rather than ability.

Chapter 9 recasts the earlier material on behaviorism, with B. F. Skinner now joining Ivan Pavlov and John B. Watson in the same chapter. Chapters 10 and 11 are updated and slightly modified versions of the original chapters on the early hypnotists, and on Freud and psychoanalysis. Chapter 12 focuses on the general subject of intelligence, beginning with a completely new section on Alfred Binet and the psychometric approach, and concluding with the contrasting (but historically related) genetic epistemology of Jean Piaget — one of the "Modern Pioneers" from the first edition. A brief afterword speculates on the nature of tomorrow's pioneers, and brings the book to a conclusion.

Summarized in another way, the new edition contains extended treatment of the lives as well as the works of fifteen major characters:

Descartes, Locke, Leibniz, Helmholtz, Fechner, Wundt, Darwin, Galton, James, Pavlov, Watson, Skinner, Freud, Binet, and Piaget. Here I have again tried to make the history of psychology come alive by blending the biographical with the theoretical, and showing the real-life circumstances under which these fifteen major figures made their major contributions. Some twenty-five other characters are also covered in substantial detail, although with relatively greater emphasis on their works than their lives. These include the six principal brain physiologists in Chapter 3, the eight hypnotists in Chapter 10, and the important students and successors of Wundt and James. A much larger number of other psychological pioneers receive brief but highlighted mention in the text, which instructors may wish to use as jumping-off points for lectures on their own favored topics.

Work on this book was greatly facilitated by a Faculty of Arts Fellowship from York University, which I was privileged to hold during the 1987–1988 academic year. Like its predecessor, this edition has also benefited greatly from the counsel and criticism of many individuals. Howard Baker, Norman Guttman, Alex Kozulin, and Michael Wertheimer provided informed critiques of aspects of the first edition that were useful in planning the second. John Kennedy, Paul McReynolds, and Ryan Tweney commented usefully on my original proposal for the new edition. For their expert comments on various chapters of the new manuscript, I thank Adrian Brock, Kurt Danziger, Scott Greer, Walter Heinrichs, Peter Kaiser, Gregory McGuire, Mark Micale, and Theta Wolf. John Meacham and Ryan Tweney provided exceptionally sensitive and constructive readings of the complete text. I have sometimes lacked the expertise to follow through on these commentators' suggestions, but the book is immeasurably stronger for their efforts. Joëlle Fancher and Judith Fraser made valuable comments regarding style and organization. The staff at Norton—especially Donald Fusting, Debra Makay, and Rachel Lee—provided their customary editorial wisdom throughout.

Raymond E. Fancher
July 1989

Pioneers
of Psychology

1

René Descartes and the Foundations of Modern Psychology

On 10 November 1619, most residents of the south German city of Ulm celebrated the St. Martin's Eve holiday with drink and frivolity. A visiting French soldier named René Descartes did not join in the festivity, however, spending the day in his heated room engaged in almost obsessional meditation. Over and over again he mentally tested the surprising ideas that had recently occurred to him, scarcely daring to hope they might resolve a personal conflict that had tormented him for years.

Finally, as a stormy night fell, the young man lay down exhausted on his bed and began to dream. At first all was fever, panic, thunderstorms, and whirling phantoms. Caught in a whirlwind on a street near his old college, he could not walk normally, although other people did so as they spoke of a missing person and a melon from a foreign land. He wished to enter the chapel and pray, but the wind blew him violently against its wall, then died down as he woke up.

After murmuring a prayer to exorcise the evil genius he thought was plaguing him, Descartes fell back asleep. He now dreamed — or was it real? — that a terrific lightning flash filled the room with sparks, and then his sleep and dreams became calm. He dreamed of a book of poetry with the line, "What path in life shall I follow?"

A stranger came and conversed about a poem beginning with the words "Yes and no." The man and book vanished, then the book reappeared newly decorated with engravings. As Descartes gradually woke up and reflected on his dreams, he interpreted them to mean his long crisis in fact was over.

He concluded that his first dream meant his old way of life, which involved putting trust in authorities, had been mistaken. The terrifying wind represented an evil authority trying to drive him by force into the chapel, a place he ought better to visit under his own initiative. Lightning and sparks then marked the descent of the spirit of truth, which inspired the final dream with its theme of indecision ("Yes and no") and vocational choice ("What path in life shall I follow?"). The improved book at the end of the dream seemed a benediction on Descartes's new ideas: If he followed them on his own, without recourse to the authorities, great results might follow.

The literal accuracy of these interpretations need not concern us (though no less an authority than Sigmund Freud would later remark that they seemed reasonable to him). More important was the fact that *Descartes* believed them, and thus they marked a turning point in his life. Previously he had been a shy, reclusive, perhaps even mentally disturbed young man drifting aimlessly through life. Now he was a man with a mission, embarked on a course that would make him the most influential philosopher of his time, and the promoter of a theory of mind and body that set the stage for the modern science of psychology.

At the heart of Descartes's inspiration in Ulm lay the idea for a new *method* of obtaining knowledge. Partly a reaction against the traditional authorities, which Descartes shared with several other intellectual leaders of his time, the method also derived from Descartes's own remarkable and unique personality. To appreciate this method fully, we thus must begin with the story of Descartes's background, early life, and education.

Descartes's Early Life and the Development of His Method

Always an intensely private person, Descartes intentionally kept many of the details of his life a secret. He even tried to hide the date of his birth, lest he become the object of speculation by astrologers. Only because an indiscreet artist wrote the date 31 March 1596 beneath one of Descartes's portraits do we know that he was born that day near the small French town of La Haye. Just a few other sketchy details of his early life are known. His mother

René Descartes (1596–1650). *The National Library of Medicine, Bethesda, Maryland.*

died shortly after his birth, and he grew up on his grandmother's estate near La Haye. His father, a wealthy lawyer, practiced mainly in Brittany, 150 miles away. Childrearing duties fell mainly to his grandmother, an older brother and sister, and a nurse. In later life Descartes dealt with these people rather formally and distantly, suggesting that he had formed few close attachments within his family.

Still, young René's intellectual precocity impressed his father, who sent him at age ten to the best and most progressive school in France, the College at La Flèche. There the curriculum included not just the traditional academic subjects of literature, languages, philosophy, and theology, but also a certain amount of science and mathematics — though the science was still strongly tinged with theology, and the mathematics had not yet been integrated with science. With only slight exaggeration, Descartes could later argue that he had been taught everything there was to be taught from books by the time he completed his education at La Flèche.

Young Descartes learned an approach to science dominated by **Aristotle** (384–322 B.C.), whose writings from the Golden Age of Greece had later been integrated into Christian thought by the so-called **scholastic philosophers** of the Middle Ages. The Aristotelian view of the universe placed the earth at the center, surrounded by a series of revolving, concentric, "crystalline spheres" carrying, in order, the moon, the sun, Mercury, Venus, Mars, Jupiter, Saturn, and the fixed stars. Beyond the sphere of the stars was the "unmoved mover" — equated with God — who set the spheres in motion about the earth, and kept them in order. The Polish astronomer **Nicholas Copernicus** (1473–1543) had published a book in 1543 hypothesizing that the sun rather than the earth was the center of the system, but his view was not taken seriously at La Flèche or any other school of the time.

Descartes was taught a biology dominated by the Aristotelian concept of the **soul** (called the *psyche* in Aristotle's original Greek, and the *anima* in his many Latin translations). Souls were taken to be the animating principle in all living things, and to come in varying degrees of complexity according to their possessors' places in the hierarchy of nature. All organisms, including the simplest plants, supposedly had **vegetative souls** which enabled them to nourish themselves and to reproduce. Animals were said to have additional **sensitive souls** (sometimes also called **animal souls**), which provided the more complex functions of locomotion, sensation, memory, and imagination. And alone among the living creatures, human beings presumably possessed **rational souls**, enabling them to reason consciously and take on the highest moral virtues. While the vegetative and sensitive souls supposedly perished with the death of an organism's body, the rational human soul was viewed as immortal and capable of existing without the body.

Aristotle and his scholastic followers had made some astute observations about the various organic functions they attributed to souls, but from the viewpoint of modern science their approach suffered from a major limitation. They regarded the functions of the soul as elemental explanatory factors, incapable of being explained themselves in terms of more basic units. Thus living organisms were believed to reproduce, to move, or to think *because* they had vegetative, animal, or rational souls — and the analysis went no further. Modern biologists and psychologists, of course, think of these functions as things to be explained rather than units of explanation in themselves. As we shall see, Descartes became one of the major creators of this reversal of strategy.

As a student, however, Descartes absorbed the doctrine of the soul along with everything else he was taught, becoming the best pupil in his school. He even succeeded in convincing his teachers that he did his best thinking while meditating in bed, earning the extraordinary privilege of lying abed in the mornings while his fellow students were up and about their chores. He evidently did not abuse this privilege, for there is no sign his special treatment was resented by others. When he graduated at age sixteen, he was the top student from the top school in his country.

Soon after graduation Descartes migrated to Paris, where, as an independently wealthy young man with no adult supervision, he at first gambled and engaged in other mild debauchery. Then he briefly came under the wholesome influence of **Marin Mersenne** (1588–1648), a Franciscan monk and older alumnus of La Flèche with broad intellectual interests and wide acquaintance with the scholarly world. Mersenne took Descartes under his wing, and provided intellectual as well as personal support. All too soon, however, Mersenne's clerical order transferred him from Paris. Desolated by the loss of his mentor, Descartes retreated from society altogether. Without notifying anyone, even his family, he rented an apartment in the country suburb of St. Germain and secretly moved in.

Descartes now experienced a deep emotional and intellectual crisis, brought on by his feeling that all of his hard-won academic knowledge was useless or uncertain. In a manner that many students may still sympathize with today, Descartes listed the deficiencies and inanities of all his academic subjects. The *classics* were occasionally interesting but also treacherous because "those who are too interested in things which occurred in past centuries are often remarkably ignorant of what is going on today." *Literature* was dangerous because it "makes us imagine a number of events as possible which are really impossible, and . . . those who regulate their behavior by the examples they find in books are apt to fall into the extravagances of the knights of romances." Great achievements in *poetry* or *theology* resulted from natural gifts or divine inspiration rather than study, so it was foolish to try to teach those subjects in school. *Mathematics* offered a pleasing certainty of result, but seemed trivial because it had not yet been applied to the solution of practical problems. And worst of all was *philosophy*, which had been studied for centuries by the most highly reputed minds "without having produced anything which is not in dispute and consequently doubtful and uncertain." Descartes concluded, "When I noticed how many different opinions learned men may hold on the same subject, despite the fact that no more than one of them can ever be right, I resolved to consider almost as false any opinion which was merely plausible."[1]

Descartes summarized his youthful condition as follows:

From my childhood I lived in a world of books, . . . taught that by their help I could gain a clear and assured understanding of everything useful in life. . . . But as soon as I had finished the course of studies which usually admits one to the ranks of the learned, . . . I found myself so saddled with doubts and errors that I seemed to have gained nothing in trying to educate myself unless it was to discover more and more fully how ignorant I was.[2]

For all his intellectual brilliance and accomplishment, Descartes felt the attainment of *perfectly certain* knowledge was beyond him.

The intellectual and emotional foundations cut from beneath him, he entered a crisis of profound doubt.

While at St. Germain, Descartes had an incidental experience that would markedly influence his later thought. He visited the small town's most famous attraction, an intricate series of mechanical statues constructed by the queen's fountaineers in grottoes in the banks of the River Seine. When visitors stepped on plates hidden in the floor, water flowed through pipes and valves in the statues and caused them to move. As one approached a statue of the goddess Diana bathing, for example, she retreated modestly into the depths of the grotto; upon further approach, a statue of the god Neptune came forward waving his trident protectively. Though intended only as ingenious amusements, these statues would later serve Descartes as important models for a theory of *living* bodies set into motion by mechanical means.

How these struck Descartes on first viewing is impossible to know, just as it is impossible to know the exact severity of his personal crisis at the time. The general feelings Descartes expressed in his autobiography were obviously intense, but not terribly far out of the ordinary. Very possibly, the whole episode represented little more than a temporary "identity crisis" in an over-schooled young man who needed to broaden his horizons. One commentator has argued, however, that the crisis may have been considerably more severe than that. Tendencies to withdraw into isolation and private meditation while avoiding close emotional attachments characterize patients diagnosed today as suffering from schizophrenia. Schizophrenic patients also sometimes "depersonalize" themselves and others, seeing people in general as machine-like and bereft of emotions. Since these symptoms are at least *consistent with* the little that is known about Descartes during his St. Germain period, Descartes arguably may have suffered a schizophrenic breakdown at this period of his life.[3]

Fortunately, one does not require an exact psychiatric diagnosis in order to appreciate the general relationship between Descartes's youthful personality and his later intellectual style. It suffices merely to note that he was a person who preferred solitude to society, his own ideas to those of others, and a skeptical as opposed to a credulous orientation to the world.

9

In any event, Descartes finally ended his self-imposed isolation and rejoined society. In 1618, he decided to see if the "real world" of practical experience could offer more satisfying knowledge than the academic ivory tower. The twenty-two-year-old ex-scholar became a soldier. Europe just then lay on the brink of the Thirty Years War, a conflict that would pit Catholic against Protestant armies in an outgrowth of the Lutheran Reformation. Although a Catholic, Descartes first enlisted in the Protestant army of Prince Maurice of Nassau. Simple proximity may have determined his choice, since this army was billeted relatively nearby, in the Dutch city of Breda.

The actual battles of the war had not yet begun, so Descartes experienced several months of boredom. Further, he disgustedly observed that soldiers possessed no more useful wisdom than scholars. "I found nothing there to satisfy me," he complained. "I noticed just about as much difference of opinion as I had previously remarked among scholars."[4]

Then a turning point occurred on 10 November 1618, exactly one year before his climactic experience in Ulm. As Descartes tried to read a mathematical puzzle that had been posted on a public wall, he asked the help of a bystander in translating its unfamiliar Flemish language. The bystander happened to be **Isaac Beeckman** (1588–1637), a physician and internationally known mathematician. Surprised and amused by a soldier with an interest in mathematics, Beeckman engaged Descartes in conversation, and then befriended him. Like Mersenne in Paris, he became a mentor and revitalized Descartes's intellectual interests. At Beeckman's urging Descartes wrote his first extended original scholarly work, an essay on music that he gratefully dedicated to his friend. "You alone have drawn me from my idleness," he wrote. "If I produce anything of merit, you will be entitled to claim it entirely for yourself." He also showed characteristic caution, however, by making Beeckman promise never to have the work published, or even show it to others, who "would not overlook its imperfections, as I know you will."[5]

Years later the friendship was strained when Beeckman incautiously showed these words of Descartes to others, and implied that he was the real originator of the then-famous philosopher's ideas.

Infuriated, Descartes upbraided Beeckman: "When you boast of such things in front of people who know me, it injures your own reputation. . . .[Everyone] knows that I am accustomed to instructing myself even with ants and worms, and one will think that is how I used you."[6]

This breach still lay far in the future, however, when Beeckman had to leave Breda in early 1619. Descartes now saw no strong reason why he should remain there either. With no personal commitment to Prince Maurice's cause, he decided to try life with the other side, and set out to join the Catholic forces of Maximillian of Bavaria, some 350 miles to the south. Rather than going directly, however, he took a leisurely and meandering route through Poland and northern Germany. Early in this journey, Descartes reputedly had a crucial insight that led to his invention of **analytic geometry**.

According to legend, the inspiration struck Descartes one morning during his habitual meditation in bed, as he watched a fly buzzing in the corner of his room.[7] He suddenly realized that the fly's position at any instant could be precisely defined by three numbers, representing the fly's perpendicular distances from the two walls and the ceiling. Generalizing from this, he recognized that *any* points in space could similarly be defined by their numerical distances from arbitrarily defined lines or planes. (These reference lines, since named *Cartesian coordinates* in honor of Descartes, include the *abscissa* and the *ordinate* so well known to generations of mathematics students.) Now, geometrical curves could potentially be defined by numbers, as the paths traced by points as they moved with respect to the coordinates; in short, Descartes had devised a means of uniting and integrating the previously separate mathematical disciplines of geometry (involving shapes) and algebra (involving numbers). Soon this would have tremendous practical applications — helping astronomers to describe and calculate planetary orbits, for example. Since Descartes's major earlier complaint about mathematics concerned its lack of practical usefulness, he had special reason to feel pleased with this invention. If he had done nothing else in his life, he would have won a major place in the history of science for his analytic geometry.

11

Descartes's Method In fact, Descartes's creative life was just beginning. By the fall of 1619 he reached the city of Ulm on the Danube,
still some distance from Maximillian. Finding a comfortable and
heated apartment, Descartes decided to spend the winter there and
postpone further soldiering until the spring. In his room he gave
himself over to intense meditation, particularly on the question of
how the non-mathematical disciplines might be granted the same
certainty of results as analytic geometry. His doubting of all
knowledge reached obsessional proportions once again, until at last
he had two ideas that precipitated his climactic dreams on St.
Martin's Eve.

First, the thought struck him: "Frequently there is less perfection in a work produced by several persons than in one produced
by a single hand. Thus we notice that buildings conceived and completed by a single architect are usually more beautiful and better
planned than those remodeled by several persons."8 And most
academic learning, acquired from an assortment of different teachers
and books, was obviously a group product. How much better it
might be if *all* knowledge could be the product of systematic experience and reflection by a single person! Here was a perfect rationale for Descartes to indulge his proclivity for solitary investigation, to dismiss the presumptuous "expertise" of the authorities, and
to follow his own inclinations instead.

Descartes's second major insight pointed to a way of applying
a geometry-like mode of reasoning to all fields of knowledge. In
geometry, one began with a small number of self-evident and certainly true *axioms*, such as the assertion that a straight line is the
shortest distance between two points. Then one proceeded to link
the axioms together by small but logically certain steps to arrive
at complex and often surprising — but nonetheless certain — conclusions or *theorems.* Thus the most obvious rules in Descartes's new
"method" prescribed a similar step-by-step and systematic reasoning process for the other disciplines as well. Less obvious, however,
was Descartes's new idea about how to generate the self-evident
starting points or "axioms" for non-mathematical fields. This "first
rule" of the method was:

never to accept anything as true unless I recognized it to be certainly and
evidently as such: that is, carefully to avoid all precipitation and prejudg-

ment, and to include nothing in my conclusions unless it presented itself so clearly and distinctly in my mind that there was no reason or occasion to doubt.[9]

In essence, Descartes here argued that the route to certainty was *to doubt everything*, and then to take as axiomatic whatever proved to be incapable of sustaining doubt. Yet as he entertained this exciting possibility, he could not avoid being overcome by a final paroxysm of uncertainty. How could he know that his method would work? How could he know that if he gave himself up completely to systematic doubting, he would *ever* come up with ideas whose truth was certain? He feverishly ruminated on these themes, until finally he had his dream.

The dream — or rather his optimistic interpretation of it — gave him confidence to proceed. Inspired by the thought that the ideas of individuals were generally superior to those of groups, he now could go his solitary way with a clear conscience. And his predilection for skepticism and doubt, previously a source of torment, could now be creatively employed in the search for positive truth. If Descartes had previously been emotionally ill, he now was on the road to recovery, secure in his vocation as a solitary philosopher and scientist. Knowing at last what he wanted to do, Descartes gave up all thought of continuing as a soldier, and began applying his method to a host of intellectual questions.

True to form, he worked in obscurity for nine years following his experience at Ulm, sometimes in Paris but often in other cities he visited throughout Europe. His major project for that period, an unfinished work entitled "Rules for the Direction of the Mind," attempted to show how his method could be applied to the analysis of the physical world. First, he argued, the most elementary and axiomatic units of a subject, which he called **simple natures**, had to be determined. A simple nature was an idea or impression that was at once *clear*, meaning that it was given immediately in experience, and *distinct*, meaning that it was incapable of further analysis or doubt. A primary source of error arose from accepting as simple natures ideas that were clear but not distinct; that is, that had been insufficiently doubted. The misleading image of a bent stick partly immersed in clear water exemplified an idea that was clear but not distinct. Doubting the impression would lead to removing the stick from water and discovering it was really straight, its "bend" the result of light refraction in the water.

After Descartes systematically doubted the phenomena of the physical world, he hypothesized that just two properties were ultimate simple natures, incapable of further analysis or doubt: **extension** (the spatial dimensions occupied by a body) and **motion**. Thus he believed that all phenomena of the physical world should be ultimately explainable in terms of just these two properties. Light, heat, sound, and all other physical qualities presumably resulted from some sort of extended, material particles in motion. It also occurred to Descartes that *living bodies* could be thought of as mechanical contrivances, explainable according to the same principles.

Just as Descartes was developing these ideas, the great Italian scientist **Galileo Galilei** (1564–1642) published something very similar. In a 1623 work called *The Assayer*, Galileo distinguished between what he called the **primary and secondary qualities** of physical matter. The three primary qualities of shape, quantity, and motion presumably resided inherently in matter, whereas the secondary qualities arose only after the primary qualities impinged on the human senses. Thus the sight, sound, smell, and feel of an object were secondary qualities, while the size, shape, and motion of its constituent particles were primary. The science of physics, for Galileo, entailed the analysis of the primary qualities of matter.

The obvious similarity between Descartes's and Galileo's ideas may have been more than coincidental. The two men probably knew about each other's work through Mersenne, who corresponded regularly with them and many other scientific figures of the time.* Descartes, despite his avowed mistrust of other people's work, might even have read *The Assayer* and been impressed by its consonance with his own thought. Or perhaps the general idea of a physics based

---

*Mersenne was one of a number of individuals who, while not original scientists themselves, nevertheless contributed greatly to the advancement of science because they were convivial and knowledgeable *correspondents* of scientists. In an age before scientific periodicals had been established for the easy dissemination of information, these sociable go-betweens helped scientists keep up with each other's work.

entirely on material particles in motion was simply "in the air," and was developed independently by these two great figures. In any case, Descartes postulated a physical system much in tune with the ideas of his most able contemporaries, despite his penchant for isolation and solitary thought.

Still, Descartes published nothing and remained a largely anonymous figure until 1628. That year, however, he attended a public lecture in Paris on chemistry, which was well received by most of the audience but unacceptable to Descartes because it employed concepts that seemed to him only clear and plausible, but not distinct. Aroused to unusual boldness, Descartes spoke out in the public discussion following the lecture, and his critique greatly impressed an influential cardinal in the audience. The cardinal invited Descartes home after the performance, and upon learning that the shy philosopher had extended his ideas into physiology as well as physics, implored him to publish.* Encouraged by this support, Descartes decided to write a work synthesizing his physics and his physiology—or, as he called them, his "mechanics" and his "medicine."

But even with this new motivation, Descartes proceeded very slowly. The Parisian atmosphere became distracting, and he fled again to Holland. This time he stayed for twenty years, preserving his privacy by moving twenty-four times during that period and seldom leaving a forwarding address. He worked for five years to perfect his physical analysis of the world and his mechanical analysis of the animal body. At last in 1633 he completed a lengthy manuscript in French entitled *Le Monde* (*The World*), subdivided into one part on physics called "Treatise of Light," and another on physiology, "Treatise of Man."

The World: Descartes's Physics and Physiology

Just as Descartes was about to entrust his new book to the printer, he received the staggering news that Galileo had been condemned

---

*The chemist whose lecture inspired all this, a man named Chandoux, was less fortunate. Following his humiliation by Descartes he tried to employ his scientific talents as a counterfeiter; unsuccessful there,too, he was finally arrested and hanged for his crime.

by the Inquisition for supporting the Copernican theory of the universe. Previously, the Catholic Church had tolerated publication of the theory so long as it was clearly labeled a hypothesis, and not presented as established truth. But now the Church declared it heretical to express the idea at all, and Galileo had publicly recanted upon threat of torture. Descartes's "Treatise of Light" entertained the Copernican theory too, and while he was in no personal danger in Protestant Holland, he wanted his work and name to be acceptable in the Catholic universities of France. Thus he withdrew his book from publication, but fortunately preserved the manuscript, which his admirers managed to publish soon after his death.

Among the striking features of *The World*, as of Descartes's thought generally, was the way it integrated several previously separate branches of science. Ever since Ulm, Descartes had sought to construct a "universal science" connecting all the arts and sciences within a single set of fundamental principles. This integrating quality made *The World* one of the first modern textbooks, not only of physics and physiology, but of psychology as well. Physical laws were applied to an understanding of physiology, which in turn was used to explain certain psychological phenomena. Few of Descartes's physiological ideas are still accepted today exactly as he conceived them, and he did not carry his psycho-physiological integration as far as many scientists do today. But still, *The World* clearly set the style for the future emergence of psychology as a member of the family of sciences.

Physics "Treatise of Light" presented Descartes's physical ideas, based on the analysis of material particles in motion. Following Aristotle, Descartes believed there could be no void, so he saw the entire universe as completely filled with different kinds of material particles in different kinds of motion. When a particle moves, it leaves no empty space behind it, for that space is instantaneously filled by other particles—just as when a fish swims the space it leaves is instantaneously refilled with water.

Descartes hypothesized three different basic types of particles in the universe, corresponding roughly to the classical elements of fire, air, and earth. He conceptualized the fire, or heat particles, as the smallest ones—so unimaginably tiny, in fact, that when aggregated they constituted "a virtually perfect fluid" capable of filling up space of any shape or size. Descartes argued that these particles would naturally sift through all of the other larger particles in the universe, so as to congregate in particular intensity at its center and form the sun. Such was Descartes's justification for the now-heretical Copernican theory.

Descartes thought of "air" particles as somewhat larger, but still too small to be directly perceived. The most numerous of all the particles, these completely filled all the spaces between objects and, again like the water in a fish pond, instantaneously moved into the space just vacated by a moving object. All such objects—including the planets and comets as well as the earth and the things on it— were supposedly composed of accretions of "earth" particles, the third and heaviest variety in Descartes's hypothetical universe.

As its title suggests, much of this first treatise dealt with the various phenomena of light. Descartes argued that "air" particles naturally arrange themselves into columns between objects, forming the material basis of light rays. Thus when we look at an object, innumerable light rays or columns of invisible air extend directly between it and our eye. Descartes further argued that the "earth" particles constituting the object are in constant vibratory motion, and these vibrations are inevitably transmitted to the columns of light rays extending to the eye. The vibrations of the rays in turn stimulate the material particles of the eye into sympathetic motion, and such is the physical basis for the sensation of light in the perceiving individual.

In elaborating on this notion, Descartes used the analogy of a blind man sensing objects in the world with a stick. As he probes with his stick and encounters a solid object, pressure at the tip of the stick is transmitted its length and perceived by the hand. The stick is thus analogous to a Cartesian light ray, transmitting the motion of a stimulus from one end (the perceived object) to another (the hand or eye). Descartes's theory implied that the speed of light was instantaneous, since both ends of the light rays (like both ends of the blind man's stick) were presumed to move together, and he acknowledged that the theory would be discredited by any evidence of a finite speed for light. Such evidence did not appear until 1676, however, so the theory remained plausible for many years. And even though incorrect regarding the physical structure of light, Descartes's system still facilitated the analysis of many optical phenomena, such as the refracting or bending of straight rays in lenses and other devices, in much the general manner still done today.

Moreover, in conceptualizing the eye as a physical mechanism activated by the physical properties of light waves, Descartes introduced another idea of great and permanent influence: namely, that the structures of a living body could be thought of as physical systems operating according to physical laws. This mechanistic view of the body was more fully developed in the second, physiological part of *The World*, the "Treatise of Man."

Mechanistic Physiology A few others before Descartes had approached animate bodies mechanistically. Galileo, for example, had analyzed the bones and joints of the body as if they were a system of levers, and the great British doctor **William Harvey** (1578–1657) had analyzed the heart as a physical pumping mechanism in his revolutionary demonstration that blood is not constantly created and dissipated anew, but instead *circulates* constantly throughout the body.

Thus Descartes's unique contribution lay not in the idea of physiological mechanism per se, but rather in the *scope* of the functions to which he applied the idea. He mechanistically analyzed the following ten different physiological functions in his treatise: the digestion of food; the circulation of blood; the nourishment and growth of the body; respiration; sleeping and waking; sensation of the external world; imagination; memory; the appetites and passions; and the movements of the body. The net result was to obviate the traditional concepts of the vegetative and animal souls. Descartes argued that the body's ten functions occur mechanically,

no more nor less than do the movements of a clock or other automaton, from the arrangement of its counterweights and wheels. Wherefore it is not necessary on their account to conceive of any vegetative or sensitive soul or any other principle of movement and life than its blood and spirits, agitated by the heat of the fire which burns continually in its heart and which is of no other nature than all those fires that occur in inanimate bodies.[10]

18

Descartes conspicuously omitted just one major animate function from his mechanistic treatment — namely, *reason*. Though he replaced the vegetative and animal souls with new explanatory concepts, he could not bring himself to do the same for the rational soul. Instead, he dealt with the "highest" psychological processes in an altogether different way that we shall take up later. For now, however, we shall consider his revolutionary mechanistic treatment of several of the "lower" psychological functions, which he accounted for as consequences of the workings of the brain and nervous system. This work began a tradition of **neuropsychology** that continues to the present day.

Descartes was particularly interested in the brain's internal cavities, or **ventricles**, filled with the clear yellowish liquid called **animal spirits** in his day and **cerebrospinal fluid** today. He speculated that these spirits were the smallest and finest particles in the blood, after being filtered from the grosser particles by passing through tiny arteries en route to the brain. He further adopted an idea proposed centuries earlier by the Greek physician **Galen** (ca. A.D. 130–200), that the animal spirits might somehow flow through the body's network of *nerves* to activate specific muscle groups throughout the body. Without benefit of a microscope, Descartes convinced himself (falsely, we now know) that the narrow nerve fibers were hollow. With liquid animal spirits and supposedly hollow nerves, animal bodies could be construed as mechanisms similar to the statues in St. Germain, set into motion by the flow of fluids through internal pipes. Descartes made the connection explicit when he wrote:

In the same measure that spirits enter the cavities of the brain they also leave them and enter the pores (or conduits) in its substance, and from these conduits they proceed to the nerves. And depending on their entering . . . some nerves rather than others, they are able to change the shapes of the muscles into which these nerves are inserted and in this way to move all the members. Similarly you may have observed in the grottoes and fountains in the gardens of our kings that the force that makes the water leap from its source is able of itself to move diverse machines . . . according to the various arrangements of the tubes through which the water is conducted.[11]

19

Thus Descartes conceived of the brain as a complicated system of tubes and valves for shunting animal spirits into specific nerves, thereby initiating specific actions. *Memory* and *learning* occurred when repeated actions in the brain caused certain "pores," under certain circumstances, to be particularly open and receptive to animal spirits.

Having hypothesized a mechanism for animal movement, Descartes next addressed the question of what *starts* the mechanism in the first place; that is, what regulated the opening or closing of the valves in the brain to start or stop the flow of animal spirits to the nerves? Again, St. Germain suggested a clue, for there the statues were activated by *external pressure on sensing devices* — the pressure of spectators' feet on special floor plates. Descartes imagined something similar in a living body. According to his physics, all sensory stimuli from the external world had to be material particles in motion, exerting pressures from their motion onto the various sense organs. Light, sound, and heat, for example, were vibrating columns of infinitesimal particles pushing themselves against the eye, ear, or skin. The movements thus initiated in the sense organs might in turn get transmitted via the nerves to the brain, causing selected valves to open and trigger specific actions.

Descartes even believed he saw a mechanism for the transmission of vibratory motions from sense organ to brain. While dissecting some of the larger nerves, he *thought* he saw extremely fine filaments running their length inside. Just as a fisherman's line transmits the swimming motion of a fish to the hand of the fisherman, these filaments could presumably transmit vibrations in the sense organs to the brain, as tugs and pulls that could open or close specific valves, releasing a flow of animal spirits to specific muscles.

Though Descartes did not use the exact term, he had here formulated the general idea of what we now call the **reflex** — a neurophysiological sequence in which a specific **stimulus** from the external world automatically elicits a specific **response** in the organism. Your doctor tests two of your reflexes by tapping your knee (stimulus) to produce an involuntary kick of your leg (response) and shining a light in your eye (stimulus) to produce a contraction of the pupil (response). The specific mechanism Descartes imagined for the reflex is now known to be incorrect; the nerves do *not* contain minute filaments for transmitting sensory messages, as he thought, and they are *not* hollow conduits for flows of cerebrospinal fluid as motion initiators. (One contemporary historian[12] has jokingly called Descartes's conceptions a "flush-toilet model" of the reflex, since the hypothetical mechanism he proposed closely resembles that of a chain-operated water closet.) But Descartes's *general* conception of the reflex has been enormously useful to physiologists and psychologists, and we shall see later how his successors developed more accurate theories for the mechanisms underlying nervous transmission.

Descartes's theory enabled him to differentiate two kinds of reflexive responses. In one, the vital spirits presumably flowed immediately down the same nerve whose fiber had been tugged, resulting in an automatic and immediate response. When the hand is held too close to a fire, for example, signals from hand to brain trigger an immediate return of animal spirits to the hand, causing it to withdraw reflexively from the heat.

The second type of reflex accounted for *learned* reactions, where the response is not innately connected with its stimulus. Here Descartes postulated a sort of flexible shunting system in the brain, whereby incoming tugs can activate the opening up of nerves *other than* the one stimulated. Thus the sound of a bell may initiate a response originally unconnected with it, such as participating in a fire drill. Descartes did not elaborate on exactly *how* the brain performs this mechanical shunting, but his general differentiation between innate and learned reflexes, with the latter presumably entailing more activity in the brain, has been an enduring and productive idea in Western psychology.

While innate and learned reflexes could explain the activation of an organism by stimulation from the external world, Descartes also recognized that people and animals do not always respond in the same ways to the same stimuli. Internal factors such as **emotions** also play a role in animal response, and Descartes proposed a mechanistic account of these in terms of variations in the animal spirits. He suggested that localized currents, eddies, or what he called "commotions" may develop in parts of the animal-spirit reservoir, influencing the receptiveness of nearby nerves to flows of spirit toward the muscles. Through such variations, different emotional predispositions such as anger or fear might be created:

When it is a question of forcefully avoiding some evil by overcoming it or driving it away — as anger inclines us to do — then the spirits must be more evenly agitated and stronger than they usually are. Whereas, when it is necessary to avoid harm with patience — as fear inclines us to do — then the spirits must be less abundant and weaker.[13]

In this way, Descartes explained the animate body's mechanical responses as occurring because of an *interaction* between the effects of external stimulation on the nervous system and the internal, "emotional" preparedness of the animal spirits to respond in particular ways.

Further mechanistic consequences of the animal spirits included the states of *sleeping* and *waking*. An alert waking state presumably arose when an ample supply of spirits in the brain cavities caused the brain tissue to expand somewhat, pulling the nerve fibers to a state of tautness and maximal sensitivity to the vibrations of external stimulation. Descartes saw the sleeping brain, by contrast, as relatively devoid of spirits, with flaccid tissues and slack nerve fibers incapable of transmitting most external vibrations. Only sporadically do random eddies in the depleted reservoir of spirits cause isolated parts of the brain to expand and stretch taut a few nerve fibers — much as a weak, intermittent wind occasionally pulls taut just a few of the ropes supporting sails on a ship. Thus the sleeping organism is generally unresponsive to external stimulation, with just a few isolated and disconnected experiences, or *dreams*, created by the momentary tautness in the nerves.

Descartes believed his analyses demonstrated how all of the traditional functions of the vegetative and animal souls could be regarded mechanistically — which was to say that those Aristotelian concepts were outmoded and needed to be replaced. He argued that animals could be understood *completely* in mechanistic terms, as automata. Their hydraulic mechanisms might be more complicated than those of man-made machines, containing more pipes more intricately interconnected with each other, but in principle they were the same. As Descartes summarized to a friend, "The soul of beasts is nothing but their blood."[14]

But Descartes would not go so far regarding human beings, in spite of the fact that their bodies resembled the bodies of animals in many ways, and obviously operated like machines as well. The point of difference, Descartes believed, lay in human capacities for *consciousness* and *volition*. It seemed obvious to him that his own actions often occurred because he *wanted them to*, or because he freely chose them following rational deliberation. This supremely important, subjective side of human experience did not lend itself to mechanistic analysis. Accordingly, Descartes attributed it to the presence of a soul or **mind**, which he thought interacted with the bodily machine in human beings. In sum, he got rid of the Aristotelian vegetative and animal souls, but retained the rational soul.

Much of Descartes's most important work after *Le Monde* — including the first books he actually brought himself to publish — centered on the features of the rational mind and its interactions with the body. Since he ruled out a mechanistic approach to the full analysis of the mind, this writing naturally strikes a modern reader as less "scientific" and more "metaphysical" in tone. Given certain trends in modern psychology deemphasizing the subjective side of experience, it may also seem old-fashioned or naive. But as we shall see, these writings actually highlighted some of the most fundamental questions psychology can ask, questions which remain problematical to the present day.

Descartes's Philosophy of Mind

After suppressing publication of *The World*, Descartes started on new projects he hoped would be more acceptable to the Church. He spent four years writing detailed treatises on optics, meteorology, and geometry — all subjects he could discuss without raising the question of a sun-centered universe. And he also prepared a brief autobiographical "Discourse on Method," describing how his method based on systematic doubt came into being, and summarizing its major conclusions regarding the body and the soul.

In 1637, all of these works were finally published in a single volume bearing the lengthy title: *Discourse on the Method of Rightly Conducting the Reason and Seeking the Truth in the Field of Science; plus Dioptric, Meteorology, and Geometry, which are some of the Results of that*

Method. Characteristically shy, Descartes omitted his name from the title page, and was annoyed when Mersenne wrote an introduction to the Paris edition that made its authorship clear. Nonetheless, he was eager to have his book widely read, and in lieu of royalties accepted two hundred copies which he distributed to Europe's intellectual leaders. In an attempt to appeal to as large an audience as possible, he had written the work in vernacular French, rather than the Latin of most scholarly books of the time.*

The autobiographical *Discourse on Method*, with a succinct analysis of the rational human soul, quickly became a philosophical classic. Here Descartes described his earliest attempts at systematic doubt, after Ulm. He related that, at first, *everything* seemed to be doubtable, even the most clear and distinct sensory impressions and the simple natures of the physical world. For example, he could imagine that those impressions were merely illusory, that he dreamed them rather than really experienced them. But as he continued to doubt, he at last came upon one idea that seemed absolutely certain, and that he described in his *Discourse* in one of the most famous passages in modern philosophy:

Finally, as the same percepts which we have when awake may come to us when asleep without their being true, I decided to suppose that nothing that had ever entered my mind was more real than the illusions of dreams. But I soon noticed that while I thus wished to think everything false, it was necessarily true that I who thought so was something. Since this truth, *I think, therefore I am, or exist*, was so firm and assured that all the most extravagant suppositions of the sceptics were unable to shake it, I judged that I could safely accept it as the first principle of the philosophy I was seeking.[15]

Almost paradoxically, the act of doubting provided Descartes with evidence of the certainty he desired. He could doubt the reality of

*Galileo had also published much of his work in vernacular Italian. This self-conscious appeal by Galileo and Descartes to readers who were not necessarily classically educated represented part of the general movement they led toward the "democratization" of science, and away from the acceptance of ideas simply because of the authority or credentials of those proposing them. Galileo's works would have been (correctly) regarded as less of a threat to the authority of the Church had they been written in Latin.

his senses, or even the material existence of his body and the physical world, but he could not doubt the subjective reality of his own doubting mind. The experience of doubt itself was unquestionably real. Thus one unquestionable reality was the activity of his own rational mind, or soul.

It followed logically — at least to Descartes — that the mind must stand in marked contrast to the body, as something altogether distinct:

I concluded that I was a thing or substance whose whole essence or nature was only to think, and which, to exist, has no need of space nor of any material thing or body. Therefore it follows that this ego, this mind, this soul, by which I am what I am, is entirely distinct from the body and is easier to know than the latter, and that even if the body were not, the soul would not cease to be all that it is now.[16]

The body, like all physical things, consisted of extended particles in motion. The soul, whose essence was consciousness and thought, existed independently of spatial and material considerations as a separate kind of immaterial "substance."

Reflecting further on the soul, Descartes concluded that it never appeared directly or immediately in consciousness like a sensory experience. Although he was absolutely certain it existed, he never experienced its totality all at once. This stimulated a search for other ideas which, while "real," also seemed incapable of being represented by a single sensory experience: Notions such as "perfection," "unity," "infinity," and the geometrical axioms came to mind. Descartes concluded that such ideas, independent as they are of specific sensory experience (but capable of being *suggested* or *alluded to* by experience), must derive from the nature of the thinking soul itself. Accordingly, he called them the **innate ideas** of the soul.

Descartes's belief in innate ideas provided an anchor for much of the rest of his philosophy. The presumably innate idea of "perfection," combined with his certainty of the reality of his own mind, suggested to Descartes that there must exist a real God who embodies all aspects of perfection. Now certain of the existence of a perfect God as well as of his conscious soul, Descartes felt he could accept his sensorily based conclusions regarding the makeup of the physical world. That is, knowledge from the senses could be trusted — not because it was inherently certain itself, but because the integrity of the mind that perceived it, and the perfection of the God that created both matter and mind, *were* certain.

Thus Descartes's philosophy rated reason and the intellective functions of the conscious mind as more fundamental than, and potentially independent of, sensory experience. For this reason Descartes is commonly labeled a **rationalist**. And because his system posits innate ideas existing prior to concrete experience, he is also called a **nativist**. Opponents of these positions — arguing in various ways that the mind *arises* primarily out of concrete experience, or that there can exist no innate ideas independent of sensory experience — are referred to as **empiricists**. We shall meet several of them, as well as other sorts of nativists and rationalists, in later chapters.

Descartes is also called a **dualist**, because of his sharp division between the two substances of body and mind. Of course, philosophers and theologians long before Descartes had differentiated between the perishable body and the immortal rational soul, so his dualism per se was scarcely new. But he added something new by emphasizing that many important phenomena are the result of neither body nor mind acting alone, but rather of the many different possible kinds of *interactions* between the two. Descartes elaborated on this **interactive dualism** in a number of works following his *Discourse on Method*, but most extensively in his 1649 work, *Treatise on the Passions of the Soul*.

Here he argued that a body without a soul would be an automaton, completely under the mechanistic control of external stimuli and its internal hydraulic or "emotional" condition — and completely without consciousness. Conversely, a soul or mind without a body would have consciousness, but only of the innate ideas; it would lack the sensory impressions and ideas of material things that occupy normal human consciousness most of the time. Thus the body presumably adds richness to the contents of the soul's consciousness, while the soul adds rationality and volition to the causes of behavior.

From a modern perspective, some of Descartes's most peculiar theorizing concerned the *location* of these interactions between mind and body. From one point of view, the soul as an immaterial substance could not be said to be located anywhere in material space. But from another, it had to affect and be affected by the actions of the body, which *was* localized in space. Thus Descartes was led to search for a place in the body where interactions with the soul were most likely — though recognizing that the soul was not confined to that location. He felt the most logical place was somewhere in the brain, the control center for the body's sensations and movements. Yet he worried because the brain was a physically *divided* organ with two symmetrical halves, whereas the soul seemed a unified, single entity. He expressed his dilemma as follows:

I observe . . . the brain to be double, just as we have two eyes, two hands, two ears, and indeed, all the organs of our external senses double; [yet] since of any one thing at any one time we have only the single and simple thought, there must be some place where the two images which come from the two eyes, and where the two impressions which come from one single object by way of the double organs of the other senses, can unite before reaching the soul, and so prevent their representing to it two objects in place of one.[17]

From the purely mechanistic standpoint of the body, the double nature of the brain and senses posed no problem. So long as specific stimuli produced specific distinctive signals for the brain's mechanism to respond to, it made no difference whether those signals were single, double, or even resembled the objects that excited them at all. Only after consciousness entered the picture did the problem arise, for while the body received double representations of an object in the world, the soul consciously perceived only one. Further, Descartes believed that the conscious percept must accurately replicate the real world — that the single tree he saw in his head as he looked out the window, for example, corresponded accurately to a real, single tree in the external world. Thus, somewhere the double images of the senses must reunite and reassemble to form the unitary percepts of the soul.

Descartes thought it probable that this happens in the only undivided structure he could find within the brain: the **pineal gland**, a small, roughly spherical organ lying near its center. Further, this

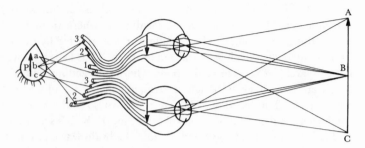

Figure 1-1. *Descartes's conception of visual perception.*

gland extends into the largest ventricle, ideally situated to influence
and be influenced by variations in the pool of animal spirits. And
finally, Descartes erroneously believed the gland was a unique
feature found only in human brains.* What better place could there
be for the body and soul to interact?

Figure 1-1 illustrates Descartes's conception of how visual images
are transmitted to the soul.[18] Light rays from an external object
(the arrow) are refracted so that miniature, inverted images are projected onto the retinas of the two eyes. Vibrations thus initiated
on the retinas stimulate nerve filaments, which open valves in the
brain at their ends (the points 1, 2, and 3 mark the valves opened
by stimulation from points A, B. and C on the arrow, respectively).
At this point, an animal's processing of visual stimulation would
end, as the resulting flow of animal spirits would produce
mechanistic reflexes. In human beings, however, the process goes
further, as signals from the double points 1, 2, and 3 are reinverted
and reunited (presumably by further neural messages) on the *single*
points a, b, and c on the pineal gland (marked P in the figure).
The soul, interacting with the body at P, accordingly encounters
and brings to consciousness a single and upright image of the arrow.

By some necessarily unspecifiable process, the soul may now play

*Had Descartes paid slightly more attention to the work of established
authorities, he would have known the gland was not unique to humans,
but had first been discovered by anatomists in an *ox*'s brain, where its
generally pine-cone shape suggested its name (*conarium* in Latin).

upon the various valves in the brain in light of its perception, somewhat as an improvisational musician plays upon the keys of a piano. Depending on its particular rational interpretation of the image, it may inhibit, abet, or otherwise modify the mechanistic reflexive responses to which the body itself is predisposed. In other words, the soul mediates behavior with reason, making it conscious, and at least to some extent deliberate and freely willed.

Further important consequences of the body-soul interaction hypothesized by Descartes are the **passions**, defined as the conscious experiences accompanying the body's emotions. When the emotion-causing eddies and currents in the animal spirits flow past the strategically located pineal gland, and cause it to move slightly, the soul responds to this information in two ways. First, as it senses the particular nature of the gland's movement it has conscious sensation of a passion—a feeling such as love, hatred, fear, wonder, or desire. Second, the soul may take a conscious *attitude* toward that passion, and attempt to influence it by initiating voluntary movements in the pineal gland that enhance or inhibit the emotional perturbations of animal spirit. If the soul experiences anger, for example, it can *will* to attack the offending person, and influence the pineal gland to splash even more spirits into the nerves initiating attack responses. Alternatively, it can will to inhibit the attack, situating the gland so as to block the flow of spirits into those nerves.

While the soul may sometimes consciously will to oppose or modify the body's responses, Descartes emphasized that it is not always successful. Indeed, he saw the soul's control over emotions as similar to its control over external sensory impressions. For relatively mild emotions, the soul can will to ignore or override their influences, just as it can ignore or override mild background stimulation while in a state of concentration. But with very intense emotions, the rational influence of the soul may be insufficient; people often strike out in anger or run away in panic even when rational consideration would recommend otherwise. Descartes thought that, here, the strong commotions of animal spirits simply overpower the conscious soul's countervailing efforts.

Descartes asserted that such conflicts never occur within the soul itself, but always involve the soul *against* the body. He chided those who characterized the soul as other than a perfectly unified and

29

harmonious entity, in a passage that epitomized his interactive dualism:

The error committed in representing [the soul] as displaying diverse personalities that ordinarily are at variance with one another arises from our failure to distinguish its function from those of the body, to which alone we must attribute whatever in us is observed to be repugnant to our reason. There is, therefore, no contest save that which takes place in the small gland which is the center of the brain, when it is impelled to one side by the soul, and to another by the animal spirits.[19]

For Descartes the soul was perfectly rational, consistent, and unified—but also limited in the power it could exert over the often unruly body. If the soul willed to augment the body's mechanical tendencies, all was well and harmonious. If it decided to oppose them, however, a struggle was played out in the pineal gland, in which neither side had the complete or consistent advantage; sometimes the soul prevailed, and sometimes it was overwhelmed by the strength of the body's demands. Thus Descartes saw competition between body and soul as the essence of the human condition.

In sum, Descartes presented an overall view of human beings that was curiously mixed. On the one hand, he taught that people's bodies were like machines, capable of being studied by the methods of the physical sciences. But he also taught that the soul—the most valuable and unique of human attributes—lay beyond the reach of scientific method and could be approached only by rational reflection. And he approached the presumed interaction between these altogether different substances with a mixture of anatomical inference, psychological introspection, and logical analysis that strikes a modern reader as particularly empty. Today, Descartes's discussions about how and where an immaterial but unified entity like the soul could interact with a material but divided organ like the brain seem meaningless—perhaps in the same way that his medieval predecessors' debates over how many angels could dance on the head of a pin seemed meaningless to him.

But despite the archaic quality of some of his formulations, Descartes's interactive dualism has had a lasting appeal. Minds and bodies are still commonly thought of as different and often opposed entities today, in catch phrases such as "Mind over matter," "Strong

30

bodies and sound minds," and the physician's "psychosomatic illness." And Descartes's basic contention that there is something scientifically *different* about subjective consciousness, placing it beyond the reach of ordinary "objective" investigation or explanation by mechanistic analysis, has exercised psychologists ever since. We shall see how some of his successors disagreed with him, and others deliberately tried to avoid the issue altogether. But the general issue has remained alive, and at the heart of psychology's development as a science.

Descartes's Influence

The final decade of Descartes's life brought conflict, change, and tragic irony. He had followed his successful *Discourse on Method* with two more published philosophical works, the *Meditations on First Philosophy* (1641) and *Principles of Philosophy* (1644). To his disgust, however, these works aroused public controversy. After going out of his way to make his works acceptable to the Catholic Church, he found himself under attack by Protestant clergy in Holland, who succeeded for a time in getting his books banned from Dutch universities because they allegedly promoted freethinking and atheism. For Descartes, a man of sincere religious faith and tolerance, this was almost too much to bear. He drastically slowed down his rate of publication, sending only the 1649 *Passions of the Soul* to the printer, and confining the rest of his thought to unpublished manuscripts and long, discursive letters to a few trusted individuals. (Fortunately, much of this correspondence was saved, and has been published since Descartes's death.)

One such correspondence began in the late 1640s with Christina, the imperious but intellectually curious queen of Sweden. When she invited Descartes to come to Sweden and be philosopher-in-residence at her court, he was inexplicably tempted, and in 1649 gave up his blessed Dutch anonymity in favor of the fashionable life of a courtier. The venture spelled disaster from the beginning, as the philosopher was asked to spend part of his valuable time writing verses to accompany frivolous theatrical productions celebrating Christina's accomplishments. Most ironically of all, the queen demanded her philosophical lessons at five o'clock in the morning. Regularly forced to abandon his meditational bed before sunrise during the bitter Swedish winter, Descartes promptly contracted pneumonia. On 11 February 1650, just six months after arriving in Sweden, he died at the age of fifty-three.

Like many other philosophers of meditational bent, some of whom we shall meet later, Descartes never married. He fathered and provided for one illegitimate daughter, born to one of his servants, but she died in childhood. Thus Descartes left no direct descendants. Few people, however, have ever left greater intellectual legacies. Besides his contributions to mathematics, philosophy, and the physical sciences, he provided many seminal ideas for a new science of psychology, which we shall investigate further in the following chapters.

In Chapter 3, for example, we shall see how Descartes's successors continued his analyses of the brain. The specific "hydraulic" mechanisms he proposed, and the central organizing role he gave to the pineal gland, both turned out to be wrong. But his general point — that the brain is the most important individual organ in the mediation of behavior — was certainly correct, and his mistaken specific hypotheses proved valuable starting points for future research.

The filament-and-fluid method of neural transmission was another of Descartes's conceptions wrong in its specifics but immensely productive in general. In Chapter 4, we shall see how the nerves have continued to be recognized as the purveyors of sensory information from sense organ to brain; now, however, electrochemical mechanisms of transmission replace the ones proposed by Descartes. Further, his general idea of the reflex as a stimulus-response sequence mediated by the nervous system remains a basic psychological concept. Chapter 9 will show how the concepts of innate and acquired reflexes lay at the heart of the tremendously influential approach to psychology known as behaviorism.

In appreciating the importance of *inner* functions such as emotions and passions as complements to external stimulation in the causation of behavior, Descartes also anticipated the main tenets of modern "dynamic psychology." Chapter 11 will describe Sigmund

Freud's psychoanalysis—a conception of human beings as creatures in conflict, constantly impelled in contradictory directions by their inner instincts for sex and aggression, their rational and moral precepts, and the constraints of external reality. Freud's model parallels Descartes's vision of the human body as a machine controlled by the combined and often conflicting influences of the animal spirits, the rational soul, and external stimulation.

Perhaps most seminal of all has been Descartes's general philosophy of mind, with its diverse aspects of nativism, rationalism, and interactive dualism. His successors have responded to various aspects of this philosophy in innumerably different ways, accepting and rejecting its various components in varying combinations. One particularly important successor, the Englishman John Locke (1632–1704), admired Descartes's mechanistic physical analyses, but reacted against his nativism and rationalism while establishing the most important tradition of empiricism in psychology. And the German Gottfried Wilhelm Leibniz (1646–1716) accepted much of Descartes's philosophy of mind but rejected his physics, while furthering a powerful; countervailing tradition of nativism. Many further aspects of modern psychology have derived from these two great heirs to Descartes, whose lives and works are the subject of the next chapter.

Suggested Readings

A good English biography of Descartes is Jack R. Vrooman's *René Descartes: A Biography* (New York: G. P. Putnam's Sons, 1970). Readers proficient in French will enjoy the classic biography by Descartes's younger contemporary, Adrien Baillet, *La Vie de Monsieur Des-Cartes*, included in Volume 13 of the complete edition of Descartes's *Oeuvres*, edited by Charles Adam and Paul Tannery (Paris: Cerf, 1897—1913). For a provocative discussion of Descartes's personality and its relation to his thought, see Julian Jaynes, "The Problem of Animate Motion in the Seventeenth Century," in Mary Henle, Julian Jaynes, and John J. Sullivan, eds., *Historical Conceptions of Psychology* (New York: Springer, 1973).

The best single introduction to Descartes's thought is unquestionably his own *Discourse on Method*, available in numerous editions; it is included along with several other of his important works in *Descartes: Philosophical Writings* (New York: Modern Library, 1958). *Treatise of Man* has been translated, and published with a useful introduction and facsimile of the original French edition, by Thomas Steele Hall (Cambridge, MA: Harvard University Press, 1972).

For useful explications of Descartes's works, see Norman Kemp Smith, *New Studies in the Philosophy of Descartes* (New York: Russell and Russell, 1963). Herbert Butterfield's *The Origins of Modern Science: 1300–1800* (London: Bell and Sons, 1957) describes the larger scientific context in which Descartes worked.

2

Philosophers of Mind: John Locke and Gottfried Leibniz

In early 1697, the German philosopher **Gottfried Wilhelm Leibniz** (1646–1716) tried unsuccessfully to get in touch with the Englishman **John Locke** (1632–1704). Leibniz had read and been impressed by Locke's recent book, *An Essay Concerning Human Understanding*, which discussed the nature of human knowledge from an empiricist's point of view — that is, as the exclusive result of concrete sensory experience. But Leibniz had also felt the Englishman's empiricism went too far, and overlooked the role of several important properties innate to the mind. He ventured to express these nativist reservations in a short paper, which he asked a mutual friend to transmit to Locke along with the assurance that "it is not possible to express in a letter the great character Monsieur Leibniz has of you."

Locke reacted coolly to Leibniz's comments, however, and did not condescend to reply. He told a friend, "Mr. L's great name had raised in me an expectation which the sight of his paper did not answer. This sort of fiddling makes me hardly avoid thinking that he is not the very great man as has been talked of him."[1] Upon learning that Locke had "not understood" his criticisms, Leibniz elaborated on them in a book-length manuscript entitled *Nouveaux Essais sur l'Entendement Humain (New Essays on Human Understanding)*, in which a fictional representative of Locke engages in Platonic-style dialogue with a mouthpiece for Leibniz himself. Unfortunately, Locke died just as Leibniz finished this work. Averse to disputing with dead authors, Leibniz put his manuscript aside and it remained unpublished until a half century after his own death.

It was unfortunate that these two greatest philosophers of their time never entered into real dialogue, for Leibniz had some issues of genuine substance to argue, and Locke's replies would have been of great interest. Moreover, despite their theoretical differences, the two had much in common. Both had extremely wide interests, ranging from history and economics to science and religion. Both had rejected opportunities to pursue academic careers in favor of participation in the "real world" of politics and public affairs. Politics then being largely the domain of the wealthy aristocracy, both of these middle-class men had had to function as courtiers, working under the patronage of aristocratic sponsors who valued their services. And both had tried to integrate their political ideas with a larger and general philosophy of mind, derived in part from the earlier work of Descartes.

But here was the rub, for while each had been greatly influenced by the Frenchman, each had reacted for and against different aspects of his system. Locke had accepted many of Descartes's basic ideas regarding physics and physiology, while strenuously rejecting the notion of a constantly active conscious soul, brought into the world with a ready-made supply of innate ideas. He revived Aristotle's suggestion that the mind resembles a blank slate at birth, capable only of recording impressions from the external world, and subsequently recalling and reflecting upon them. Arguing that *all* human knowledge comes from experience, and that the best models for obtaining truth were set by Galileo, Newton, and the new breed of scientists who arrived at conclusions by observation and experiment, Locke became the leading proponent of the empiricist reaction against Descartes.

Leibniz, by contrast, strongly objected to aspects of Descartes's physics. On logical grounds, he disputed that infinitely divisible material particles (Descartes's "simple natures") could ever be taken as the ultimate units of reality. He did agree with Descartes about the unquestionable reality of the conscious soul, however, and therefore concluded that the ultimate "substance" of the universe must be some consciousness-bearing, soul-like entity which precedes all apprehension of the physical world. Thus he propounded a philosophy of mind emphasizing the nativist and rationalist tendencies of Descartes.

From Locke and Leizniz have sprung two major and often competing traditions in the history of psychology. The empiricistic, Lockean tradition has been particularly influential in English and American psychologies, which have emphasized the role of experience in forming the mind, and the functions of the mind in learning to predict and control events in the external, peripheral environment. The Leibnizean tradition, relatively stronger in Germanic countries, has placed greater emphasis on the controlling and central functions of an active and innately given mind. To see how these contrasting points of view actually developed, we turn now to the individual stories of their two great originators.

John Locke: Child of Revolution

The son of a minor attorney, John Locke was born in the English Somerset town of Wrington on 29 August 1632. He later said he had been born "in a storm," for England then lay on the brink of revolution, and his family was involved. Like most people in their region, the Lockes favored the Puritan "roundheads," who shortly would battle for the rights of Parliament and dissenting religious groups, against the Royalist "cavaliers," who endorsed the absolute and divine rights of the monarchy and the central religious authority of the established Church of England.

When civil war broke out in 1642, Locke's father fought briefly and somewhat ingloriously under Colonel Alexander Popham, the local Member of Parliament and one of his legal clients. Both retired from the military after some early losses, Popham to concentrate on parliamentary politics, and the elder Locke to become a county clerk for sewers. But when the war turned decisively in their side's favor in 1647, Popham was in a position to do his lawyer's son a favor. The famous Westminster School in London had come

John Locke (1632–1704). *The Bettmann Archive.*

under parliamentary control, and Popham sponsored fifteen-year-old John Locke for admission.

Little is known of Locke's life until that time, save that he had grown up in a small, middle-class, provincial household. At Westminster, however, his experience broadened considerably under the influence of Richard Busby, the able Royalist headmaster who had been allowed to remain by his new parliamentary overseers in an act of tolerance that Busby reciprocated. Without hiding his own opinions—for example, he led the school in public prayer when King Charles I was executed nearby in 1649—Busby taught his pupils to think for themselves and to beware of *anyone* who tried to influence them by mere propaganda. From Busby and some fellow pupils who were also Royalists, Locke learned the lasting lesson that there are two sides to most stories.

After five years at Westminster, Locke won a scholarship to Christ's Church College at Oxford University, which would remain his home for many years. There he temporarily became an arch-conservative, and following the failure of Oliver Cromwell's Commonwealth he greeted the 1660 restoration of the monarchy with King Charles II as enthusiastically as any hereditary aristocrat. But while he may have seemed to have put his own family's values behind him, other moderating and liberalizing influences were also at work.

Prime among these were the anti-authoritarian attitudes implicit in the work of several *scientists* he encountered, who stressed concrete observation and experiment rather than the traditional study of classical texts. Although Oxford's official curriculum contained no science except for a medicine based on the classical Greek and Latin texts, a few members of the faculty practiced and taught the new observational approach to medicine. **Thomas Willis** (1621–1675), for example, studied brain anatomy in unprecedented detail, and made several fundamental discoveries about the brain that we shall review in the next chapter. After earning a degree in classics, Locke studied seriously with Willis and some other progressive Oxford physicians. While he never took the classically oriented courses necessary for a medical *degree*, such was not then required in order to practice, and Locke became a skillful doctor.

Another proponent of the new experimental science, **Robert Boyle** (1627–1691), had settled privately at Oxford and built a home laboratory. There he conducted the experiments that demonstrated what came to be known as *Boyle's law*, that the volume of a gas varies inversely with the pressure upon it. This work laid one of the major foundations of modern chemistry. Sociable as well as scientifically ingenious, Boyle regularly invited others to his home for scientific discussion — gatherings that helped form the nucleus for the future British Royal Society. Locke often attended, somewhat to the irritation of one fellow guest, who remembered him as follows:

John Locke was a man of turbulent spirit, clamorous and never contented. The club wrote and took notes from the mouth of their master, who sat at the upper end of a table, but the said John Locke scorned to do it, so that while every man besides of the club were writing, he would be prating and troublesome.

But far from minding these shows of independence, the "master" himself became Locke's lifelong advisor, friend, and sharer of small jokes. Boyle helped Locke to open a small scientific laboratory of his own in Oxford, and to solicit funds from fellow students to enlarge it. This led Locke to jest that they thus engaged upon "a new sort of chemistry; i.e., extracting money out of the scholars' pockets."[2]

About this same time, Locke also encountered Descartes's works, which reinforced his growing belief that nothing should be taken on mere authority. He later recalled that Descartes's books first gave him "a relish of philosophical studies," and that "he rejoiced in reading of these because though he very often differed in opinion, . . . yet he found that what he had to say was very intelligible."[3]

In 1665, Locke's interests widened still further when he accepted a temporary post as secretary of a diplomatic mission to the German city of Cleves. There he got his first taste of practical politics, and observed at first hand a higher degree of religious toleration than prevailed in England. Locke pleased his superiors, and after returning home in 1666 was offered another diplomatic post in Spain. He had not enjoyed all aspects of foreign living, however, and felt reluctant to accept.

Indeed, as the summer of 1666 began, John Locke had little sense of where his life was leading. Now nearly thirty-four, he had tried and succeeded moderately in classical scholarship, medicine, science, and diplomacy. Each had held its attractions, but none had sufficiently gripped him for a permanent vocation. And while he had inherited a modest independent income from his parents, this could not support him indefinitely. At this point, he had a fortuitous but crucial meeting with one of England's most important political leaders.

Shaftesbury and the Political Origins of Locke's Works Sir **Anthony Ashley Cooper** (1621–1683) had begun the Civil War a Royalist, but

changed sides to become one of Cromwell's major roundhead commanders in 1644. He then served in Cromwell's government, but
when the Commonwealth failed he joined those advocating the
restoration of the monarchy. One of the parliamentary commissioners appointed to escort the new king, Charles II, back from the
continent in 1660, he won the new monarch's favor and became
a privy councillor. In 1661 he was named Baron Ashley and appointed Chancellor of the Exchequer, a post he retained until he
was elevated to Lord Chancellor and made the first **Earl of Shaftesbury** in 1672. Thus when he met Locke in 1666, he was still called
Lord Ashley (the title of address for a baron), and his political star
was very much on the ascent.

The meeting occurred because Ashley, in chronic ill health from
a liver cyst, visited Oxford to drink medicinal waters drawn from
a nearby spring. The doctor originally hired to bring him bottles
of the water became indisposed, and asked his colleague John Locke
to fill in for him. A mixup prevented the first day's delivery, so a
deeply embarrassed Locke had to apologize to his eminent new
client. Evidently he did so effectively, for Ashley wound up inviting
him to stay for dinner.

Friendship developed, as Ashley found Locke to be a sensible,
broadly educated gentleman as well as a knowledgeable physician,
and Locke found in Ashley a mature political mentor whose views
meshed perfectly with his own developing inclinations. Both men
had sided at various times with each of the two great factions that
divided England, and been repulsed by the violent extremes of each
side. Both men favored toleration in religion and moderation in
government. Ashley actively supported the religious rights of the
numerous dissenting Protestant sects who sought protection from
Parliament against persecution by the established Church of England
and the aristocracy. And even as he now enjoyed the king's favor,
he advocated a constitutional as opposed to an absolute monarchy,
and strongly supported parliamentary rights as a counterbalance
to the king's power. Eventually these views would bring Ashley into
severe conflict with Charles. But they proved highly congenial to
John Locke from the first, and when invited by his new friend to
move to London as his personal physician, Locke happily accepted.

He quickly earned his keep when Ashley's cyst became dangerously inflamed and other doctors despaired of his life. After consulting the famous physician Thomas Sydenham, Locke took the radical step of inserting a silver drainage tube into the cyst through an abdominal incision. Ashley recovered wonderfully, and shortly had Locke replace the silver tube with a gold one that he left in place for the remaining fifteen years of his life.

London life stimulated Locke in other, nonmedical ways. Boyle had recently moved to town, and helped found the Royal Society — soon to be recognized as Britain's most important scientific organization — as an enlarged continuation of his Oxford groups. Locke became a Fellow of the Society in 1668, and thus kept abreast of the most important new scientific developments.

On the political front he became even more actively involved, emerging as an important and trusted advisor to Ashley. He wrote several papers on government and religion that served as drafts for his patron's official memoranda, and met regularly — both formally and informally — with other politically active London figures. One informal but particularly momentous gathering occurred in early 1671, when Locke met with a group of colleagues to discuss the vexed issue of "the principles of morality and revealed religion." With so many religious groups propounding different and sometimes mutually exclusive beliefs, the question arose as to how one might rationally choose among them. Locke recalled the meeting as follows:

Five or six friends, meeting in my chamber and discoursing . . . , found themselves quickly at a stand by the difficulties that arose on every side. After we had awhile puzzled ourselves, without coming any nearer a resolution of those doubts which perplexed us, it came into my thoughts that we took a wrong course; and that before we set ourselves upon enquiries of that nature it was necessary to examine our own abilities, and see what objects our understandings were or were not fitted to deal with.[4]

Locke accordingly proposed a simple-seeming idea: to examine the nature of knowledge itself, and of the mind or "understanding" that obtains that knowledge, in order to discover exactly what it is possible to know — and just as important, *not* to know — with certainty. He optimistically thought he could resolve this preliminary issue in a page or two of analysis, and then move on to the original religious and moral questions. In fact, it took nineteen years of intermittent work before he was satisfied, as his page or two expanded into his great book, the *Essay Concerning Human Understanding*.

In the meantime, political crises dominated much of Locke's attention, for in 1679 his patron confronted the most important and difficult battle of his life, regarding the succession to the monarchy. Charles II had no legitimate offspring, and under prevailing rules his younger brother James — a Catholic — would succeed. This troubled Shaftesbury and his allies because they feared that a Catholic king would owe primary allegiance to a non-English power, the pope. Thus Shaftesbury successfully promoted an Exclusion Bill through Parliament, disqualifying Catholics from the succession. When Charles II refused to acquiesce, insisting on his brother's divine right to succeed him, a crisis ensued.

Shaftesbury now organized the first political party in England, the "Whigs,"* to champion the Protestant cause and limit the absolute, divine right claimed by Charles for the monarchy. Locke wrote several papers in support of the cause, including drafts for *Two Treatises of Government* — a work justifying the right of subjects to rebel against tyrannical authority — which laid the philosophical foundations of future American as well as British governments.

At first Locke prudently withheld publication of the *Treatises*, as matters went very poorly for the Whigs. In 1681 Shaftesbury was seized by Charles's agents and imprisoned in the Tower of London. Although freed after a few months when a grand jury refused to indict him, he emerged a broken man. He fled to Holland and shortly died, leaving behind a party temporarily in retreat. Locke returned to Oxford, but upon discovering himself under unfriendly surveillance by the king's spies, fled to Holland himself in 1684.

There he remained for five years, assuming the false name "Dr. van der Linden" and moving frequently to avoid being traced. While prudent, such secretiveness was also much in Locke's character. His

---

*This name was coined derisively by Shaftesbury's opposition from the Scottish "Whiggamore," a term for cattle rustlers and horse thieves. In return, the Whigs labeled their opponents "Tories," a then-derogatory name applied to Irish-Catholic bandits who harassed the English in Ireland. While the term "Whig" has largely lost its political meaning today, "Tory" is still customarily applied to the Conservative parties in Canada and the United Kingdom.

major biographer has described him as "never a candid man," with an "almost Gothic fondness of mystery for the sake of mystery."[5] Even before coming to Holland Locke had kept notes in secret codes and shorthand, and sometimes used invisible ink in correspondence. A handsome bachelor, he had exchanged romantic letters with women he addressed only as "Scribelia" and "Philoclea" while calling himself "Atticus" and "Philander." And while it was obvious to all who knew him that he had fled to Holland because of its congenial political climate, he insisted publicly that it had been mainly for the beer.

Still, Locke overcame his secretiveness sufficiently to meet fellow English libertarians such as William Penn when they visited Holland, and to befriend several liberal Dutch scholars. And most important, he found leisure to work on his manuscripts for *Essay Concerning Human Understanding* and *Two Treatises of Government.* As he polished them in Holland, events occurred in England to clear the way for their eventual safe publication. Charles II died in 1685 and was in fact succeeded by his Catholic brother, James II. But after an abortive rebellion in 1685, the Whigs succeeded in overthrowing James three years later, replacing him with his own Protestant daughter Mary and her Dutch husband, William of Orange.

Shortly after this so-called "Glorious Revolution,"* Locke returned to England openly and in triumph, as part of the new queen's personal party. Back home under the new regime, he at last felt safe to entrust his manuscripts to the printer. The first editions of his *Essay* and *Two Treatises* both appeared in 1690, followed by a stream of other works on philosophy, religion, education, and economics. For these works Locke became the most widely recognized and honored of English philosophers, rivaling in his own sphere the great Isaac Newton in science.

Throughout this final phase of his life Locke lived as a paying guest on the Essex estate of Sir Francis and Lady Masham. Lady

---

*Unsurprisingly, this name was coined by historians sympathetic to the Whig cause. The dangers and misrepresentations implicit in such "Whig history"—that is, history written exclusively from the standpoint of the victors, or which interprets and evaluates the past exclusively according to the standards and values of the present—have been pointed out by Herbert Butterfield in his influential book, *The Whig Interpretation of History* (New York: Norton, 1965).

Masham, the former Damaris Cudworth, was not only an accomplished philosophical and theological scholar in her own right, but also the "Philoclea" of one of Locke's earlier passionate correspondences. Nevertheless, all lived harmoniously under the same roof until Locke's death in 1704, when he was buried in the churchyard of the small Essex town of High Laver. He composed his own epitaph, which reads in part: "A scholar by training, he devoted his studies wholly to the pursuit of truth. Such you may learn from his writings, which will also tell you whatever else there is to be said about him more faithfully than the dubious eulogies of an epitaph."[6] In conformity wih this advice, we turn now to the most important of Locke's writings.

An Essay Concerning Human Understanding

In introducing his *Essay*, Locke explicitly tied his own thought to the work of his great contemporary scientists. With perhaps just a touch of false modesty he wrote: "Everyone must not hope to be a *Boyle* or a *Sydenham*; and in an age that produces such masters as the great *Huygenius* and the incomparable *Mr. Newton* . . . , it is ambition enough to be employed as an under-labourer in clearing the ground a little, and removing some of the rubbish that lies in the way of knowledge."[7] Locke believed the recent discoveries of these men represented the pinnacle of human knowledge, and accordingly adopted their observational and inductive methods as his ideal model for how the human mind operates best. At least in theory, they had succeeded by making many concrete observations of the subjects they wished to understand, without initial presuppositions as to what to expect. Within such masses of observations, they detected recurrent patterns and regularities that formed the basis of their scientific laws.* Locke's *Essay* assumed a human mind that operates basically according to this inductive model,

---

*Modern philosophers of science emphasize that this model was never followed completely in practice, since it is impossible to make observations absolutely "neutrally," without having some presupposition about what to look for. As we shall see, a variant of the same argument was made against Locke's general philosophy of mind by Leibniz.

developing *all* of its knowledge from observations of things in the external world.

Locke thus saw the mind as essentially receptive and often passive, with the primary functions of sensing and perceiving. With a touch of sarcasm, he denied Descartes's conception of the mind as constantly active:

> I confess myself to have one of those dull souls, that doth not perceive itself always to contemplate ideas; nor can conceive it any more necessary for the soul always to think, than for the body always to move: the perception of ideas being (as I conceive) to the soul what motion is to the body: not its essence, but one of its operations.[8]

Locke further disagreed with Descartes by denying the reality of innate ideas. He argued that the ideas and principles most often claimed to be innate do *not* occur in inexperienced or enfeebled minds. Thus the ideas of "infinity" and "perfection," considered by Descartes to be beyond experience and therefore innate (see page 25), seemed to Locke to be the results of abstraction beyond the capabilities of the very young and the mentally disabled. The notion that the same thing cannot both be and not be — another idea widely held to be universal and part of the inborn widsom of the mind — was according to Locke manifestly *not* understood and accepted by young children and deranged adults. Since such "universals" were really not universal at all, but existed only in reasonably well-functioning minds that had already had a certain amount of experience, they seemed the very opposite of innate.

Thus Locke postulated a mind devoid of ideas at conception, but passively receptive to sensation — a *tabula rasa* (blank slate) or "white paper void of all characters." And then, in one of the *Essay*'s most ringing passages, he asked:

> How comes [this blank slate] to be furnished? Whence comes it by that vast store which the busy and boundless fancy of man has painted on it with an almost endless variety? Whence has it all the materials of reason and knowledge? To this I answer, in one word, from *experience*; in that all our knowledge is founded, and from that it ultimately derives itself.[9]

Moving to the issue of what *sorts* of experiences the mind has, Locke proposed just two general categories: **sensations** of objects in the external world, and **reflections** of the mind's own operations. Such experiences produce representations or **ideas** in the mind, which not only occupy consciousness immediately, but also remain potentially recallable in the form of memories.

Locke argued that the inexperienced mind's earliest sensations and reflections give rise to a variety of **simple ideas**, such as redness, loudness, coldness, or saltiness from sensation; and willing, perceiving, liking, or disliking from reflection. With further experience, simple ideas may be combined by the mind in varying combinations to produce **complex ideas**. For example, redness, roundness, and sweetness may combine in producing the idea of an apple; the ideas of apple and desiring may combine to produce part of the still more complex idea of hunger.

Although some complex ideas may represent things that do not exist in reality, Locke insisted that all of the simple components of such ideas must have been previously experienced concretely. For example, we can have the idea of a man with green hair without ever having seen such a person, but not without previous experience of men, hair, and greenness. Without a concrete experiential basis in simple ideas, even the most obviously "true" of complex ideas are impossible. The Irish scientist **William Molyneux** (1656–1696) suggested a famous illustration of this point in a letter Locke quoted in his *Essay*:

Suppose a man born blind, and now adult, and taught by his touch to distinguish between a cube and a sphere of the same metal . . . . Suppose then the cube and sphere placed on a table, and the blind man made to see: *quaere* [query], whether by his sight, before he touched them, he could now distinguish and tell which is the globe, which the cube?

Such an experiment had never been performed, but Molyneux and Locke had no doubt the answer would be no: "Though [the blind man] has obtained the experience of how a globe, how a cube affects his touch, yet he has not yet obtained the experience that what affects his touch so and so must affect his sight so and so; or that a protuberant angle in the cube, that pressed his hand unequally, shall appear to his eye as it does in the cube."[10] That is, visual components cannot be part of the complex ideas of a cube or a sphere until they have first been experienced as simple ideas, and then connected with the appropriate tactile ideas. (The general truth of this position has been dramatically demonstrated since Locke's time, as surgeons have been able to remove congenital cataracts, and thus bestow sight on patients blind since birth. Such patients quite literally had to *learn* how to see — a prolonged and often difficult process.[11])

The Nature of Human Knowledge   After asserting these basic principles regarding the nature of ideas, Locke discussed what human minds can *know* about them. "Knowledge," he insisted, is "nothing but the perception of the connexion and agreement, or disagreement and repugnancy, of any of our ideas."[12] A very few such perceptions are immediate and irresistible, as when we recognize the difference (disagreement) between something black and something white, or between a circle and a triangle. Such knowledge — that black is not white or a circle not a triangle — Locke called **intuitive knowledge**. Less immediate but equally certain is **demonstrative knowledge**, arrived at by stepwise logical deductions, each of which is intuitively certain, but the total pattern of which is not. The conclusions arrived at in Euclidean geometry — for example, that the three internal angles of a triangle always add up to 180 degrees or that the sum of the squares of the sides of a right triangle exactly equals the square of the hypotenuse — exemplify demonstrative knowledge.

By far the largest part of human knowledge is neither intuitively nor demonstrably certain, however, but depends upon the patterns of specific sensory experiences one happens to have with objects in the world. This **sensitive knowledge**, concerning the existence and nature of those objects and experiences, is problematical for Locke and, as we shall see, can be accepted as "true" only subject to certain conditions.

Following Galileo and Descartes, Locke posited a distinction between those **primary qualities** which actually inhere in perceived objects (akin to Descartes's "simple natures," as described in Chapter 1) and the **secondary qualities** imposed on objects by the senses. As primary qualities, Locke proposed *solidity, extension, figure,* and *mobility*; all material objects presumably truly "have" these qualities, which accordingly constitute the fundamental units for constructing a true picture of the world.

But the mind also perceives objects to have "secondary" qualities such as sounds, colors, temperatures, tastes, and odors — characteristics that inhere as much in the perceiving sense organs as in the objects themselves. The sound of a bell and the taste of an apple, for example, reside just as much in the perceiving ear and tongue as in the objects themselves. Locke saw the ideas produced by secondary qualities as less certain and true than those of the primary qualities, and illustrated this supposition with a now-famous example. If you immerse one hand in cold water and the other in hot, and then place both in tepid water, the tepid water "may produce the sensation of heat in one hand and cold in the other, whereas it is impossible that the same water, if those ideas were really in it, should at the same time be both hot and cold."[13]

Thus our sensations of secondary qualities may deceive, and Locke accordingly saw the acquisition of "true" sensitive knowledge as requiring the explanation of secondary qualities in terms of the more basic primary ones, on which they ultimately depend. A body's "true" temperature lies not in inherent qualities of warmth or cold, but in the speed of vibration of its particles — which may appear fast to a hand whose own particles have been slowed down by previous insertion in cold water, but slow to the one previously speeded up by hot water. The sound of a bell can be reduced to the effect of its primary qualities — its vibrations or "motility" — in creating sound waves that produce complementary motion in the receptive organs of the ear. Such analyses, of course, were precisely the goals of the great physical scientists whose work Locke admired so much.

Locke saw further impediments to "true" sensitive knowledge in the inevitable fact that any one person's experience of the world must be incomplete, and to some degree random. In the fourth edition of the *Essay* he introduced the term **association of ideas**, while arguing that experience can cause ideas to become linked together in infinitely varying combinations. While some of these combinations have "a natural correspondence and connexion with one another," others, "not at all of kin," come to be connected "wholly owing to chance or custom."[14] The first category, "natural" associations, includes the redness and roundness of apples, and (especially) the lawfully interconnected phenomena discovered by scientific analysis. The second category includes all of one's "accidentally" linked ideas — for example, customs dictated by culture rather than nature, superstitions, and one's idiosyncratically connected experiences. Although only the first class of associations constitutes truly valid knowledge, both kinds can seem equally compelling. Thus a child who has been repeatedly told that goblins inhabit the dark may come to believe in the association between darkness and danger as strongly as in that between the redness and roundness of apples.

Locke's *Essay* did not specify exactly *how* ideas come to be associated, although his examples suggest the importance of factors such as **contiguity** (the experiencing of two or more ideas either simultaneously or in rapid succession) and **similarity**. These themes would be substantially elaborated upon by his philosophical successors. His own primary intention was simply to emphasize the provisional and uncertain nature of much of what passes for knowledge, but is in fact not truly grounded in nature.

Locke's Influence

The *Essay*'s essential message — that all knowledge comes from experience, but that no one person's experience can be sufficient to acquire a complete and error-free knowledge of the world — accorded well with the new British political climate. Since no single person could claim absolute wisdom or exclusive access to truth, toleration was in order on religious questions, and wide participation in the affairs of government. Locke spelled out these implications in his second major book of 1690, *Two Treatises of Government*.

Here he modified and elaborated upon the theory of the **social contract**, earlier introduced by his countryman **Thomas Hobbes** (1588–1679) to account for the origins and purposes of civil government. Hobbes had seen human beings as naturally and essentially aggressive, self-centered, and predatory. Left on their own in the state of nature, such people's lives would inevitably be "solitary, poor, nasty, brutish and short." Thus expediency led our ancestors to join together in groups, with supreme authority invested in centralized powers to organize defenses against other groups, and to curtail wanton aggression within their own groups. For Hobbes, survival itself required acquiescence to a centralized authority; therefore such acquiescence was obligatory regardless of the specific form one's particular authority took. Thus Hobbes supported the absolute powers of the monarchy, or any other established government.

Locke, too, saw rulers and their subjects as bound together by an implicit social contract, but he held a more positive view of humanity in its "state of nature." His *Essay* implied that humans have the capacity to gain increasing amounts of valid knowledge from their experience, and to profit from the combined experiences of groups of people. (In science, organizations such as the Royal Society provided excellent examples of the collective benefits to be had from the sharing of information.) Thus Locke saw the establishment of the social contract as a *rational* choice, bringing real advantage to individuals by investing protective and regulatory functions in a centralized authority. Under most circumstances, reason and concern for the common good dictate that individuals obey that authority. But Locke argued that governments could and sometimes did exceed the reasonable limits of their authority. He saw the contract as being two-way, and when a government grossly violates its subjects' interests, they have a "natural" right to be heard. And if the government's excesses persist, subjects have a right to rebel and establish a new authority. Here was justification for the "Glorious Revolution" in England, and here was the philosophy of government later to be adopted by America's founding fathers. The United States Constitution's system of participatory democracy, and checks and balances among the executive, legislative, and judicial branches of government, were expressly designed to enshrine the values implicit in Locke's analysis.

Locke also profoundly influenced subsequent philosophy and psychology, inspiring a tradition or "school" of mental philosophy commonly called **British associationism**. Its most prominent early member, the Irish bishop **George Berkeley** (1685–1753), applied Locke's associationistic principles to the systematic analysis of visual depth perception. Berkeley argued that the ability to see things in three dimensions is not innate, but the result of learned associations between the visual impressions of objects at different distances and the concurrent sensations of muscular movements in the eyes and body as one moves toward or away from the objects. More controversially, Berkeley disputed Locke's distinction between primary and secondary qualities, arguing that *all* sensory ideas, including those of solidity, extension, figure, and mobility, were only "in the mind," and essentially mental creations rather than independently existing qualities.

Later, the Scotsman **David Hume** (1711–1776) revived an old Aristotelian notion while defining two specific **laws of association** that determine how and when ideas get linked together by experience. The law of **association by contiguity** asserts that ideas experienced either simultaneously or in rapid succession (that is, contiguously in time) will tend to be linked together in the future; the law of **similarity** holds that ideas or experiences that resemble each other will also tend to be associated together. As we shall see in Chapter 4, Hume questioned the reality of any meaningful relationships among ideas *apart from* their associations by contiguity and similarity: He reduced even the cherished scientific notion of "causality" to the assumption that patterns of association experienced in the past will continue in the future.

Hume's contemporary **David Hartley** (1705–1757), a physician, attempted to integrate associationism with neurophysiology by arguing that specific "ideas" are occasioned by minute vibrations in specific locations of the brain and nerves. Nerve fibers presumably transmit vibrations from one location to another, thus constituting a physical basis for the association or linkage of specific ideas. In the nineteenth century, the father-and-son team of **James Mill** (1773–1836) and **John Stuart Mill** (1806–1874) claimed that virtually all important individual differences among people in character, conduct, and intellect arise according to associationistic principles; that is, people differ from each other mainly because of differences in their experiences and associations, rather than because of their innate endowments. Others have taken exception to the Mills' claim, and we shall later see several occasions where this "nature versus nurture" question has inspired important psychological developments.

Chapter 9 will show that many of these basic Lockean ideas came together, although stripped of their "mentalistic" terminology, in the important twentieth-century movement known as **behaviorism**. Behavioristic psychologists explained all learning as the acquisition and interconnection (association) of various neurologically mediated stimulus-response connections or reflexes, and emphasized the extent to which individuals may be trained or "conditioned" by their experience.

But even as Locke inspired a large number of successors to accept and develop his basic empiricism and environmentalism, he also stimulated others to stress certain mental phenomena that his philosophy deemphasized, ignored, or denied. His great contemporary Leibniz first called attention to a number of these, thereby initiating a competing and equally influential school of thought for the subsequent development of psychology.

Leibniz's Life and Career

Gottfried Wilhelm Leibniz was born in Leipzig, Germany, on 1 July 1646. His father, a professor of moral philosophy at the city's famous university, taught Gottfried at home to read and love books, but unfortunately died when his son was six. Sent to school to continue his education, young Gottfried quickly astonished his teacher by translating a Latin text usually read only by university students. This created debate, for the teacher thought any child should be kept away from books so unsuited to his age, while another family friend said it proved Gottfried should be granted access to his father's locked-up library. Fortunately the latter advice prevailed, and by twelve Leibniz had read most of the Latin classics and the works of the Church fathers, and made a good start at Greek. At fourteen he was admitted to the University of Leipzig.

There he quickly completed the standard classical curriculum, and at nineteen wrote a dissertation on combinatorial logic and finished studies for a doctorate in law. Now his age worked against him, however, for the university awarded only twelve law doctorates each year, and if there were too many candidates priority was determined by age. Leibniz was told to wait until the next year. Enraged, he left Leipzig for the smaller University of Altdorf, submitted his dissertation, and won his degree within six months. The impressed Altdorf authorities offered him a professorship but Leibniz — perhaps understandably disgusted by academic politics — said he had

Gottfried Wilhelm Leibniz (1646–1716). *The Bettmann Archive.*

"different things in view." In an age when paying positions for intellectuals outside universities or the Church were rare, he began his lifelong quest for work that would both support him materially and satisfy his voracious intellectual appetites.

At first he became secretary to a Nuremberg alchemical society, a position he later said he won by submitting a letter full of obscure alchemical terminology that even he did not understand, but that somehow impressed the society's officers. While there Leibniz developed an enduring interest in the project of transmuting base metals into gold (a possibility then taken seriously by many leading scientists, including Locke and Newton in England), but the job itself failed to satisfy and he soon decided to move on.

In the city of Mainz he met by chance Baron Johann Christian von Boineburg, an important statesman in the service of the Elector of Mainz (one of the eight major German princes entitled to elect the Holy Roman Emperor, hence his title). Much as Lord Ashley had taken to John Locke a few years earlier, Boineburg recognized Leibniz as a young man of great general promise and secured him a position as legal advisor to the Elector. Leibniz now began his lifelong career as a courtier, earning his keep by meeting the demands of his aristocratic patrons, while also trying to find time for his own multitudinous interests. At first things went well, as Leibniz worked with the Elector's blessing on such varied projects as a new method for teaching law, a cataloging system for libraries, a book on China, a study of doctrinal differences and similarities between Catholics and Protestants, and a scheme for the systematic review of new scholarly books. And in 1672 he was dispatched to Paris, on a delicate diplomatic mission, for what became the most intellectually satisfying and exciting four years of his life.

Discoveries in Paris Leibniz's diplomatic goal was to persuade King Louis XIV to invade Egypt, as a means of deflecting French bellicosity away from the German states. He had even devised a detailed invasion plan almost identical to the one actually followed by Napoleon more than a century later. But like many of Leibniz's other ideas, this was ahead of its time and Louis refused to rise to the bait. Leibniz's diplomacy failed of its immediate purpose.

Nevertheless, he found much else to do in the French capital, managing to complete enough official business to satisfy his patrons while pursuing innumerable private interests. An inveterate tinkerer, he invented a new kind of watch with two symmetrical balance wheels, a prototypical submarine, and a mathematical calculating machine far superior to anything previously developed. He took the last to London in 1673, where it greatly impressed the members of the Royal Society and helped him gain election as one of that organization's first non-British members. (Although John Locke was then in London and a fellow member, there is no evidence that they met then or at any other time.)

Back in Paris, Leibniz met and befriended many leading intellectuals including the mathematician Christian Huygens (the "great Huygenius" to whom Locke modestly compared himself in the introduction to his *Essay*) and the Cartesian philosopher Nicolas de Malebranche. Through such contacts he gained access to Descartes's unpublished as well as published works, which he studied deeply and with great interest. He also greatly expanded his sophistication in mathematics, and made two fundamental discoveries in that field before leaving Paris in 1676.

One was **binary arithmetic** — the representation of all numbers with just ones and zeros, as is done electronically in modern digital computers and calculators. In the 1670s, however, this application remained far in the future. Leibniz's own mechanical calculator, using cogs and gears, worked much better using the standard decimal system of arithmetic. Thus in Leibniz's time, binary arithmetic remained a creation of intellectual and logical interest, but limited practical application.

The usefulness of his second and greater mathematical discovery, the **infinitesimal calculus**, became apparent immediately. Leibniz did not and could not know that Newton had already developed the calculus a few years earlier, for the secretive Englishman had not deigned to share his ideas with others. Leibniz had no such compunction, however, and thus became the first person to *publish* the calculus. Moreover, he employed a notation system much more flexible and convenient than Newton's, which has remained in standard use ever since. Nowadays the two men are usually granted shared credit for the great discovery.

Essentially, Leibniz's calculus represented an extension of Descartes's analytical geometry, which had represented algebraic equations geometrically and graphically as lines and curves drawn on systems of coordinates. Its applications were limited, however, to curves definable as conic sections; that is, those circles, ellipses, and parabolas that may be produced by slicing through cones at various angles. With the calculus, Leibniz (and Newton) provided a technique for subjecting many more kinds of curves and continuously varying quantities to precise calculation — a development that made it possible to analyze mathematically physical phenomena such as the orbits of planets, the motions of pendulums, and the vibrations of musical strings; and to calculate such values as the centers of gravity of three-dimensional objects and the moments of inertia of rotating flywheels.

Very briefly, the calculus works by conceptualizing any continuously varying quantity as an infinite series of imperceptibly changing "instants" or "infinitesimals." As a car constantly accelerates from zero to sixty miles per hour, for example, it passes through every intermediate speed, but remains at each one for only an imperceptible instant. With each minutely fractional passage of time its speed increases minutely, and although we know there must be an instant when the speed is exactly thirty miles per hour, that exact instant must be infinitely brief. Earlier mathematics could not deal with such an instant, because speed equals the distance traveled divided by the time elapsed, and here the time involved is zero, a nonpermissible divisor. The calculus, however, enabled mathematicians both to calculate the sums of infinite series of such infinitesimals (the integral calculus) and to extract the properties of individual infinitesimal instants from given curves (the differential calculus).

Quite apart from its enormous scientific and practical importance, the calculus embodied two general notions or attitudes that extended into all of Leibniz's subsequent philosophical and even psychological theorizing. First, the calculus dealt with variables undergoing *constant and continuous change*, and Leibniz would henceforth see the linked phenomena of continuity and change as essential features of the world in general. Second, Leibniz's calculus analyzed the physical world in terms of mathematical concepts that were literally mental "fictions." The calculus's individual infinitesimals were not themselves concretely experiencable in reality, yet they could figure as fundamental elements in mathematical equations that *did* mirror and predict concrete reality. As we shall see, Leibniz's philosophy reflected these ideas by positing a universe undergoing constant "organic" development in stages that imperceptibly merge one with the other, and by challenging the assertion of Locke and others that the fundamental elements of the world had to be the concrete and palpable "primary qualities" of particles of extended matter.

Serving the House of Hanover Unfortunately, Leibniz's productive sojourn in Paris had to end after both of his major patrons — Boineburg and the Elector of Mainz — died within a few months of each other. Failing to find another position that would allow him to remain in the French capital, he reluctantly accepted a position as court councillor to the House of Hanover, rulers of a German state then less important than Mainz. He remained in this post for the rest of his life, but started out characteristically by taking almost a year to travel by a meandering route from Paris to his new German headquarters. He stopped in London for a return visit to the Royal Society, and then spent time in Amsterdam where he met both the philosopher **Benedict Spinoza** (1632–1677) and the lens-grinder who developed the modern microscope **Anton van Leeuwenhoek** (1632–1723). Amazed by the living microorganisms he saw in Leeuwenhoek's microscope, he had a vision of the entire cosmos as composed of hierarchies of living, organic units:

In the smallest particle of matter there is a world of creatures, living beings, animals, entelechies, souls. Each portion of matter may be conceived as like a garden full of plants, and like a pond full of fishes. But each branch of every plant, each member of every animal, each drop of its liquid parts, is also some such garden or pond. Thus there is nothing fallow, nothing sterile, nothing dead in the universe; no chaos, no confusion save in appearance.[15]

Before he could fully reflect on such thoughts, however, Leibniz had to establish himself in Hanover. Once finally arrived, he plunged into official duties as court librarian, political advisor, international correspondent, and technological advisor. The last function soon dominated his attention, as he became obsessed with the idea of using windmill power to drain water from mines in the Harz Mountains. Promised a lifetime pension if he succeeded, Leibniz designed countless windmills, gear mechanisms, siphons, and pumps. Unfortunately, he overestimated the average winds for the region, and his designs did not work. As he desperately pressed ever newer and "improved" versions on the beleaguered mining engineers, he became both a nuisance and an object of ridicule. A book entitled *Foolish Wisdom and Wise Folly* satirized Leibniz for designing impossible and fantastic contrivances, such as a coach capable of the unbelievable speed of thirty-five miles per hour!

Finally in 1685, Leibniz and his patrons struck a new bargain. He would get his pension, but for a historical rather than a technological project: He was to write an extended history of the House's family, tracing it back to its earliest recorded origins. For Leibniz, the job carried the important fringe benefit of justifying extensive travel to archives throughout Europe. For the Hanoverians, it diverted their gifted but troublesome employee away from the mines.

Although this job provided Leibniz with a lifetime stipend, it also hung over him like a black cloud for the rest of his life. Never one to do things by halves, he accumulated huge masses of data and produced nine volumes of historical essays before he died. But these only brought the family history up to the year 1024, and his employers grumbled constantly that he devoted his time primarily to projects he had not been commissioned to do, while leaving the history centuries short of its goal. Their complaints bore at least a grain of truth, for Leibniz regularly undertook an almost unbelievable variety of ambitious projects, and he sometimes could not help but spread himself thin.

A few of these activities did directly serve his patrons' immediate interests. For example, he wrote briefs supporting Hanover's case to become the ninth German Elector state, on a par with Mainz in selecting the emperor. He also assisted in negotiations concerning succession to the British throne, when the shortage of Protestant heirs in England made it possible that succession would eventually pass to Georg Ludwig of Hanover, a great-grandson of England's James I. In the civic arena, Leibniz promoted a public-health system and fire-fighting service, street lighting, and the establishment of a state bank. He also worked to introduce silk production into Germany, growing in his own garden the mulberry trees on which silkworms must feed.

But these represented only a fraction of Leibniz's activities. He interested himself in everything, and corresponded with people about *almost* everything. He wrote at every possible moment, even when traveling about in his coach, and more than fifteen thousand of his letters still survive today. A staunch believer in the importance of information exchange, he promoted several new scientific societies and scholarly journals.

He also worked independently in the fields of mathematics,

physics, and logic, and with vast erudition in so many different fields, he tried to integrate all forms of knowledge together in a unified philosophical system. Yet for all these talents and ambitions, Leibniz's life remained ironically unfulfilled. One biographer has summarized as follows:

Leibniz's life was dominated by an unachievable ambition to excel in every sphere of intellectual and political activity. The wonder is not that he failed so often, but that he achieved as much as he did. His successes were due to a rare combination of sheer hard work, a receptivity to the ideas of others, and supreme confidence in the fertility of his own mind. Whenever he tackled a new subject, he would read everything he could lay his hands on, without submitting to orthodox concepts and assumptions. On the other hand, his desire to produce monuments to his genius, which would be both complete and all his own work, made it impossible for him to finish anything. Despite all his notes, letters and articles, he never wrote a systematic treatise on any of his special interests. His assistant Eckhart put it nicely when he said of the [Hanover family history] that, as with numbers [in the calculus], Leibniz knew how to extend his historical journey to infinity.[16]

Thus Leibniz's contemporaries saw only fragmentary evidence regarding the range and depth of his thought, and later generations of scholars have had to sift through his enormous private correspondence and unpublished private papers in order to appreciate him fully.

In his own lifetime, Leibniz was often ridiculed. With his enormous jet-black wig and overly ornate, old-fashioned clothes, he was described by one of his Hanoverian masters as "an archeological find" likely to be mistaken for a clown by those unfamiliar with him.[17] Some observers complained that he strove excessively to ingratiate himself with female members of the aristocracy by presenting watered-down and overly "optimistic" versions of his philosophy to them, while keeping his real opinions private. Indeed he became the model for the ridiculous philosopher Pangloss in Voltaire's satire *Candide*, who consistently asserts that this is the best of all possible worlds, in the face of repeated catastrophes.

The final decade of Leibniz's life was blackened by an unseemly priority dispute with Isaac Newton over who invented the calculus. On the basis of false evidence and questionable testimony from the pathologically secretive Newton, English mathematicians officially branded Leibniz a plagiarist. Leibniz, who had originally tried to be conciliatory, responded with some unseemly slanders of his own, and the result was an unfortunate, long-standing breach between English and continental mathematics.*

Ironically, Leibniz's fall from grace in England was followed in 1714 by the accession of his patron, Georg Ludwig, the Elector of Hanover, to the English throne as George I. Leibniz, who had had a hand in the negotiations leading to his accession, proposed to follow him there and become the official historian of Great Britain. The new king, only too aware that Leibniz's presence in England could produce diplomatic disaster, insisted that he remain home and finish the Hanover family history.

Leibniz, now approaching seventy, somewhat guiltily tried to acquiesce while still doing some serious philosophical writing. Sadly, however, he soon became acutely ill with gout and colic, and died on 14 November 1718. Although he was buried with proper ceremony, no one of importance attended his funeral. Another half century would pass before publication of his private papers began to reveal the true scope of his genius, and the full dimensions of a philosophy of mind that set the stage for the emergence of scientific psychology in Germany.

Leibniz's Philosophy of Mind

Among Leibniz's posthumously published works was *Nouveaux Essais sur l'Entendement Humain (New Essays on Human Understanding)*, his extended commentary on Locke's *Essay*. (Leibniz chose to write this in French because he lacked fluency in English, and he did not regard his native German as well suited for philosophical discussion.) Finally appearing in print in 1765, this work contained his most incisive discussions of explicitly psychological issues, and vividly presented the main themes that have defined the "Leibnizian" tradition in subsequent psychological writing. To appreciate it fully,

---

*The English lost out in the long run here, as their mathematicians patriotically continued for more than a century to use the inconvenient and clumsy notation system for the calculus devised by Newton. Continental mathematicians used the clearer and more flexible one developed by Leibniz, and made greater progress as a result.

however, we must begin by reviewing the basic philosophical concepts Leibniz had developed elsewhere, before writing the *New
Essays*.

The Monadology Like Locke, Leibniz had been stimulated by the
works of Descartes, and moved to disagree with some aspects of
the Frenchman's thought while accepting others. His *pattern* of acceptance and disagreement, however, differed markedly. As we have
seen, Locke accepted Descartes's project for mechanistic analysis
of the physical world and animal body, while rejecting or ignoring
most of his doctrine of the soul. Leibniz's major disagreement centered precisely upon the mechanistic assumptions that Locke so
enthusiastically adopted.

While Locke, following Galileo and Descartes, accepted extension and motion as the "primary" or "ultimate" qualities of the universe, Leibniz argued that logically they could not be such. As his
infinitesimal calculus illustrated, every extended material object is
potentially divisible to infinity: No matter how small the pieces into
which it is divided, each piece may be further subdivided still. Thus,
as he put it, "we should never reach anything of which we could
say, here is a real [ultimate] being." Motion, detectable only as
changes in the relative positions of non-ultimate physical bodies,
logically could not be ultimate either.

But while denying ultimate status to either matter or motion,
Leibniz thought there must be *forces* or *energies* that produce the impressions of matter in motion: "Motion, that is change of place,
is not something entirely real. . . . But the force or proximate cause
of these changes is something more real."[18] Thus the ultimate units
of the world must be dynamic rather than static, containing within
themselves energies and forces. And how may one conceptualize
energies and forces? For Leibniz, the only answer seemed to be as
a sort of "willing" or "striving," akin to the motives and drives that
human beings perceive in themselves. Thus the energies that drive
the physical world have much in common with *spiritual* or *mental*
qualities, attributed by Descartes to the soul rather than the body.
Further, Leibniz accepted Descartes's *I think, therefore I am* argument, shown in the last chapter to assert the unquestionable and

"superior" reality of the conscious soul. Accordingly, Leibniz adopted as his ultimate units of reality not material particles in motion, but rather an infinitude of energy-laden and soul-invested units that he called **monads** — a term derived from the Greek *monos*, meaning "unit."

Among the most important qualities of souls and hence monads, apart from their motives and energies, is their capacity to *perceive* — to register impressions of the rest of the world. Leibniz saw the universe as composed of four different kinds of monads, differing primarily in the clearness, distinctness, and completeness of their perceptions of the world. At the top of the hierarchy he posited a supreme monad, equated with God, from whose purposes and perceptions all other monads are created. Omniscient and omnipotent, this supreme soul knows and controls all else, but is itself apprehendable only incompletely and to varying degrees by its creations, the three classes of "finite monads."

First and closest to God in the hierarchy are **rational monads**, corresponding to the conscious souls of human beings. These exceed all other finite monads in the completeness, clearness, and distinctness of their consciousness. They have the capacity not just for simple perception but also for **apperception**, a new term Leibniz coined to denote the ability to reflect upon and rationally contemplate phenomena, and to comprehend them as governed by underlying laws and principles. Apperception also entails an ongoing sense of the "I-ness" of the "self" of the rational monad, so it not only reacts to the world, but also is fully conscious of its own activity in doing so.

Beneath the rational monads in Leibniz's system lie **sentient monads** which comprise the souls of living but nonhuman organisms; lower still are the **simple monads** that make up the "bodies" of both organic and inorganic matter. Sentient monads presumably have the capacity for simple perception and memory, with varying degrees of clearness and distinctness, but lack the self-consciousness and reasoning capacity of rational monads. Simple or bare monads react to the world in a still more confused, indistinct, and unconscious way.

Leibniz saw the monads as organized hierarchically. Inorganic matter presumably consists simply of collections or aggregations of simple monads, acting under minimal organizing energies. When such an aggregation comes under the domination of a sentient monad, however, it constitutes a living organism — the activities of its parts coordinated and organized consistently with the purposes of that dominant monad. And as the vision of Leeuwenhoek's micro-organisms within organisms suggested, these sentient organisms may themselves be hierarchically arranged. That is, aggregates of smaller sentient organisms may be dominated by "higher" sentient monads. Still further, some complex aggregations of sentient monads are dominated by individual *rational* monads, in the constitution of individual human beings. And at the final level of the hierarchy, all of the simple, sentient, and rational monads of the universe fall under the perfect control and apperception of God, the supreme monad which created them.

As the supposed creations of a single perfect and supreme consciousness, all of the finite monads were said by Leibniz to possess a "pre-established harmony." That is, they do not mutually *influence* one another, but rather pursue independent but parallel and harmonious courses. Thus while the rational and sentient monads were described in the last paragraph as "dominant" over aggregates of simple monads, their dominance consists not in the physical power to control action, but entirely in their higher levels of *awareness*. The view of the universe afforded to each rational monad is broader, clearer, and more distinct than that of the others — but still only a part of the whole as apperceived by the supreme monad. Minds (or rational monads) and bodies (the aggregated sentient and simple monads "dominated" by the rational monads) thus do not truly *interact* with each other, as Descartes had it, but rather reflect differing aspects or perspectives on the same harmonious universe. In a famous metaphor, Leibniz likened the monads to a vast number of perfectly constructed clocks all set to the same time; each one runs independently of all the others, but records exactly the same time. In contrast to Descartes's "interactive dualism," Leibniz's conception of the mind-body relationship is traditionally called **psychophysical parallelism**.

In sum, Leibniz posited a universe consisting of an infinity of energized, soul-like substances called monads, with varying capacities for the apperception or perception of subordinate levels of monads. Each monad has its own innate purposes and destiny, but pursues them in preestablished harmony with all other monads because all are the creations of the single, perfect, and supreme monad. Thus Leibniz saw the universe as an *organic* entity, comprised of hierarchical levels of awareness and purpose.

Such metaphysical speculation about the ultimate nature of the cosmos had not concerned the more practically minded and commonsensical Locke, who simply followed the scientists in assuming a universe composed of palpable particles interacting in a comprehensible mechanistic way, and drew the implications for how best to manage affairs in that real world. Unsurprisingly, Leibniz saw Locke's analyses as limited and incomplete, and expressed these reservations in the *New Essays on Human Understanding*, to which we now turn.

New Essays on Human Understanding The *New Essays* consist of a preface, which may be read by itself as a succinct summary of Leibniz's psychology, followed by a Socratic-style dialogue between "Philalethes," a fictional proponent of Locke's point of view, and "Theophilus," who speaks for Leibniz himself. Here Philalethes presents Locke's arguments in the same order and often exactly the same words as they appeared in his *Essay*, and Theophilus reacts to them.

The preface opens by describing Locke's system as basically derived from Aristotle, and Leibniz's own from Plato:

There is the question whether the soul in itself is completely blank like a writing tablet on which nothing has as yet been written — a *tabula rasa* as Aristotle and the author of the *Essay* maintain, and whether everything which is inscribed there comes solely from the senses and experience; or whether the soul inherently contains the sources of various notions and doctrines, which external objects merely rouse up on suitable occasions, as I believe and as [does] Plato.[19]

To support his view, Leibniz cited the rules of arithmetic, the geometrical axioms, and the rules of logic, all of which he called

necessary truths. While we feel a perfect certainty as to their absolute correctness, such correctness is not *proved* by concrete experience, but only *instanced* or *demonstrated* by it. Thus, as Leibniz put it, necessary truths "must have principles whose proof does not depend on instances nor, consequently, on the testimony of the senses, even though without the senses it would never occur to us to think of them."[20]

In elaboration, Leibniz likened the mind not to a neutral, blank slate, but to a veined block of marble whose internal lines of cleavage predispose it to be sculpted into some shapes more easily than others. Such shapes are "innate" in the marble, even though a sculptor's work is necessary to expose them and bring them to clarity. Leibniz declares, "This is how ideas and truths are innate in us — as *inclinations, dispositions, tendencies, or natural potentialities,* and not as actions." Locke, he complains, "seems to claim that there is nothing *potential* in us, in fact nothing of which we are not always actually aware."[21]

Leibniz's view here derived from his monadology. He supposed human beings to be constituted of countless energized and willfully striving simple and sentient monads, under the dominance of rational monads that strive to apperceive the world as fully as possible and that contain the "necessary truths" implicitly within themselves. Thus inclinations, dispositions, and specific intellectual potentialities are part of human nature.

Leibniz conceded that *animals,* who lack a dominant rational monad with inherent necessary truths, may in fact function in much the way prescribed by Locke. The thought sequences of animals represent "only a shadow of reasoning," he wrote, and "are just like those of simple empirics who maintain that what has happened once will happen again in a [similar] case, . . . although that does not enable them to judge whether the same reasons are at work." Lacking the innate necessary truths required for logical reasoning, animals cannot grasp the underlying *reasons* for the empirical regularities they perceive. Thus, Leibniz concludes, "what shows the existence of inner sources of necessary truths is also what distinguishes man from beast."[22]

Leibniz saw these considerations as not so much *contradicting* Locke as filling in details on points left implicit or unspoken by the Englishman. Locke had seen *two* sources of ideas, in the sensations of the external world and the reflections on the mind's own operations, but had not much elaborated on the latter. Leibniz argued that many of the innate tendencies and dispositions he himself emphasized were implicit in Locke's notion of reflection. In discussing precisely the same mathematical and logical proofs in which Leibniz had seen evidence for innate "necessary truths," Locke had seen evidence of "intuitive and demonstrative knowledge," with a higher order of certainty than "sensitive knowledge." From where might this added certainty come, except from innate stores of knowledge implicit in the processes of reflection?

Locke's point of view here seemed summarizable in the old Latin saying *"Nihil est in intellectu quod non prius fuerit in sensu"*—"There is nothing in the intellect that was not first in the senses." Leibniz simply added the tag line: *"nisi ipse intellectus"*—"except the intellect itself." That is, Locke took for granted the mind's own activity in processing its sensations, subsuming a large number of important and interesting features under the general term "reflection." Leibniz chose to emphasize and elaborate upon those features.

Another difference, however, proved more difficult to reconcile. Locke had steadfastly insisted the mind is *not* constantly active, and can sometimes be without thoughts just as the body can sometimes be without movement. Leibniz just as steadfastly insisted that the mind *is* constantly active, even during such states as dreamless sleep. Part of this conviction derived from the theory of monads as the constantly active and striving sources of the mind. Another part— more momentous for the future history of psychology—lay in Leibniz's belief in *unconscious* mental activity.

Leibniz postulated a continuum of consciousness, ranging from the clear, distinct, and rational *apperceptions* through the more mechanical and indistinct *perceptions* and terminating in what he called **minute perceptions**. While real, these last never actually enter consciousness. Leibniz described them as follows:

At every moment there is in us an infinity of perceptions, unaccompanied by awareness or reflection; that is, of alterations of the soul itself, of which we are unaware because these impressions are either too minute and too numerous, or else too unvarying, so that they are not sufficiently distinctive on their own.[23]

Some minute perceptions may rise to the level of full perceptions or apperceptions, as when we shift our attention to a previously unnoticed background noise. Others, however, are inherently too vague and indistinct to be consciously perceived at all. To illustrate these, Leibniz wrote:

I like to use the example of the roaring noise of the sea which impresses itself upon us when we are standing on the shore. To hear this noise as we do, we must hear the parts which make up this whole, that is the noise of each wave, although each of these little noises makes itself known only when combined confusedly with all the others, and would not be noticed if the wave which made it were by itself.[24]

The minute perceptions held both metaphysical and psychological importance for Leibniz. Metaphysically, they enabled him to argue that all monads respond to and reflect all of the universe. Most perceptions remain minute, however, and out of consciousness; indeed for simple monads, *all* perceptions are such. Rational and sentient monads bring constantly varying degrees of apperception or simple perception to a small portion of the universe, while the vastly larger part remains beyond full consciousness for them, too. Presumably, only the supreme monad could constantly apperceive the entire universe.

On the psychological level, Leibniz called the minute perceptions "more effective in their results than has been recognized" in creating several important phenomena. He argued that our sense of continuity as individual, distinctive *selves*, for example, is maintained by innumerable minute perceptions and unconscious memories of our previous states — some of which may occasionally be brought to consciousness but most of which remain in the subliminal state. He saw unconscious perceptions as adding to experience "that *je ne sais quoi*, those flavours, those images of sensible qualities, vivid in the aggregate but confused as to the parts."[25] And in a brief but significant anticipation of his nineteenth-century successors, Leibniz saw unconscious perceptions as playing a telling role in human *motivation*: "It is these minute perceptions which determine our behaviour in many situations without our thinking of them, and which deceive the unsophisticated."[26] He added:

[Minute perceptions resemble] so many little springs trying to unwind and so driving our machine along. . . . That is why we are never indifferent, even when we appear to be most so, as for instance whether to turn left or right at the end of a lane. For the choice that we make arises from these insensible stimuli, which, mingled with the actions of objects and our bodily interiors, make us find one direction of movement more comfortable than the other.[27]

Sigmund Freud and other successors would find more momentous examples of unconsciously motivated behavior than this, but Leibniz was ahead of his time in even calling attention to the possibility.

Elsewhere in the *New Essays*, Leibniz comments from his own perspective on Locke's most striking images and passages. Thus he notes Locke's discussion of how tepid water may seem hot to one hand and cold to another, in demonstration of the presumed uncertainty of secondary qualities. Leibniz adds, however, that similar contradictory perceptions may also occur with the supposed "primary" qualities of extension and number. When you cross your fingers and touch a marble or a pencil with the now-adjacent outside edges of your fingertips, for example, the single object will *feel* like two. Back in Britain, George Berkeley would shortly use a similar argument to deny the entire Lockean distinction between primary and secondary qualities.

On the "Molyneux problem" — the blind man suddenly granted the ability to see and confronted with a cube and a sphere — Leibniz agreed that *in practice* the outcome would probably be as Locke and Molyneux expected. He insisted, however, that the *ideas* underlying such geometrical distinctions must be to some degree independent of the specific sensory *images* that illustrate them. Thus a blind person and a paralyzed person may both be taught geometry, the one in completely tactile terms and the other in completely visual terms. Yet while the specific images of the two differ completely, they learn the same underlying geometrical ideas and principles — showing once again that experience does not *create* the necessary truths, but merely brings them out or illustrates them. Following from this, Leibniz argued that *if* the hypothetical blind man could somehow be instructed that his new visual experience contained two stimuli, one a sphere and the other a cube, and *if* he could actually differentiate the one stimulus from the other, he would be able by rational principles to say which was which. Leibniz conceded, however, that such could probably never happen in reality. A real person in such a situation would probably be dazzled and confused by the strangeness of his visual sensations, and unable to make sense of them at all until correlating them with specific and familiar sensations of touch.

This analysis nicely epitomizes the differences of approach between Locke and Leibniz. For while the Englishman tried to analyze the *limits* of knowledge, and to establish rules for the solution of everyday practical problems, Leibniz focused more on the *potential* of the mind. Locke concerned himself with the understanding of events largely *peripheral* to the mind, with an analysis of the components of external reality. The mind itself interested him only secondarily, as the instrument necessary for understanding the external world and learning how to control it. But for Leibniz the mind itself, with its central organizing principles and innate necessary truths, was a primary object of interest in its own right.

Leibniz thus established a point of view equally as important and influential as Locke's. In Chapters 4 and 5, we shall see how Immanuel Kant and Wilhelm Wundt explicitly adopted a Leibnizean as opposed to a Lockean perspective while establishing the idea of psychology as an independent intellectual discipline. In Chapters 10 and 11 we shall hear echoes of Leibniz's ideas in the "dynamic" psychologies of several early investigators of hypnosis, and the psychoanalyst Sigmund Freud, with their emphases on internal and unconscious motivational factors. And in Chapter 12 we shall see how the Swiss psychologist Jean Piaget has analyzed the growth of intelligence in children as an organic, biologically based *development* of capacities in an active mind; his basic conception follows directly in the tradition of Leibniz.

Suggested Readings

For full details on Locke's life see Maurice Cranston's *John Locke: A Biography* (London: Longmans, 1957). A good briefer account of his life and work appears in Ricardo Quintana's *Two Augustans: John Locke, Jonathan Swift* (Madison, WI: University of Wisconsin Press, 1978). *An Essay Concerning Human Understanding* appears in several inexpensive editions.

For Leibniz's life see E. J. Aiton, *Leibniz: A Biography* (Bristol, UK, and Boston: Adam Hilger Ltd., 1985). An abridged edition of Leibniz's *New Essays on Human Understanding*, preceded by a valuable Editors' Introduction, has been translated and edited by Peter Remnant and Jonathan Bennett (Cambridge: Cambridge University Press, 1982). For a lucid summary of Leibniz's thought see G. MacDonald Ross, *Leibniz* (New York: Oxford University Press, 1984). Leibniz's influence on psychology is usefully analyzed in Chapter 14, "The Rationalism of Leibnitz and the Psychology of Wolff," of D. B. Klein, *A History of Scientific Psychology: Its Origins and Philosophical Backgrounds* (New York: Basic Books, 1970).

Bertrand Russell presents useful and witty accounts of both Locke and Leibniz in his classic *A History of Western Philosophy* (New York: Simon and Schuster, 1945); his biases, however, lie clearly in favor of his countryman Locke.

3

Physiologists of Mind: Brain Scientists from Gall to Penfield

Today, we take it for granted that the bodily organ most responsible for our intelligence and higher mental abilities is the brain. An intelligent person is said to "have brains" or to *be* "a brain," while the opposite number is a "lamebrain." Indeed, the assumption seems so obvious to us that it may be surprising to learn that it has been universally accepted by scientists only for the past two hundred years or so. Before that, scholars disagreed widely about the nature of the brain, and its importance for the functions of the mind or soul.

Aristotle, the greatest scientist of ancient Greece, dismissed the importance of the brain because of some accurate but misleading observations. Although richly supplied with blood in life, the brain's vessels rapidly drain after death. Thus the dissected brain struck Aristotle as unprepossessing in appearance, nearly uniform in its bloodless, grayish color and spongelike consistency. Moreover, he knew of soldiers whose brain surfaces had been exposed by battle wounds, and who had reported no sensation whatsoever when their brains were touched. Aristotle found it hard to believe that such a "bloodless," "insensitive," and generally unimpressive-looking organ could be the seat of the highest human faculties. He assigned that role to the heart, and saw the brain as a relatively minor organ serving as a "condenser" for overheated vapors or "humors" that presumably rose to the top of the body. The cerebrospinal fluid in the ventricles, which Descartes later interpreted as "animal spirits," was for Aristotle the product of the brain's condensations.

While the brain also had some supporters, Aristotle's dismissive assessment of it continued to be echoed in various forms by other influential investigators for two thousand years. We saw in Chapter 1 how in the seventeenth century Descartes localized some important functions in the brain, but did not believe a perfect and unified entity like the rational soul could be housed in a divided structure like the brain. And while the pineal gland—his nominee for the most likely point of interaction between body and mind—was physically *in* the brain, it constituted but a very small part of the total structure.

Following Descartes, however, the brain attracted increasing attention. John Locke's teacher, the Oxford physician **Thomas Willis** (1621–1675), published the first accurate and detailed *Anatomy of the Brain* in 1664, illustrated with plates by the celebrated architect Christopher Wren. In relating anatomy to function, Willis emphasized the *substance* of the brain's various structures, rather than the ventricles and cerebrospinal fluid, as Descartes had. He observed that brain tissue was not undifferentiated, as Aristotle had thought, but consisted of two kinds of substances: (1) a pulpy **gray matter** occupying the outer surface or "cortex" of the brain, the inner part of the spinal cord, and several discrete centers within the brain; and (2) a fibrous **white matter** in the other regions. Willis speculated that the white matter consisted of narrow canals whose function was to distribute "spirits" generated in the gray matter.* Willis also accurately described the blood vessels of the brain, firmly establishing that it was far from a bloodless organ in life. He speculated

---

*Since the late nineteenth century, it has been recognized that the brain and spinal cord are composed of billions of cells called **neurons**, each with an electrochemically active **cell body** or **nucleus** interconnected to others by branchlike **dendrites** (which receive electrochemical stimulation from other neurons) and the long, fibrous **axon** (which transmits stimulation to other neurons). The axons tend to cluster together to form the brain's white matter, while the cell bodies and dendrites constitute the gray.

with less accuracy on the roles that specific parts of the brain might play in the mediation of specific functions.

Other doctors contemporary with Willis discovered that interruptions to the brain's blood supply could cause **strokes**, also called **apoplexy** — sudden attacks that left their victims without the power of speech, partly paralyzed, or with sensory disabilities of varying kinds. And by the early 1700s it was recognized that injuries to one side of the brain often produced paralyses or losses of feeling somewhere on the *opposite side* of the body.

But despite these gains in knowledge, the brain did not become an object of major scientific interest until the 1800s, when it became implicated in a sort of pseudoscientific craze that captured the imagination of the general public as much as of scientists. The German physician **Franz Josef Gall** (1758–1828) played a major role in these developments, as he convincingly demonstrated the general importance of the brain for all of the higher human functions, while also originating the popular nineteenth-century movement known as **phrenology**. We turn to Gall's story for the origins of an important tradition in brain science that continues today.

Gall and Phrenology

Although some of Gall's ideas aroused instant suspicion and hostility among "establishment" scientists, he was also quickly recognized as a brilliant anatomist — the greatest since Willis. Using new and delicate dissection techniques, he confirmed and elaborated upon many of Willis's basic findings regarding gray and white matter. He showed that the two halves of the brain are interconnected by stalks of white matter called **commissures**, for example, and that other, smaller tracts of white fibers cross over from each side of the brain to connect with the opposite sides of the spinal cord. The latter finding helped explain how damage to one side of the brain could result in paralysis or other debility to the opposite side of the body.

Also the first great *comparative* anatomist of brains, Gall carefully examined the similarities and differences among brains of many different animal species, children, elderly and brain-damaged people, as well as normal human adults. In a general but convincing way, these studies showed that higher mental functions correlated with the size and intactness of the brain in question, particularly its outer surface or cortex. We shall later see that the correlation is imperfect, and can give rise to some misleading assumptions about intellectual differences *within* an adult human population. But Gall demonstrated an undeniable tendency for animals with larger brains to manifest more complex, flexible, and intelligent behavior. More than any other single argument, this demonstration convinced scientists once and for all that the brain was in fact the center of all higher mental activity.

These contributions should have earned Gall a secure and respected place in the history of science. Unfortunately for his reputation, however, he embedded these noncontroversial ideas within another doctrine his followers labeled "phrenology" (meaning "science of the mind," from the Greek root *phrenos*, for "mind"). Not content to stop at the assertion that the higher functions were localized *generally* within the brain, Gall held that discrete psychological "faculties" were housed within specific *parts* of the brain. Moreover, he believed that the bumps and indentations on the surface of an individual skull reflected the size of the underlying brain parts, and hence of the different faculties.

A curious mixture combining a few astute observations with some fanciful logic, phrenology never won the respect of the most orthodox scientists. And when Gall failed to win over the professionals, he appealed increasingly to the general public. Phrenology became very popular, earning Gall and a host of followers a good living; but its popularity only increased the disdain with which it was regarded by many establishment scientists. One prominent figure labeled phrenology a "sinkhole of human folly and prating coxcombry."[1]

Gall's controversial theory had an appropriately idiosyncratic origin in his childhood experience. According to his autobiography, he was irritated as a schoolboy by some fellow students who, while less intelligent than himself (or so he judged them), nevertheless got higher grades because they were better memorizers. As he thought about these exasperating rivals, he realized that they all had one prominent physical characteristic in common: namely, large and protuberant eyes.

75

At that time, people commonly associated particular facial characteristics with specific psychological qualities. The art of **physiognomy** — the reading of a person's character in his or her physical features — had been effectively promoted by the Swiss mystic and theologian **Johann Kaspar Lavater** (1741–1801) in the 1770s, and remained a popular pastime throughout the 1800s.* But Gall's physiognomic observation took on a new and different significance when he recalled it as an adult, in the context of his emerging view of the brain.

Already convinced that the higher intellectual and psychological qualities were associated with large brains in a general way, he now speculated that perhaps specific parts of the brain were the seats of specific functions or faculties. If one of those parts of the brain happened to be unusually large and well developed, then the specific function it housed should be unusually strong. Thus people with especially good "verbal memories," like his schoolboy rivals, might have particularly well-developed "organs of verbal memory" somewhere in their brains. And Gall believed he knew exactly where this was: in the region of the frontal lobes directly behind the eyes, where the pressure of the enlarged brain caused the eyes to protrude.

After tentatively localizing verbal memory in one part of the brain, Gall naturally began to look for other faculties in other locations. Of course, in an era before CAT (computerized axial tomography) scans and other modern techniques, he had no direct means of observing living people's brains, and so had to make an important but questionable assumption. Just as the brain part responsible for verbal memory causes the eyes to protrude, he argued, so will the conformation of the rest of the brain cause observable irregularities in the skull that surrounds it. Through "craniometry" — the measurement of the physical dimensions of the skull — Gall hoped to draw conclusions about the shape of the brain beneath.

---

*In Chapter 6, we shall see how the youthful Charles Darwin was almost rejected for the post of naturalist aboard the ship H.M.S. *Beagle* in 1831 because the captain thought his nose inappropriately shaped for a seafarer. Later in the century the Italian criminologist **Cesare Lombroso** (1836–1901) presented an influential physiognomic theory of the "criminal type," part of which still persists today in the myth that evildoers must have shifty eyes and irregular features.

Thus he sought correspondence between particular bumps and depressions on the skull and the particular psychological characteristics of the people who had them.

Once embarked on this search, Gall quickly developed further hypotheses. One of his patients, a woman whose most marked personality trait earned her the title of "Gall's Passionate Widow," one day conveniently collapsed into his arms in such a way that his hand supported the back of her neck. Gall could not help but notice that her neck and the base of her skull were unusually thick, leading him to suspect that her **cerebellum** — the structure at the base of her brain — was unusually well developed. Observations of other people with strong sexual drives convinced Gall that they too had well-developed necks and skull bases, and led him to localize the personality characteristic of "amativeness" in the cerebellum.

Gall's further researches led him to befriend a gang of lower-class boys who did errands for him. After gaining their confidence, he found that the boys' attitudes toward petty theft varied greatly — some expressing an abhorrence of it, and others openly admitting to committing it, even bragging about it. Gall measured the boys' heads, and discovered that the inveterate thieves had prominences just above and in front of their ears, while the honest boys were flat in that region. Thus Gall hypothesized an "organ of acquisitiveness" in the brain beneath. He justified this hypothesis with further cases, including a man with an unusually large bulge in the region who had been repeatedly jailed for theft until he gained insight into his acquisitive nature. Gall reported that when the man realized he could not resist temptation, he decided to become a *tailor* so "he might then indulge his inclination with impunity."[2] (Gall must have had bad personal experience with his own tailor, although he did not explain his remark.)

Through similar observations of other people with outstanding characteristics, Gall localized the qualities of veneration, benevolence, and firmness in separate locations on the top of the brain, love of food and drink just below the organ of acquisitiveness, and a host of other qualities in other regions. While it is easy today to laugh at this phrenological theorizing, we should observe that it did have a certain naive plausibility, and was properly "scientific"

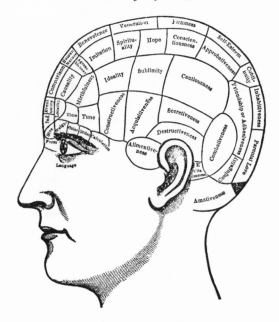

Figure 3-1. *The phrenological organs.*

in being derived from direct empirical observation. The ultimate weakness of Gall's theory lay in three other factors.

First, Gall incorrectly assumed that the shape of one's skull accurately reflects the shape of the underlying brain. But while recognition of the incorrectness of this "fact" obviously invalidated the phrenologists' practical claims to be able to read character in head shapes, it did not discredit their more basic hypothesis of a relationship between *brain* shapes and character.

A second and more fundamental defect lay in Gall's choice of specific psychological qualities to localize within the brain—a collection of twenty-seven highly specific "faculties" for qualities such as "mirthfulness," "secretiveness," and "philoprogenitiveness" (parental love), in addition to the ones discussed so far. Gall's followers quickly added more, yielding complex configurations like that illustrated in Figure 3-1.[3] Thus phrenologists saw these particular faculties

78

as *basic* to human character, constituting the elemental building blocks out of which all significant personality variations are constructed. But in fact their arbitrary list included complex qualities that were themselves the result of many different interacting factors. The question of just what the basic dimensions of personality variation really are remains in dispute to the present day, but the faculty solution was unquestionably oversimplified. And so long as phrenology lacked an adequate classification of psychological characteristics, its attempts to localize those characteristics in the brain were doomed.

Phrenology's third and fatal defect lay in the feckless methods by which its hypotheses were often tested. Gall always maintained his theory was grounded in observation, a claim literally true but unreflective of the selectivity and arbitrariness of many of the observations. Further, with twenty-seven or more interacting faculties to work with, it became almost ridiculously easy to explain away apparently discrepant observations. When confronted with a huge organ of acquisitiveness in a highly generous person, for example, Gall could claim that a large organ of benevolence (or some other convenient faculty) *counteracted* the acquisitive tendencies that would otherwise show clearly. Or he could claim that certain organs of the brain became selectively or temporarily impaired by disease, accounting for intermittent alterations in people's behavior. Between the presumably counterbalancing effects of several faculties and the "illnesses" that arbitrarily interfered with some faculties but not others, Gall explained away virtually any observation that ran counter to his theory.

And if *Gall* was cavalier in his interpretations of evidence, he attracted some followers who raised that tendency to an art form. When a cast of Napoleon's right skull predicted qualities markedly at variance with the emperor's known personality, one phrenologist replied that his dominant side had been the left — a cast of which was conveniently missing. When Descartes's skull was examined and found deficient in the regions for reason and reflection, phrenologists retorted that the philosopher's rationality had always been overrated.

Such tactics, and the promise of easy but "scientific" character analysis, helped phrenology to retain a hold on the public imagination throughout the early and mid-1800s — in much the same way that astrology, biorhythm analysis, and ESP do today. Some practicing phrenologists undoubtedly actually helped some of the clients who flocked to them for readings, using their general knowledge of people (rather than any specific phrenological theories) to offer shrewd advice. But in contrast to the general public, most in the established scientific community regarded phrenology as a joke — exemplified by their widely circulated story that Gall's own skull, when examined after his death, turned out to be twice as thick as the average.

This attitude reflected not only the scientists' disdain for phrenology, but also their respect for a series of experiments conducted in the early 1800s by the young French scientist **Pierre Flourens** (1794–1867). Flourens's investigations, to which we turn now, ran dramatically counter to several of Gall's hypotheses, and initiated a classic controversy about the nature of the brain that remains alive today.

Flourens and the Discrediting of Phrenology

In style and personality, as well as in the course of his career, Flourens contrasted dramatically with Gall. Whereas Gall was always an outsider, never accepted by orthodox scientists, Flourens epitomized the man of the establishment. Born near Montpellier in the south of France, he was graduated from that city's famous medical school at nineteen. He had already published his first scientific article, and won the sponsorship of the famous botanist **Augustin de Candolle** (1778–1841). Moving to Paris with Candolle's letter of introduction, the young Flourens quickly became a special protégé of **Georges Cuvier** (1769–1832), the most celebrated scientist in France, known appropriately as the "Dictator of Biology." Cuvier's endorsement guaranteed that Flourens's work would be greeted respectfully — although it was in fact good enough to stand out on its own.

Appalled by the cavalier observational strategies of the phrenologists, Flourens determined to study the functions of the brain strictly by controlled **experiment** — that is, where particular **independent**

Franz Joseph Gall (1758–1828) and Pierre Flourens (1794–1867). Early opponents in the localization-of-function controversy. *The Bettmann Archive* and *The National Library of Medicine, Bethesda, Maryland.*

variables would be deliberately and systematically manipulated, and the resulting effects on **dependent variables** carefully observed. To do this he used the technique of **ablation**, surgically removing or ablating specific small parts of an animal subject's brain and observing any consequent changes in the behavior or function of the animal after recovery from the surgery. He knew that brain tissue does not regenerate after removal. Thus when he observed specific functions to be permanently missing or altered following an ablation, he hypothesized that the excised brain parts must normally be involved in the production of those functions.

Flourens did not actually invent the brain ablation experiment, but he refined it to a new degree. Showing great surgical skill, he removed more precisely defined areas from the small brains of his animal subjects than his predecessors had been able to do, with a higher survival rate. He always carefully nursed his animals back to as healthy a state as possible before drawing any conclusions, to avoid confusing the transient effects of surgical shock or postoperative complications with the permanent effects of his ablations.

Flourens tested Gall's hypotheses by ablating brain regions associated with particular phrenological faculties. Since he worked with animals, he could most directly investigate those few "faculties" presumably shared by animals and humans. Sexual responsivity obviously qualified, so some of Flourens's earliest and most influential experiments involved ablations of the cerebellum — Gall's "organ of amativeness." His ablations produced alterations of behavior all right, but scarcely of the type that phrenological theory predicted:

I removed the cerebellum in a young but vigorous dog by a series of deeper and deeper slices. The animal lost gradually the faculty of orderly and regular movement. Soon he could walk only by staggering in zig-zags. He fell back when he wanted to advance; when he wanted to turn to the right he turned to the left. As he made great efforts to move and could no longer moderate these efforts, he hurled himself impetuously forward, and did not fail to fall or roll over. If he found an object in his path, he was unable to avoid it, no matter what means he took; he hurled himself right and left; nevertheless he was perfectly well; when one irritated him he tried to bite; in fact, he bit any object one presented to him when he could reach it, but often he could no longer direct his movements with precision so as to reach the object. He had all his intellectual faculties, all his senses; he was only deprived of the faculty of coordinating and regularizing his movements.[4]

This classic description of a cerebellar lesion, originally published in 1824, has scarcely been improved upon to the present day (though such an experiment would perhaps understandably be frowned upon by animal rights activists today). Flourens clearly established the cerebellum's major role in the integration and "programming" of all the innumerable small muscular movements that make up any organized behavior. Even a simple act like walking requires the proper ordering of thousands of discrete movements, and the cerebellum helps achieve this ordering. Flourens observed that his experimental subjects often moved about as if drunk — and we now know that persistent and heavy alcohol use can in fact produce degenerative changes in the cerebellum, and thus the odd and clumsy walking style of many chronic alcoholics. In sum, Flourens proved that the cerebellum was indeed the center of a specific function — but unfortunately for Gall and phrenology that function bore little relation to "amativeness."

Flourens's ablation studies of the **cortex** — the brain's surface area implicated by Gall in most of the "higher" faculties — seemed at first even more damaging to phrenology. As Flourens ablated progressively larger sections of cortex from birds, they gradually lost the use of all of their senses and their capacity for voluntary action. One pigeon, with its *entire* cortex removed, was kept alive by force feeding and other heroic ministrations, but became completely insensitive to visual or auditory stimulation, and never initiated a movement on its own. Only when prodded or physically disturbed would it move, to resume its customary resting position. In describing this bird's state, Flourens imagined it had lost all capacity for consciousness: "Picture to yourself an animal condemned to perpetual sleep, and deprived even of the faculty of dreaming during this sleep."[5] In his view, the animal had lost its **will** along with its cortex.

Flourens believed his findings demolished phrenology. Although he had demonstrated localization of a sort, with different functions attributed to the cerebellum and cortex, he believed these separate functions were evenly distributed *within* each organ. As increasingly larger sections of cortex were removed, for example, all of the various sensory and voluntary functions tended to disappear *together*. Flourens argued that if the phrenologists were right and the cortex housed many different specific organs, then small ablations ought to have removed some organs while leaving others intact, producing more specific effects than he had in fact observed.

Actually, Flourens skated on thin ice here, since by his own description he had ablated progressively deeper "slices" of cortex. Any "slice," no matter how shallow, very likely interfered with many different cortical regions at once, thus producing an apparently general effect. Gall, who contemptuously referred to all brain ablators as "mutilators," eagerly seized upon this point: "[Flourens] mutilates all the organs at once, weakens them all, extirpates them all at the same time."[6] With hindsight, we know that Gall was correct, and that Flourens did miss important effects of cortical localization.

More enduring, however, have been some of Flourens's other conclusions regarding the cortex's flexibility and plasticity. For example, he observed that sometimes (though not always) ablation-caused deficits improved over time, particularly if the animal was young and the ablations relatively small. Since lost brain tissue does not regenerate, this suggested that intact parts of the brain must somehow be able to take over functions previously served by the ablated portions. The exact limits and conditions of such brain plasticity continue to be explored by scientists today.

Moreover, Flourens's investigations of the brain highlighted the state of integration and harmony that normally prevails among its separate parts. While he conceded a certain *"action propre"* ("specific action") for the cerebellum and cortex considered separately, he also emphasized the cooperation and communication between the two brain parts. Actions initiated by the "will" in the cortex had to be put together and integrated by the cerebellum, and the loss of co-ordination occasioned by damage to the cerebellum had to be dealt with by voluntary reactions in the cortex. In Flourens's terminology, the *actions propres* of the parts were subject to an overall *"action commune"* ("common action") of the brain acting as a whole. In a conception somewhat reminiscent of Descartes, Flourens saw the brain as the seat of an integrated and harmonious soul.

Flourens's views seemed much more scientifically respectable than phrenology, and were generally accepted by the scientific establishment throughout the middle 1800s. In the 1860s, however, new findings came to light suggesting that even Flourens's meticulous experiments had failed to detect some important localized functions in the cortex, and that he had in some ways overemphasized the unity of brain function.

Localization Theory Revived: The Brain's Language Areas

Even during the height of Flourens's influence, one particular phrenological localization continued to attract a degree of interest and support from a vocal minority of doctors: the placement of "verbal memory" in the brain regions directly behind the eyes. These doctors studied the mysterious speechlessness that sometimes followed strokes or other injuries to the brain.

Several such cases had been well documented, including that of the famous English author of *Gulliver's Travels*, Jonathan Swift (1667–1745). Following a stroke the year before he died, Swift became unable to speak with ordinary declarative language, even though he seemed to understand everything that was said to him, and he could sometimes utter highly emotional commands or exclamations. Thus he once angrily shouted at a servant trying to break up a large piece of coal: "That is a stone, you blockhead!" Another time when upset with *himself*, he bitterly exclaimed, "I am a fool!" In circumstances calling for ordinary conversation, however, Swift remained completely mute.[7] His emotional outbursts showed that his muscles necessary for the uttering of words remained intact, even while his capacity for discursive speech was lost.

A respected French physician named Jacques Lordat left a remarkable first-person account of a similar condition, from which he ultimately recovered. He recalled the onset of his illness, in 1825, as follows:

I was informed that a person who had come to the house to enquire about my health had refrained from paying me a visit for fear of disturbing me. I tried to utter a few words to acknowledge this courtesy. My thoughts were ready, but the sounds that should convey them to my informant were no longer at my disposal. Turning away in dismay, I said to myself: *So it's true that I can no longer speak!*[8]

Lordat reported that *subjectively* his mental processes seemed unimpaired during his illness; he could think, recognize what was happening in the world, even prepare lectures in his head. Only when he tried to communicate did his deficiency appear. After several months of painstaking labor, he regained his capacity for language and described his illness in words.

Gall had known of such cases and accounted for them as the result of injury or disease to the "organ of verbal memory," the region behind the eyes involved in his first phrenological hypothesis. He had produced one striking supporting case in his own practice, a soldier who had suffered a sword wound to the brain behind his left eye. Afterward, this soldier could no longer easily name things or people, resorting to vague catch-all terms like "Mr. Such-a-one" in referring even to people he knew very well. Gall's description of this case was probably the first published observation of a specific correlation between speech deficit and injury to the left frontal lobe of the cortex.

Though largely ignored in the general devastation following Flourens's attack on phrenology, Gall's hypothesis was kept alive by his former student **Jean Baptiste Bouillaud** (1796–1881). Bouillaud eventually rejected much of phrenology, but felt there was at least a grain of truth to the notion of a "language center" in the frontal region of the cortex, and collected what evidence he could on the issue. This was scanty, since no one had thought it important to perform autopsies on the brains of deceased patients who had suffered from speech losses. Nevertheless, Bouillaud became something of a fanatic on the issue, speaking out at medical meetings and offering to pay five hundred francs to anyone who could demonstrate a case of severe frontal lobe damage unaccompanied by speech disorder. Apparently, no one took him seriously enough to accept his challenge.

One doctor *had* to take Bouillaud seriously, however: his son-in-law **Ernest Aubertin** (1825–1893). Moreover, Aubertin found one very interesting patient whose symptoms supported Bouillaud's theory. A soldier, wounded by gunshot on the left front of his head, had recovered completely except for a soft spot in his skull at the point of the wound. When the spot was gently pressed, he lost his otherwise normal power of speech. This case posed obvious opportunities for conscious or unconscious dissimulation by the patient, and failed to impress skeptics. But Aubertin believed in the patient's sincerity, and now took up cudgels for his father-in-law's theory himself. When he presented his views at the Paris Anthropological Society in 1861, he precipitated one of the critical incidents in the history of brain science.

Paul Broca and the Case of "Tan" **Paul Broca** (1824–1880), a young chief of surgery at a major Parisian hospital, had founded the Paris Anthropological Society in 1859. Through his surgical work Broca had become interested in variations among different people's skeletal structures, particularly their skulls. He invented several instruments for measuring such variations, and founded the Anthropological

Society to bring together other people with similar interests (which in today's terminology would be considered part of *physical* as opposed to *cultural* anthropology). Several experts on head and brain anatomy joined, including Aubertin.

Most of these experts accepted Flourens's general argument about the brain, and regarded Aubertin's contrary view very skeptically. On 4 April 1861, however, Aubertin made an announcement to the Society in the tradition of his father-in-law:

I have studied for a long time a patient . . . who has lost his speech, who nevertheless understands all that is said to him, replying by signs in an intelligent manner to all questions put to him. This patient . . . is now at the Hospital for Incurables [and] will die, without doubt, in a short time. In view of the symptoms which he presents, I have made a diagnosis of softening of the anterior [i.e., frontal] lobes. If at autopsy the anterior lobes are found intact, then I shall renounce the ideas which I have sustained.[9]

Just five days after this challenge, an event occurred which led to Aubertin's patient being largely forgotten, along with Aubertin himself. A patient with similar symptoms turned up on *Broca's* surgical ward, terminally ill with gangrene of the right leg. Twenty-one years earlier he had lost his speech, while remaining otherwise healthy and intelligent. He could understand what was said to him, point correctly to named objects, and answer numerical questions by holding up the appropriate numbers of fingers. Like Swift, he could use words only when angry, uttering the oath *"Sacre nom de Dieu!"* Otherwise his only vocalization was the syllable "tan," which he repeated rhythmically when he wished to speak, and which led to his being nicknamed "Tan" on the wards.

Ten years after Tan's speech loss, his right arm and leg gradually became paralyzed. Early in 1880 he began to go blind and took to his bed almost constantly—a solitary and pathetic creature. When an infection developed in his insensitive right leg, neither he nor the hospital staff noticed until it became gangrenous and he was sent to Broca's surgical ward. Lacking modern antibiotics, Broca immediately saw the case as hopeless. He summoned Aubertin to ask if Tan fit the requirements for a test of his hypothesis; Aubertin replied that he did.

When Tan died a few days later, Broca promptly autopsied the brain and brought it to the Anthropological Society. An egg-sized portion of the left frontal hemisphere had clearly been damaged, with its center very close to Gall's "organ of verbal memory." Though it could not be proved, it seemed likely that Tan's speech problem had begun with progressive brain deterioration starting at that center, his other symptoms developing as the degeneration spread.

One confirming case could not prove a theory, of course, and Broca reserved judgment until he found more. This was more difficult to do than one might think, because he could not experimentally create frontal lesions in humans as Flourens had in animals, and cases of patients who had had both speech impairments and brain autopsies were rare. Thus while Broca may have been lucky to steal Aubertin's thunder in producing the first demonstration case, he proved his real mettle as a scientist by collecting more supportive evidence. Over the next two years, he found autopsy information from some dozen further cases of speech loss. While the extent of brain damage varied considerably among these cases, it always included the same region of the frontal lobe. A surprise finding, for Broca and everyone else, was that the damage almost always occurred on the left side. The crucial region, shown in Figure 3–2, came to be known as **Broca's area**. After some debate, the speech debility resulting from damage to that area came to be called **aphasia**, after the term used by Plato to denote the state of being at a loss for words.

With his investigations of aphasia, Broca became the first establishment figure seriously and effectively to challenge Flourens's conception of the undifferentiated cerebral cortex. His findings ushered in a new period of interest in the localized functions of the brain. In short order, individuals sometimes called the "new phrenologists" discovered many further important localizations.*

---

*In a more dubious achievement, Broca also became known for promoting the idea that differences in brain size correlated positively with differences in intelligence, and that European males — with allegedly larger average brain size than all women and the males of other racial backgrounds — were consequently innately superior to all other groups. Although both ideas were widely accepted for a time (mainly by other European males), neither has been confirmed by later and better research.

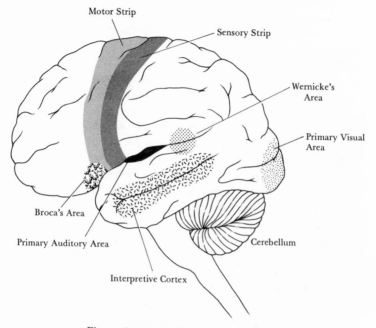

Figure 3–2. *Left side of the human brain.*

<u>Sensory and Motor Areas</u> In 1870, two young German physiologists named **Gustav Fritsch** (1837–1927) and **Eduard Hitzig** (1839–1907) had the bright idea that the brain might not be the totally insensitive organ Aristotle had thought, but might respond to direct *electrical* stimulation. Recent discoveries about the electrochemical nature of the nervous impulse lent plausibility to this idea, and electricity in general was a fashionable and exciting scientific topic of the day, whose possible applications were being explored in many different fields — somewhat in the way that laser technology is today. Thus Fritsch and Hitzig surgically exposed the cortex of a dog, and applied mild electrical stimulation to various specific points with a penlike electrode.

Conducted with makeshift equipment on an unanesthetized animal in Fritsch's kitchen, the experiment partly resembled a scene from a Gothic novel, and would certainly not be approved by ethics committees today. But the results revolutionized brain science, for Fritsch and Hitzig discovered that stimulation to specific points in the region now known as the **motor strip** (see Figure 3–2) elicited specific movements on the opposite side of the body. Stimulation to one particular point on the right motor strip always produced a flexion of the left forepaw, for example, while a neighboring point's electrification caused extension of the left hind leg. Here was evidence for a previously unsuspected kind of localization in the brain, as well as a new experimental technique for studying it.

Many other scientists quickly followed Fritsch and Hitzig's lead, none more skillfully than a young Scottish neurologist named **David Ferrier** (1843–1928). Throughout the 1870s he demonstrated several other functionally distinct "centers" in the cortex, to accompany Broca's area and the motor strip. When he electrically stimulated the rear portion of the occipital (rear) lobe of a monkey's brain, for example, the animal's eyes moved rapidly and synchronously, as if looking at something. Ablation of the same region produced blindness, but no deficiency in any other sense. Thus the occipital cortex contained a **visual area** (see Figure 3–2). Ferrier also discovered an **auditory area** in the temporal (side) lobe, and a strip immediately behind the motor strip that mediated *sensory* functions for the same body parts. Ablations from this **sensory strip** produced *losses of sensitivity* in specific parts of the body, while oblations from the bordering motor strip caused *paralyses*.

While these findings confirmed the reality of cortical localization, they also conclusively undermined the old phrenology, even in the popular view. Although Broca's area resembled Gall's organ of verbal memory in some ways, all of the other newly discovered localizations differed greatly from phrenological organs in that they mediated elementary sensory or motor functions, instead of complex and highly developed "faculties." One diehard phrenologist tried to claim that the leg movements produced by electrical stimulation of the "organ of self-esteem" were really rudimentary acts of *strutting*, but such desperate rationalizations generally received the contempt they deserved. Very quickly, an entirely new conception of brain function came into vogue, attempting to explain not only the newly discovered localizations but also the numerous "blank" areas on the cortical map — that is, areas whose stimulation or ablation produced no clear-cut observable effects in animal subjects.

According to this conception, the brain *receives* sensory information at the various sensory centers, and then *stores* it in the surrounding regions. Thus visual *memories* are presumably stored in specific locations surrounding the visual area, auditory memories around the auditory area, and so on. (Animal subjects could not talk about their memories, of course, so stimulation or ablation of these memory regions had produced no clearly observable effects.) Further, all of these localized memories were hypothesized to be potentially *interconnected* with one another by fibers of white matter. Brain parts particularly rich in white matter were called "association areas." The frontal lobes of human brains — very large compared to other species, and also particularly rich in white matter — were speculated to contain the large association areas responsible for humans' superiority over other animals in thoughtfulness and intelligence.

Wernicke's Theory of Aphasia In 1874, the young German neurologist **Carl Wernicke** (1848–1905) used this new conception of the brain as the basis of an extremely fruitful theory of aphasia. He started by noting that Broca's area lay directly in front of the part of the motor strip responsible for movement of the mouth, tongue, and face — precisely where one would expect to find memories of the movements involved in speech, according to the new conception. Thus, localized damage to Broca's area alone (that is, without extending onto the adjoining motor strip) should theoretically afflict the *memories* for spoken words but not the physical capacity for speaking. This could account for cases like Tan and Jonathan Swift.

Wernicke went on to describe a group of ten patients he had discovered with a very different sort of language disorder, which he called **sensory aphasia** to contrast with the **motor aphasia** previously investigated by Broca. These patients could speak perfectly fluently with correct syntax, but their *understanding* of spoken language was severely impaired, and their speech was marked by numerous peculiar words and mispronunciations that Wernicke called **paraphasias**. The speech of such patients sounded like something from the Theater of the Absurd, as in the following responses of a modern patient with sensory aphasia to the question of what brought him to the hospital:

Boy, I'm sweating, I'm awful nervous, you know, once in a while I get caught up, I can't mention the tarripoi, a month ago, quite a little, I've done a lot well, I impose a lot, while on the other hand, you know what I mean, I have to run around, look it over, trebbin and all that sort of stuff.[10]

Wernicke showed that patients with sensory aphasia had suffered lesions to a part of the left temporal lobe close to the auditory area — precisely where the auditory memories of words should theoretically be stored. This made sense, because so long as the auditory regions themselves remain intact such patients should hear what is said to them and recognize when they are being engaged in conversation, but without remembering what the heard words *mean*. If Broca's area also remains intact, such patients retain the *motor* memories of words necessary for fluent spoken responses, and they may try to reply out of social habit. But since they have not understood what was said to them, their responses seem bizarre to the listener. Wernicke observed that such patients are likely to be misdiagnosed as suffering from a psychotic mental illness if their brain injuries go undetected.

Wernicke explained his patients' mispronunciations, or paraphasias, as the result of the same lesions. Normally, he argued, people listen to themselves as they speak, constantly monitoring and correcting themselves as they go along. If they start to mispronounce a word, they rapidly stop, correct themselves, and begin again with scarcely a break in their sentence. Since sensory aphasics lack comprehension of their own as well as others' spoken words, however, they also lack this self-correcting ability and utter many paraphasias.

The brain region implicated in sensory aphasia has come to be known as **Wernicke's area**, and is shown in Figure 3–2. Wernicke's terms, motor and sensory aphasia, are still commonly used, though the two conditions are also sometimes called **Broca's aphasia** and **Wernicke's aphasia**, respectively.

In a final impressive theoretical achievement, Wernicke successfully predicted the existence of still another kind of aphasic speech disorder, previously undescribed and undetected by doctors. He reasoned that an intact brain must contain association fibers connecting the sensory speech memories in Wernicke's area with the motor ones in Broca's area; these connections make possible the silent monitoring and correcting of one's own speech. If these association fibers become damaged while Broca's and Wernicke's areas remain intact, a condition Wernicke called **conduction aphasia** should occur — marked by paraphasias because of the loss of self-monitoring, but with comprehension and general fluency unimpaired. Such cases should be rare, since damage to the small connecting region would usually be accompanied by injury to the nearby Broca's or Wernicke's area, producing motor or sensory aphasia. Further, the predicted symptoms of conduction aphasia would be relatively mild, making it likely that many cases would be overlooked.

Once placed on the alert by Wernicke, however, neurologists everywhere went on the lookout for cases of conduction aphasia, and soon found several. In addition to their paraphasias, these patients suffered from a striking inability to repeat aloud things that were said to them. Though not specifically predicted by Wernicke, this symptom too clearly accorded with his theory: Without connections between their auditory and motor word memories, the patients lacked a mechanism for modeling their own speech after something they had just heard.

This remarkable vindication of Wernicke's theory indicated that brain science had entered a new era of sophistication. Previously, work had been largely descriptive and atheoretical, directed simply toward the empirical localization of functions in the cortex. Most of these functions turned out to involve elementary sensory and motor reactions rather than complex faculties. Wernicke used that information to construct a theory of one complex function, language, as the result of an *interaction* among several simple sensory, motor, and associative factors. Following his lead, scientists no longer looked for high-level "faculties" localized in the brain, but sought instead to demonstrate how complex psychological processes in general might be created out of the basic elements of sensations, movements, and their memory traces.

Memory and the Equipotentiality of the Brain

Even as Wernicke demonstrated the power of localization theories, certain other facts were coming to light suggesting the brain's potential flexibility and plasticity. Flourens had already shown that some of the functions lost with ablation could sometimes be recovered over time, particularly in young and developing organisms. Language turned out to be one such function. Children suffering damage to Broca's or Wernicke's area were much more likely to recover from aphasia than adults. Moreover, if infants suffered damage to the normal language areas in the left brain while the right side remained intact, language functions still developed normally; the right side apparently "took over" functions normally housed in the left. Such findings suggested that the brain was *not* a pre-formed structure with certain specific slots inevitably pre-destined for specific functions. At least under some conditions, its predispositions for localization could be altered.

Attempts by brain scientists to study the phenomena of **memory** and **learning** provided further evidence of the brain's plasticity. Wernicke's model, of course, assumed that specific memories were somehow "stored" in specific brain cells. Learning presumably occurred whenever previously separate memories became connected with each other via the association fibers. Thus the memories themselves, as well as the connections among them, were assumed to be localized in specific brain cells.

Despite this theory's general plausibility, however, it received a severe challenge from a classic series of experiments conducted in the 1920s by the American psychologist **Karl Spencer Lashley** (1890–1959). As an early "behaviorist," Lashley ruled out any experimental methods involving introspection or reports of conscious states, and restricted his data to the strictly observable and "objective" behaviors of his subjects.* Tame white rats were favored subjects in behavioristic research because they could be easily and constantly observed, their environments could be carefully controlled, and, since they could not talk, they could not mislead the experimenter with un-

---

*Lashley had been the first Ph.D. student of **John B. Watson** (1878–1958), the founder of the behaviorist movement, whose life and career are detailed in Chapter 9.

to stimulus intensity as further "distortions" or "incongruities" imposed by the senses, consistent with his general perspective. Fechner, however, took a different approach. He thought it should be possible to *measure* the perceived as well as the physical intensities of sensory stimuli, and to determine the *mathematical relationships* between the two measures. His sudden intuition in October of 1850 told him the relationships would turn out to be harmonious, and illustrative of the basic underlying unity of the psychological and physical worlds.

Of course, an immediate practical question arose: How might one hope to measure the subjective intensities of stimulation? The yardsticks, scales, and light meters used to measure physical intensities could not be placed inside people's heads to measure their subjective responses. Indeed, Kant had argued against the possibility of psychology's ever becoming a true science precisely because subjective mental phenomena seemed incapable of quantification or measurement.

Fechner saw an answer to this problem, as well as a strong hint as to what his final psychophysical relationships would look like, in some previously little-appreciated work by his Leipzig friend and colleague, the physiologist **Ernst Heinrich Weber** (1795–1878). Several years before, Weber had investigated people's ability to discriminate accurately between different weights of similar appearance, and reported:

In observing the disparity between things that are compared, we perceive not the difference between the things, but the *ratio* of this difference to the magnitude of the things compared.[12]

That is, Weber found that accurate discrimination depended on the relative rather than the absolute difference between the weights. The finest discriminations that could be made always involved judgments where one weight was approximately 1/30th lighter than the other. For example, a weight of 29 drams was the heaviest that could be reliably detected as lighter than one of 30 drams, and one of 58 drams the heaviest that could be differentiated from one of 60 drams. The absolute difference had to be twice as large in the second case as it was in the first, but then the weights themselves were twice as heavy in the second case. In sum, Weber determined that the **just noticeable difference** (commonly abbreviated as **jnd**) for weight discrimination — that is, the minimum amount of difference between two weights necessary to tell them apart — was always an amount equal to 1/30th of the heavier of the weights being compared.

Weber observed similar regularities for other kinds of sensory discriminations — though the specific fraction for the jnd differed with each sense. In comparing the length of lines, for example, the jnd was always about 1/100; a line of 99 millimeters could be differentiated from one of 100, one of 198 from one of 200, and so on. For musical pitches, the jnd seemed to be about 1/161 of the vibrations per second. Weber suspected, though he did not prove, that a constant fraction could be determined for all of the other senses as well.

Weber's findings suggest a new way of looking at the phenomena discussed at the beginning of this section: The sound waves created by a dropped pin become noticeable only if the ratio of their intensity to that of the background noise exceeds the critical fraction for the jnd. Of course that ratio will be higher, and more likely will exceed the critical fraction, when the intensity of background noise is lower.

This work gave Fechner a crucial clue as to how he might empirically demonstrate the harmony between physical and psychological. If one accepted that the jnd was in fact a constant fraction within each of the senses, then the jnd itself could be taken as the unit of measurement for psychological intensities of stimulation. One could then take the smallest intensity of a stimulus that can be perceived at all — a value Fechner called the **absolute threshold** — as the zero point on a scale of psychological intensities. On a graph, successive jnd's above the threshold could be plotted against the measured increases in physical intensities necessary to produce them. Weber's findings suggested that the resulting graph should always show a striking mathematical regularity, as illustrated in the following hypothetical example.

Assume that the absolute threshold for a sense has been shown to be 8 units of physical intensity, and that the jnd fraction has been determined to be 1/2. Thus when the subjective intensity of the stimulation (abbreviated "*S*") is at the starting point, or 0, the corresponding intensity of physical stimulation ("*P*") is 8. To get 1 jnd above the threshold, the physical intensity must increase by 1/2, or 4 units, thus becoming 12; to increase 1 jnd further requires an increase of half of 12, or 6, so the physical intensity now must be 18. Another jnd beyond that requires 9 units of *P*, and so on as in the chart below:

S:	0	1	2	3	4	5	6
P:	8	12	18	27	40.5	60.75	91.125

When these figures are plotted in a graph, they define a regular curve as in Figure 4–4.

Any of the sensory functions we have discussed so far would yield a graph of the same general shape (though with different individual values), because their characteristic feature is an ever-increasing number of units of *P* to produce each succeeding jnd. The *rate* of increase varies from sense to sense, according to its particular jnd fraction; but for every sense some increase is required, and thus its curve will show the gradually accelerating upswing demonstrated in our hypothetical figure. Note that if there were a perfect, one-

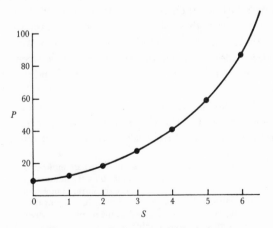

Figure 4–4. *Fechner's psychophysical curve.*

to-one relationship between P and S—that is, if every unit increase in physical stimulation produced an exactly corresponding unit increase in subjective intensity—the graph would not be a curve, but a straight line.

Fechner recognized that these observed relationships between physical and subjective stimulus intensities for many different senses could be expressed by the single, general mathematical formula

$$S = k \log P.$$

That is, the subjective intensity of a stimulus (in jnd units) will always equal the *logarithm* of its physical intensity times some constant (k) which will vary for each sense, but which may be experimentally determined.* Fechner modestly referred to this equation as "Weber's law" when he first published it, but it is now customarily called **Fechner's law** instead.

Nearly ten years passed between Fechner's crucial insight in 1850 and the publication of his law in his 1860 book *Elements of Psychophysics*. During that time he developed new methods for measuring jnd's for senses that had not been investigated by Weber, and expanded upon some implications of his work. On the one hand, of course, the lack of perfect correspondence between subjective and physical stimulus intensities provided another sample of the way human senses "distort" their representations of the physical world. But on the other hand, these distortions occurred in a regular, lawful way, expressible in a beautiful mathematical equation. To Fechner, this provided evidence of an underlying harmony between the "two faces" of nature; that is, between the psychological and the physical worlds.

Fechner's book and law aroused great interest, and some criticism. Critics pointed to studies showing that his law was accurate only approximately, and tended to break down at the extremes of high

---

*A number's logarithm is the power to which some base number must be raised to produce it. For example, the logarithms in base 10 for the numbers 10, 100, 1,000, and 10,000 are 1, 2, 3, and 4, respectively, since the former numbers represent 10^1, 10^2, 10^3, and 10^4, respectively. Note that each unit increase in the logarithms is associated with a progressively larger increase in the numbers they represent: When the logarithm goes from 1 to 2 the number increases by 90; from 2 to 3 by 900; and from 3 to 4 by 9,000. Thus a graph representing the relationship between numbers and their logarithms assumes the same general shape as Figure 4-4.

verifiable subjective reports. Behaviorists studied learning by constructing mazes and other physical puzzles for their animal subjects, and observing their progress in solving them. They found that hungry white rats could gradually learn to solve quite complicated mazes if they were rewarded with food pellets whenever their trial-and-error explorations brought them to the ends of the mazes. The numbers of false turns or "errors" tended to decrease with each succeeding trial, and provided objective indices of the animals' learning.

Lashley originally hypothesized that this learning resulted from the establishment of specific reflex pathways in the brain. That is, brain centers representing the sensory images of specific choice-points in the maze presumably became linked with other centers representing motor memories of either left or right turns. In other words, Lashley believed the specific stimulus-response connections constituting an animal's "memories" of a maze were localized in the brain. And if this were so, he reasoned, ablations of small portions of the cortex theoretically ought to have a selective effect on memory and learning, interfering only with those connections localized in the removed tissue, and leaving others intact.

Lashley tested his hypothesis by first training large numbers of rats to run mazes of varying difficulty, then ablating varying amounts and parts of their brains, and finally observing how impaired their maze performance was after recovery from the surgery. The results surprised him, for the *locations* of the ablations made almost no difference at all. Of much greater importance were the absolute *sizes* of the ablations, and the *difficulty levels* of the mazes involved; that is, large ablations tended to interfere with *all* mazes more than did small ablations, and the greatest learning losses always occurred for the more difficult mazes. Thus memory seemed to pervade the entire cortex, rather than being selectively localized on it. Lashley's results are summarized in Figure 3–3,[11] which graphs the numbers of errors made by rats running mazes of three difficulty levels, after six varying degrees of ablation.

Just as Broca, Ferrier, and Wernicke revived memories of Gall and the early localizationists, so Lashley hearkened back to Flourens and the brain's *action commune* — though for Lashley it was memory rather than the will that seemed evenly distributed throughout the

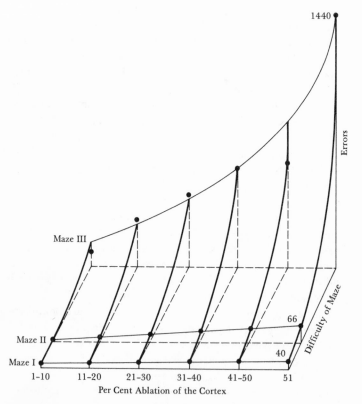

Figure 3-3. *Results of Lashley's ablation studies.*

cortex. In summarizing his results, Lashley contributed two new terms that Flourens would undoubtedly have approved. First, he said that the brain is marked by **equipotentiality**, which he defined as "the apparent capacity of any intact part of a functional brain to carry out . . . the [memory] functions which are lost by the destruction of [other parts]." But the brain's equipotentiality may sometimes be offset by Lashley's second factor, the **law of mass action**, "whereby the efficiency of performance of an entire complex function may be reduced in proportion to the extent of brain injury."[12]

ingram

In sum, Lashley's experiments seemed to rule out any simple theory of memory localization in the brain, and toward the end of his life he wryly expressed his own frustration with the problem: "I sometimes feel in reviewing the evidence on the localization of the memory trace, that the necessary conclusion is that learning just is not possible. It is difficult to conceive of a mechanism which can satisfy the conditions set for it."[13]

The mechanism of memory remains a mystery today, though Lashley's successors have proposed some promising possible solutions. Some have suggested that his original theory oversimplified the problem, and that even elementary maze learning actually involves much more than the coupling of single sensory stimuli with single motor responses. In learning to run a maze, a rat must inevitably associate *many different stimuli* (involving touch, smell, and hearing as well as vision) with the various "correct" motor responses. Thus even if localized stimulus-response connections really do underlie learning and memory, there should be many of them in many different parts of the brain for any single completed act of maze learning. Damage to just a small part of the brain would remove just a few of these, and have a small effect on overall learning; damage to larger areas would remove a larger portion of the total, and produce a larger decrement in performance.

The so-called **redundancy hypothesis** offers a related explanation, suggesting that each individual memory gets stored in several different locations throughout the cortex, with the number increasing as the memory becomes better established and more widely associated with other memories. Ablation of an isolated brain area then would be expected to remove some but not all of the traces of any particular memory.

The contemporary American surgeon and neuropsychologist **Karl Pribram** (b. 1919) has borrowed from modern laser technology in proposing an altogether different sort of explanation, the **holographic theory**. A hologram, he notes, is a photographic plate on which visual information from a scene has been *evenly* dispersed and stored (through a laser process whose description lies beyond the scope of this chapter). A laser beam shone through the plate projects a three-dimensional image of the holographed scene. Moreover, if the plate is cut into pieces and a laser shone through just

97

one piece, the entire scene will be projected, but with less fidelity and sharpness. Thus each small element of visual information is spread throughout the entire holographic plate—just as individual memory traces seem to be spread throughout the cortex. Pribram has argued that the hologram may offer a useful physical model for the way the brain operates.

Much work remains to be done to confirm the holographic or any other theory of memory, for here is one area in which the venerable localization-of-function debate remains very much alive. One certainty, however, is that any final solution will have to account for some relatively recent and very *non*-behavioristic experiments, involving the electrical stimulation of the conscious human brain. While many of their implications remain unclear, these studies represent one of the most intriguing and exciting phases of the localization-of-function controversy.

Stimulation of the Conscious Human Brain

Stimulation studies of the conscious human brain got off to a poor start in 1874, shortly after Fritsch and Hitzig first stimulated the conscious animal brain. A mentally retarded young woman with a cancerous lesion of the scalp and skull came under the care of the Cincinnati doctor **Roberts Bartholow**. Bartholow later reported that, since part of her brain was visible through the opening in her skull, he "supposed that fine needles could be introduced without material injury to the cerebral matter." Following Fritsch and Hitzig's lead, Bartholow connected his needles to a mild electrical supply and stimulated the exposed surface, producing involuntary muscular contractions on the opposite side of the body. When the needle was inserted deeper, the patient complained of an unpleasant tingling in her arm. Then, "in order to develop more decided reactions, the strength of the current was increased," with the following sad results:

Her countenance exhibited great distress, and she began to cry. Very soon the left hand was extended as if taking hold of some object in front of her; the arm presently was agitated by clonic spasms; her eyes became fixed, with pupils widely dilated; her lips were blue, and she frothed at the mouth;

her breathing became stertorous; she lost consciousness, and was violently convulsed on the left side. The convulsion lasted five minutes, and was succeeded by coma.

The patient's general condition worsened after the experiment, and she died before Bartholow could carry out a planned repetition. He examined her brain at autopsy, and concluded that "although it is obvious that even fine needles cannot be introduced into the cerebral substance without doing mischief, yet the fatal result in this case must be attributed to the extension of [her original cancer]."[14] Despite Bartholow's attempt to minimize the harmfulness of his procedures, the grisly experiment created such an outcry that he shortly had to leave Cincinnati.

More than a half century passed before the next stimulation experiments on conscious human subjects. These, by the Canadian neurosurgeon **Wilder Penfield** (1891–1976), had much greater ethical justification and yielded much more valuable scientific results. Penfield began in the 1930s by seeking new surgical treatments for intractable cases of **epilepsy**, which he knew to be caused by abnormal activation of cerebral neurons beginning at a small "focus," and then spreading over larger and larger areas of the brain. When the abnormal activation spreads sufficiently far, patients lose consciousness and have convulsions. Shortly before the convulsions, patients frequently experience peculiar subjective warning signs called **auras**. These vary from patient to patient, and include sensations such as a particular smell, a tingling or other feeling in some particular part of the body, an intense but inexplicable feeling of familiarity or *déjà vu*, or the unexplained arousal of an emotion such as rage, guilt, depression, or elation. One famous epileptic, the great writer Dostoyevsky, experienced two contrasting kinds of emotional auras. One was a feeling of irrational guilt, the conviction that he had committed some unknown but unspeakable crime; the other was "a feeling of happiness such as it is quite impossible to imagine in a normal state, . . . for a few seconds of such bliss, one would gladly give up ten years of one's life."[15]

Penfield had the idea that auras might result from early activation at the focus, before it spread so far as to cause the convulsion and seizure per se. Further, he thought the specific *content* of an aura might depend on the *location* of the focus; an aura of tingling in the left arm, for instance, might be associated with a focus in the right sensory strip. This suggested a daring experimental treatment, to be tried only on the small proportion of epileptic patients whose seizures could not be controlled by ordinary medication.

Using a local anesthetic, Penfield surgically exposed the brains of his fully conscious, volunteer patients. He then gently stimulated different locations with an electrode, seeking specific spots whose stimulation would cause his patients to experience their auras. He often found such spots, and concluded that they marked diseased brain tissue responsible for the epilepsy. Thus he surgically removed the suspect areas, unless they happened to lie near a language region whose ablation might produce aphasia. Most patients reported a subsequent lessening of their epilepsy that justified any side effects from the procedure.

Apart from its therapeutic value, Penfield's remarkable procedure provided invaluable information about localization of function in general. While searching for aura-producing spots, Penfield naturally stimulated many different *normal* regions of the cortex and observed the effects on fully conscious, intelligent, and cooperative individuals. Some of these effects were predictable from earlier localization studies. Stimulation of the motor strip, for example, produced movements on the opposite side of the body — movements that surprised the patients themselves because they occurred involuntarily. When Penfield stimulated the sensory strip his patients reported tingling, quivering, or pressure in various parts of the body. Stimulation of the visual area produced flashes of light, color, and abstract patterns, while the auditory area yielded clicks, buzzes, chirps, rumbles, and other sounds.

There were also many surprises. When Penfield stimulated the regions *surrounding* the primary visual and auditory areas, for example, patients experienced full visual or auditory hallucinations replete with meaning, as opposed to the "contentless" flashes, clicks, and buzzes produced by the primary regions. Thus stimulation of one patient's **secondary visual region** (as Penfield called this surrounding area) led the patient to say, "Oh gee, gosh, robbers are coming at me with guns." He actually *saw* the robbers coming, from behind and to the left.[16] When Penfield stimulated another patient's **secondary auditory region**, one spot produced the sound of a mother calling a child, and another a Beethoven symphony. So real and surprising was the latter sensation that the patient accused Penfield of secretly turning on a radio.

Stimulation of the temporal lobe — the side area of the cortex above the ear — produced the most surprising effects of all. Apart from the relatively small auditory region and Wernicke's area, the temporal lobe had previously been a blank zone on the brain localizationists' map, unimplicated in any of the functions they knew about. But Penfield found what he called the **interpretive cortex** (see Figure 3-2), a temporal region whose stimulation produced two kinds of "psychical responses." First were "interpretive responses," in which patients suddenly and unexplicably saw their immediate situations in new lights. Depending on the points of stimulation, interpretive responses included feelings of *déjà vu*, the opposite sensation that everything was suddenly alien or absurd, senses of foreboding and fear, or sudden euphoria and exhilaration. These interpretive sensations duplicated some patients' epileptic auras, of course, which now became understandable for the first time as the results of focal discharges in the interpretive cortex. Moreover, Penfield had shown that highly specific emotional and orienting attitudes were localized in the brain, just as sensations and movements were.

Penfield's stimulation of other parts of the interpretive cortex produced "experiential responses," described by his patients variously as hallucinatory "dreams" or "flashbacks" of real events from the past, usually with unremarkable content. For example, one patient reported: "Oh, a familiar memory — in an office somewhere. I could see the desks. I was there and someone was calling to me — a man leaning on a desk with a pencil in his hand." Other typical responses included: "A scene from a play; they were talking and I could see it," and "A familiar memory — the place where I hang my coat up — where I go to work."[17] Unlike normal "memories," however, these scenes were vividly *experienced* subjectively, and not merely thought about.

Penfield's exciting findings actually raised more questions than they answered. They demonstrated new and unexpected localized functions of some sort, but the real nature of those functions remains in some doubt today. At first thought, for example, it may be tempting to argue that Penfield's "experiential responses" provided the long-sought evidence for the localization of memories. Their vivid detail suggests that even inconsequential experiences may become permanently recorded in specific brain cells, potentially available for exact recall. But Penfield himself hesitated to equate these responses with "memories."

First, he noted that patients described their experiential responses as being qualitatively different from normal memories—more on the order of vivid dreams than of ordinary thoughts or recollections. Thus the normal functioning of memory must involve something different from the specific stimulation of neurons artificially produced by Penfield. He himself thought the electrical stimulations initiated a "scanning" of experiences recorded in the brain that is part but not all of the normal memory process.

Penfield further cautioned that no one understood the exact effects of artificial electrical stimulation on the cerebral neurons. He personally suspected that electrical stimulation and abnormal epileptic discharges both tend to *inhibit* rather than to activate the normal functions of the neurons involved. Thus interpretive and experiential responses may really be caused by the operation of unknown parts of the brain whose functions are normally *opposed* by the neurons of the interpretive cortex. When the cortical neurons are temporarily knocked out of commission by artificial electrical stimulation or epileptic discharge, the opposed functions are permitted to express themselves.

Even as these issues become resolved, the understanding of the brain will barely have begun. After brain scientists learn *where* specific functions take place, they still have to determine *how* they occur in all their complexity. Penfield observed, for example, that experiential responses were much more like moving pictures than still pictures, indicating that cerebral neurons must somehow represent the "flow" of experience and not just stationary images of it. Much more must be involved than the simple storage of individual static "ideas" in single neural cells. Scientists of the future will be challenged to discover how the complex circuitry of the "organ of the mind" can accomplish such marvelous feats of engineering.

Toward the end of his life, Penfield published a surprising opinion about the ultimate fate of such brain research. He admitted that his own work had originally been inspired by the assumption that the mechanisms of the brain *account for* the phenomena of the mind. He assumed that once the brain was fully understood, all mental and psychological phenomena would be explained in consequence. But by 1975, he had doubts; certain elements of experience — particularly the conscious *willing* or *deciding* to do something, or *believing* in something — had never been produced by electrical stimulation or any other mechanistic process. Penfield now doubted that they ever would be, and wrote:

Because it seems to me certain that it will always be quite impossible to explain the mind on the basis of neuronal action within the brain, and because it seems to me that the mind develops and matures independently throughout an individual's life as though it were a continuing element, . . . I am forced to choose the proposition that our being is to be explained on the basis of two fundamental elements.[18]

In other words, Penfield came to regard "brain" and "mind" as two independent though interacting entities, each with its own separate levels of explanation. He thus finally opted for a dualism not very different (except in detail) from Descartes's.

Penfield admitted that he could not *prove* this opinion, and many contemporary brain scientists would contest it. And they would note that Penfield's original assumption of a unity between brain and mind had been highly productive, helping to suggest his important work in the first place. But still, Descartes's issue obviously remains very much alive, and will continue to animate brain scientists as well as philosophers well into the future.

Suggested Readings

For general accounts of the history of the localization-of-function controversy see David Kretch's "Cortical Localization of Function" in Leo Postman, ed., *Psychology in the Making* (New York: Knopf,

1962), and Robert M. Young's *Mind, Brain and Adaptation in the Nineteenth Century* (Oxford: Clarendon Press, 1970). For more specific aspects of the story see: Owsei Temkin, "Gall and the Phrenological Movement," in *Bulletin of the History of Medicine* (*21*:275–321, 1947); Byron Stookey, "A Note on the Early History of Cerebral Localization," in *Bulletin of the New York Academy of Medicine* (*30*:559–576, 1954); and Norman Geschwind, "Wernicke's Contribution to the Study of Aphasia," in *Cortex* (*3*:448–463, 1967).

Karl Lashley cogently summarized his own findings in his book *Brain Mechanisms and Intelligence* (Chicago: University of Chicago Press, 1929), as did Wilder Penfield in Wilder Penfield and Lamar Roberts, *Speech and Brain-Mechanisms* (Princeton: Princeton University Press, 1959). Penfield's late doubts about *ever* being able to account for the "mind" totally in terms of brain function are expressed in his *The Mystery of the Mind* (Princeton: Princeton University Press, 1975).

4

The Sensing and Perceiving Mind: Immanuel Kant, Hermann Helmholtz, and Gustav Fechner

In middle age, the German philosopher **Immanuel Kant** (1724–1804) arose from what he called "my dogmatic slumbers." Trained in the Leibnizean tradition of German philosophy, he had previously written respected but unspectacular works on topics such as the existence of God and the difference between absolute and relative space. But now, stimulated by a challenge from one of John Locke's successors in the British associationist school, Kant embarked upon a program of "critical philosophy" that subtly but crucially refashioned the German view of humanity and nature. Among its unintended results was a climate of opinion conducive to the scientific study of the mind, and the development of a new and experimental psychology.

The Scottish philosopher **David Hume** (1711–1776) had aroused the intellectually slumbering Kant, by carrying Lockean empiricism and associationism to an extreme and questioning the logical status of the concept of **causality** — our intuitive belief that certain events have been directly "caused by" certain other preceding events. When one billiard ball strikes another, for example, we usually interpret the motion of the second as having been directly *caused* by the impact of the first. Classical scientific theories assume that specific antecedent conditions *cause* specific and predictable consequences. These uses of the term "cause" imply a *necessary* sequential relationship between certain antecedent and consequent events, and that we immediately apprehend this necessity when we perceive the events and attribute causality to them.

Hume doubted this. All we can ever really know, he argued, is that certain regular sequences of events have occurred in the past, leading us to expect their repetition in the future. Our conviction that one billiard ball's motion has been caused by its impact with another thus really amounts to the recollection of associated impact-movement sequences from the past, and the assumption that such will continue in the future. "Causality" is nothing more than that. The presumed *necessity* of the connection between the events is never directly perceived, and causality thus has only a probabilistic instead of an absolute basis. As Hume summarized: " 'Tis not, therefore, reason, which is the guide of life, but custom. That alone determines the mind, in all instances, to suppose the future conformable to the past."[1]

From a practical point of view, of course, these considerations make no difference. We fare best in the real world by anticipating lawful regularities in nature, whether their causation be real or merely assumed. But to a philosopher like Kant, concerned with the essential nature of human knowledge, the issue was crucial. If one could not actually "know" causality in nature, then the logical underpinnings of science and the entire structure of knowledge seemed challenged.

Kant responded to this challenge with a simple but revolutionary variant of Leibniz's nativist argument. He argued that since causality cannot be proven to exist in the external world, but nevertheless seems an inescapable part of our experience, it must represent an innate contribution of the mind. He postulated two separate domains of reality, one completely inside the human mind, the other completely outside. The external or **noumenal world** consists of "things-in-themselves" — objects in a "pure" state independent of human experience. Although presumed to exist, and to interact with the human mind, the noumenal world can never be known directly, for once it encounters a human mind it becomes transformed by that mind into the inner or **phenomenal world**. The term "phenomenal" comes from the Greek *phainomenon*, meaning "appearance," and reflects Kant's argument that human beings never directly experience the pure reality of things-in-themselves, but a series of "appearances" or "phenomena" that are partly the *creations* of an active mind encountering the noumenal world. Thus the mind for Kant does not just passively reflect or record the external world, but actively participates in the creation of each person's experience of that world.

In creating the phenomenal world, the Kantian mind inevitably follows certain rules of its own. It always localizes phenomena in *space* and *time*, for example — dimensions that Kant referred to as the **intuitions**. In addition, Kant argued that the mind automatically organizes phenomena in terms of twelve **categories**, defining their quality, quantity, relationships, and mode. Among the relational categories is the concept of causality. Thus human beings inevitably experience the world as organized in time and space, and as operating according to causal laws — not because the noumenal world is "really" that way, but because the mind can do nothing else but structure phenomenal experience that way.

Kant expounded on the implications of his critical philosophy in a series of books between 1781 and 1798, beginning with the *Critique of Pure Reason* and concluding with *Anthropology from a Pragmatic Point of View*.[2] The importance of these works for the future science of psychology lay not in his specific list of intuitions and categories, but in his general insistence that the mind itself contributes importantly to our experience of external reality, in ways that are capable of systematic analysis and description. In the Kantian context, the inherent properties of mind assumed a crucial new importance, worthy of study in their own right.

Ironically, after staking a claim for the importance of the study of the mind's organizing properties, Kant went on to assert that such study would never be able to achieve the status of a true "science" like physics. He argued that mental phenomena, in contrast to the physical objects investigated by physical scientists, (1) have no spatial dimension; (2) are too transient to pin down for sustained observation; (3) cannot be experimentally manipulated; and (4) perhaps most important of all, cannot be mathematically described or analyzed. In other words, many of the categories and intuitions necessary for scientific thought seemed inapplicable to mental phenomena, and for this reason Kant thought psychology must always remain a "philosophical" rather than a "scientific" discipline.

Throughout the century after Kant, however, a number of un-questionably scientific investigators began serious study of human sensory processes, and focused attention on many situations in which one's conscious experience was demonstrably different from, or a transformation of, the "objective" external stimuli giving rise to the experience. In the wake of Kant's philosophy, these transformations seemed interpretable as the effects of an active, creative agency, analogous to, if not identical with, the Kantian mind.

Among the simplest and most obvious of these situations were **optical illusions**, where one's conscious impression of a visual stimulus differs demonstrably in some respect from its "objective" properties. In Figure 4–1, for example, a test with a ruler will show the two horizontal lines to be of exactly the same length. The simple imposition of seven converging lines, however, has made the top line *seem* markedly longer than the bottom one. The real difference in length, of course, lies not in the lines themselves, but has been somehow contributed by the mind's perceptive process.

In a related vein, neurophysiologists in the early nineteenth century discovered the so-called **law of specific nerve energies**, asserting that each sensory nerve in the body conveys one and only one kind of sensation. First proposed by the Scottish scientist **Charles Bell** (1774–1842) in a privately published monograph of 1811, the law's implications were most fully explored and developed in the 1830s by the German physiologist **Johannes Müller** (1801–1858). The better reception and development of the law in Germany was no historical accident, for Kant's philosophy had created a particularly receptive intellectual climate there for appreciating its implications.

Essentially, the law of specific nerve energies contradicted the

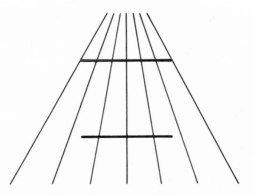

Figure 4-1. *An optical illusion.*

traditional concept of a sensory nerve as something like a hollow tube, capable of conveying light, sound, pressure, or any other kind of stimulation that happened to be introduced into it. Instead, each sensory nerve produces only one type of sensation — for example, visual, auditory, or tactile — regardless of how it becomes stimulated.

A simple experiment will demonstrate the visual specificity of the **optic nerve**, which leads into the brain from the retina at the back of the eye. In normal vision, the optic nerve becomes stimulated by photochemical reactions of light on the retina, and transmits signals to the brain which result in conscious visual sensations of light. If, however, you turn your eyes as far to the right as you can, close your eyes, and then press gently on the left side of your left eyeball, you will see a spot of colored light in the right-hand side of your visual field. You have here stimulated the retina and hence the optic nerve with tactile pressure rather than the normal light rays — but the effect is still a *visual* sensation. You have literally *seen* the pressure on your eyeball, because the stimulated optic nerve can convey no other sensations except visual ones. The same sort of specificity characterizes the other sensory nerves.

The law of specific nerve energies seemed especially interesting in the general context of Kantian philosophy, since now particular sensations could no longer be taken as infallible representations of external "reality." Seeing a particular pattern of light, for example, now only meant that the visual nerves had somehow been stimulated — and while the stimulation *might* have originated in light rays from a real external object, there could be no guarantee of the fact. The *immediate* source of sensory experience was revealed to be not the external world alone, but a sensory nervous system that has interacted with the external world and added its own contribution to the contents of consciousness.

Further, physical scientists had increasingly demonstrated the usefulness of conceptualizing the physical, "external" world as ultimately composed of various forces, waves, and energies, which, like Kant's things-in-themselves, are not directly apprehendable by the senses. Light, sound, or heat waves, for example, presumably impinge on the nervous system, but instead of being perceived as *waves* they somehow get transformed into the phenomenal experiences of color, sound, and warmth and cold. But while the ultimate qualities of the external world were not *directly* perceivable by the human senses, they became increasingly so *indirectly* thanks to new techniques of scientific measurement and analysis. Physicists devised apparatuses to give them precise, numerical values for the wavelengths and frequencies of light or sound waves, for example. Thus the nineteenth-century physicists' external world remained like Kant's noumenal world in being only indirectly knowable by the senses, but increasingly differed from it by being describable in mathematical and other scientific terminology.

Two nineteenth-century Germans helped psychology to gain recognition as a genuine *science* — Kant notwithstanding — by investigating and discovering lawful relationships between these newly specifiable aspects of the physical world, and the ways they are consciously experienced by people. **Hermann Helmholtz** (1821–1894), a student of Johannes Müller working in what he explicitly saw as the tradition of Kant, carried the doctrine of specific nerve energies to far-reaching conclusions while becoming one of the greatest scientists of his time. And **Gustav Theodor Fechner** (1801–1887) laid the groundwork for a mathematically based experimental psychology, by studying how differences in the physical intensities of stimulation are perceived psychologically.

Hermann Helmholtz (1821–1894). *The National Library of Medicine, Bethesda, Maryland.*

Helmholtz's Early Life

Hermann Helmholtz was born on 31 August 1821 in the Prussian town of Potsdam near Berlin. His father, a high school teacher with strong interests in Kantian philosophy, encouraged Hermann's early enthusiasm for science. Physics became the boy's consuming passion from the moment he found some old textbooks in his father's library. He worked on optics diagrams beneath his school desk when he should have been studying Latin, spoiled the family linen with chemistry experiments, and in due course became the most promising young scientist in town.

At that time, however, a young man had to show more than promise in order to practice science seriously. Although the educated classes were beginning to appreciate the importance of science, job opportunities were scarce. The pursuit of "pure science" as a vocation remained the prerogative of the independently wealthy — whose numbers did not include the Helmholtz family. Fortunately, however, the Prussian government had instituted a program offering free medical training for poor but talented students at Berlin's Royal Friedrich-Wilhelm Institute, in exchange for eight years' service as army surgeons after graduation. While not as appealing to young Helmholtz as physics, medicine at least involved science; he applied at seventeen and was accepted. According to his letters home he did little for the next year but study medicine, relieved only occasionally by piano playing, reading Goethe and Byron, and "sometimes for a change the integral calculus."

In the second year of the program Helmholtz began to study physiology with Johannes Müller, the eminent propounder of the law of specific nerve energies. He also befriended a brilliant group of fellow students including **Émile du Bois-Reymond** (1819–1892), who would later establish the electrochemical nature of the nervous impulse; **Rudolf Virchow** (1821–1902), who would pioneer the field of cell pathology; and **Ernst Brücke** (1819–1893), who would become the favorite teacher of Sigmund Freud. Helmholtz shone even among this exceptional group of students, largely because of his unusual grasp of the physics concepts Müller frequently employed in accounting for physiological processes. For example, he analyzed the eye as an optical device like a camera, and the ear as a propagator of sound waves through solid and liquid media.

Even with his respect for physics, however, Müller still clung to an old physiological doctrine known as **vitalism**, according to which all living organisms are imbued with an ineffable "life force" which gives them their vitality, and which is not analyzable by scientific methods. Müller did not deny that ordinary physical and chemical processes often take place in living organisms; his willingness to use physical principles in analyzing the eye and ear testified to that. But he also believed these processes are somehow harnessed and controlled in living organisms by the vital force. With death, the vital force presumably departs and physicochemical processes are allowed to run free, leading to the putrefaction and decay of the body, rather than to its maintenance. Belief in vitalism implied that there was a limit to the possible scientific understanding of physiological processes, since the life force itself was presumably beyond scientific analysis.

Although respectful of their famous teacher, Helmholtz and his friends refused to accept this implied limitation on science. To them, the gains from using physical principles in physiology had been so great that it seemed foolish to postulate any limits to the approach. Accordingly, they rejected vitalism and adopted the doctrine of **mechanism**, declaring *all* physiological processes to be potentially understandable in terms of ordinary physical and chemical principles. The processes might be highly complex and beyond present comprehension, but ultimately they must be subject to the same universal physical laws as inanimate processes. Mechanism became an article of faith among the students, which they duly solemnized by composing and swearing to the following formal oath:

No other forces than the common physical-chemical ones are active within the organism. In those cases which cannot at the time be explained by these forces one has either to find the specific way or form of their action by means of the physical-mathematical method, or to assume new forces equal in dignity to the physical-chemical forces inherent in matter, reducible to the force of attraction and repulsion.[3]

The students' avowal of mechanism led them to differ from their teacher more in emphasis and attitude than in the actual methods of physiological research. No "ultimate experiment" could be done to choose between vitalism and mechanism, and Müller was quite happy to apply physical principles to physiology as far as they would go. He disagreed with his students only in his certitude that a limit to mechanism would be reached at *some* point, when the vital force entered the picture. Nevertheless, this difference subtly influenced the kinds of problems selected for investigation. Müller, for example, believed that the deepest mysteries of nervous functioning probably involved the life force and so remained impervious to scientific understanding. He believed that nervous impulses traversed nerve fibers with infinite or near-infinite speeds, probably because of their close involvement with the life force. Accordingly, he did not seriously contemplate research into possible physicochemical properties of the nervous impulse. Helmholtz and his mechanistic friends operated under no such constraint, and partly as a result they revolutionized physiology.

The Triumph of Mechanism   At twenty-one, Helmholtz completed a dissertation on the microscopic nerve structure of invertebrates, received his medical degree, and faced his eight-year military obligation. As an army surgeon in his hometown of Potsdam he found his medical duties tedious but scarcely all-consuming of his time, so he built a small physiological laboratory in his barracks where he studied metabolic processes in frogs. Conceived and conducted within the mechanistic framework, his experiments demonstrated that the amount of muscular energy and heat generated by a frog was consistent with the amount of energy released by the oxidation of the food it consumed. That is, he showed that ordinary chemical reactions were *capable* of producing (though not necessarily that they *did* produce) all of the physical activity and heat generated by a living organism.

In 1847, Helmholtz's fifth year in the army, he turned his attention to an idea implicit in the above research, namely, the **conservation of energy**. According to this notion, all the different kinds of forces in the universe — heat, light, gravity, magnetism, etc. — were potentially interchangeable forms of a single huge but quantitatively fixed reservoir of energy. Energy could be transformed from one state to another, but never created or destroyed by any physical process. Thus the total amount of energy in the universe was constantly conserved.

Under this hypothesis, a machine was simply a device for transforming energy from a less useful to a more useful kind. A steam engine, for example, transformed the heat from a fire into the motion of steam molecules, whose energy was transformed into the motion of pistons, which in turn activated the usefully moving parts of the engine. The frog's muscles Helmholtz had studied could be thought of as machines that transformed the potential chemical energy stored in food and oxygen into movement and body heat.

Several different scientists had hypothesized the conservation of energy in the early 1840s, but Helmholtz approached the topic in a unique and particularly influential manner in his 1847 paper, "The Conservation of Force." Here he began by arguing that a perpetual-motion machine, if it could be successfully built, would necessarily violate the conservation-of-energy principle. Any machine with moving contiguous parts would inevitably generate heat by friction, for example, which would represent a loss of total energy in the system. Under the conservation principle, motion could never be "perpetual," but would have to be maintained by the constant input of new energy or fuel from without, to compensate for the energy lost as heat. Helmholtz proceeded to show that a successful, conservation-violating perpetual-motion machine had never been built, and never *could be* given the accepted laws of gravity, heat, electricity, magnetism, and electromagnetism — thus suggesting that the conservation of energy must hold for each of those kinds of forces. After discussing these subjects from the domain of physics, Helmholtz concluded by noting that all *organic* processes studied so far had also seemed governed by conservation of energy — thus implying that the range of this physical principle extended into physiology.

In recognition of this brilliant work, the Prussian government released Helmholtz early from his military obligation and appointed him lecturer on anatomy at Berlin's Academy of Arts in 1848. The next year he was made professor of physiology at Königsberg, Kant's old university.

Two major achievements marked Helmholtz's six-year tenure at Königsberg. First, while preparing an optics lecture during his first year, he realized that a partially silvered mirror could be arranged in such a way as to allow an observer to look directly at the retina of a living subject's eye. This inspired him to invent the **ophthal-**

moscope, an invaluable tool for eye examination quickly appreciated by eye doctors around the world, and still used today.

Helmholtz's second major project at Königsberg held greater import for psychology. He became interested in the question of the speed of the nervous impulse, which Müller and other authorities had taken to be instantaneous or almost so, and thus immeasurably fast. During the 1840s, however, Helmholtz's mechanist friend du Bois-Reymond had studied the chemical structure of nerve fibers, and hypothesized that the nervous impulse might be an electrochemical wave traveling along the nerve at a slower rate than anyone had imagined. Helmholtz speculated it might even be slow enough for measurement in a laboratory.

To test this startling idea, Helmholtz devised an instrument capable of measuring smaller fractions of seconds than were detectable by existing timepieces. He used a simple laboratory galvanometer, an electricity-detecting device with a needle that deflected in proportion to the strength of current passing through it. Helmholtz knew that when current first came on, a short but measurable and consistent amount of time occurred before the needle reached its maximum deflection. If the current were switched on and off almost immediately, before the maximum deflection had been reached, the proportion of full needle deflection achieved corresponded to the proportion of time necessary for full deflection.

With this galvanometric "stopwatch," Helmholtz ingeniously measured the speed of neural impulse in a severed frog's leg. He knew that mild electrical stimulation of the nerve in the leg would cause the foot to twitch, and arranged his apparatus so a foot twitch could turn his electrical supply *off*. His electrical circuit also passed through the time-calibrated galvanometer. Thus when he turned on the current the galvanometer needle began to move, but it stopped as soon as the foot twitch turned things off; its extent of deflection measured the fraction of a second the current had flowed.

Helmholtz compared these fractions of seconds when the originating current was applied to different locations on the nerve fiber, and found the farther the location from the foot, the longer the reaction took. A stimulation four inches from the foot began a reaction that took 0.003 second longer than one begun with a stimulation just one inch away. Helmholtz concluded that this must have represented the time necessary for the nervous impulse to travel the extra three inches, and calculated that the speed of the impulse must therefore have been about eighty-three feet per second—approximately fifty-seven miles per hour. This was fast, but certainly far from instantaneous or the speed of light.

Helmholtz next turned to *human* subjects whom he trained to make a response such as pressing a button whenever a stimulus was applied to their legs. Subjects took slightly but measurably longer to respond when the toe was stimulated, as opposed to the thigh. Assuming that a nervous impulse had to travel from the point of stimulation to the brain to initiate the response, Helmholtz estimated that its speed in the human leg was somewhere between 165 and 330 feet per second. High variability made these results less certain than those from the frog, but they at least confirmed that the speed of nervous impulse was finite and measurable. Helmholtz himself soon abandoned these studies of human **reaction times**, but we shall see in the next chapter how they were later expanded and developed by his followers in the earliest laboratories devoted explicitly to experimental psychology.

At first, however, most scientists failed to appreciate the significance of Helmholtz's experiments on the nervous impulse because of his opaque literary style. His friend du Bois-Reymond chided: "Your work, I say with pride and grief, is understood and recognized by myself alone. You have, begging your pardon, expressed the subject so obscurely that your report could at best only be an introduction to the discovery of method." Helmholtz's father attended a lecture and found his son "so little able to escape from his scientific rigidity of expression, . . . that I am filled with respect for an audience that could understand and thank him for it."[4]

Further, some of the implications of Helmholtz's research were simply too surprising to be easily believed. Mental processes are generally experienced subjectively as occurring instantaneously, and physiologists naturally assumed that any neurological events responsible for them must be nearly instantaneous too. Yet Helmholtz's experiments suggested that a whale receiving a wound to its tail could not become conscious of the injury until a full second had passed to allow an impulse to travel from tail to brain, and that another second would pass before a message triggering defensive reaction could be relayed from brain back to tail. Such long reaction times are now known to be characteristic of large animals, but many scientists in the 1850s found that hard to believe.

Despite their initial implausibility, Helmholtz's results gradually gained acceptance and immeasurably strengthened the general case for mechanism. His biographer noted: "The unexpectedly low rate of propagation in the nervous system [was] incompatible with the older view of an immaterial or imponderable [vitalistic] principle as the nervous agent, but quite in harmony with the theory of motion of material particles in the nerve substance."[5] Such results showed mechanism to be more productive than vitalism, suggesting important experiments and ideas that vitalism discouraged. Had Helmholtz and du Bois-Reymond not been mechanists, they would never have thought even to try their experiments. In the wake of their success, a "new physiology" came into vogue, with ambitions of accounting mechanistically even for those processes in the brain and nervous system that presumably underlay higher mental functioning.

Helmholtz on Sensation and Perception

Helmholtz would have won a place in the history of psychology for his experiments on nervous transmission alone, but he followed these with an even more monumental series of studies of **vision** and **hearing** that still stand as a foundation of the modern psychology of sensation and perception. While at the universities of Königsberg, Bonn, and Heidelberg between 1853 and 1868, he not only conducted much original research in these fields, but also personally replicated all the major experiments of other scientists to ensure their accuracy. (He even taught himself Dutch so he could read one important article in the original.) In his *Handbook of Physiological Optics* (1856–1866) and the ponderously titled *The Theory of the Sensation of Tone as a Physiological Basis for the Theory of Music* (1863) he attempted to summarize *all* of the available knowledge about the senses of vision and hearing. By most accounts he nearly succeeded, and both books are still widely used today.

Helmholtz approached both senses with a similar strategy, which we shall illustrate here by discussing his treatment of vision. He started by dividing his general subject into primarily physical, primarily physiological, and primarily psychological categories, although recognizing that they were all interrelated. The physical studies regarded the eye as an optical instrument, examining the processes by which light from the external world comes to be focused into an image on the retina. The physiological analyses concerned the problem of how an image on the retina conveys signals to the brain which result in conscious **sensations** of light. Psychological analysis followed the process a step further, asking how sensations of light become converted into meaningful **perceptions** of objects and events.

His distinction between sensations and perceptions bears elaboration. Sensations are the "raw elements" of conscious experience, requiring no learning or prior experience. In vision, they include the spatially organized patches of light with varying hues and brightnesses that fill one's visual field, quite independently of any "meaning." Perceptions, by contrast, are the meaningful *interpretations* given to sensations. As you look outside a window, for example, your sensations might include patches of blue and white in the upper field of vision, with green, brown, and yellow areas below. Your perceptions of the same scene might be of a landscape, with sky and clouds above trees and fields. For Helmholtz, the conversion of an image on the retina of the eye into conscious sensations of color was a physiological process, mediated by neurological mechanisms between the eye and the brain. The further conversion of sensations into perceptions was a psychological process involving activities in the brain, but also dependent upon the learning and experience of the individual. Since both processes transform input of one kind into conscious output of another, however, Helmholtz regarded both as examples of the sort of creative activities of the human mind that had been postulated by Kant.

We turn now to some of Helmholtz's specific points regarding the physical, physiological, and psychological aspects of the visual system.

119

Physical Properties of the Eye Helmholtz showed how the optical properties of the eye could be described as if it were a microscope, camera, or other manufactured optical instrument. As is shown in Figure 4–2, the eye has a curved and transparent surface called the **cornea**, in front of a transparent and elliptically shaped **lens**. Because of its curvature, the cornea-lens system refracts, or bends, incoming light rays such that a miniature and inverted image of the external object is projected onto the light-sensitive **retina**, analogous to the film in a camera, at the back of the eye.

In a camera, the images of nearby or distant objects may be brought to sharp focus by altering the distance between the lens and film. The eye achieves the same end, but by a different mechanism in the lens itself called **accommodation**: The lens assumes a relatively flat shape for sharply focusing distant objects on the retina, and bulges in the middle for nearby ones.

Helmholtz also observed, however, that virtually all of the eye's physical features have "defects" or imperfections that would be considered unacceptable in a high-quality camera, telescope, or other manufactured instrument. The eye's field of maximum sharpness is very small, for example, consisting only of that part of the image that falls on a tiny section of the retina known as the **fovea**. The fovea's size can be appreciated by extending an arm fully and focusing on the nail of the forefinger; the image of the nail completely fills the fovea, whose size relative to the retina is thus the same as the size of the nail's image relative to the rest of the visual field. Visual acuity within the fovea is excellent, and a normal observer

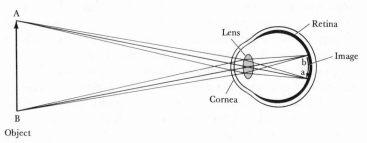

Figure 4–2. *Optical features of the eye.*

can distinguish images on it that are separated by less than one percent of its diameter. Acuity decreases rapidly for images falling outside the fovea, however, and images at the edge of the visual field are very imprecise indeed. A photograph providing an image like that recorded by the eye would be very unsatisfactory, because everything but the very center would be blurred. The eye compensates for this, so we do not normally notice it, because of its ability to "scan" a scene, shifting its focus very quickly and flexibly from one part of the visual field to another.

Helmholtz observed many other "deficiencies" in the optical properties of the eye. Colors are imperfectly reproduced on the retina, for example, because the fluid in the eyeball is not perfectly colorless, and because the lens refracts the relatively longer rays of red light less than the shorter rays at the blue-violet end of the spectrum. An imperfect alignment of refractive surfaces known as **astigmatism** distorts images in all people's eyes, though to highly varying degrees. Perhaps the most dramatic defect of all is the **blind spot**, which occurs because a small part of the retina where the optic nerve leaves it contains no light-sensitive receptor cells. To demonstrate your own blind spot, draw two X's on a sheet of paper, side by side and two inches apart. Then hold the paper at arm's length, close your left eye, and focus on the left-hand X with your right eye. Now slowly draw the paper toward your eye; at some point the right-hand X will suddenly disappear as its image falls upon your blind spot.

For Helmholtz, these "defects" had philosophical as well as practical significance, supporting what he regarded as a Kantian interpretation of experience. He argued that even at the level of the eye, the registered image of external "reality" on the retina is not a perfect reproduction of the external stimulus. A certain amount of change and distortion inevitably takes place because of the features of the eye. And at the next, physiological level of processing, as the image on the retina becomes converted into conscious visual sensations, the transformations and distortions increase further. Our conscious visual sensations are *not* exact reproductions of the physical objects that give rise to them, or even of the images on the retina. Nothing better illustrates this point than Helmholtz's influential treatment of the subject of color vision.

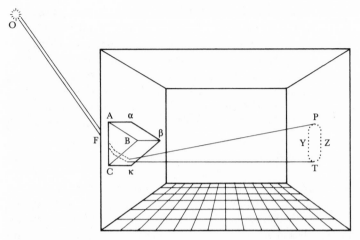

Figure 4-3. *Newton's diagram of the solar spectrum (from his* Optical Lectures).

Color Vision A century and a half before Helmholtz's birth, Isaac Newton discovered that the "white" light from the sun is more complicated than it seems. He shone a narrow band of ordinary sunlight through a transparent crystal prism as represented at the left of Figure 4-3, and observed the light to emerge on the right as the elongated, multicolored band known as the **solar spectrum**, with red at the bottom (T) followed by orange, yellow, green, and blue to violet at the top (P).

Newton's observation was explained by hypothesizing that the different spectral colors represent light of different wavelengths, and that the white light of the sun is composed of all of the different wavelengths mixed together. When the mixture of sunlight passes through the prism, shorter waves get bent or "refracted" more than longer ones; thus the emerging light is sorted out in the order of its wavelengths, with the relatively long red light having been bent relatively little, and the blue-violet light relatively much. At first thought, then, it might seem that our color sensation is simply a means of differentiating the various wavelengths of light we encounter: When we see orange, for example, we are encountering light whose waves are shorter than red but longer than yellow.

This idea turned out to be oversimplified, however, holding true only in certain circumstances. Experiments with **color mixing** revealed the true situation as more complex, showing that the visual sense sometimes responded to *mixtures* of wavelengths in exactly the same way it did to individual spectral colors. For example, if light from the red part and light from the yellow part of the spectrum are superimposed upon each other, the visual result is a sensation of orange indistinguishable from the orange of the spectrum. Thus widely differing physical stimuli (in terms of the wavelengths of light striking the eye) can produce identical conscious sensations of color.

Several scientists studied the details of color mixing, with the most complete analysis being reported by the Scot **James Clerk Maxwell** (1831–1879) in 1855, just as Helmholtz was beginning his own studies of color vision. By then, many different pairs of **complementary colors** had been identified; that is, pairs of spectral colors which when mixed together created a sensation of white light indistinguishable from sunlight. A certain red mixed with a certain blue-green always produced white, for example, as did a certain yellow when mixed with a certain blue-violet. Moreover, a particular combination of *three* spectral colors—a certain red, a green, and a blue-violet—not only produced white when mixed equally together, but also could be mixed in various other combinations so as to produce *any other* color. These three, which seemed to be building blocks for all of the kinds of color sensation, came to be known as the **primary colors.***

Helmholtz explained these phenomena by means of the **trichromatic theory,** according to which the retina contains three different kinds of receptor cells, each one responding most strongly to light waves of one of the three primary colors, and with diminishing strength to light waves increasingly different from it. Nerves attached to the receptors presumably transmit messages to the brain whenever their receptors are stimulated. Here was an elaboration

---

*Children usually learn from experience with paintboxes that the primary colors are red, blue, and yellow, since those are the best constituents for making other colors. The discrepancy arises because paints contain pigments which selectively absorb as well as reflect light waves. The absorbing capacities of the pigments cause them to give different results when mixed, as compared to the simple mixture of projected lights on a screen.

of Müller's specific energy theory, suggesting that individual nerves transmit sensory messages not only of a specific *kind* (visual, auditory, tactile, etc.), but also of a specific *quality* (red, green, or blue-violet).

Helmholtz acknowledged that the English scientist **Thomas Young** (1773–1829) had suggested a similar idea in 1802, so the name **Young-Helmholtz theory** is often used as well as the trichromatic theory. In fact, the idea had been published as early as 1777, by an obscure and somewhat disreputable English pharmacist named G. Palmer.[6] Thus one might be tempted to argue for the "Palmer-Young-Helmholtz theory." For scientific recognition, however, being first is not really enough; one must also successfully demonstrate and communicate the relevance and usefulness of the theories one proposes. On these scores, Young's writings had more influence than Palmer's, and Helmholtz greatly surpassed them both; thus the standard name is not altogether inappropriate.

Helmholtz clearly demonstrated the trichromatic theory's ability to explain many facts of color vision and mixing. According to the theory, when spectral red, green, or blue-violet light strikes the retina, only one kind of receptor is strongly stimulated and results in a sensation of a "pure" primary color. Light of the non-primary colors, or some combination of colors, results in the stimulation of some combination of the three receptor types, and the sensation of a non-primary color. Thus if the red and blue-violet receptors are simultaneously excited, the sensation of purple results; red and green together produce sensations of orange or yellow (depending on the proportions). When *all three* types of receptors are simultaneously and equally excited, sensations of *white* occur. Sunlight, consisting of all the wavelengths of light, naturally stimulates all three receptor types. Complementary colors do the same: In the combination of red and blue-green, for example, red light stimulates the red receptors and the blue-green light simultaneously stimulates both the green and the blue-violet receptors; in the combination of yellow and blue-violet, yellow simultaneously stimulates the red and green receptors, while blue-violet stimulates the third. In both cases, the combined excitation of all three receptor types produces a sensation of white.

Helmholtz thus explained the laws of color mixture as functions of the human visual apparatus itself, having relatively little to do with the "objective" physical properties of light waves. In evaluating the visual color sense as an accurate detector of physical "reality," Helmholtz observed: "The inaccuracies and imperfections of the eye as an optical instrument . . . now appear insignificant in comparison with the incongruities we have met with in the field of sensation. One might almost believe that Nature had here contradicted herself on purpose in order to destroy any dream of a pre-existing harmony between the outer and the inner world."[7] And since colors were now seen more as products of the human sensory system than as properties of physical reality, Helmholtz explicitly recognized their consistency with Kantian philosophy when he wrote: "That the character of our perceptions is conditioned just as much by our senses as by the external things is of the greatest importance. . . . What the physiology of the senses has demonstrated experimentally in more recent times, Kant earlier tried to do . . . for the ideas of the human mind in general."[8]

Visual Perception When Helmholtz turned his attention from visual sensation to perception, he agreed less completely with Kant's point of view. In agreement, he recognized that as sensations are interpreted and given meaning by the perceptual process, they undergo further transformations worthy of a Kantian "mind." Sometimes, in fact, the mind imposes features on its perceptions that *contradict* the raw sensations that give rise to them, as in optical illusions. Thus in Figure 4-1 at the beginning of the chapter, the two parallel lines are exactly the same length, even though you consciously perceive the top line as longer. Here, your mind makes a mistake in its interpretation of visual sensations.

Helmholtz's disagreement with Kant concerned the *origins* of many perceptual processes, including those involved in illusions. Kant's theory implied that spatial perception was mainly determined by the *innate* intuitions and categories. Helmholtz, while regarding the processes of sensation as innate, laid greater emphasis on the role of experience and learning in perception.

Of course, no one denied that *some* perceptual processes are acquired by experience. Locke had already successfully argued that a person born blind and granted sight only later would still quite literally have to *learn* how to see — would have to have concrete experiences connecting specific ideas of objects to the new and initially bewildering visual sensations. The question separating empiricist from nativist — Helmholtz from Kant — was not whether *any* perceptual processes were acquired through experience, but *how many* and *to what extent*.

Helmholtz conceded that he could never conclusively disprove nativism, but chose as a matter of strategy to regard *all* perception as acquired through experience (much as he had earlier adopted mechanism as a matter of strategy). He then demonstrated the usefulness of his strategy by showing that many observed facts about perception could be explained on the basis of experience and learning.

One classic series of experiments demonstrated how space perception could be altered by experience. Helmholtz fitted subjects with spectacles that systematically distorted the visual field in some way, such as by shifting the images of objects several inches to the right of their normal locations. When subjects were asked to look at an object, then close their eyes and reach out to touch it, their first responses were invariably to the right — toward the apparent rather than the real position. But if the subjects were given a few minutes to handle objects while looking at them through the glasses, something Helmholtz called **perceptual adaptation** occurred. At first they had to instruct themselves consciously to place their hands to the left of the apparent objects they saw, but soon this became natural, automatic, and unconscious. Now they could easily perform their original task, and touch remembered objects with their eyes closed. And now, with spectacles *removed* they began to make errors once again, but this time to the left instead of to the right. So complete and automatic had their adaptation become that it took them a minute or two to resume their normal spatial orientation.

Helmholtz theorized that perceptual adaptation and other perceptual phenomena might result from a process he called **unconscious inference**. Visual experience — such as the manipulation of objects while wearing distorting spectacles — might lead to the unconscious adoption of certain rules that operate like the major premises in logical syllogisms. For example, experience might teach that an object that fills a very small part of the visual field is farther away than a similar object filling a larger part. This would produce a rule or major premise that could operate as in the following syllogism:

Major premise: The size of an object's image varies inversely with its distance from the eye.
Minor premise: The size of the image of a ball currently in my visual field is getting smaller.
Conclusion: The ball is moving away from me.

The difference between perception and syllogistic reasoning lies in the fact that perception occurs instantly and effortlessly, while the working out of a syllogism may be laborious and time consuming. Helmholtz accounted for this difference by assuming that the major premise of a perception has become so well learned as to be automatic and unconscious. As he put it: "[Perceptual] inferences are unconscious insofar as their major premise is not necessarily expressed in the form of a proposition; it is formed from a series of experiences whose individual members have entered consciousness only in the form of sense impressions which have long since disappeared from memory. Some fresh impression forms the minor premise, to which the rule impressed on us by previous observation is applied."[9]

Just as syllogisms may lead to false conclusions if based on false premises, so may unconscious inferences sometimes lead to faulty perceptions such as optical illusions. In Figure 4–1, for example, the perceptual error may be blamed on the incorrect premise that converging straight lines indicate depth. In *three* dimensions the premise is valid, because the retinal images of parallel lines do in fact appear to converge with increasing distance from the eye. In *two* dimensions, however, the convergence of lines gives the false impression that the top horizontal line is farther away than the bottom one. Since the retinal images of the two lines are equal but the top one is interpreted as being farther away, the top line is also perceived as being of greater real length. Since all of these inferences are unconscious, however, their result — the perceived difference in length — comes to consciousness directly and irresistibly, more like an intuition than a rational thought.

Helmholtz's Place in Psychology Even as he studied sensation and perception, Helmholtz retained his original passion for physics and found spare time to write occasional articles on such topics as vortex motion in liquids and the motion of air waves in open-ended tubes. At last in 1871 he realized his childhood ambition by being appointed professor of physics at the University of Berlin. From then on, physiology and psychology became sidelights as he focused his research mainly on thermodynamics, meteorology, and electromagnetism. Indeed, he earned his greatest fame as a physicist, and in 1882 was elevated by the emperor to the ranks of nobility; Hermann *von* Helmholtz became his legal name. Following his death in 1894, von Helmholtz was mourned at home and abroad. A monument in his honor was erected in Berlin, and in Britain a popular "Ode to Helmholtz" employed verse considerably less elegant than Helmholtz's scientific theories to proclaim:

> When Emperors, Kings, Pretenders, shadows all,
> Leave not a dust-trace on our whirling ball,
> Thy work, oh grave-eyed searcher, shall endure,
> Unmarred by faction, from low passion pure.[10]

But even though he won his greatest honors as a physicist, and had earlier regarded himself as more of a physiologist than a psychologist, Helmholtz still earned a place as one of psychology's greatest pioneers for two important achievements. First, he helped show how the neurological processes underlying mental functions, previously thought to be ineffable, could be subject to rigorous laboratory experimentation. And second, he helped to develop a scientific conception of the Kantian "mind" with his integrated physical, physiological, and psychological studies of vision and hearing. No longer just a metaphysical entity, the sensing and perceiving mind was shown to operate by lawful and mechanistic principles as it created its phenomenal reality.

Many of Helmholtz's ideas and theories are still accepted today, much as he originally presented them. The trichromatic theory of color vision, for example, has been amply confirmed by modern research.* The retina is now known to contain millions of tiny color

---

*It is further understood today that color processing does not end with the cones on the retina, but that certain "opponent processes" occur in the thalamus of the

receptor cells called **cones**, which come in three varieties, each one containing a photopigment that maximally absorbs light of one of the three spectral primary colors. The absence of one or more of these pigments or irregularities in their distribution cause the types of visual defects popularly known as "color blindness."

In general, Helmholtz's work on perception has been modified more than that on sensation. His term "unconscious inference" has given way to a variety of concepts such as "apperception," "set," and the recent terminology of the "information-processing" approach. His relatively extreme empiricism has been challenged, perhaps most effectively by the "visual cliff" experiments of Cornell University's **Eleanor Gibson** and colleagues in the 1950s. These experiments showed that visually inexperienced animal and human infants systematically avoided walking or crawling on parts of a glass platform with no visible surface directly below. That is, they showed elements of depth perception, even though they lacked the sorts of experiences that Helmholtz believed were necessary for such perception.

Despite these partial contradictions, however, Helmholtz's perceptual theories have had a continuous influence on the experiments psychologists perform. Perceptual adaptation is still studied, often with distorting spectacles much like Helmholtz's originals. And even with the altered terminology and interpretations of some of the modern work, Helmholtz's basic ideas are still relevant, and he would feel very much at home in a modern perception laboratory.

Fechner's Early Life

Gustav Theodor Fechner resembled Hermann Helmholtz in some important ways, but differed dramatically from him in others. Like Helmholtz, he held broad interests in physics as well as physiology and psychology, and he studied the relationship between external

---

brain itself which help produce color *afterimages* (for example, if you stare fixedly at a red stimulus and then shift your gaze to a neutrally colored background, you will see an afterimage of the same stimulus, only in the complementary color of blue-green). Such findings do not invalidate the trichromatic theory, however, but only show that it does not tell the *complete* story of human color vision.

Gustav Fechner (1801–1887). *Archives of the History of American Psychology,
University of Akron.*

"physical reality" and one's conscious or phenomenal experience of
that reality. Fechner's great contribution, like Helmholtz's, was to
help determine the laws by which our sensory system converts external physical stimulation into conscious sensation and perception.
But while both men contributed to the same general problem, they
did so in different styles and for different reasons, and they reacted in
opposite ways to some of the major intellectual currents of their day.

Fechner was born into a family of Lutheran ministers on 19 April
1801 in the east German region of Lusatia. His father and grandfather were men of the cloth, and when his father died in 1806 young
Gustav went to live with an uncle, another clergyman. His father,
at least, seems to have appreciated science as well as religion, for

he is reported to have startled his congregation by installing a lightning rod on his church's steeple, declaring that the laws of physics had to be honored just as those of God. The elder Fechner created another stir by preaching in the manner he insisted Jesus must also have done — without the then-customary minister's wig. Although Gustav's father may have died too soon to have had much direct influence on the molding of his character, these stories must have been known to him, and must have encouraged his own sense of independence and moderate iconoclasm.

Gustav grew up with strong philosophical and broadly "religious" interests, but felt no inclination to follow in his family's vocational tradition. At first, medicine seemed a more desirable profession than the ministry, so he entered the University of Leipzig's medical school at the early age of sixteen. But medicine proved to be his calling no more than the ministry had, and he never took up practice after completing medical studies in 1822. Indeed, even while a student he had begun publishing satirical attacks on medicine under the pen name of "Dr. Mises." He ridiculed the then-current medical fascination with iodine in "Proof that the Moon Is Made of Iodine," and lampooned old-school doctors for rationalizing their medical blunders in "Panegyric on Contemporary Medicine and Natural History." The latter paper portrayed a doctor who amputated the wrong leg of a patient, and then proposed a new theory of medicine in which *all* treatments are best applied to the opposite side of the body from the one afflicted. Over the rest of his life, Fechner would publish several more times as Dr. Mises, retaining that pen name for much of his speculative, philosophical, or non-scientific writing.

After rejecting medicine, Fechner had to find some other way of making a living, and so began translating French textbooks on physics and chemistry. This tedious and poorly paid work at least had educational benefits, enabling Fechner thoroughly to learn the physical sciences. He learned enough to undertake his own research on electricity, and this became well enough recognized to gain him appointment as a lecturer on physics at the University of Leipzig in 1824. Over the next few years he enhanced his reputation by original research on direct electrical current, and became a full professor of physics in 1833.

While becoming an accomplished physicist, Fechner also indulged his more speculative side by studying *"Naturphilosophie"* (literally, "Nature-philosophy") — a semi-mystical, semi-scientific movement then popular in Germany. Part of the Romantic development of Kantian philosophy, this movement regarded the entire universe as an organic entity imbued with consciousness and other animate functions; at death, one's individual consciousness presumably merges with this "over-consciousness" of the whole universe. And throughout the phenomenal universe (that is, the universe as we know it in this life), the essential wholeness and organic unity of things is presumably revealed in the observable parallels and symmetries in nature.

Fechner recognized that some nature-philosophers carried their search for mystical regularities to ludicrous extremes. As Dr. Mises, he satirized them in an article entitled "The Comparative Anatomy of Angels." Here he argued, tongue in cheek, that spheres are perfect shapes and angels are perfect beings, hence angels are spherical like planets — in fact, *are* living planets.

But while he recognized certain excesses in nature-philosophy, Fechner also believed it offered an antidote to the rising tide of *materialism* that accompanied the increasing domination of the Newtonian world view. While sensing the potential scientific power of mechanistic analysis, Fechner also felt oppressed by its implications. Almost a generation older than Helmholtz and his cohorts, and of a different temperament, Fechner saw unbounded mechanism not as a means for liberating physiology, but as a philosophically deadening and depressing doctrine. (We shall see in later chapters that he was not alone in this reaction.)

Fechner was upset by the apparent "two-facedness" of nature: the fact that the immutable laws governing the physical, external side of the world seemed to contradict or be irrelevant to the impression of free will and volition that one actually experiences in consciousness. He became obsessed with the question "Does Nature or the world have a soul?"[11] As Dr. Mises, he wrote a series of works depicting two alternative conceptions of the universe, each suggesting a different answer to his question. The materialist conception, which he called the *Nachtansicht* (literally, "night view"), regarded the universe as essentially a dead mechanism, with life and consciousness occurring only as incidental and fully predetermined by-products of mechanistic laws. The contrasting *Tagesansicht* ("day view") had roots in Leibniz's monadology (see Chapter 2). It took consciousness itself as the fundamental characteristic of a "besouled" universe, and regarded mechanistic laws as offering only a partial, "external" view of reality. As his choice of names implies, Fechner found the brighter day view more appealing than the gloomy night view, though he obviously harbored some doubts about its truth.

For several years, Fechner waged a mental battle between his night and day views, even as he successfully followed his career in physics. Then in 1839, apparently near the peak of his powers, he suffered a major prostration. The exact circumstances are unclear, though a severe eye injury caused by looking too long at the sun while studying afterimages played some part. Emotional and philosophical factors undoubtedly exacerbated the situation, as conflicts between the night and day views — and the Gustav Fechner and Dr. Mises aspects of his own personality — became increasingly acute. Whatever the exact causes, Fechner became almost a complete invalid, often unable to speak or even to eat. He had to resign his professorship, and retreated into a penurious isolation for several years.

He finally solved his eating problem by following a mystic's advice to subsist entirely on a diet of fruit, strongly spiced ham, and wine. He now began to engage in increasingly mystical speculation himself, and published under his own name the arcanely entitled *Nanna, or on the Soul-life of Plants* in 1848, followed by *Zend-Avesta, or on the Things of Heaven and the Beyond* in 1851. Understandably, these works did not enhance Fechner's scientific reputation.

But on 22 October 1850, while lying abed and meditating, Fechner had a sudden insight whose working out eventually brought him back into the scientific mainstream — and to a position as one of the fathers of modern experimental psychology. He was reflecting on the relationships between the material and the mental worlds — the same general problem that preoccupied Helmholtz. But while Helmholtz emphasized the *differences* between the two worlds —

writing of the "inaccuracies and imperfections" of the eye as an optical instrument and of the "incongruities" imposed by the color-sensing apparatus — Fechner was suddenly impressed with a previously unappreciated and partly hidden example of *harmony* between the two worlds. Indeed, he joyfully took his insight to be a confirmation of the day view, since it signified the basic oneness of the physical and mental universes.

The particular subject that so roused Fechner involved the sensation of *stimulus intensities*. His subsequent experiments on this topic laid the groundwork for a new scientific discipline that he believed united the physical with the psychological and that he called, appropriately enough, **psychophysics**.

The Invention of Psychophysics

Some simple, everyday observations about our hearing and vision help to introduce the subject of Fechner's psychophysics. With hearing, we take it for granted that a very slight sound will be "drowned out" by a lot of background noise, but easily audible when the background is "so quiet you can hear a pin drop." A similar phenomenon occurs with vision: A single lit match is much more noticeable in a darkened than in a brightly lit room, and the stars are easily visible against the dark background of the night sky but are overwhelmed by the greater brightness of daylight.

These apparently obvious facts have some interesting implications. They indicate that our conscious sensations of stimulus intensity do *not* perfectly reflect physical reality, because the same stimuli create different impressions of their magnitude under different circumstances. A dropped pin, a particular star, or a lighted match always emits sound or light waves of the same intensity, yet those waves are perceived differently depending on the background stimulation — sometimes being highly noticeable, sometimes dimly so, and sometimes completely unnoticeable. Here are further examples of the general Kantian point of this chapter — namely, that the sensory system processes and transforms impressions from physical stimuli before bringing them to consciousness.

Helmholtz would undoubtedly have interpreted these reactions

or low sensory intensities. They found that "absolute thresholds" differed somewhat from person to person, or even within the same person from time to time. Some objected theoretically to the use of the jnd as a unit of measurement, since it was not intuitively obvious that the first jnd above the threshold and, say, the twenty-first were identical to each other in the same way that the first and the twenty-first inches on a yardstick are.

But still, *Elements of Psychophysics* became generally accepted as representing a breakthrough for experimental psychology. Following Weber's lead, Fechner had demonstrated that a purely psychological phenomenon — subjective stimulus intensity — might at least approximately be quantified and mathematically related to other variables in apparently lawful ways. Since a field's susceptibility to mathematical expression was regarded as an index of its "scientific" status, Fechner's book gave an enormous boost to psychology's status as a potentially mathematical and experimental *science*. No longer would psychology be regarded as the merely metaphysical discipline described by Kant.

Further, Fechner's basic concepts and methods have remained in constant and productive use for more than a century. His most important successor, the Harvard psychophysicist **S. Smith Stevens** (1906–1973), studied the intensity or magnitude judgments of subjects for scores of different sensory stimuli. For a very few situations — such as reporting conscious impressions of how long an auditory stimulus had been turned on — the subjective judgments in fact corresponded almost perfectly with the objective durations of the stimuli. And for a few other stimuli, subjective intensities increased at a *faster rate* than the objective intensities — the opposite of the Weber fractions. When a person experiences increasing levels of electric shock to the finger, for example, small increases in voltage were relatively unnoticeable when the total current was weak, but were markedly noticeable at higher intensities.

Stevens recognized that these cases were not covered by Fechner's law, but that both they *and* the ones studied by Fechner could be covered by a still more general mathematical equation. This was the so-called **power law**, or **Stevens's law**, which asserts that S is a function of P raised to a particular power times a constant:

$$S = kP^n.$$

When the power represented by the exponent n is less than 1, this equation becomes roughly equivalent to Fechner's law and accounts for the traditional cases. When the exponent is exactly 1, the equation becomes equivalent to $S = kP$; its graph becomes a straight line and it represents stimuli, such as the duration of a sound, that are subjectively judged very similar to their objective properties. And if the exponent is greater than 1, the equation applies to stimuli like electric shock, whose subjective intensities increase at a faster (exponential) rate than their physical intensities.

Like Fechner's law, Stevens's law must be recognized as an approximation, holding most accurately for the middle ranges of physical stimulation, and subject to certain fluctuations across individuals and situations. But it still confirms the general robustness of Fechner's original inspiration: namely, that certain sensory judgments can be quantified, and related in a meaningful way to events in the physical environment.

Conclusion Neither Helmholtz nor Fechner considered themselves to be psychologists. In both cases, their backgrounds had been primarily in physics and physiology, and in both cases their primary achievement was to bring certain psychological phenomena into lawful relationships with physical or physiological data. But their work demonstrated conclusively that it was possible to study the phenomena of the mind in the same general ways that the physical world was studied: in terms of general, mechanistic laws (Helmholtz) or mathematically specifiable ones (Fechner). Thus they demonstrated the *promise* of a genuinely experimental psychology. This promise was promptly fulfilled by other individuals, especially a younger colleague of both Helmholtz and Fechner named **Wilhelm Wundt** (1832–1920), whom we shall meet in the next chapter.

Suggested Readings

For discussion of Kant's influence on the development of psychology, see Chapter 15, "The Kantian Background," in D. B. Klein's *A History of Scientific Psychology* (New York: Basic Books, 1970). The classic description of the development of the law of specific nerve energies appears in Chapters 2 and 5 of Edwin G. Boring, *A History of Experimental Psychology* (New York: Appleton-Century-Crofts, 1957).

A good sampling of Helmholtz's work—including his paper on conservation of energy, a brief autobiographical sketch, and popularized accounts of his theories of vision and hearing—has been collected and edited by Russell Kahl in *Selected Writings of Hermann von Helmholtz* (Middletown, CT: Wesleyan University Press, 1971). The standard biography of Helmholtz is Leo Koenigsberger's *Hermann von Helmholtz*, translated by Frances A. Welby (New York: Dover, 1965).

For a lucid account of the origins of psychophysics, see David J. Murray, *A History of Western Psychology*, 2nd edition (New York: Prentice Hall, 1988), pp. 176–185. William R. Woodward's article, "Fechner's Panpsychism: A Scientific Solution to the Mind-Body Problem," *Journal of the History of the Behavioral Sciences* (*8*: 367–386, 1972), usefully discusses the relationship between Fechner's philosophical and scientific concerns.

5

Wilhelm Wundt and
the Establishment of
Experimental Psychology

In 1861, a young German physiologist named **Wilhelm Wundt** (1832–1920) rigged his pendulum clock into a "thought meter" for a simple but clever home experiment. He wanted to test the commonsense assumption that when two different stimuli strike our senses at the same time—as when we hear a person speak and simultaneously watch his lips move—we become *consciously aware* of both stimuli at the same instant.

Figure 5–1 illustrates Wundt's apparatus.[1] The clock's pendulum, marked *B* in the diagram, swung above the calibrated scale *M*. A knitting needle (*S*) was attached to the shaft of the pendulum so that it would strike a bell (*g*) at precisely the instant the pendulum reached an extremity of its swing (position *b*). Thus the bell sounded at exactly the instant the pendulum was at position *b*.

When Wundt tested his own reactions, however, he discovered an anomaly. As he looked at the swinging pendulum and judged the position it *seemed* to occupy at the instant he heard the bell, he found it was never exactly at position *b* but always somewhere on the swing *away* from there. He calculated that the time necessary for the pendulum to swing this extra distance was between one-

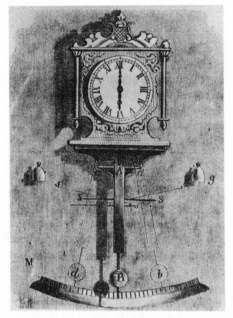

Figure 5-1. *Wundt's "thought meter."*

tenth and one-eighth of a second. He concluded that he had *not* consciously experienced the auditory and visual stimuli simultaneously, even though they had actually occurred together. Instead, separate acts of **attention** had apparently been required, first to register the bell in consciousness, and then the position of the pendulum. Each act of consciousness had presumably taken up a tenth to an eighth of a second.

This result carried important implications for Wundt. As Hermann Helmholtz's assistant at the University of Heidelberg, Wundt knew all about his chief's pioneering studies (reviewed in the previous chapter) measuring the speed of the nervous impulse. Those studies, however, had been restricted to the speed of neural events on the *periphery* of the nervous system — that is, impulses in the sensory and motor nerves, transmitting messages to or from the brain. Wundt's new study demonstrated how the reaction-time experiment

143

could be refined to measure the exact duration of a *central* process, presumably mediated by neurological activity within the brain itself, and responsible for the psychological reaction of attention.

Wundt further recognized that he had just joined Hermann Helmholtz and Gustav Fechner (whose *Elements of Psychophysics* had just been published) in subjecting a clearly psychological process to experimental study. He was struck by the fact that suddenly *several* different experimental approaches to mental phenomena had been developed, contrary to Kant's influential opinion that such was impossible. In fact, Wundt concluded that there now were sufficient grounds for establishing a whole new field of **experimental psychology**, which might be explicitly pursued in the universities along with traditional subjects.

Wundt proposed this possibility in the introduction to his 1862 book, *Contributions to the Theory of Sensory Perception*, and then worked on and off for many years to make it a reality. Finally, in 1879, he established an official "institute" at the University of Leipzig, where graduate students could come for the express purpose of earning Ph.D. degrees in experimental psychology. He attracted students from around the world, many of whom returned to their home countries to establish experimental psychology programs there. By 1900, more than a hundred psychological laboratories had been established worldwide, and psychology was widely recognized as an important and independent academic subject. Today, little more than a century after Wundt started things, psychology is one of the most frequently taken subjects in Western universities. For having started these institutional developments, Wundt is often regarded as the "father" of modern academic and experimental psychology.

Of course, progeny do not always turn out exactly as their fathers might wish, and such was also the case with Wundt's intellectual offspring. The strong-minded founder held very clear notions of what psychology should and should not be, and despite his advocacy of experimental methods he also retained a strong sense of their limitations. Many important psychological problems, he believed, could only be approached with non-experimental techniques. Not all of Wundt's students and immediate successors agreed with him,

Wilhelm Wundt (1832–1920). *Archives of the History of American Psychology, University of Akron.*

and some promptly pushed the fledgling science farther and in different directions than he thought appropriate. As these trends gained popularity, Wundt gained the reputation of being an old-fashioned father, one who got things started but then lacked the vision or modernity to carry his ideas to fulfillment. One historian of psychology in 1964 went so far as to characterize Wundt's psychology as "an interruption in the development of a natural science of man."[2]

Recently, however, Wundt's reputation has been rehabilitated. Many of his views turn out to have been misinterpreted or misrepresented by his successors, and at least some of his cautions about experimentalism now seem better founded than they once did. Thus as we turn now to the story of Wundt's life, and of his "founding" of experimental psychology, we take up issues that have more than antiquarian interest.

Wundt's Early Life

Wilhelm Maximilian Wundt was born near Mannheim, Germany, on 16 August 1832, in a small village where his father was an Evangelical pastor. The family had solid academic connections, for his father's father had been a professor of history at the University of Heidelberg, and two of his mother's brothers were physicians and professors of physiology. One of these, Wilhelm's "Uncle Friedrich" (Philipp Friedrich Arnold, 1803–1890), would play a particularly important role in his later life.

As an infant Wilhelm contracted malaria. His worried parents, who had already lost two children in infancy, moved to less lucrative but climatically healthier parishes in farming villages near Heidelberg. They sent their only other surviving child, eight-year-old Ludwig, to live with an aunt and attend school in Heidelberg. Thus Wilhelm grew up essentially as an only child, in small rural communities.

Wundt's earliest memory was of falling down a staircase, his head striking painfully on every step. A similar depressive tone pervaded most of his other childhood reminiscences. A clumsy and unathletic youth saddled with the further social stigma of being a pastor's son, he was ostracized and frequently manhandled by the rough-and-ready country boys who were his only peers. In his loneliness he became a chronic daydreamer, and while he liked to imagine himself as a prolific author of scholarly tomes on comparative religion, the habit severely interfered with his schoolwork. Once his father visited his school and became so incensed at Wilhelm's inattentiveness that he slapped the boy publicly.

One moderately happy interlude began at age eight, when his

father's assistant pastor also became Wilhelm's private tutor. Wilhelm idolized this kindly young man, who taught Latin quite proficiently, mathematics less so. Independent reading in his father's library aroused lifelong interests in literature and history. Wilhelm continued to daydream, however, and the habit brought disaster once again when he had to go to *Gymnasium*, or high school, at age twelve. In this "school of suffering" he was constantly humiliated by students and teachers alike, and he completely failed his first year.

Wundt's despairing parents sent him to Heidelberg to live with his aunt and brother Ludwig, now a university student. In this cosmopolitan university town, he found not only a studious older brother to emulate, but also some new schoolmates with interests similar to his own. Under these improved circumstances he at last curbed his daydreaming, and was graduated at nineteen with a respectable academic record.

He had not done well enough to win a university scholarship, however, and he had no occupational goal except to avoid the ministry. His family had just enough money to finance four years of university study, but worried that it might be wasted on him. At this point his uncle Friedrich Arnold, a physician and professor of anatomy and physiology at the University of Tübingen, emerged as a role model. Wundt enrolled in medical school at Tübingen, and after a slow start the first year suddenly became inspired as never before by his uncle's course on brain anatomy.

The next year Arnold became professor of anatomy at Heidelberg, and Wundt followed his uncle back home to complete his training. Still inspired and now working prodigiously, he enjoyed genuine academic success for the first time in his life. He finished first in his class in several subjects, and after three years passed his final medical examinations *summa cum laude*. Even more important, he had begun to experience the pleasures of conducting his own experimental research.

Early Research Wundt's first independent experiment at Heidelberg was supervised by Robert Bunsen (1811–1899), the eminent chemist whose name is still memorialized today in the laboratory "Bunsen

burner" he invented. Wundt studied the influence of salt depriva-
tion on the composition of his own urine, and reported the results
in 1853—his first scientific publication. The next year he studied
the effect of the vagus nerve on respiration. Working at home with
the loyal assistance of his mother, he severed the vagus nerves on
experimental animals, observed the effects, and submitted a report
to the Heidelberg faculty. This effort won a gold medal from the
university, and publication in Johannes Müller's prestigious journal
of anatomy and physiology. Wundt evidently found real-life authorship to be just as rewarding as it had seemed in his childhood
daydreams, for these student papers marked the beginning of an
extraordinarily prolific publishing record that eventually totaled
almost sixty thousand printed pages.

After taking his degree, Wundt briefly practiced medicine as an
assistant pathologist, but then went to Berlin to study physiology
with Johannes Müller and Émile du Bois-Reymond. Finding he
enjoyed research and academics more than medical practice, he
returned to Heidelberg and became accredited by the University
as a *Privatdozent*, or lecturer. This lowest rung on the academic lad-
der carried no salary, but authorized him to offer courses privately
while he sought to enhance his reputation by research. Wundt's first
course, taught in his home on experimental physiology, attracted
only four students and was prematurely terminated when Wundt
contracted mild tuberculosis. He used his convalescence period to
write his first book, a not terribly original treatise on the physiology
of muscular movement, published in 1858.

That same year, thanks largely to Uncle Friedrich's recruiting,
the young but already famous Hermann Helmholtz came to Heidelberg to establish an Institute of Physiology. Wundt became Helmholtz's assistant—a salaried but low-paying position that carried
responsibility for much of the actual *teaching* of physiology at the
university. (Like many eminent professor-scientists today, Helmholtz stayed in the laboratory and out of the classrooms as much
as possible.) Wundt held this post for six years, although he buried
himself in private research as much as possible and kept rather aloof
from both Helmholtz and his fellow assistants.

Wundt later suggested that he and Helmholtz never became close because of the similarity of their research interests. While one might expect similarity of interest to *attract* an aspiring young scientist to an eminent elder, Wundt was no ordinary young scientist. Over the years he had somehow developed a fierce drive for independence and dominance, a desire to be a leader rather than a follower in his chosen field. Thus while he was unquestionably influenced by Helmholtz in his choice of subjects to investigate, he kept much to himself in the actual conduct of his research.

While working as Helmholtz's assistant, Wundt independently studied and wrote on vision and the perception of space — both topics close to the heart of his employer. In one paper he postulated a process of "unconscious inference" in the conversion of visual sensations into perceptions — and completely failed to mention that Helmholtz had already used exactly that term in accounting for optical illusions! It was a mark of Helmholtz's tolerance, as well as his respect for his assistant's industry and ability, that he later wrote Wundt favorable recommendations for several university positions.

Wundt's crucial "thought meter" experiment also occurred during this time, and we have seen that this too had clear connections with Helmholtz's prior work on nervous velocity. Wundt knew that his study also had roots predating Helmholtz's work, for certain aspects of the reaction-time problem had long concerned *astronomers*. In 1796, the English Astronomer-Royal Nevil Maskelyne had discovered that his own "transit readings" for stars — that is, the precise times he noted when stars under observation crossed grid lines in his telescope — regularly differed by more than half a second from those of his assistant, Kinnebrook. As often happens when employee differs with employer, Kinnebrook was fired. But twenty years later, the German astronomer **Friedrich Wilhelm Bessel** (1784–1846) showed that *all* astronomical observers differed from one another in their transit readings, and in generally consistent ways; that is, some observers tended to mark the transits consistently earlier or later than others. With knowledge of one another's "personal equations," as these consistent individual differences came to be called, astronomers could render their readings equivalent to one another.

Helmholtz's research on the nervous impulse suggested that part of the differences among astronomers' personal equations could be explained by individual differences in the lengths of their sensory and motor nerves, or in the speed with which those nerves transmitted impulses. Wundt reasoned that the differences might also be partly the result of differences in the speeds of *central* processing in their brains. By demonstrating with his thought meter experiment that a measurable amount of time was required for one such central process — the shifting of attention from one stimulus to another — Wundt added to the plausibility of his hypothesis, and contributed to the venerable debate about personal equations.

But while Wundt's study related to earlier work in physiology and astronomy, it also carried implications for a future science of psychology. In detecting and following up these implications, Wundt at last established his own originality and began to make the name he sought for himself.

Experimental Psychology and Völkerpsychologie   As we have seen, Wundt's thought meter experiment highlighted the importance of central as opposed to peripheral processes — of events in the very core of the nervous system, occurring between the reception of stimuli by the sensory nerves and the activation of responses by the motor nerves. Stimuli were not simply received by the senses and responded to instantaneously and mechanically by motor nerves, but were registered in consciousness by an attentional process whose independent reality was proven by the extra time required for it to occur. Wundt believed this finding supported the general philosophical tradition of Leibniz as opposed to Locke, requiring a psychology that accounts for the receptive and creative properties of the mind itself, above and beyond the influence of external stimuli in creating "ideas."

Wundt also believed that times for other central processes besides attention could be studied by refinements of the reaction-time experiments, in a systematic program of **mental chronometry**. The details remained to be worked out, but here was a possible experimental program that could join Fechnerian psychophysics and Helmholtzian studies of sensation and perception to form the basis of a new science of experimental psychology. As we have noted,

Wundt expressed this idea publicly in the preface to his 1862 book, *Contributions to the Theory of Sensory Perception*, a work whose main body reprinted his recent articles on vision, unconscious inference, and reaction time. The *idea* for a new and separate discipline of experimental psychology traditionally dates from then.

But even as he proposed a new discipline of experimental psychology, Wundt also firmly believed that experimentation could never be the *only* method for psychology as a whole. He thought experimental methods would have to be confined to the study of *individual* consciousness, that they could not be readily applied to mental processes that were essentially *collective* or *social* in nature. Preeminent among the collective human processes was *language*, and since language seemed crucial to all of the "higher" mental functions including thinking and reasoning, Wundt saw those functions as immune to experimental investigation. Accordingly, he proposed a second and complementary branch of psychology that would use comparative and historical methods rather than experiments, and that he chose to call **Völkerpsychologie**.

Wundt borrowed this name from a recently created journal, the *Zeitschrift für Völkerpsychologie und Sprachwissenschaft*. *Zeitschrift* translates easily as "journal" and *Sprachwissenschaft* as "linguistics," but *Völkerpsychologie* has no clear English equivalent. German *Völk* refers to "people, nation, tribe, or race," and so the term has sometimes been translated as "ethnic psychology," "folk psychology," or even "social psychology," but none of these is totally accurate. Basically, Wundt meant to signify a type of non-experimental psychology that deals with the *communal* and *cultural* products of human nature: religions, mythologies, customs, and, above all, languages and their derivative higher processes.

After formulating the two branches of psychology, Wundt lost little time in actively pursuing both. In the summer of 1862 he offered a new course of lectures on the experimental side, for students in physiology and medicine, entitled "Psychology from the Standpoint of Natural Science." At the same time he started writing *Lectures on the Human and Animal Mind*, a two-volume work published in 1863 and 1864, covering issues such as the origin of speech and the sensual, aesthetic, intellectual, and religious feelings. Although

Wundt would later call this book a "youthful indiscretion," it started him on the path to his mature *Völkerpsychologie*.

But even with these accomplishments, Wundt had to struggle to earn a decent living. In 1863 he resigned as Helmholtz's assistant, under conditions that remain uncertain. One rumor had it that Helmholtz found Wundt lacking in mathematics and physics, and dismissed him. Wundt denied this, claiming that his duties did not involve mathematics or physics, and scoffing at the idea that Helmholtz required "assistance" in those fields in any case. But for whatever reason, Wundt lost his only steady source of income with his resignation. The university granted him a new title of assistant professor, but this carried no salary and left him even more dependent on privately paying students at his lecture courses.

Wundt's three published books to this point were all on highly specialized topics and had sold poorly. He now decided that at least temporarily he must write to make money, and so wrote three more popular books in three years: a textbook on human physiology, a handbook of medical physics, and a philosophical analysis of the physical basis of causality. These books did sell reasonably well, and the last had the great advantage of helping to establish Wundt's credentials in philosophy — a field in which he had taken only one undergraduate course as a student.

Wundt continued his private courses on psychology, and the subject returned to the forefront of his consciousness in early 1867 with an invitation to write on "Recent Advances in the Field of Physiological Psychology" for a new interdisciplinary journal. In response he wrote a thirty-three-page review of recent work on visual space perception and mental chronometry, and promised a further work in which he would elaborate on the connections between physiology and psychology.[3] This article aroused more attention than anything he had previously written, and convinced many that a new scientific psychology was truly on the horizon. Among those so convinced was a young American named **William James** (1842–1910), who read it and wrote:

It seems to me that perhaps the time has come for psychology to begin to be a science — some measurements have already been made in the region lying between the physical changes in the nerves and the appearance of consciousness (in the shape of sense perceptions), and more may come of it. . . . Helmholtz and a man named Wundt at Heidelberg are working on it.[4]

As we shall see in Chapter 8, James went on to become the major promoter of psychology in the United States.

But even this enhanced international recognition did little to help Wundt's position at Heidelberg. When Helmholtz left for Berlin in 1871 Wundt was passed over as his replacement in favor of a rival five years younger than he. The defeat stung badly, for the intensely ambitious Wundt had already gone overboard in his zeal to succeed. He had engaged in some unseemly priority disputes with other scientists, and had labeled himself as "Professor" on the title pages of his books while omitting the important modifier, "Assistant." Nevertheless, he had also worked enormously hard, producing seven books and scores of articles in several different fields. He had also been politically active, serving a term as elected representative to the Baden legislative assembly and acting as president of the Heidelberg Workers' Educational Association. Yet for all his effort and real accomplishment, he approached the age of forty still holding a minor and poorly paid academic position.

Principles of Physiological Psychology Wundt's fortunes improved markedly after 1874, when he fulfilled the promise in his 1867 paper and completed the two volumes of *Principles of Physiological Psychology*. In this landmark book Wundt not only defined a "new domain of science" whose task was to conjoin the two previously separate disciplines of physiology and psychology, but also provided detailed examples of how the task could be accomplished. In providing the first genuine textbook for the new field, Wundt emphatically established himself as its leader.

In defining the new field, Wundt observed that physiology investigates living organisms "by our external senses," while psychology examines things "from within" and tries to explain those processes that "inner observation discloses." Physiological psychology was to be the discipline in which "psychological introspection goes hand in hand with the methods of experimental physiology," to study processes simultaneously accessible to *both* kinds of observation.[5]

Wundt saw two major examples of such processes: sensation, where externally observable stimuli give rise to describable psychological states, and voluntary movement, where psychological impulses give rise to externally observable muscular reactions. Most of his book was devoted to detailed descriptions of studies that conformed to this definition. Since this "physiological psychology" used experimental techniques along with introspection, Wundt suggested it could also be called "experimental psychology," the name he had used before 1867.

Enthusiastic reviewers observed that *Principles of Physiological Psychology* "corresponds exactly to the need for a *specialized* scientific treatment of the actual relations between body and consciousness,"[6] and that it "fills a lacuna, and circumscribes in a very convenient way all those phenomena of human life which can be studied both by introspection and by objective investigation."[7] Thus even though Wundt himself had not done a great deal of actual research in the new experimental psychology, as its definer and documenter he became the person most closely identified with it.

Wundt now found himself in unwonted but highly pleasing professional demand. In 1874 he won a full professorship in philosophy at the University of Zurich, despite the fact that he had taken only one philosophy course in his own education. A year later he accepted an equivalent position at Leipzig — one of the largest and most prestigious of German universities, and home of the aging but still active Gustav Fechner and E. H. Weber. Here, in due course, Wundt created the first full-fledged *program* in experimental psychology.

Wundt at Leipzig

For all the promise of his new position, Wundt could not get physiological psychology off to a fast start at Leipzig. He had accepted the job on condition that the university provide storage space for the large collection of apparatus he had assembled, and which for the past ten years he had used for demonstrations to augment his lectures on experimental psychology. Disappointingly, the university proved unable to provide the space during his first year, and his first courses were on language, anthropology, and logic rather than on experimental psychology.*

Another difficult situation marred Wundt's early years at Leipzig, although in a very different way, when he became embroiled in a disagreeable controversy with Johann Zöllner, a Leipzig colleague who had previously been an enthusiastic supporter. An astrophysicist by training, Zöllner had also done research on optical illusions, was a close friend of the psychophysicist Fechner, and had warmly welcomed Wundt as the leader of the new experimental psychology.

Zöllner became estranged from Wundt after an 1877 visit to Leipzig by the American "spiritualist" and "medium" Henry Slade. Slade had already confessed to fraud in America, but still found ready audiences for his séances in Europe. Then as now, many people believed in the reality of paranormal or occult powers, and were willing to pay those who purported to have them; then as now, some trained scientists were among the believers. Slade held séances for several leading Leipzig scientists including Fechner, Zöllner, and Wundt. Here Slade caused tables to tip, produced knots in a taut piece of string, and purported to receive messages "from a departed spirit," which he wrote down in broken German on a slate board. Fechner was impressed but noncommittal about the performance, while Zöllner became enthusiastically convinced of Slade's genuineness. Wundt viewed the proceedings skeptically, however, and published an article entitled "Spiritualism as a Scientific Question" that can still be read today as a model challenge to many claims for the paranormal.[8]

Wundt pointed out that the effects he observed occurred only when Slade had the opportunity to cheat. Everyone had to sit in a tight circle around a table, and Slade permitted no one to observe

---

*History of psychology textbooks standardly but mistakenly report that Wundt and William James shared priority for establishing the first psychological demonstration laboratories in 1875, James at Harvard and Wundt in his new position at Leipzig. Actually Wundt was *prevented* from doing experimental demonstrations in 1875 because of the unavailability of his equipment—but he had already begun the practice a decade earlier in his Heidelberg courses—Thus the standard story errs in that Wundt actually preceded James by several years, but ironically was unable to continue his practice the very year James began his.

from outside. Slade's hands, and the slate on which he received "spirit messages," were frequently out of sight beneath the table. Most of these messages had nonsensical content, and came in English or poor German even though the presumed "senders" and all the sitters except Slade were German. Wundt added that scientists, despite their reputations for brilliance, are probably very *poor* judges of the reality of psychic phenomena; themselves devoted to the disinterested pursuit of truth, they do not expect deceit in others and are ill-equipped to detect it. Thus magicians or conjurers would make much better judges than scientists, because they would know what kinds of tricks to look for. Wundt concluded that he himself lacked the competence to judge definitively, but he strongly suspected Slade had produced his effects by "jugglery."

Wundt's article greatly offended Zöllner, who also seems to have been becoming mentally unbalanced at this time. This former ally wrote a sarcastic and defamatory reply, claiming that Wundt should be jailed for five years for lying and calling him a "suckling child" who had directly copied skeptical and materialistic opinions from his "lord and master" Helmholtz and "the Berlin vivisectionist" du Bois-Reymond. Wundt, perhaps realizing that Zöllner was no longer fully in control of himself, refrained from replying. He reprinted his article a few years later, however, and added an introduction stating that belief in the paranormal, while unfounded, perhaps filled a useful social purpose "like beer and tobacco." As a form of superstition, it was likely to recur from time to time in "epidemics," and "like pain and illness, [to] disappear from earth only with humanity."[9]

Despite his early problems, Wundt gradually established himself very well in Leipzig. In 1876 he got his storage space and resumed teaching experimental psychology, and by 1879 he had several students clamoring to do research under his supervision. Late that year, two German students named Max Friedrich and Ernst Tischer joined with the visiting American G. Stanley Hall (whom we shall meet again in Chapter 8) to work on a reaction-time study that Friedrich later presented as his Ph.D. dissertation. Thus 1879 is traditionally given as the date of the first working research laboratory explicitly devoted to experimental psychology, and Friedrich is credited with earning the first Ph.D. in experimental psychology.

From this modest start, the discipline grew rapidly. In 1881 Wundt founded the journal *Philosophische Studien (Philosophical Studies)* to publish the new laboratory's research.* Two years later, after threatening to move to Breslau, Wundt was rewarded with a quadrupling of his laboratory space and a forty percent salary increase at Leipzig. The university now officially designated his laboratory and program as the *Institute* for Experimental Psychology, lending them enhanced prestige and prominence in the university catalog. So popular was the Institute that it had to be physically enlarged again in 1888, 1892, and 1897.

Wundt's institutional and organizational accomplishments were aptly summarized by one of his earliest American students in 1888:

> Professor Wundt, by the publication of his *Physiologische Psychologie* in 1874 and the establishment of a psychological laboratory at Leipzic [sic] in 1879, has made himself the representative of the efforts to introduce experimental methods into psychology. Weber, Lotze, Fechner and Helmholtz . . . had cleared the way, but their books and researches remained to a certain extent isolated attempts, until Wundt directed toward one centre the divergent lines, and persuaded men of science on the one hand and students of philosophy on the other to accept the new science.[10]

For these organizational accomplishments alone, Wundt could have earned the title of father of experimental psychology. But he also played a major role as designer, supervisor, and sometimes subject in the multitudinous experiments that were conducted in his laboratory. He habitually *assigned* research topics to his students, only rarely allowing those who struck him as unusually mature to propose their own studies. He took a keen interest in every project, and was extremely helpful to students as they prepared for their oral examinations; some reported that he seemed as nervous as they, and that he coached them to let them know what kinds of questions to expect from their non-psychological examiners. Moreover, the results of many of his students' experiments helped shape Wundt's voluminous mature theoretical writings about psychology. Thus we

---

*Wundt had considered calling the journal *Psychological Studies*, but abandoned the idea because a journal with a similar name already existed, and dealt with the scientifically unrespectable subjects of spiritism and parapsychology. Further, he genuinely believed that psychology was a subdiscipline of philosophy, and wished to emphasize that fact in the title of his new journal.

shall consider first some of the important experiments conducted at Leipzig, and then take up Wundt's more general theories.

Research at Leipzig Early experimental research at Leipzig fell into three general areas: psychophysics; studies of the time sense; and mental chronometry. The psychophysical studies tested Fechner's general law on previously uninvestigated sensory stimuli, such as the loudness or pitch of sound and the brightness of light. Although not outstandingly original in conception, these studies often required ingeniously constructed apparatus, and helped fill out the psychophysical program by confirming the general (although not perfect) accuracy of Fechner's law in a variety of new situations.

Studies of the time sense investigated the amount of time by which stimuli had to be separated in order to be recognized as distinct. Visual stimuli, for example, had to be separated by at least one-tenth of a second, or else they would fuse together into a single continuous impression — a fact soon to be taken advantage of by the inventors of motion picture cameras. For sound and touch, the smallest detectable intervals were much shorter. And when stimuli for two different senses were presented (for example, a sound and a touch), separations ranging from one-twentieth to one-sixth of a second were necessary before subjects could accurately say which one occurred first. Like the psychophysical studies, these lacked theoretical momentousness, but added valuable facts to the growing store of detailed information about the senses.

The studies of mental chronometry lay closest to Wundt's heart, for these not only provided new factual observations, but also bore directly on his own innovative psychological theory. Most of these studies used the **subtractive method**, a technique originally developed in 1868 by the Dutch physiologist **F. C. Donders** (1818–1889). Donders had started by measuring simple reaction time, where a subject responded to a single visual stimulus as quickly as possible. Then he complicated the experimental task by randomly presenting two different kinds of visual stimuli, but instructing the subject to respond only to one of them. Reaction times became somewhat longer than for the simple situation, presumably because the subject required extra time to differentiate one stimulus from the other.

158

Donders subtracted the average simple reaction time from the average for the complex task, and concluded that the difference — about a tenth of a second — had been the time required for a mental act of "discrimination."

Max Friedrich elaborated on Donders's study for his thesis research, and many other subtractive studies followed. The most systematic and extensive of these were done by Wundt's American student **James McKeen Cattell** (1860-1944), and we shall describe them in some detail as illustrative of Leipzig research.

Like many other successful pioneers in experimental psychology, Cattell showed great ingenuity in designing apparatus. He invented the instrument shown in Figure 5-2A[11] to present various kinds of visual stimuli in reaction-time studies. The stimulus for any trial would initially be hidden behind the sliding black metal screen, suspended at the top of the apparatus by an electromagnet. To start a trial, the experimenter would turn off the magnet, thus causing the screen to drop and to reveal the stimulus. At precisely the instant the stimulus was uncovered, the falling screen would trigger a switch starting a chronoscope, or timing device. The subject would then make a response to turn off the chronoscope, whose reading accurately reflected the full reaction time.

Most reaction-time experiments before Cattell's had the subject respond by pressing a simple finger-key, but Cattell also invented keys activated by movement of the lips (Figure 5-2B), or by sound vibrations from the subject's voice. Thus he could measure the reaction times for *verbal* responses as well as for ordinary finger presses. In sum, he devised ways to measure reaction times more accurately, and in a wider and more interesting variety of situations, than had ever been done before.

Using just himself and one fellow student as subjects, Cattell measured thousands of reaction times under varying conditions. In the simplest situation, where the revealed stimulus was always a blank white patch and the response a press of the finger-key, reaction times averaged about fifteen-hundredths of one second. In the first complication, two kinds of stimuli were randomly presented — for example, a red patch and a blue one — and the subject was told to respond only to one of them. Here, as in Donders's study, reac-

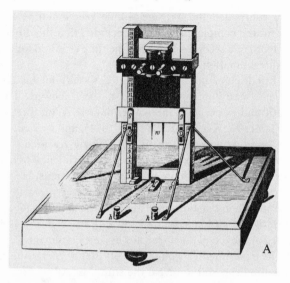

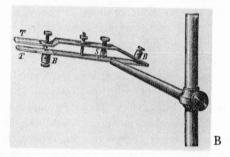

Figure 5-2. *Cattell's stimulus-presenting apparatus* (A) *and "lip-key"* (B).

tion times increased by about one-tenth of a second — the time presumably required for "discrimination" or "perception." When the
subject had to perform a separate response to each stimulus — say,
press a right-hand key for red and a left-hand one for blue — average
reaction times increased by another tenth of a second. Wundt believed the subject here had to make a voluntary decision to move
either the right or left hand, and referred to this increment as the
"will time." Cattell preferred the more neutral term "motor time."

160

Some of Cattell's most interesting findings occurred when he presented *verbal* stimuli such as letters or words, and required spoken responses rather than finger presses. When letters and colors were presented as stimuli and named in response, average reaction times were three-hundredths to four-hundredths of a second longer for the letters. The times also varied surprisingly from letter to letter, however, with the relatively common "E" requiring considerably longer than the less common "W." When short *words* were presented as stimuli, reaction times were only negligibly longer than for individual letters. This important finding led Cattell to conclude, "We do not therefore perceive separately the letters of which a word is composed, but the word as a whole."[12]

Cattell measured verbal "association times" by presenting verbal stimuli and requiring as responses words associated with them. For example, subjects reacted to German words with their English translations, or to the names of cities with the countries in which they are located, or to famous authors' names with the languages in which they wrote. These diverse association tasks required reaction times ranging between thirty-five-hundredths of a second and one second — a good deal longer than the simple and nonverbal reactions. The range indicates there was considerable variation, however, not only across tasks but also between the two subjects. Sometimes Cattell and at other times his colleague was significantly quicker on a particular type of task. In speculating on the implications of these differences, Cattell suggested that some people may have *generally* quicker association times than others. If so, he believed the quick reactors not only would think faster, but also would literally experience more ideas in the same objective period of time, and thus "live so much the longer in the same number of years."[13] Here was a suggestion that differences in people's average reaction times might reflect differences in their *intelligence* — a notion that Cattell and others would later pursue, and that we shall return to in later chapters.

Shortly after Cattell's thesis, another student performed a further reaction-time experiment that greatly interested Wundt. In 1888, **Ludwig Lange** (1863–1936) compared simple reaction times when the subject's attention was focused on the expected *stimulus* with those obtained when attention was on the *response* to be made.

That is, in one case the subject paid particular attention to what he was about to see, and in the other to what he was about to do. Reaction times in the first case were about one-tenth of a second longer than those in the second.

In interpreting these results, Wundt borrowed Leibniz's distinction between the processes of simple perception and **apperception**, described in Chapter 2. In perception, he argued, one simply responds to a stimulus automatically, mechanically, and "thoughtlessly." In apperception, one's full *attention* is focused on the stimulus, and it is consciously recognized, interpreted, and "thought about." As an example, compare the reaction to a street sign reading "Main Street" by a neighborhood local with that of a stranger trying to locate an unfamiliar address. To the native, the sign is a familiar landmark on a well-known path, and on encountering it he turns right on his way home without giving it a thought. He has *perceived* the stimulus and responded to it, but without deliberation. To the stranger, however, the Main Street sign is something he has been carefully looking for, because his directions have told him to turn right there to get to his destination. Thus the sign fully enters and occupies his attention — in Wundt's language is *apperceived* — at least for a brief period of time.

Wundt believed that Lange's subject merely perceived the stimulus in the condition where he was concentrating on the response; although fast, this "thoughtless" reaction was also relatively error prone and liable to be triggered by inappropriate stimuli. The subject concentrating on the stimulus apperceived it, requiring an extra fraction of a second for its full registration in consciousness.

Apperception became a major concept in Wundt's psychology, both experimental and theoretical. His students conducted experiments to measure the *span* of apperception; that is, to determine the number of separate stimuli that can be fully grasped in consciousness at once. Arrays of random numbers, letters, or words were flashed on a screen for one-tenth of a second (the time presumably necessary for a single act of apperception), and subjects were asked to recall as many of them as they could. The number of correctly recalled stimuli almost always lay between four and six, regardless of the level of complexity of the stimuli. Thus if a four-by-four array of random *letters* was flashed, subjects typically apperceived four to six of them; if the array comprised sixteen random *words* of six letters each, subjects recalled four to six of *them*, for a total of twenty-four to thirty-six individual letters. This reinforced Cattell's earlier finding that familiar words could be reacted to as quickly as individual letters, and his contention that such words are responded to as wholes rather than as collections of individual letters. In these cases, subjects did not "see" all of the individual letters of the words, but apperceived the complete words as independent entities. Of course, if unfamiliar words were flashed, apperception was reduced to the level of individual letters. Thus while typical English-speaking subjects would easily apperceive familiar words like *taller* with little more than a glance, they would have trouble with its equally long Polish equivalent, *wyzszy*, being able to remember it only as a collection of six individual letters.

Voluntaristic Psychology The concept of apperception took a central place in Wundt's theoretical writings on psychology, in which he likened it to the events occurring in the very center of the visual field. In normal vision, a large number of individual stimuli may be present in the field, but only the very few whose images have fallen on the tiny fovea in the retina are sharply focused. Since the eye is extremely mobile, however, it constantly shifts its sharpest focus from object to object. As you read this page, for example, your eye movements constantly bring new words into sharp focus as previous ones fade into the periphery. Wundt argued the same sort of thing happens with consciousness in general. At any given moment, a maximum of six ideas are apperceived in direct attention, while many others may be perceived peripherally and indistinctly. Like visual focus, attention can shift rapidly from one small group of ideas to another.

Wundt further believed that perceived and apperceived ideas are subject to different rules of organization and combination. Perceived ideas organize themselves mechanically and automatically, along lines laid down by past experience: the *associations* a person has experienced in the past. Apperceived ideas, however, may be combined and organized in many different ways, including some that have never been experienced before. In Wundt's terminology, a **creative synthesis** takes place at the center of attention.

Consider a simple example: a person's conscious response to a card on which the digit 1 has been printed immediately above the digit 2. If the stimulus is merely perceived, it will elicit the idea most strongly associated with it in the past — perhaps the number "three" since the stimulus resembles an elementary arithmetic problem. This straightforward reaction has been fully determined by past experience. But later, if apperceptive attention becomes focused on the stimulus, a host of new and "creative" responses may occur: the idea of "minus one," perhaps, or "twelve," "twenty-one," notions of a secret code or cipher, or anything else depending on the imagination of the subject.

Theoretically, if one knew a person's complete history in advance, one could predict that person's reactions to perceived stimuli with complete accuracy. But Wundt believed reactions to apperceived stimuli are *not* predictable, subject as they are to unobservable and "inner" influences such as motives, innate predilections, emotions and feelings, and the ineffable effects of the will itself. Accordingly, he argued that an entirely different order of causality determines apperceptive versus merely perceptive processes, a **psychic causality** whose rules are not reducible to the purely mechanistic processes of physical causality. In a sense, Wundt here rejected the complete mechanism of the Helmholtz school in favor of Descartes's old contention that at least some central mental processes closely connected with consciousness and "will" require an altogether different kind of analysis.

Wundt did not deny the power and usefulness of mechanistic physiology for explaining events on the periphery of conscious experience. But he insisted that something further was needed for full explanation of that experience itself. Believing that this something — responsible for apperception, creative synthesis, and psychic causality — closely involved the conscious experiences of "will" and "voluntary effort," Wundt often referred to his entire theory as a **voluntaristic psychology**.

Wundt further believed that mental processes determined by psychic as opposed to physical causality must logically be largely insusceptible to laboratory experimentation. Here was another strong argument for the development of a non-experimental *Völkerpsychologie* to deal with such issues, and he accordingly devoted the final years of his career to that project.

Völkerpsychologie and Its Implications   Higher and central mental processes such as apperception and thinking had been experimentally demonstrated to *exist* by mental chronometry, and a few of their features, such as the span of apperception, had been measured in the laboratory. But Wundt believed their most essential features would always resist experimental analysis, and would have to be studied naturalistically by comparative and historical rather than experimental methods. Wundt himself tried to do this between 1900 and 1920, publishing his results in the ten large volumes of his *Völkerpsychologie*. Here he dealt with the *collective* products of human culture: myth, religion, custom, and — the heart of his analysis — language.

Several theorists before Wundt had equated *thought* with language, arguing that even silent thinking was a sort of low-level talking to oneself. Wundt believed otherwise, however, and cited several common situations in which people's words apparently do *not* accurately or uniquely represent their thoughts. Sometimes, for example, we suddenly realize that our speech is not expressing our thoughts properly, and exclaim something like, "That's not what I meant to say; let me start over again." Other times we listen to someone else speak and *recognize* a point of disagreement before we can put it in words; we interject a "What?" or "No!" or "Wait a minute!" long before we can actually describe what it is that disturbs us. Or again, we can often repeat the gist of ideas or messages in words totally different from those of their original speaker. The fact that we often have to work to put our thoughts into words, and that the same thoughts can be represented by different patterns of words, suggested to Wundt that words and thoughts cannot be exactly the same thing.

Accordingly, Wundt concluded that the most basic unit of thought is not the word or other linguistic element, but rather a "general impression" or "general idea" (*Gesamtvorstellung*) that is independent of words. The process of speaking begins with an apperception of the general idea, followed by its analysis into linguistic structures that represent it more or less adequately. In listening, we first apperceive the language, and then connect it with some appropriate general idea.

In analyzing language itself, Wundt argued that the fundamental linguistic unit was not the word but the *sentence*, the overall structure that somehow "contains" a complete thought or general idea. When we use language, our attention is focused not only on the specific words as they are uttered, but also on the role of each word in an overall sentence structure. As we speak, we somehow know that each of our words has a specific role in the larger structure of our sentence — as subject, object, verb, or the like. And conversely, as we listen, we automatically assign each word to a vacant place in our awaiting thought structure. Wundt thus described the sentence as a structure that is at once "simultaneous" and "sequential":

> It is simultaneous because at each moment it is present in consciousness as a totality even though individual subordinate elements may occasionally disappear from it. It is sequential because the configuration changes from moment to moment in its cognitive condition as individual constituents move into the focus of attention and out again one after the other.[14]

As this brief discussion shows, Wundt's *Völkerpsychologie* made use of, and was consistent with, concepts derived from his experimental psychology. Apperception of words, sentences, and general impressions all presumably followed the rules of speed and capacity that had been demonstrated in the laboratory. But a full understanding of thought and language also involved the comparative study of many different languages, to determine what they had in common and thus was presumably universal in human speech. And it involved the introspection and analysis of ongoing naturalistic speech processes — processes Wundt believed were too complicated to be manipulated experimentally in the laboratory.

Thus Wundt actually practiced the two-sided approach to psychology he had prescribed early in his career. Among the first to apply the emerging mechanistic, deterministic, and experimental approaches of the "new psychology" to central psychological processes, he is justly remembered as the father of experimental psychology. But he also believed these approaches were useful mainly in studying the relatively simple and peripheral aspects of psychological functioning: sensation, muscular activation, and the times required for mental processes to occur. For studying the complex and central functions — those at the farthest remove from easily observable sensory and motor interactions with the physical world — Wundt relied on non-experimental techniques, and posited a non-mechanistic psychic causality.

Not all of Wundt's students and immediate successors agreed completely with this conception of psychology, and two particularly lively debates arose during the latter part of his career. Both of these debates centered partly on the role of **introspection** — the observation and reporting of one's own subjective "inner experience" — in psychological experiments.

Since Wundt saw psychology as the science of conscious experience, he saw introspection as the most direct source of much psychological data. On the basis of introspection, he concluded that the contents of consciousness could be usefully described as composed of varying combinations of specifiable **sensations** and **feelings**, which in turn could be classified according to basic dimensions. Thus he believed sensations could be categorized as to their **modes** (that is, whether visual, auditory, tactile, etc.), their **qualities** (for example, their colors and shapes if visual, their pitches and timbres if auditory), their **intensities**, and their **durations**. Wundt classified feelings according to the three basic dimensions of **pleasantness-unpleasantness**, **tension-relaxation**, and **activity-passivity**.

But while accepting introspective analysis of consciousness as a useful descriptive tool, Wundt firmly expressed two kinds of reservations about it. First, he warned that the introspectively revealed dimensions of consciousness ought *not* be taken overly seriously as "elements of consciousness" analogous to the chemical elements — that is, as ultimate units capable of combining together to form complex psychological states in the same way chemical elements combine to create physical compounds. He noted that chemical elements such as hydrogen, oxygen, and carbon can actually exist and be seen in their pure states, while the dimensions of sensation and feeling *only* exist in combination with each other, and are in fact really abstractions rather than concrete conscious experiences. One of

167

Wundt's most influential students, **Edward Bradford Titchener** (1867–1927), came to disagree with this, and to propound an experimental psychology whose major goal was the atomistic analysis of the elements of consciousness. Titchener's atomism in turn aroused considerable opposition, most strikingly in a group of investigators who called themselves **Gestalt psychologists**.

Wundt's second reservation about introspective psychology derived from the essentially private and unverifiable nature of subjective reports, and the fact that memory often plays tricks with the recollection of psychological states. Accordingly, he set strict limits on the use of introspection in experiments — restricting it to simple and immediately recallable experimental situations, or to the generation of hypotheses that could be tested by non-introspective experiments. To Wundt, the higher mental processes seemed much too complicated to be accurately recalled and introspected — part of the reason they could never be studied experimentally. In contradiction of Wundt's belief, his former student **Oswald Külpe** (1862–1915) supervised a series of experiments at the University of Würzburg in which several of the higher processes were in fact approached introspectively. And in Berlin, **Hermann Ebbinghaus** (1850–1909) devised a non-introspective but still experimental approach to studying memory — one of the higher processes that Wundt had ruled out of bounds to experimental methods of any kind.

Both of these debates led to developments that endure in modern psychology, and we turn now to each of them in more detail.

The Atomism Debate: Titchener versus Gestalt Psychology

An Englishman who had absorbed the predilections of his native associationist tradition before studying with Wundt, Edward Titchener completed his Ph.D. in 1892 and then moved to Cornell University in New York State to establish a laboratory in the general Wundtian mold. There he ruled with an iron hand, lectured in academic robes (which he reputedly said gave him the right to be dogmatic), and quickly built the largest psychology Ph.D. program in the United States. He also staunchly advocated an introspective approach to psychology he called **structuralism**.*

Titchener represented himself as a loyal student of Wundt, and in the absence of translations of most of the German's work, structuralism came to be accepted in English-speaking countries as synonymous with Wundtian psychology. In fact, however, Titchener had adopted only part of Wundt's psychology and rejected much that was essential to it. He agreed with his teacher that introspection must be used carefully and only under precisely controlled conditions. But he did not share Wundt's distrust of the chemical-element analogy, and indeed argued that the *primary goal* of experimental psychology was the introspective analysis of conscious experience into its elements of sensation and feeling.

Titchener himself had strong visualizing tendencies, holding very concrete images even for abstract terms. He literally *saw* the concept of "meaning," for example, as "the blue-grey tip of a kind of scoop which has a bit of yellow above it . . . and which is just digging into a dank mass of . . . plastic material."[15] Predisposed as he was toward such vivid imagery, it is perhaps unsurprising that he believed *all* conscious experience could be reduced to introspectively accessible sensory images—if only one knew how to introspect properly.

Accordingly, introspection for Titchener was no casual inner pondering, but a rigorous procedure that one had to be carefully trained to perform. Introspectors had to reduce all of their mental contents into their most basic elements, while assiduously avoiding what Titchener called the **stimulus error**—the imposition of "meaning" or "interpretation" on their subject. Titchener's own quotation above would not qualify as a proper introspective report because it contained such meaning-laden terms as "scoop" and "digging." To

---

*Titchener selected this name because he believed experimental psychologists' first task should be to discover the *structure* of the phenomena they dealt with, before concerning themselves with their *function*—following the example of biologists who supposedly had to know the anatomy of organs before being able to understand their physiology. Titchener's "structuralism" died with him, and bears no relationship to the movement of the same name associated with recent figures important to cognitive psychology, such as Jean Piaget, Noam Chomsky, and Claude Levi-Strauss.

qualify, those images would have to be further reduced to their pure sensory elements: to minutely described patches of light with different colors, shapes, intensities, and durations. Titchener's introspection attempted to cut through the learned categories and concepts that define everyday experience, and to arrive at the pristine building blocks of consciousness from which everything presumably begins. From such painstaking introspections, Titchener concluded that there exist more than forty-three thousand distinguishable elements of sensory experience, more than thirty thousand being visual and eleven thousand auditory in nature. He found just four specifiable elements involved in taste, and three in the sensations of the alimentary tract.

True to his premise, Titchener believed he found an elemental sensory base for virtually everything he analyzed introspectively, even including Wundt's key processes of apperception and attention. Attention, he argued, was simply a matter of the *clarity* of the imaginal process—one of the elemental sensory attributes. He interpreted the vague sense of concentration and effort that accompanies attention as nothing more than sensations from the minute frowns, movements, and muscle contractions that occur simultaneously with a thought.

To Wundt, such analyses distorted the essential nature of central psychological processes, which he saw as much more than the sum of their constituent elements. Indeed, Titchener's goal of avoiding the stimulus error, and stripping experience of its "meaning," ran counter to Wundt's whole approach to psychology. Titchener's elements struck Wundt as barren, sterile, and largely beside the point.

This anti-elementistic position was elaborated—mainly in the years immediately following Wundt's death—by the Gestalt psychologists. Although none of these individuals had studied with Wundt, or even acknowledged a direct indebtedness to his views, at least some of their writing was in a tradition he would have approved.

The German term *Gestalt*—roughly translatable as "form" or "shape"—entered psychological vocabularies in 1890. That year the Austrian **Christian von Ehrenfels** (1859–1932) wrote of certain perceptual "form qualities" — *Gestaltqualitäten* — that could not be intro-spectively broken down into separate sensory elements, but instead resided in the overall configurations of objects or ideas. For example, the "squareness" of a square, or the melody of a musical piece, inhered not in the percepts' separate parts, but in their total con-figurations. A square may be constructed out of any group of four equal straight lines, so long as they are properly arranged; "square-ness" resides not in the particular lines, but in their relationships to each other. Similarly, a melody retains its distinctive and recog-nizable quality regardless of the key in which it is played or the timbre of its specific notes. "Yankee Doodle" is still "Yankee Doodle" whether played in the highest register of the piccolo or the lowest of the tuba. The essence of its melody lies not in its specific notes, but in the *relationships* among its notes.

The implications of Gestalt qualities were most fully explored after 1910, when a former student of Ehrenfels named **Max Wertheimer** (1880–1943) had a sudden inspiration while waiting for a train to take him on summer vacation. He abandoned his vacation to conduct research at Frankfurt with the assistance of two younger colleagues, **Kurt Koffka** (1886–1941) and **Wolfgang Köhler** (1887–1967). The three of them subsequently founded the movement known as Gestalt psychology.

Wertheimer's inspiration was to study the optical illusion of *apparent movement*, just then attracting much public notice because of recent developments with motion pictures. As we have already seen, early studies in Wundt's laboratory had shown that successive visual stimuli separated by less than one-tenth of a second tended to blend together into a single continuous impression. Wertheimer and his colleagues investigated this effect more systematically, em-ploying very simple visual stimuli. With a tachistoscope — a device that projects images on a screen for measured fractions of a second — they flashed light alternately through two slits, one vertical and the other tilted by thirty degrees. When the interval between the flashes exceeded one-fifth of a second, observers saw the "true' state of affairs: two separate, rapidly alternating lights. When the interval was less than one-hundredth of a second, both of the slits appeared to be illuminated constantly. Apparent movement occurred when

171

separation times lay between those values, with the strongest effect at about one-twentieth of a second. Observers then had a distinct impression of a single slit of light "falling over" from the vertical to the inclined position, then rising back up again. Wertheimer named this apparent movement—a simplified version of a motion picture—the **phi phenomenon**.

Wertheimer went on to show that an observer, presented with randomly distributed examples of real movement and comparable apparent movement, could not distinguish one type from the other. Furthermore, both real and apparent movement could produce identical **negative afterimages**—a tendency to see stationary objects as moving in the direction opposite to that of a moving object that has been observed immediately before. Here was another perceptual situation like those discussed in Chapter 4, where widely differing physical stimuli can produce subjectively identical conscious experiences. That is, in real movement light images literally sweep across the retina, falling upon all of the receptor cells lying in their path. In the phi phenomenon, only the receptors lying at the beginning and at the end of the "sweep" become physically illuminated. Yet both sets of physical conditions produce the same perception of continuous physical motion. These findings indicated that at least some of the processes responsible for the perception of movement take place at a neurological level higher than the retina. "Movement" is an attribute that may be imposed upon stationary images by the higher brain processes.

Following this work on apparent movement, Wertheimer, Koffka, and Köhler considered Ehrenfels's Gestalt qualities, and concluded that human perception in general imposes its own order and dynamic organization upon the individual "elements" of sensation. They asserted that meaningful perception entails far more than the simple addition of sensory elements, or even the unconscious inferring of logical relationships among those elements. Instead, the mind seems to organize the elements of experience into *wholes*, whose significance completely transcends that of their summed individual parts. Squares, melodies, and phi phenomena alike are not only *more* than the sums of their sensory parts, but dynamic entities on their own whose parts were defined by their relationships to the whole. Wertheimer summarized:

172

There are wholes, the behavior of which is not determined by that of their individual elements, but where the part processes themselves are determined by the intrinsic nature of the whole. It is the hope of Gestalt theory to determine the nature of such wholes.[16]

Thus the Gestalt psychologists analyzed experience not like Titchener, who started with simple elements and attempted to show how they combine to create wholes, but by starting with the wholes and then describing the functions of the parts *within* those wholes.

The Gestalt psychologists also observed that perception always occurs in a "field" divided into the **figure** and the **ground**, the figure being the whole percept immediately attended to in consciousness, and the ground the necessary backdrop against which the figure must define itself. Figure cannot exist without ground; thus the printed words you are now reading cannot be perceived (as figure) except against the lighter background of the page. Figure and ground may never both be in consciousness simultaneously (for then both would be part of the figure), but they may reverse. Figure 5-3 illustrates figure-ground reversal when you see it first as a white vase against a black ground, and then as black profiled faces against a white ground. You may *not* see both the vase and the faces at exactly the same time, because that would constitute two figures with no ground. Thus the whole figures — or "Gestalts" — in your perceptual field constantly change, but each always appears as only a part of the entire field, standing out against the background.

Figure 5-3. *Reversible figure and ground.*

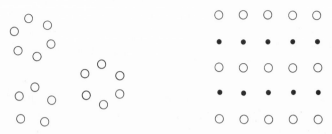

Figure 5–4. *Gestalt principles of organization.*

Wertheimer, Koffka, and Köhler also emphasized that perceived Gestalts tend to *simplify* and *organize* the perceptual fields in which they occur. Relatively complicated aggregates of stimuli inevitably become organized into simpler groups according to principles of contiguity and similarity. In the left-hand portion of Figure 5–4, for example, the circles' spacing (contiguity) leads most people to perceive "three groups of circles" rather than the more complex "seventeen scattered circles." On the right, the mind uses similarity cues to perceive "alternating rows of circles and dots" more readily than the more complicated "five columns of mixed circles and dots."

The same Gestalt principles seem to apply in other sense modalities besides vision. Perceived *sounds* for example, must always be heard against a relatively neutral background. Auditory figure-ground reversals can easily occur, as when nervous airplane passengers "listen" for the ominous periods of silence that may punctuate the droning of a faulty engine. Complex temporal sequences of sounds may be organized into simpler contiguous groups, as in the perceived regularities of a drummer's beat, and they may be grouped by similarity, as when the violin part is clearly discerned against the background of the rest of the orchestra.

History has treated the Gestalt psychologists more kindly than Titchener, for while the Gestalt principles of figure-ground and perceptual organization are discussed in virtually all introductory psychology textbooks, Titchener's atomistic introspective methods — if discussed at all — are routinely dismissed as an unproductive line of research followed only in the days before psychology became properly scientific. There is irony here, however, because while the discredited (and ultimately unproductive) methods were most enthusiastically endorsed by *Titchener*, the name most frequently associated with them in English-language textbooks is *Wundt*. It seems many English textbook writers accepted Titchener's claim to be Wundt's true student and representative, did not read Wundt in the original, and so tarred the teacher with the same brush they did the errant student. As we have seen, Wundt actually warned about the ultimate sterility of psychological atomism.

Experimenting on the Higher Functions: Külpe and Ebbinghaus

Oswald Külpe took his Ph.D. with Wundt in 1887, then remained as his chief assistant and right-hand man for seven years. In 1894, however, Külpe established his own psychological laboratory at the University of Würzberg, and soon began supervising students in introspective studies of which Wundt did not approve. Most of these involved setting relatively complex mental tasks for subjects to perform, and then asking them to recall what they had consciously experienced as they solved them. Subjects reported two kinds of experiences that Wundt found arguable.

First were **imageless thoughts**. After associating to stimulus words, or judging the relative heaviness of different weights, Würzberg introspectors recalled that they had experienced certain transitory states that were not definable in terms of sensations or feelings. They said they had been aware of their own processes of associating or judging, but these experiences had seemed impalpable and devoid of specifically definable content. Wundt refused to accept these findings, on grounds that the experimental conditions had not been sufficiently controlled, and because he believed the mental processes involved were too complex to be reliably introspected and recalled.

Studies of **directed association**, conducted by Külpe's Scottish student **Henry J. Watt** (1879–1925) and his junior colleague **Narziss Ach** (1871–1946), posed an even more direct challenge to Wundt's experimental psychology. Watt asked his subjects to associate to stimulus words in a highly specific rather than "free" manner — by naming the first superordinate or subordinate concepts to come to mind. Thus to the stimulus word "bird," associations such as "animal," "creature," and "living thing" would be appropriate superordinate concepts, while "canary," "robin," and "hawk" would be acceptable subordinate replies. Ach presented *his* subjects with pairs of numbers, after first suggesting they be added, subtracted, multiplied, or divided. Thus a card with a 4 over a 3 elicited responses of 7, 1, 12, or 1.33, depending on his instructions.

Under all of these conditions, subjects gave correct replies easily and with negligible differences in reaction time. And when they introspectively recalled their experiences, they said that the instructions, after having once been heard and registered in consciousness, played no further conscious role in the process of associating. A subject instructed to subtract responded "one" to the stimulus above just as quickly, automatically, and "thoughtlessly" as he replied "seven" when asked to add. It seemed that the instructions, or in Watt's language the **task** set by the experimenter, predetermined the subjects' associational patterns in different ways before the experiment began. Ach wrote that the instructions established different **determining tendencies** or **mental sets** that did not consciously enter into the subjects' associational processes, but that predetermined them in particular directions before the experiments began.

In one way these results accorded well with Wundt's voluntaristic psychology, for the task, determining tendency, and set were precisely the kind of central, directive, and motivational variables he had proposed to enter into the process of apperception. But Külpe, who had been suspicious of many mental chronometry experiments even before he left Leipzig, saw the Würzberg results as undermining the logic of Wundt's subtractive procedure. Külpe argued that subjects in the more complicated situations did not perform mere aggregates of simple reactions (perception plus apperception plus discrimination plus association, and so on), but instead operated under "sets" completely different from those of subjects in simpler situations. Thus the logic of the subtractive procedure grossly oversimplified the true process of thinking and reacting. Although Wundt protested, Külpe's argument here proved generally persuasive. The Würzberg experiments on directed association are still considered today as classic demonstrations of the predetermining influence of motives on association and thought.

A different and even more influential challenge to Wundt's conception of experimental psychology came from his younger compatriot **Hermann Ebbinghaus** (1850–1909). After taking history and philosophy degrees at the University of Bonn, Ebbinghaus fought in the Franco-Prussian War and then spent seven years in travel and independent study, earning his keep by tutoring. Sometime in the late 1870s he chanced upon a secondhand copy of Fechner's *Elements of Psychophysics* in a London bookshop. The book impressed him greatly, and he decided to see if he could apply the same sort of experimental mathematical treatment that Fechner had given sensation to the new subject of *memory*. Wundt had just published his *Physiological Psychology* declaring that higher processes such as memory could not be studied experimentally, but Ebbinghaus evidently took this as a challenge rather than a deterrent, and proceeded completely on his own to conduct one of the classic research programs in experimental psychology.

Using just himself as the subject, Ebbinghaus investigated the amount of time he required to study material before being able to remember it perfectly. His major experimental difficulty was to find appropriate material to memorize. He knew from experience that stimuli differed greatly in their ease of memorization, and he believed that most of this variability occurred because of differing prior associations. Because of previous experience, one finds some stimuli but not others to be particularly familiar, meaningful, and memorable. Ebbinghaus sought for his experiments a large number of stimuli to be memorized that he could feel confident were equally unfamiliar at the outset.

Thus he created **nonsense syllables** by systematically going through the alphabet and constructing some twenty-three hundred consonant-vowel-consonant combinations such as *taz, bok,* and *lef* that could serve as originally neutral or meaningless stimuli to be memorized in his experiments. He randomly assembled these nonsense syllables into lists, usually between twelve and sixteen syllables in length, and set about memorizing them under fixed conditions. Typically he read aloud through a list at a fixed rate of speed, over and over again until he thought he had memorized it perfectly. Then he would test himself, and if he made any mistakes in the syllables or their order would go back to reading the list again. For each list, he recorded the amount of learning time he had required before the first perfect recollection. On the average, he perfectly memorized a single sixteen-syllable list in about twenty-one minutes.

Having once memorized his lists, Ebbinghaus tested himself on their *retention* under varying conditions. He always had to re-study a list to get it right again, but for a shorter period of time than at first. After an interval of twenty-four hours, for example, he typically re-learned lists of sixteen syllables in fourteen minutes each — a reduction in learning time of one-third compared to the twenty-one minutes of the day before. Ebbinghaus used this fractional "savings" in learning time as a quantitative measure of his memory strength.

When Ebbinghaus calculated his average savings for various periods of time between the original and the second memorizations, he was not surprised to find that savings decreased as the interval increased. More surprisingly and delightfully, however, the rate of decrease was not constant, but fell on a regular **forgetting curve** where memory declined rapidly immediately after the initial learning, but then almost leveled off. For example, when he re-tested himself on one series of lists, the savings were fifty-eight percent after twenty minutes, forty-four percent after an hour, thirty-six percent after eight hours, thirty-four percent after one day, twenty-five percent after a week, and twenty-one percent after a month. Ebbinghaus did not fail to mention that the shape of this forgetting curve approximated a mathematical function similar to that in Fechner's psychophysical law (except that Fechner's curve *increased* at a progressively slower rate, while his own *decreased*). In sum, he demonstrated that memory *could* be studied experimentally, and yield mathematically regular results. Wundt's limitation on experimental psychology had been too extreme.

On Memory has remained for over a century one of the most cited and most highly respected works in all of experimental psychology. Wundt could (and did) argue that nonsense syllables stripped of all meaningfulness were parodies of normal mental stimuli, and thus claim that Ebbinghaus had only studied an artificial sort of memory. But even if he had a point, it was largely overlooked by later generations of experimental psychologists who seized upon Ebbinghaus's methods as a model for their research on human verbal learning.

Wundt's Reputation and Influence

Wundt remained full in saddle until the very end of his long life. He retired from teaching in 1917 at age eighty-five but continued to write his *Völkerpsychologie*. He completed his autobiography on 23 August 1920, just eight days before his death. He left behind sixty thousand pages of published works, and most of the thousands of students he had taught during his prodigious career.

In general, however, historians have been unkind to Wundt, particularly in English-speaking countries. This occurred partly because of his mistaken association with the ultra-introspectionist, structuralist school of Titchener, which turned out to be particularly out of tune with the incipient American movement toward practicality, "objectivity," and behaviorism. In addition, Wundt's personal and stylistic qualities were uncongenial to William James, the influential leader of academic psychology in the United States, whom we shall meet in Chapter 8. When these intellectual and attitudinal differences became exacerbated by the all-too-physical antagonisms of World War I, the ardent German patriot Wundt became easily dismissed in England and America. Unread and largely untranslated, he came to be caricatured as the founder of an ineffective experimental psychology, a dogmatic tyrant who suppressed everyone else's point of view, and an indefatigable author of boring tomes.

Recently, however, a few English-speaking scholars have taken the trouble to find out what Wundt *really* said, and they have found much of current relevance. Psychology's present preoccupation with central cognitive processes represents a clear return to "Wundtian" interests. Although experimental techniques and terminologies have changed since Wundt's day, he would still feel at home with modern psychologists who study such cognitive phenomena as information processing, selective attention, and perceptual masking; who study schizophrenia as a disease interfering with attention and the apperceptive processes; or who comparatively analyze languages according to the "transformational grammar" theory of linguist Noam Chomsky. Further, increasing numbers of psychologists today join Wundt in questioning whether the purely "objective" and "detached" techniques of the laboratory experiment can ever do full justice to the complexity of human experience. In sum, there seems good reason to believe that the father of experimental psychology will be better remembered by his later than by his earlier intellectual descendants.

Suggested Readings

Arthur Blumenthal initiated the modern revival of interest in Wundt with his book *Language and Psychology: Historical Aspects of Psycholinguistics* (New York: Wiley, 1970) and his paper "A Reappraisal of Wilhelm Wundt," *American Psychologist* (*30*:1081–1088, 1975). The centennial of Wundt's Leipzig laboratory in 1979 inspired two excellent collections of invited articles, containing extensive biographical as well as analytical material; these are Wolfgang G. Bringmann and Ryan D. Tweney (eds.), *Wundt Studies: A Centennial Collection* (Toronto: Hogrefe, 1980), and Robert W. Rieber (ed.), *Wilhelm Wundt and the Making of a Scientific Psychology* (New York: Plenum, 1980). Of particular biographical interest are Solomon Diamond's "Wundt before Leipzig," in the Rieber volume, and two articles by Wolfgang Bringmann et al. in the Bringmann and Tweney collection: "Wilhelm Maximilian Wundt, 1832–1874: The Formative Years," and "The Establishment of Wundt's Laboratory: An Archival and Documentary Study." For an interesting firsthand account of Wundt's Leipzig laboratory by his student Cattell, see *An Education in Psychology: James McKeen Cattell's Journal and Letters from Germany and England, 1880–1888*, edited by Michael M. Sokal (Cambridge, MA: MIT Press, 1981).

Kurt Danziger has written several important interpretive articles on Wundt and his contemporaries, including "The Positivist Repudiation of Wundt" in *Journal of the History of the Behavioral Sciences* (*15*:205–230, 1979); "The History of Introspection Reconsidered," also in *Journal of the History of the Behavioral Sciences* (*16*:241–262, 1980); and "Origins and Basic Principles of Wundt's *Völkerpsychologie*," *British Journal of Social Psychology* (*22*:303–313, 1983).

6

Charles Darwin and the Theory of Evolution

In early September of 1831, the young Cambridge graduate **Charles Robert Darwin** (1809–1882) went to London for the most important interview of his life. Unexpectedly recommended for the post of naturalist aboard the survey ship H.M.S. *Beagle,* Darwin had already had some difficulty convincing his father it would be a good thing to do. Now he faced a crucial meeting with Captain Robert FitzRoy, the ship's formidable commander, to determine if he would be finally accepted for the job.

A direct although illegitimate descendant of King Charles II, FitzRoy was already a veteran surveyor and ship's captain at age twenty-six. He now planned a multiyear voyage to survey the coasts of South America, and then proceed around the world. He wished to engage a congenial gentleman who would not only make geological, mineralogical, and biological observations, but also share his table and cabin and be very much a companion on the voyage. The post carried no pay, and several experienced naturalists had declined it before the inexperienced but wealthy Darwin had been suggested.

At first the interview went badly, partly because of political differences between the liberal Darwin and the aristocratic, archconservative captain—but mainly because of the shape of Darwin's

Charles Darwin (1809–1882)

nose! FitzRoy subscribed to the theory of "physiognomy" — which held that a person's facial features reflect his or her character — and Darwin's nose had a shape supposedly associated with a lack of energy and determination.* And indeed Darwin's modest academic record did little to contradict that diagnosis. As the interview proceeded, however, Darwin's great geniality and charm gradually won

*As noted in Chapter 3, the theory of physiognomy — originally proposed by the Swiss mystic **Johann Lavater** (1741–1801) — was a precursor of phrenology.

the captain over and encouraged him to take a chance. Darwin spent the next five years on one of the most scientifically consequential voyages of modern times.

Departing raw and untrained, Darwin returned home from the *Beagle* as an accomplished and respected geologist and collector of biological specimens. Even more important, he had made some crucial observations that started him toward developing the **theory of evolution by natural selection**, a revolutionary biological theory with vast implications for psychology. This chapter will tell Darwin's story, and that of his momentous theory.

Darwin's Early Life

Charles Darwin was born on 12 February 1809 (the same day as Abraham Lincoln) in the English town of Shrewsbury, the fifth and next-to-last child in a wealthy and distinguished family. His father, Robert Darwin, ranked among the most highly paid of English provincial physicians; his mother, born Susannah Wedgewood, came from the famous chinaware-producing family. His grandfather **Erasmus Darwin** (1731–1802) had been one of the most famous intellectual figures of his day: a doctor, inventor, poet, and general man-of-science. He had even formulated an early theory of evolution, expressing it colorfully although without the range of supporting evidence necessary for it to be taken terribly seriously by his contemporary scientists.

Educated first at home and then at the nearby Shrewsbury School, young Charles proved an indifferent scholar in the then-standard classical curriculum. He recalled, "Nothing could have been worse for the development of my mind. . . . The school as a means of education to me was simply a blank." He failed to impress his schoolmasters, and once led his exasperated father to declare, "You care for nothing but shooting, dogs, and rat-catching, and you will be a disgrace to yourself and all your family."[1]

But despite his father's immortally unprophetic lament, young Darwin already possessed two qualities that eventually stood him in good stead. First was a strong curiosity and love of nature that drove him to spend countless hours observing, collecting, classifying, and experimenting in the natural world. He maintained extensive collections of plants, shells, and minerals, and his explosive experiments in a home chemistry laboratory earned him the nickname "Gas." Although unrewarded in school, these activities provided excellent training for a scientist.

Second, Charles Darwin showed from youth onward a warm and sympathetic personality that made him almost universally liked. This quality later commended him to Captain FitzRoy and won him the post on the *Beagle*. Moreover, his warmth and sympathy extended to animals as well as people, predisposing him in a peculiar way to appreciate the functional, adaptive value of many animal behaviors that seemed incomprehensible or repugnant to others — a key insight in his evolutionary theory.

Nevertheless, Charles's academic situation improved only slightly at age sixteen, when his father finally released him from classical study and sent him to medical school at the University of Edinburgh. There he learned the art of taxidermy and presented his first scientific papers — reports on local marine life to the student scientific society. But medicine itself proved unappealing. One professor "made his lectures on human anatomy as dull as he was himself, and the subject disgusted me"; another teacher's early-morning classes were "something fearful to remember." And worst of all, Darwin witnessed two live operations performed without anesthesia, one on a child: "I rushed away before they were completed. Nor did I ever attend again, for hardly any inducement would have been strong enough to do so; this being long before the blessed days of chloroform."[2]

Darwin's father was not without sympathy, for he himself hated the sight of blood and maintained that he practiced medicine only out of economic necessity. Thus he proposed yet another change: that Charles move to Cambridge University and prepare to become an Anglican clergyman. Attracted by the prospect of becoming a country parson and pursuing natural history as an amateur, Charles accepted the plan.

At Cambridge, Darwin joined "a sporting set, [that] sometimes drank too much, with jolly singing and playing at cards afterwards."[3] His dining society — officially called the Gourmet Club but appropriately nicknamed the Glutton Club — was notorious for its "devouring raids on birds and beasts which were before unknown to human palate." It "came to an untimely end by endeavouring to eat an old brown owl." The Cambridge academic curriculum emphasized mathematics as well as classics, and although Darwin enjoyed geometry he was described by a fellow Glutton Clubber as having "a special quarrel" with the binomial theorem.[4] Thus Darwin never bothered to compete for honors, but "went out in the poll" with an ordinary or pass degree in 1831. He mastered enough geometry, classics, and natural theology to graduate tenth out of the 178 non-honors students in his class.

Although respectable, Darwin's formal academic career at Cambridge contained little to foretell that his alma mater would one day name a new college after him. He stood out only in extracurricular activity, with his passion for nature study. "No pursuit at Cambridge . . . gave me so much pleasure as collecting beetles," he recalled, and he offered the following "proof of my zeal":

One day, on tearing off some old bark, I saw two rare beetles and seized one in each hand; then I saw a third and new kind, which I could not bear to lose, so that I popped the one which I held in my right hand into my mouth. Alas it ejected some intensely acrid fluid, which burnt my tongue so that I was forced to spit the beetle out, which was lost, as well as the third one.[5]

The enthusiastic amateur entomologist attracted the attention of Cambridge's professor of botany, the Reverend **John Stevens Henslow** (1796–1861). This clergyman-naturalist earned no salary for his professorship, because the university still considered all sciences as distinctly minor subjects. But he did offer voluntary lectures for the small number of students who took extracurricular interest in botany, and organized walking tours of the local countryside. Darwin soon became known as "the man who walks with Henslow," and through his mentor's influence also became friendly with Cambridge's professor of geology, **Adam Sedgwick** (1785–1873).

Darwin's friendship with Sedgwick and Henslow proved fateful immediately after graduation in 1831. He accompanied Sedgwick on a summer geological tour of north Wales, which kindled a real interest in a science he had found rather dull at Edinburgh. And upon returning home to Shrewsbury, another great surprise awaited in the form of a letter from Henslow.

Henslow had just been offered the naturalist's post on Captain FitzRoy's *Beagle*, but had declined because of family commitments. He told Darwin:

I have stated that I consider you to be the best qualified person I know who is likely to undertake such a situation — I state this not on the supposition of your being a *finished* Naturalist, but as amply qualified for collecting, observing, and noting anything worthy to be noted in Natural History. . . . The Voyage is to last 2 years and if you take plenty of Books with you, any thing you please may be done. . . . In short I suppose there never was a finer chance for a man of zeal and spirit.[6]

Darwin's father, who would have to pay his son's expenses on this venture, at first called it a "wild scheme" that would interfere with a clerical career. Thus Charles wrote Henslow regretfully declining the offer, and went off to console himself on a shooting expedition with his uncle Josiah Wedgewood. Fortunately, however, Robert Darwin had also said that if Charles could find "any man of common sense, who advises you to go," he would reconsider his objections. And Uncle Josiah — universally regarded as a man of eminent common sense — thought the offer a wonderful opportunity. Instead of hunting, uncle and nephew together confronted the elder Darwin, who relented with good grace. To mollify his father, the often extravagant Charles told him "that I should be deuced clever to spend more than my allowance whilst aboard the *Beagle*." Robert answered with a resigned smile, "But they all tell me you are very clever."[7]

Thus Darwin had his fateful interview with FitzRoy, where his amiable manner triumphed over the weak shape of his nose and won him the position. Learning the news, a Glutton Club crony wrote a congratulatory letter saying: "Woe unto the Beetles of South America, woe unto all tropical butterflies."[8] Although Darwin in fact would collect thousands of insect specimens on this two-year voyage that expanded to five, these would be among the least of the journey's consequences.

The Voyage of the *Beagle*

Darwin's voyage on the *Beagle* began unpropitiously in December of 1831, as fierce gales in the Bay of Biscay left the former land-lubber constantly and miserably seasick. "Nobody who has only been to sea for 24 hours has a right to say that sea-sickness is even uncomfortable," he lamented. "I found nothing but lying in my hammock did me any good."[9] But when the seas calmed slightly, Darwin found he could read and work. He devised a specimen-catching bag to drag behind the ship, capturing thousands of marine creatures which he studied and classified aboard. He read voluminously on geology, geography, and biology, and kept a detailed journal of his observations and thoughts. With his good humor he soon became a favorite of the crew, who affectionately called him "Philosopher." FitzRoy wrote of him: "I never saw a 'shore-going fellow' come into the ways of a ship so soon and so thoroughly."[10]

This was a good thing, as the projected two-year voyage stretched to five. After two years only the east coast of South America had been surveyed, and the *Beagle* spent another two years on the west coast before finally starting the long westward voyage home via the Galapagos Islands, Tahiti, New Zealand, Australia, and the Cape of Good Hope. Figure 6-1 maps the entire voyage.

Geological Discoveries During his first months at sea, Darwin spent much time studying the recently published first volume of *Principles of Geology*, by the English geologist **Charles Lyell** (1797–1875). This book promoted a controversial theory called **uniformitarianism**, which held that the earth's major features have resulted from gradual processes occurring over vast stretches of time, and which continue in the present much as they have in the past (hence the "uniform" nature of geological development). Lyell disputed the then-predominant alternative theory of **catastrophism**, according to which geological features arose because of a few relatively sudden and massive cataclysms or catastrophes on the earth's surface. Catastrophism's appeal lay partly in its compatibility with a literal interpretation of the Bible, with Noah's flood representing the most important geological cataclysm. Catastrophism accorded well with the then widely

187

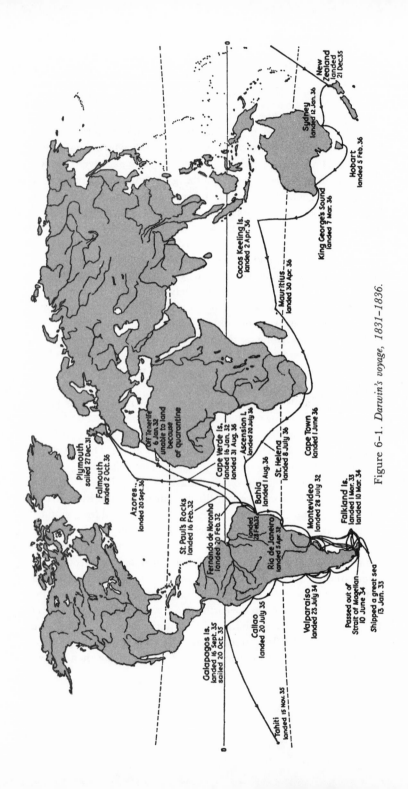

Figure 6–1. *Darwin's voyage, 1831–1836.*

accepted estimate of the earth's age as only about six thousand years, as calculated by the Irish archbishop **James Ussher** (1581–1656) after adding up the ages of the Old Testament patriarchs after Adam and Eve, as given in the Bible. Uniformitarianism required an immensely longer period of time than that for gradual processes to have built mountains and worked their other cumulative effects.

Before Darwin's departure, Henslow and Sedgwick had encouraged him to read and *think about* Lyell's book, but not to *believe* it. But as he read and thought, and then observed the geological features of the exotic places he visited, he became increasingly impressed. For example, he found seashells embedded in rock high in the Andes, and then witnessed an earthquake in Chile that left coastal features a few feet higher above sea level than they had been before. Although terrible for those caught in it, this earthquake hardly constituted a catastrophe of the order required by the older geological theory. But similar events occurring over vast periods of time — as prescribed by uniformitarianism — could easily have produced a gradual raising of land from sea-level in the distant past to a present mountainous height.

After examining the geology of several oceanic islands and atolls, Darwin became convinced that these too could be accounted for by gradual uniform processes — such as lava flows from undersea volcanoes, coral growth, and the slow rising and subsidence of the ocean floor. He wrote of all this to Henslow, who passed his letters on to Lyell and other geologists. Although Darwin did not know it at the time, these won him a reputation in England as a gifted geological observer, and helped turn the tide of informed scientific opinion in favor of uniformitarianism. Even more important, Darwin began in his own mind to accept a very ancient age for the earth — a necessary precondition for his later theory of evolution.

Biological Discoveries The inveterate collector also found and shipped home thousands of biological specimens. FitzRoy wrote of "our smiles at the apparent rubbish [Darwin] frequently brought on board,"[11] but many of the specimens won immediate scientific recognition back home. Among these were the fossilized remains of several large extinct creatures, found embedded in the stratified cliffs of Argentina. The *megatherium*, for example, had the skeletal structure of a modern sloth, but the size of an elephant. Bones from a giant armadillo, a wild llama the size of a camel, and a strange, rhinoceros-sized but hornless creature called the *toxodon* also fascinated the English naturalists.

Such fossil finds bore on the uniformitarianism-catastrophism debate, when the question naturally arose as to how and when they came to be embedded in rock. Aboard the *Beagle*, the devoutly religious FitzRoy offered a catastrophist explanation: The extinct species represented animals who had not made it onto Noah's ark, and therefore succumbed in the deluge. Darwin privately doubted this, but for the time being kept a discreet silence on the issue.

Darwin also collected and described thousands of *living* plant and animal species, many previously unknown in science. While reflecting on his biological findings, he adopted two general lines of thought. First, he habitually asked himself about the possible *functions* of all animal characteristics. When he saw an octopus change color to match its background, the camouflage value of such a reaction seemed obvious. And even when a marine iguana in the Galapagos behaved in a repetitive and seemingly "stupid" way, Darwin still could imagine a function:

I threw one several times as far as I could into a deep pool left by the retiring tide; but it invariably returned in a direct line to the spot where I stood. . . . As often as I threw it in, it returned. . . . Perhaps this singular piece of apparent stupidity may be accounted for by the circumstance, that this reptile has no [natural] enemy whatever on shore, whereas at sea it must often fall a prey to the numerous sharks. Hence, probably, urged by a fixed and hereditary instinct that the shore is its place of safety, whatever the emergency may be, it there takes refuge.[12]

While an ordinary observer would simply have remarked on the oddity or stupidity of such behavior, Darwin sought to understand its possible *usefulness*. This sensitivity to the functional adaptiveness of all biological phenomena later helped lead him to his theory of evolution.

A second important line of thought began almost casually, when Darwin began noting the *geographical distributions* of species. He saw that many entirely different animals existed on either side of the

Andes, for example, even though climate and other conditions were generally similar. His most surprising observations of this kind came in the Galapagos Islands, six hundred miles off Ecuador in the Pacific Ocean. These geologically recent volcanic islands supported many animals who closely resembled species found on the South American continent, and whose predecessors had presumably originated there. But despite the resemblances, the Galapagos creatures had developed distinctive characteristics of their own, some of which even varied discernibly from island to island within the chain. Thus giant tortoises (whose Spanish name *galapagos* had given the islands their name) showed slight but characteristic differences in the shapes of their shells that enabled an experienced observer to know on which island they had been born. And several populations of common brown finches differed only in the shape and size of their bills: On some islands they were long, pointed, and well suited for digging out insect prey, while elsewhere they were short but powerful and capable of cracking open hard nuts and seeds. These casual observations later assumed great importance when Darwin began thinking about the possible origins of different animal species.

The Return Home After leaving the Galapagos in October of 1835, nearly a year's sailing still lay ahead of the *Beagle* — to Tahiti, New Zealand, Australia, and south Africa. These places held little charm for Darwin, however, who now only wanted to return home to his family, and to enter English scientific life. His eagerness increased when family and friends wrote to tell him that his name was already becoming well known in scientific circles. His shipped specimens had been well received, and Henslow had excerpted geological passages from his letters in a pamphlet published by the Cambridge Philosophical Society — Darwin's first scientific publication.

At last on 2 October 1836, the *Beagle* docked at Falmouth, England, and Darwin took the first coach to Shrewsbury. Arriving in the middle of the night, he stayed at an inn before strolling home to surprise his family before breakfast the next morning. A delighted Robert Darwin exclaimed to his daughters, "Why, the shape of his head is quite altered."[13] In fact, Charles Darwin *was* a matured and transformed person, now ready to begin some momentous theorizing about the significance of his *Beagle* observations.

191

The Theory of Evolution by Natural Selection

Darwin won election to the London Geological Society in 1836, and the still more prestigious Royal Society in 1839. That year he also married his cousin Emma Wedgewood, and published his first book, the edited journal from his voyage. Despite its deceptively ponderous title—*Journal of Researches into the Geology and Natural History of the Various Countries Visited during the Voyages of the H.M.S.* Beagle, *under the Command of Captain FitzRoy, R.N., from 1832 to 1836*—this lively book became an immediate best-seller and established Darwin as a leading popular naturalist and travel writer.

Even more significant events occurred privately, for in 1837 Darwin had begun reflecting on the implications of his *Beagle* observations, and recording his thoughts in a series of notebooks.[14] Here he deliberately and specifically addressed one of the most puzzling and controversial questions in all of biology, sometimes called "the mystery of mysteries": namely, how the millions of different species that inhabit the earth originally came into being.

The traditional answer had each species being created at a single time, as a complete, distinctive, and unchangeable entity. This view was cogently summarized by one of Darwin's leading contemporaries as follows:

I assume that each organism which the Creator educed was stamped with an indelible specific character, which made it what it was, and distinguished it from everything else, however near or like. I assume that such a character has been, and is, indelible and immutable; that the characters which distinguish species from species *now*, were as definite at the first instant of their creation as now, and are as distinct now as they were then.[15]

Upholders of this traditional view claimed support from the first chapter of Genesis, which declares that on the fifth day of creation God created "every living creature that moveth." On more scientific grounds, they cited the so-called **argument from design**, originally promulgated by the philosopher-theologian **William Paley** (1743–1805). According to Paley, the marvelously complicated organs of various species—the delicate but strong hinge muscle of a bivalve shellfish, for example, or the mammalian eye—are so perfectly constructed and adapted that they must have been *designed* as finished products by some powerful and knowledgeable creator. Paley saw "an invisible hand, . . . the hand of God," in these adaptive wonders, and said that to study the structure of an eye was "a cure for atheism."[16]

Darwin had read and been impressed by Paley at Cambridge, even though he knew that a rival theory of **evolution of species** had already been proposed by some, including his grandfather Erasmus Darwin. In both prose and poetry, Erasmus Darwin had written that individual species had gradually evolved or developed out of one or more original ancestor stocks.* And in 1809 — the year of Charles Darwin's birth — the French zoologist **Jean-Baptiste Lamarck** (1744–1829) had proposed that species evolve and change owing to the inheritance of bodily changes produced by the voluntary exercise or disuse of particular organs. Presumably the giraffe, for example, had begun as a short-necked animal that browsed off tree foliage above its head, thus exercising its neck muscles; the slightly strengthened and stretched muscles of each generation were subsequently inherited by its successor, until eventually the modern giraffe evolved.

Although Lamarck and Erasmus Darwin helped bring the *idea* of evolved species to scientific awareness, neither was widely accepted. The elder Darwin had proposed no plausible *mechanism* by which evolution might occur, and the mechanism proposed by Lamarck — the voluntary use or disuse of particular muscles and organs — could not account for evolution of non-voluntary characteristics such as protective coloration. Thus when Charles Darwin returned from his voyage the notion of evolution was in the air, but had not yet been proposed in a form that could be taken seriously as an alternative to the argument from design.

In the months following his return, however, Darwin concluded that the idea of evolution or "transmutation" of species had to be taken seriously. The staggering number of different species in nature, often varying from each other only slightly and subtly, seemed more compatible with a long-standing and ongoing species-

---

*For a time, Erasmus Darwin even had the half-joking motto *E conchis omnia* ("Everything from shells") painted on the side of his traveling carriage, but he removed it after his patients and neighbors found it sacrilegious.

generation process than with a separate creation of each. Further, he had personally observed extinct fossil species that resembled modern species in all but size, and Galapagos finches whose slight but distinct differences in bill structure suggested that gradual changes and developments over generations were in fact possible.

Darwin also knew that breeders had been able to produce strikingly different *varieties* or *breeds* of domestic animals by careful selection of parental stock over many generations; thus bulldogs, sheepdogs, and dachshunds had all been created by the careful and selective breeding of originally similar canine stock. No domestic breed had ever become a genuinely separate *species*, however, capable of inter-breeding only with its like. Purebred dogs can all interbreed or "mongrelize" with other breeds, producing fertile offspring who lack the distinctive characteristics of the pure parent breeds. By con-trast, genuine species in a state of nature maintain their distinctive qualities automatically, by breeding successfully only like with like.

In the autumn of 1838, Darwin suddenly thought of a plausible mechanism for the gradual evolution of countless stable species in a state of nature. He later recalled that he had been reading, "for amusement," the rather gloomy economic theories of **Thomas Mal-thus** (1766–1834). Malthus believed that most human beings are destined to live in poverty because their capacity to increase popu-lation greatly exceeds their capacity to increase food production. When a small population settles in a fertile region, good times may persist for a while. Malthus argued that eventually, however, popu-lation growth must inevitably outstrip food production, leading to a general state of scarcity and poverty. And then disease, famine, and the other effects of poverty will act as a *check* on future popula-tion growth, so a stable population living at a bare subsistence level becomes established as the "normal" outcome of human social and economic existence.

This idea of a naturally occurring check on population growth seized Darwin's imagination. In *any* species, he reasoned, countless individuals will be conceived over many generations, but only a proportion of them will survive the rigors of their environment to propagate their kind. Those who survive will disproportionately tend to be the ones *best adapted* to overcoming the particular dangers of their own particular environments. And if their adaptive characteristics are *inheritable*, their offspring will also tend to have them and to survive and propagate in greater numbers than *their* less-advantaged fellows. Here was a mechanism for the evolution of species!

Consider the Galapagos finches, all of whose progenitors presumably arrived from South America with slightly varying but generally medium-sized bills. Assume that one group arrived at an island rich in nuts and seeds, but lacking in crevice-hiding insects. Here, a slight survival advantage accrued to individual birds with relatively strong and stout beaks for breaking open and eating the seeds. These birds must have survived and propagated at a slightly higher rate than their slim-billed brethren, producing a second generation with slightly stouter bills than the first, on the average. After many generations of the same process, a stable population of broad-billed birds evolved. A second group of progenitor finches, arriving in an island environment poorer in seeds and nuts but richer in concealed insects, presumably underwent the complementary process. Here the advantage would have lain with slender bills for digging out prey, and a population so equipped would gradually have evolved.

Thus Darwin hypothesized that different environments inevitably and constantly impose a **natural selection** on their inhabitants, disproportionately favoring certain kinds of individuals to survive and propagate their kind. Just as the original breeders of basset hounds selected only animals with floppy ears and other desirable basset characteristics to be their breeding stock, so "nature," or the environment, constantly selects the individuals best suited to survive and propagate. The selective effects of nature go on inexorably and for countless more generations than the efforts of any domestic animal breeder, leading to the creation of stable species rather than vulnerable breeds or varieties.

Thus Darwin saw "nature" — that is, the presence or absence of food, competitors, predators, and the other ever-varying exigencies of the environment — as not only imposing checks on the unrestricted increase of any species' population, but also *selecting* which individuals, with which inheritable characteristics, will tend to survive and propagate. Acting over vast ages of time (and here the new uniformitarian geology suggested a time span at least in the millions rather than the thousands of years), changes and variations in the natural environment must have produced countless localized changes in selection pressures, leading to the gradual evolution of countless different species. Thus natural selection provided the "engine" or mechanism theoretically necessary to support an evolutionary process.

The Origin of Species Darwin knew his new theory would not gain easy acceptance, for it challenged a long-held view of the origin of animal species and also carried disturbing implications for the role of *human beings* in nature. The literal Bible story placed humanity in a category separate from animals—formed on the sixth and final day of creation, in God's own image, and granted dominion over the rest of the earth's inhabitants. But Darwin recognized that human beings, with their evident anatomical similarities to many animals, would logically have to be included in any consistent evolutionary system. Animals and humans "partake from our origin in one common ancestor, [so] we may be all netted together," he wrote in an early notebook.[17]

Recognizing his theory's disturbing implications, Darwin tried to an unusual degree to consider seriously every possible objection to it. He adopted a personal "golden rule" that whenever he encountered a fact or argument apparently contrary to his theory "to make a memorandum of it without fail and at once; for I had found by experience that such facts and thoughts were far more apt to escape from the memory than favourable ones."[18] He long agreed, for example, that the "perfect" mammalian eye cited in the argument from design posed difficulties for the theory of evolution. Only after reading Helmholtz's discussion of the eye's optical *imperfections* (see pages 120–121) did he feel fully comfortable about describing the eye as an evolved (and evolving) organ rather than a finished product of deliberate design.

For years Darwin proceeded cautiously, collecting more and more evidence regarding his theory while keeping it mainly to himself. In 1842 and 1844 he wrote out abstracts of the theory, but never published them. He told just a handful of trusted friends, including the geologist Lyell and the botanist **Joseph Hooker** (1817–1911), about his belief in evolution, and even then very cautiously; "it is like confessing a murder," he confided to Hooker.[19] Only in 1856 — eighteen years after his original inspiration — did Darwin feel he had enough evidence to publish his theory. He now finally began a work entitled *Natural Selection*, which he expected to reach three thousand pages in length.

In the spring of 1858, however, Darwin was rudely interrupted by a letter and manuscript from the naturalist **Alfred Russel Wallace** (1823–1913). While recovering from malaria in the East Indies, Wallace had thought of a new theory of evolution, written it up in a short paper, and sent it to Darwin, whom he knew by reputation as one of the most congenial as well as generally knowledgeable naturalists in Britain. A shocked Darwin now read a brief outline of essentially his own theory, independently conceived by Wallace. At a loss how to respond, he sent the manuscript to Lyell and Hooker — who had long been *warning* him to publish his theory before someone else beat him to the punch.

His friends quickly arranged an honorable compromise: Excerpts from Darwin's unpublished abstract of 1844 and Wallace's new paper would both be read, in the absence of both authors, at the next meeting of the Linnean Society. Thus priority for the public presentation of the theory of evolution by natural selection was jointly shared by Darwin and Wallace in July 1858. Ironically, however, the session attracted little attention and the Linnean Society's official report for 1858 declared that the year had *not* produced "any of those striking discoveries which at once revolutionize, so to speak, the department of science on which they bear."[20]

That statement shows how correct Darwin had been in assuming his theory would not receive serious attention until buttressed by a tremendous amount of supporting evidence. But now that his secret was out, he wanted to get a substantial exposition of natural selection quickly into the public eye — less substantial than the projected three thousand pages of *Natural Selection*, perhaps, but long enough to illustrate the theory's power. Thus he spent a year feverishly writing *On the Origin of Species by Means of Natural Selection, or the Preservation of Favoured Races in the Struggle for Life*, a 490-page book published at the end of 1859. Arguably the most important book of the century, this detailed, systematic, and plausible presentation of an evolutionary theory demanded to be taken seriously, and in fact created the sensation Darwin had expected and feared.

Although *Origin of Species* dealt almost exclusively with plants and animals, debate immediately raged over its implied question of whether human beings were a separate and special creation of God, or had "descended from the apes." The noncombative Darwin shrank from polemics himself, but attracted one particularly outspoken advocate in **Thomas Henry Huxley** (1825–1895). This expert on primate anatomy wrote to Darwin immediately after reading *Origin of Species*, pledging willingness "to go to the stake" in support of the theory. He added, "I am sharpening up my claws and beak in readiness" against "the curs which will bark and yelp."[21]

Appropriately nicknamed "Darwin's Bulldog," Huxley defended natural selection most spectacularly in an 1860 debate with Samuel Wilberforce, the bishop of Oxford, at a public meeting of the British Association for the Advancement of Science. Although lacking scientific training, the smooth-talking Wilberforce had been primed on some of the scientific arguments against evolution. Unwisely, however, he resorted to sarcasm in debate and asked Huxley whether it was through his grandfather or his grandmother that he claimed descent from a monkey. Hearing this, Huxley whispered "The Lord hath delivered him into mine hands," then expertly countered Wilberforce's scientific objections before turning to him to say:

If the question is put to me, "would I rather have a miserable ape for a grandfather, or a man highly endowed by nature and possessed of great means of influence, and yet who employs these faculties and that influence for the mere purpose of introducing ridicule into a grave scientific discussion"—I unhesitatingly affirm my preference for the ape.[22]

To rebuke a bishop in public was highly unusual, to say the least, and Huxley's retort created a sensation. But most observers, and particularly the undergraduates in attendance, felt Huxley had been justified, and, more important, had carried the day for Darwin and evolution.

The following year, two new scientific discoveries further advanced the case for evolution. First, fossil remains of the extinct **archeopteryx**, the most ancient of birds, were found in Bavaria. Although feathered, this creature had "fingers" on its wings, and verbebrae and tail like a reptile's. Darwin had speculated that birds had evolved from reptiles in the distant past, and here was a transitional form fully consistent with that unlikely seeming idea. And also in 1861, an African explorer recovered the skulls and stuffed bodies of gorillas, a form of great ape previously unknown to Western science. Anatomically similar to human beings, the gorilla had several features previously argued by anti-evolutionists to be *exclusively* human and thus proof of humanity's biological uniqueness. Although neither of these finds alone could "prove" the case for the evolution and interrelatedness of species, they offered dramatic evidence of the plausibility of that view. Further evidence rapidly accumulated, and within a very few years the *Origin's* general case was won.

Darwin and Psychology

Although Darwin largely ignored his theory's implications for human beings in the *Origin of Species*, he did include one short and prophetic paragraph near the end of the book suggesting that human *mental* qualities would eventually be understood as the results of evolution:

In the distant future I see open fields for far more important researches. Psychology will be based on a new foundation, that of the necessary acquirement of each mental power and capacity by gradation. Light will be thrown on the origin of man and his history.[23]

For the next decade, Darwin left the *public* working out of this idea to others, including his cousin **Francis Galton** (1822–1911), whom we shall meet in the next chapter. Privately, however, he never ceased to think about human issues, and finally in the 1870s he published three seminal works about them: *The Descent of Man, and Selection in Relation to Sex* (1871), *The Expression of the Emotions in Man and Animals* (1872), and "A Biographical Sketch of an Infant" (1877).

The Descent of Man   Here Darwin finally argued explicitly and publicly that human beings have descended from animal ancestors. He opened his argument by noting the structural similarities between humans and the higher animals with respect to bones, muscles, blood vessels, internal viscera, nerves, and that "most important of all the organs," the brain: "Every chief fissure and fold in the brain of man has its analogy in that of the orang."[24] In addition, humans share many diseases with animals, possess certain "rudimentary organs" (such as projecting points on the ear) that assume considerable importance in other animals, and pass through stages of embryological development in which they closely resemble other animals. All of these features plausibly located *Homo sapiens* within the domain of physically evolving species.

Next, Darwin tried to show "that there is no fundamental difference between man and the higher mammals in their *mental* faculties."[25] He cited cases of animals showing "higher" qualities such as courage (in defending themselves, their young, or their human masters) and kindness (sometimes taking in and caring for orphaned members of other groups and species). He argued that dogs manifestly experience many of the same *emotions* as humans, including jealousy (when a rival pet receives its master's attention), pride (when carrying the master's basket, with head held high), shame (when reprimanded), and even a rudimentary sense of humor (when playfully and repeatedly running off with a ball or stick, just before the master can get it). Animals obviously demonstrate memory, attention, and curiosity, and since dogs seem often to *dream* when they sleep — twitching, quietly yelping, and breathing irregularly exactly as if imagining themselves in some exciting situation — they must have the capacity for imagination. Darwin further argued that animals show the rudiments of *reason* — the only faculty of the soul that Descartes had reserved exclusively for human beings: They profit and learn from experience, communicate with each other by sound and gesture, and appreciate "beauty" through distinctive mating preferences for various body markings and adornments. After considering many of these examples, Darwin concluded categorically: "The difference in mind between man and the higher animals, great as it is, certainly is one of degree and not of kind."[26]

The Expression of the Emotions Darwin originally planned to include a chapter on emotions in *Descent of Man*, but when it ballooned in size he deferred the subject for a book all its own, *The Expression of the Emotions*. Here he argued that human emotional expressions are inherited and evolved characteristics, best understood as the direct or indirect consequences of reactions that had adaptive or survival value.

The functional origins and purposes of many emotional expressions seemed straightforward. The wide staring eyes of surprise, for example, presumably originated as a mechanism for seeing the surprising object more fully and clearly. The bared teeth of rage naturally followed the adoption of a fighting and biting posture, while the curled lip of a sneer may have originated in a wrinkling of the nose after smelling something unpleasant.

Some other, less obviously "adaptive" emotional expressions presumably arose because they were *antitheses* of directly serviceable reactions. A dog expressing affection or playfulness, for example, assumes an attitude directly opposite to its angry or aggressive posture: Instead of walking upright with hair and tail erect and teeth bared, the affectionate animal crouches, flexes and wiggles its forward body, lowers and wags its tail, and relaxes its lips. While all of the angry expressions are directly interpretable as preparations for attack, the affectionate ones are only indirectly intelligible as the opposites of aggression.

Darwin thought that still other emotional expressions occur as side effects from the general activation of the nervous system that accompanies emotional arousal. In states of fright, flight, and anger, for example, a general arousal of the body into an active, excited state has adaptive value. Darwin believed that sometimes this excess excitation "spills over" into the body and produces trembling, grimacing, or flexion and contortion as a side effect.

In summary, Darwin concluded that these three general principles — direct serviceability of the expression, antithesis, and direct activation of the nervous system — could account for all emotional expression in animals and human beings alike.

One major purpose of *The Expression of the Emotions* was to show that many human reactions with no obvious survival or utilitarian value now, once did have it back in the evolutionary past. Thus Darwin explained the act of *blushing* — widely regarded in Victorian times as a uniquely human characteristic bestowed by the creator along with an innate conscience and sense of morality — as the consequence of several interacting but perfectly intelligible "animal" reactions. These included flushing and the engorgement with blood of body parts that become the subject of conscious attention, combined with the self-consciousness that is made possible by language.

In general, *Descent of Man* had argued that animals possess the rudiments of human mentality. *The Expression of the Emotions* made the complementary case that human beings possess many remnants of "animality." Not always guided by conscious and rational thought, people often betray unconscious and instinctive signs of their long animal ancestry. Other theorists, including Sigmund Freud, would soon expand upon the implications of that point.

Finally, Darwin noted that human emotional expressions tend to be similar throughout all known human groups. Smiles and laughter, weeping and shrieks of rage, contortions of pain, cringings of fear — all of these emotional manifestations are universally recognized. Darwin argued that this similarity of expression points to the common descent of all human groups from the same earlier, pre-human ancestor. "It seems to me improbable," he wrote, "that so much similarity, or rather identity of structure, could have been acquired by independent means. . . . It is far more probable that the many points of close similarity in the various races are due to inheritance from a single parent-form."[27]

"Biographical Sketch of an Infant" Five years after *The Expression of the Emotions*, Darwin made his final specific contribution to psychology. After reading an article describing the acquisition of language by a young child, Darwin recalled that he had kept a detailed log on the development of his own firstborn infant, thirty-seven years earlier. He now reexamined those notes, and wrote them up in an article entitled "A Biographical Sketch of an Infant," published in *Mind* in 1877. Only ten pages in length, this modest work still stands as a landmark in the history of child psychology — among the very first in the genre of "baby biography."

Darwin's notes on his son William, or "Doddy," began during the first week of life with the observation that numerous reflexes such as sneezing, yawning, stretching, sucking, and screaming were "well performed by my infant, . . . the perfection of these reflex movements show[ing] that the extreme imperfection of the voluntary ones is not due to the state of the muscles or the coordinating centres, but to that of the seat of the will."[28] In his first successful voluntary movements, William moved his hands to his mouth at about the age of forty days. Over the next several months he acquired several more complex intentional movements, the first ones involving the hands and arms, later ones the legs and trunk.

William's earliest obvious emotional expression was of startle or fear, after hearing a loud sudden sound during the first few weeks of life. Anger first appeared at ten weeks, when William frowned after being given insufficiently warm milk. By four months the baby could be worked into a "violent passion" by small causes such as dropping a lemon he was playing with.

Clear evidence of "association of ideas, reason, etc." first occurred at five months when William became angry after being dressed in his outdoor hat and coat, but not being taken immediately outdoors. At seven months he showed that he recognized his nurse's name when he heard it, but he did not spontaneously utter a meaningful word of his own until twelve months, when he used "mum" to indicate food. The baby acquired other words rapidly thereafter, and sometimes creatively combined them — as when he coined "black-shu-mum" ("shu" was his version of sugar) for licorice. Evidence of a "moral sense" began only at thirteen months, with signs of discomfort at being chided for not kissing his father. At twenty-seven months, however, "he gave his last bit of gingerbread to his little sister, and then cried out with high self-approbation 'Oh kind Doddy, kind Doddy.' "[29]

In a small way, Darwin's paper dealt with the grand themes he had developed in his other works: the roles of instinctive reflexes, habits, emotions, and other sensibilities in an increasingly effective adaptation to the world. In general, he saw his son's development as the gradual strengthening, complication, and fusion of originally simple and separate tendencies. Language, for example, arose only after a period of emotional and associative development had enabled the child first to connect names with people or things important to him (for example, his nurse). Only after hearing and understanding words for some time did William begin to invent and utter meaningful words himself. Darwin observed that this sequence — understanding words and interpreting them as signals before making them up and using them — "is what might have been expected, as we know that the lower animals easily learn to understand spoken words."[30]

Darwin was here suggesting that an *individual's* development proceeds along roughly the same lines as the previous evolution of the *species* to which it belongs. In acquiring language, Doddy rapidly traversed the same stages it had presumably taken his pre-human ancestors countless generations to reach through natural selection. Darwin had earlier noted something similar in the development of the human embryo, which passes through stages in which it resembles increasingly higher life forms. This rapid "recapitulation" in an individual of stages and patterns consistent with earlier and less highly evolved species suggested to Darwin that each individual somehow retains rudiments of the long evolutionary past — and was one more element in his general argument for evolution.*

Darwin's Influence

In 1842, while just beginning to think about how to publish his theory of natural selection, Darwin had moved to a lovely country house sixteen miles from London, in Downe, Kent. There he found a privacy and freedom from the distractions of the big city that he cherished for the rest of his life. He raised a large and thriving family, invested his substantial inheritance shrewdly enough to be-

---

*This idea that "ontogeny recapitulates phylogeny" — that an individual's earliest development copies the antecedent evolution of its species — was later popularized and raised to the level of a literal dogma by Darwin's German follower **Ernst Haeckel** (1834–1919). In modified form it also became central to the psychology of the American **G. Stanley Hall** (1844–1924), whom we shall meet in Chapter 8. For Darwin himself, however, the idea remained a suggestive generalization rather than a literal truth — a view generally substantiated by further research.

come a rich man, and after 1859 turned out a steady stream of important books. In addition to the works already discussed, he produced major studies of orchids (1862), vines and climbing plants (1865), plants and animals under domestication (1868), the power of movement in plants (1880), and the effect of worms in producing vegetable mold (1881). Although these were specialized topics, each of them helped build the general case for evolution, and consolidated Darwin's reputation as the foremost naturalist of his age.

But while his family, his fortune, and his reputation and influence all grew steadily, Darwin suffered chronically from a mysterious digestive malady of uncertain diagnosis. The once-intrepid world traveler became something of a recluse, never again venturing out of Britain, and seldom even going to London for scientific gatherings. He did maintain a vast correspondence, however, and when physically able served as a congenial host to the many friends and admirers who came to see him at home.

Despite the original outcry that had greeted Darwin's theory in 1859, the religious establishment rapidly accommodated to it. And when Darwin died in April of 1882 — at the age of seventy-three and from a heart ailment rather than his mysterious malady — the Church consented to his being buried in Westminster Abbey, next to Isaac Newton. There the pair still rest today — the two greatest and most influential scientists that England has produced.

Shortly after Darwin's death, a movement called **social Darwinism** came much into vogue. Despite its name, this movement owed as much to the prolific philosopher **Herbert Spencer** (1820–1903) as to Darwin himself, and contained some ideas that Darwin did not endorse. Spencer had been a supporter of Lamarck's theory of evolution even before Darwin's *Origin of Species*, and had written about the general importance of an evolutionary viewpoint for psychology in an 1855 text, *Principles of Psychology*. When Darwin published his theory of natural selection, Spencer contributed the catch phrase "survival of the fittest" to summarize its effective principle — a term that quickly caught on in the public mind. Further, Spencer's own ideas — which had previously not attracted great attention — took on a new plausibility and popularity because of their association with Darwin's theory.

In an ambitious program Spencer called "synthetic philosophy," he attempted to subsume the diverse disciplines of biology, psychology, sociology, and anthropology under a basically evolutionary view. He argued that individual organisms, species, political systems, and entire societies are alike in that all tend to evolve from relatively simple and homogeneous entities into complex and heterogeneous ones. He believed such evolution to constitute highly desirable "progress," the presumed vehicle for which is unbridled *competition* among the individual units, in which only the fittest survive and perpetuate their kind. Accordingly, progress of all kinds should be maximized by societies and governments that allow free competition to reign in all spheres of activity. This idea accorded particularly well with the capitalistic spirit of the United States, where Spencer's doctrine of social Darwinism became tremendously popular, and was seen as justification for the system of unregulated free enterprise. Virtually any business practice, however predatory, could be rationalized as beneficial because it presumably contributed toward the survival of the "fittest" and the subsequent evolution of society.

Darwin himself held strong reservations about Spencer and his synthetic philosophy, writing that "his fundamental generalisations . . . partake more of the nature of definitions than of laws of nature."[31] Had he lived to see them, Darwin undoubtedly would have deplored the excesses of unbridled capitalism committed in the name of social Darwinism. Indeed, those excesses soon enough became evident to almost everyone, and led to the demise of social Darwinism everywhere, even in America.

Within the more strictly biological fields, Darwin has had a much more permanent and positive influence. Like any theory, evolution by natural selection has inevitably encountered certain problems and difficulties, and scientists still debate the correctness of some of its details. For example, biologists have recently been divided over the question of whether evolution always proceeds gradually by minutely small steps, as Darwin believed, or whether genetic mutation can produce rather sudden and dramatic "jumps" in the evolutionary succession.

The explanation of *altruistic behavior* has posed another recurrent

206

problem for evolutionary theorists. Individuals who jeopardize their own well-being for the sake of others — sometimes even sacrificing their lives — would logically seem to be at a selective disadvantage when compared to completely self-centered individuals. So the question arises as to why altruism, an apparently "maladaptive" characteristic, does not disappear as a result of natural selection. One suggested answer to this question set the unit of evolution as the *group*, rather than the individual; that is, groups of interbreeding individuals with many altruistic members might be expected to survive and prosper better than groups without them. Alternatively, the recently developed theoretical approach known as **sociobiology** has hypothesized the unit of evolution to be the individual *gene*, rather than the group or entire organism. Since altruistic acts are most often performed in the service of individuals who are genetically similar to the actor, the net effect of such acts would be to favor the survival and propagation of genes like one's own.

Despite the fact that evolutionary theorists debate these specific issues, Darwin's general conclusion — that evolution by natural selection did occur, and is responsible for the vast proliferation of life forms on earth — is almost universally accepted by informed scientists. Certain self-styled "creation scientists" have recently tried to exploit the technical debates and uncertainties among evolutionary theorists while promoting a literalist interpretation of creation much like that which prevailed before 1859. Their view remains unconvincing, however, because like its predecessor it leaves many more important problems unsolved than Darwinian theory does.

Within the broad field of psychology, Darwin also had a positive and permanent influence. Given the evolutionary interrelatedness of all species posited by his theory, human psychological functions could no longer be viewed as isolated or unconnected with their animal counterparts. Thus in Darwin's wake the study of animal behavior assumed a new importance. Shortly before his death, he granted full access to his voluminous notes on animal behavior to a younger friend, **George J. Romanes** (1848–1894). Romanes added to these with research of his own, and published two groundbreaking books: *Animal Intelligence* (1882) and *Mental Evolution in Animals* (1883). Here Romanes described his work as constituting a **comparative psychology** — a name chosen by analogy to the established discipline of comparative anatomy. Romanes argued that the study of the similarities and differences among various animals' psychological functions could shed light on their human counterparts in the same way that previous study of their physical structures had. Although Romanes's work was subsequently criticized for being too anecdotal, and for too often attributing human-like states of consciousness to lower animals, the specialty of comparative psychology has remained an important branch of the general field.

Within human psychology, Darwin's theory demanded that the brain, the mind, and behavior in general could no longer be looked at as static "givens" merely to be described and analyzed. All of these had to be understood both as "functional" entities aiding the adaptation of the individual to the environment, and as potentially transmutable phenomena that may be modified or replaced with future evolution. And since evolution proceeds by the natural selection of inheritable variations within breeding populations, the issue of *variation* and *individual differences* among people assumed great importance, for such variation and differences presumably constitute the basis for the future evolution of humanity. Thus, after Darwin, human psychology inevitably became more "functional" and "differential" — that is, more concerned with the uses and adaptive significance of psychological phenomena, and more focused on questions of variability and differences among people, as opposed to their generality or similarity. We shall see in the next chapter how Darwin's cousin, Francis Galton, laid many of the more specific foundations for the new functional and differential psychology.

Suggested Readings

Charles Darwin's published journal for the *Beagle* voyage and *The Origin of Species* are both highly recommended, and available in several paperbound editions. A good, representative collection of excerpts from his major writings is found in Mark Ridley (ed.), *The Darwin Reader* (New York: Norton, 1987). For Darwin's life, see

The Autobiography of Charles Darwin, 1809-1882, edited by his grand-daughter Nora Barlow (New York: Norton, 1969), and Ronald W. Clark, *The Survival of Charles Darwin: A Biography of a Man and an Idea* (New York: Random House, 1984). Howard E. Gruber's *Darwin on Man: A Psychological Study of Scientific Creativity* (London: Wildwood House, 1974) provides an excellent discussion of Darwin's psychological ideas.

The Measurement of Mind:
Francis Galton and
the Psychology of
Individual Differences

London's International Health Exhibition of 1884 featured a curious exhibit called an "Anthropometric Laboratory," which attracted many spectators. Enclosed behind a wall of trelliswork that afforded onlookers a partial view inside, the laboratory contained several strange-looking contrivances laid out on a long bench. As spectators watched, a volunteer subject would enter the laboratory and manipulate the device at one end of the bench while consulting with an attendant. After a minute or two, the attendant wrote something down on two small cards, and the subject moved on to the second contrivance. The procedure continued at each stop along the bench, after which the attendant filed one of the cards away and gave the other to the subject to keep. Subjects invariably left studying their cards with keen interest, and by the Exhibition's end more than nine thousand spectators had been sufficiently intrigued by what they saw behind the trellis to pay a fee of three pence and become subjects themselves.

For their time and money, subjects received both the gratification of contributing to science, and some comparative information about themselves. Each of the devices measured or tested them in some way, and the cards recorded the subjects' personal scores as well as the averages obtained by people who had gone before. Scores reflected the subjects' head size and other physical measurements, as well as their performance on several tests of reaction time and sensory acuity.

Surprisingly, from a present-day perspective, these tests were thought of by their inventor as *mental* tests, measuring aspects of *intelligence*. Today we take it for granted that intelligence involves "higher" mental processes such as thinking, reasoning, and logic, and we may find it hard to see how physical variables such as reaction time or sensory acuity could possibly be thought of as measuring intelligence. Yet the tests' inventor did have a plausible, but ultimately incorrect, rationale for them.

He reasoned that people with the highest intellectual abilities must have the most powerful and efficient nervous systems and brains. He thought the power of a person's brain would probably be related to its size, so his first and simplest test of presumed natural intelli-

The Anthropometric Laboratory. *Cambridge University Press.*

gence was to measure head size (which presumably reflected the size of the brain within). He further thought people's neurological efficiency must be related to the *speed* with which they can respond to things, and so included a test of reaction time.

He defended his tests of sensory acuity by arguing: "The only information that reaches us concerning outward events appears to pass through the avenue of our senses; and the more perceptible our senses are of difference, the larger the field on which our judgement and intelligence can act." He further shared two incorrect but widely held prejudices that suggested at least a rough correlation between sensory acuity and intelligence. First, he believed mentally retarded people were deficient sensorily as well as intellectually: "They hardly distinguish between heat and cold," he wrote, "and their sense of pain is so obtuse that some of the more idiotic seem hardly to know what it is." Second, like many other Victorian males, he simply *assumed* that women were generally less intelligent than men, and he argued that they have less acute senses as well. Otherwise how could one account for the fact that women seldom held jobs requiring fine sensory discrimination, such as piano tuning, wool sorting, or wine tasting? Ungallantly, he added: "Ladies rarely distinguish the merits of wine at the dinner-table, and though custom allows them to preside at the breakfast-table, men think of them on the whole to be far from successful makers of tea and coffee."[1] Accordingly, he felt justified in trying to assess "intelligence" by measuring subjects' relative abilities to bisect a line, discriminate weights and colors, and hear high-pitched sounds.

Note that these earliest "intelligence tests" involved measures and phenomena that had been very important in the recent rise of experimental psychology — only with a new twist. Fechner's psychophysics had explored the limits of sensory discrimination, and Wundtian mental chronometry experiments had carefully measured reaction times. But these earlier studies had aimed at establishing *general* psychological principles, applicable equally to all people, while evading or dismissing issues of *individual differences* in acuity or reaction time. The Anthropometric Laboratory's founder, by contrast, operated within the new Darwinian framework that emphasized variability and adaptation. For him, individual differences in acuity or reaction time were not "errors" or "irregularities" to be smoothed over or avoided, but the very machinery of evolution and therefore the object of prime interest.

His Darwinian orientation came naturally, for **Francis Galton** (1822–1911) was a younger cousin and friend of Charles Darwin. At age twenty-two, Galton had inherited a substantial fortune that enabled him to devote his entire life to his personal interests. Typical of many upper-class Victorian men, Galton often demonstrated a smugness and insensitivity to the position of women and others less privileged than himself. In other respects, however, he was extraordinarily atypical. An energetic, humorous, and above all *curious* individual, he had been a noted explorer, geographer, meteorologist, and biological researcher before turning his lively attention to the measurement of intelligence and other psychological attributes.

Many of Galton's psychological ideas — like his theory of intelligence testing — turned out to be incorrect or overly simplified. But this ought not mask the fact that Francis Galton numbers among modern psychology's great founders. While often wrong in their specifics, his theories provided innumerable basic foundations on which others could build. He pioneered the very *idea* that tests could be employed to measure psychological differences among people. He also offered provocative theories about the origins of those psychological differences, and prescribed controversial social policies intended to foster positive psychological qualities in the general population. He elevated the scientific study of individual differences to the level of a major psychological specialty with important social implications. Most of the general issues he raised more than a century ago still preoccupy psychologists today. We turn now to their origins, in the context of Galton's life story.

Galton's Early Life and Career

Francis Galton was born in Birmingham, England, on 16 February 1822, his wealthy banker father a descendant of founders of the Quaker religion, and his mother a Darwin — the younger half-sister of Charles Darwin's father. Francis received his earliest education

Sir Francis Galton (1822–1911). *The National Library of Medicine, Bethesda, Maryland.*

at home from an older sister, and under her doting care seemed a child prodigy as he read and wrote before the age of three, mastered the rudiments of Latin and arithmetic by five, and quoted knowledgeably from the *Iliad* and the *Odyssey* by six. At five, he said his life's wish was to win honors at the university, a goal denied earlier generations of Galtons because as Quakers they could not take the Anglican vows then required at Oxford and Cambridge. Raised as an Anglican, Francis would not be so barred.

But despite his promising start, Galton was no happier or more successful than Charles Darwin had been when sent to traditional schools that emphasized discipline, rote learning, and the classics. His schoolboy diaries recounted floggings, canings, punitive assignments, fights with local boys, and general hell-raising—but contained hardly a single reference to a scholarly or intellectual idea. He did well only at mathematics, a subject considered less important than classics.

At sixteen, Galton, like Darwin, was removed from school (to his great satisfaction), and enrolled as a medical pupil at Birmingham General Hospital. Also like his half-cousin, he experienced the horrors of operations without anesthesia, and daily confronted disease and death. But unlike Darwin, he lacked assurance that his father would support him in yet another change of plans, and so gritted his teeth and adapted to the situation. He recalled in his autobiography: "The cries of the poor fellows who were operated on were . . . terrible, but only at first. It seemed after a while as though the cries were somehow disconnected with the operation, upon which the whole attention became fixed."[2] A tendency to "objectify" other people — seeing them as cases to be studied or examples to be counted, as opposed to fellow beings to be sympathized with — remained with Galton for the rest of his life, and undoubtedly contributed to the strengths as well as the weaknesses of his later psychological theorizing.

Medical training also provided Galton ample opportunity to indulge his exceptionally lively curiosity. Required to prepare medicines and pills in the pharmacy, he could not resist trying out small quantities of his creations on himself. Samples of poppy-seed and herbal licorice proved quite delightful, while a decoction of quassia wood chips proved to be "an experiment that I recommend to the notice of students who may wish to taste the *ne plus ultra* of bitterness." Proceeding alphabetically, he started taking small doses of all the medicines listed in the pharmacopoeia, beginning with the letter "A." He found this "an interesting experience, but [it] had obvious drawbacks. . . . I got nearly to the end of the letter C, when I was stopped by the effects of Croton oil. I had foolishly believed that two drops of it could have no notable effects as a purgative and emetic, but indeed they had, and I can recall them now [as I write my autobiography]."[3]

At eighteen, Galton interrupted medical training to attend Cambridge University, where he hoped to fulfill his childhood wish by winning high honors in mathematics. There he became caught up in Cambridge's intensely competitive examination system, the culminating event of which was the Mathematical Tripos Examination, held each January for that year's graduating class. Survivors of this weeklong ordeal, which entailed forty-four hours of writing in an unheated room at the coldest time of year, were precisely ranked from first to last, with the top thirty-five or forty finishers earning the title of "wranglers." Keen interest always focused on who would take the top or senior wranglership, with university personnel often laying wagers on the outcome as if it were an athletic contest.

Galton, a better mathematician than a classicist, entered Cambridge with hopes of emerging as a high wrangler. He became keenly interested in the university's examination procedures, and noted approvingly that the tripos grading system sharply differentiated the top scorers from the rest of the class. In one class ahead of his own, for example, the first and second wranglers had been "*very* far superior to the rest, [for the second wrangler] was *1000* marks ahead of the 3rd wrangler, and the getting of *500* marks only entitles a man to be a Wrangler."[4] This observation helped convince Galton that the very best people in a given field tend to be almost in a class by themselves, and later contributed to his belief in the normal, or bell-shaped, distribution of human ability (with many people clustered around the average, and diminishing numbers toward the extremes).

On his own early, non-honors examinations, Galton obsessively compared his performance with that of his fellows. At first he did well enough to keep hopes of an eventual wranglership alive, but at the end of his second year had a second-class finish in a university-wide examination. A severe emotional breakdown followed, in which "a mill seemed to be working inside my head. I could not banish obsessing ideas; at times I could hardly read a book, and found it painful even to look at a printed page."[5] Recovery came slowly, and only after Galton had abandoned all thought of competing for honors. He was graduated from Cambridge in 1844 with an ordinary or "poll" degree like Darwin's, and then resumed medical study in London. His spirit seemed broken, however, and when his father died in 1845 and left him a substantial fortune, Galton abandoned formal study forever.

For the next several years Galton joined the idle rich. He hunted and gambled, tried the dangerous and not-quite-respectable sport of ballooning, and traveled extensively from Scandinavia in the north to Egypt and the Sudan in the southeast. Such aimless activity failed to satisfy him, however, and finally in April of 1849 he consulted a London phrenologist for a reading—based on the shape of his head—of his "natural" abilities, aptitudes, and inclinations. The shrewd phrenologist, undoubtedly relying on more than just the shape of Galton's head, reported that brains constituted like his innately lacked "much spontaneous activity in relation to scholastic affairs," but were ideally suited for "roughing it." "It is only when rough work has to be done that all the energies and capacities of minds such as this are brought to light," he advised.[6]

This judgment probably comforted Galton, who could now attribute his mediocre academic record to lack of innate scholarly ability rather than lack of effort or moral fiber. And the assurance that he had natural strengths in more *practical* fields stimulated Galton positively: Reflecting that he already enjoyed travel, and had means to do so in a big way, he decided to become an African explorer.

After consulting with the Royal Geographical Society, Galton left England on 5 April 1850 and returned exactly two years later after exploring previously unmapped territory in the part of southwest Africa now called Namibia. He found he had a talent for precise *measurement* on this expedition, using heliostat, sextant, and other surveying instruments to take readings for a highly detailed and accurate map of the country. He indulged his penchant for measurement rather more unorthodoxly after encountering some African women whose figures (he confided to his brother) "would drive the females of our native land desperate. . . . I sat at a distance with my sextant, and . . . surveyed them in every way and subsequently measured the distance of the spot where they stood—worked out and tabulated the results at my leisure."[7]

For his map and orthodox measurements of the country, Galton won the Royal Geographical Society's gold medal for 1853. That same year he published *Tropical South Africa*, an entertaining book about his expedition which first put him in the public eye. His cousin Charles Darwin, whom he had not seen in several years, wrote a note of congratulations: "I last night finished reading your volume with such lively interest that I cannot resist the temptation of expressing my admiration. . . . What labours and dangers you have gone through!" Darwin, who at this time had formulated but not yet published his epochal theory of evolution, added a typically modest personal note: "I live in a village called Downe . . . and employ myself in zoology; but the objects of my study are very small fry, and to a man [like you] accustomed to rhinoceroses and lions, would appear infinitely insignificant."[8] The cousins remained in friendly contact thereafter, but Galton would have to await *The Origin of Species* in 1859 before learning the exact nature of Darwin's "infinitely insignificant" studies.

Galton's successful expedition gave him entry into the governing councils of the Geographical Society, and for ten years he busied himself productively with geography, travel, and meteorology. He helped plan many of the epic African exploring expeditions to locate the source of the Nile, including those of Burton, Speke, Grant, and Livingstone. He developed new and improved instruments for geographical measurement, and in 1855 wrote a handbook for travelers in the wild, *The Art of Travel*. This classic guide subsequently went through eight editions and offered practical advice on such diverse subjects as pitching a tent in the sand, preventing one's asses from braying all night, and avoiding the rush of an enraged animal.

In the early 1860s Galton turned to another subject of great interest to travelers, and everyone else besides: the weather. He had the bright idea to collect simultaneous weather information from many different places and represent it on the world's first **weather maps**. From his early maps, he discovered the alternating patterns of high- and low-pressure systems now known to determine weather changes. For this meteorological accomplishment alone, Galton earned an honorable place among Victorian scientists. But beginning in the early 1860s, he turned his attention in yet another direction — with momentous consequences for the sciences of biology, genetics, statistics, and psychology. The stimulus for this shift was his cousin's *Origin of Species*.

Darwinian Theory and *Hereditary Genius*

As surprised as the rest of the world by Darwin's great work, Galton immediately wrote his cousin to say: "Pray, let me add a word of congratulations on the completion of your wonderful volume. . . . I have laid it down in the full enjoyment of a feeling that one rarely experiences after boyhood days, of having been initiated into an entirely new province of knowledge which, nevertheless, connects itself with other things in a thousand ways."[9] For a while, however, Galton was also troubled by the book. His previously orthodox religious faith and literal belief in the Bible were shattered, and for several years he suffered intermittently from his old Cambridge symptoms. But gradually, some implications of Darwinian theory combined with his own predilections to create a guiding vision that Galton pursued for the rest of his long life.

Although Darwin had not discussed human beings in *The Origin of Species*, Galton quickly grasped its implication that humans must be constantly evolving like other species. Moreover, he believed the most distinctive human characteristics, and those most likely to form the basis of future evolution and development, were *intellectual* and *psychological* in nature — although presumably mediated by small inheritable differences in the structure of the brain and nervous system.

Galton's personal experience had already led him to believe that individual differences in intelligence must be primarily innate. He himself had had high academic aspirations and come from a wealthy family and good environment, yet despite these advantages had been unable to win the honors he wanted at Cambridge. More successful students thus must have exceeded him in innate "natural ability."

Galton had also observed that intellectual eminence tends imperfectly but markedly to *run in families*. His own family had now produced two scientific superstars in Erasmus and Charles Darwin, along with many other figures of lesser but still substantial distinction. Other notable families such as the Bachs in music, the Brontës in literature, and the Pitts in politics easily came to mind. After reading Darwin's book, Galton decided to exercise his penchant for

219

measuring and counting, and approach this issue statistically. He examined biographical dictionaries similar to the *Who's Who* volumes of today, and calculated that people who achieved sufficient eminence to be listed in them represented a proportion of about one in four thousand from the normal population. Galton next examined the family trees of samples of these eminent individuals, and found that about ten percent of them had at least one close relative also sufficiently eminent to be listed in a biographical dictionary. Even accounting for the fact that each person has many relatives, this represented a far greater number of eminent relatives than would be expected by chance. Here was concrete empirical evidence of the statistical tendency for eminence to run in families.

Galton recognized that such evidence alone could not logically prove the ability necessary for eminence was *inherited*, because members of a family tend to share similar environments as well as similar heredity. One could argue that these were the more effective causes — and indeed this general heredity-environment question remains strongly alive today. But Galton was predisposed from the outset to emphasize the hereditarian side of the story, and when he presented his detailed statistical findings of eminent families in the 1869 book *Hereditary Genius* he boldly stated: "I propose to show in this book that a man's natural abilities are derived from inheritance, under exactly the same limitations as are the form and physical features of the whole organic world."[10]

Galton's book went on to offer three new arguments in support of this contention, based on the normal distribution of intellectual qualities, the specific patterns of eminent relatives Galton most frequently observed, and the comparison of adoptive versus biological relatives. As we shall see, these continued to render his case plausible, but scarcely as definitively proven as he thought.

The Normal Distribution In the first part of his case, Galton argued that measures of intellectual ability tend to fall into statistical distributions similar to those of inheritable physical traits. The great Belgian statistician **Adolphe Quetelet** (1796–1874) had earlier shown that measurements such as height or weight, when collected from large populations, invariably fall into bell-shaped, **normal distri-**

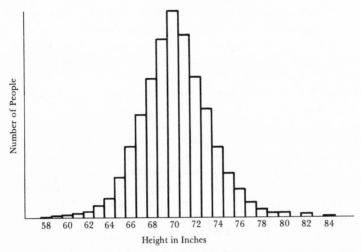

Figure 7-1. *An example of normal distribution: height measurements for 300 adult men.*

butions, like the one illustrated in Figure 7-1. In such distributions, many more measurements fall in the middle ranges than at the extremes, and successive scores tend to be more widely separated from one another at the extremes.

The greater dispersal of measurements in the tail of a normal distribution reminded Galton of Cambridge tripos examination results, in which top wranglers had scored *far* higher than anyone else. To confirm this observation he obtained the distributions of raw examination scores for the top 100 candidates in two successful Cambridge triposes, and showed that the 200 raw scores ranged from a high of 7,634 to a low of 237; the highest score exceeded the second highest by more than 2,000, while more than half of the population fell in the range from 500 to 1,500 total points. Thus the scores in fact approximated an upper tail of a normal distribution (with most of those who would have been in the lower tail presumably not even taking the honors exam). Mathematical ability — at least as measured by the Cambridge examinations — fell in a distribution closely resembling the known distributions of inheritable physical variables such as height or weight.

221

Of course, resemblance does not prove identity, and in fact it is now well known that normal distributions characterize innumerable variables that are not hereditary. Galton's study had still been worth doing, because had the distribution *not* turned out to be normal, such would have counted *against* his hypothesis. But once again his observations were merely *consistent with* his thesis, without offering positive proof of it.

Pedigrees of Genius Galton's second new line of argument — derived from a close analysis of the family trees of eminent people — had a similar limitation. He examined the family trees of twelve different groups of eminent people (Judges of England, statesmen, great military commanders, writers, scientists, poets, musicians, divines, painters, top classical scholars, champion oarsmen, and champion wrestlers) and found two general patterns throughout.

First, the eminent relatives of eminent people tended to be close rather than distant: first-degree relations (sibling or parent-child) appeared four times more frequently than those of the second degree (grandparents, grandchildren, nephews-nieces, or uncles-aunts), who were in turn four times more likely than third-degree relations (great-grandparents, cousins, etc.). Even third-degree relations, however, occurred much more frequently than would have been expected by chance. This pattern again duplicated that for inherited physical variables: Fathers and sons tend to resemble each other in height more than do grandfathers and grandsons, who in turn are more similar than average cousins.

Second, Galton found an imperfect but clear tendency for relatives to excel in the same fields. Thus the eminent relatives of eminent writers were most often writers too, although they also appeared in other occupations with greater than chance frequency. Such would be expected, Galton argued, if the requisite "natural ability" for each particular field were some complex combination of physical, mental, and emotional characteristics, each one separately and partially inherited. Each offspring of an eminent parent would then inherit *some proportion* of the requisite qualities for eminence in that same field, but not necessarily the full complement.

Note again, however, that one might expect exactly the same patterns of results if the major familial advantages predisposing to eminence were environmental rather than hereditary. Close relatives share environments to a greater degree than distant relatives do, and any specific environmental factors conducive to success in particular fields should expectably be found in some families more than others.

Studies of Adoptive versus Biological Relatives In *Hereditary Genius*, Galton acknowledged but minimized the possibility that environmental advantages within eminent families could have helped produce his results, insisting that "social advantages are incompetent to give [eminent] status to a man of moderate ability."[11] He probably had himself partly in mind as he wrote that, recalling his own disappointing academic career in spite of his socially advantaged background. He went on to suggest a research design which, if properly implemented, promised to offer concrete evidence for his contention. This involved the comparative study of *adoptive relations* of eminent people.

Galton observed that Roman Catholic popes had once commonly "adopted" young boys to be brought up in their own privileged households as their "nephews." Such boys thus shared the environmental but not the genetic advantages of their patrons, and Galton wondered if they went on to attain eminence to the same degree as the biological children of eminent fathers. He suspected they did not:

I do not profess to have worked out the kinships of the Italians with any special care, but I have seen amply enough of them, to justify me in saying that . . . the very common combination of an able son and an able parent, is not matched, in the case of high Romish ecclesiastics, by an eminent nephew and an eminent uncle.[12]

On this rather impressionistic basis, Galton concluded that social and environmental advantages count for much less than heredity in producing eminence.

Galton's *idea* of comparing similarities between adoptive versus biological relatives was a good one that has been used productively by many later generations of genetic researchers. But Galton's particular use of the idea left something to be desired. Not only did he fail to lavish the same statistical care on this analysis that he did elsewhere, but he also confined his study to a small and unusual sample of questionable general representativeness.

223

In general then, Galton's three lines of evidence in *Hereditary Genius* were consistent with his hereditarian thesis, but did not prove it conclusively. Nevertheless, he succeeded in presenting the thesis clearly and graphically, and henceforth it would have to be taken seriously by hereditarians and environmentalists alike.

The Nature-Nurture Controversy

Unsurprisingly, Galton received mixed reviews for *Hereditary Genius*. On the positive side, Charles Darwin liked the book and wrote privately to say, "I do not think I have ever in my life read anything more interesting and original." Publicly, in his *Descent of Man*, Darwin wrote: "We now know, through the admirable labours of Mr. Galton, that genius which implies a wonderfully complex combination of high faculties, tends to be inherited."[13]

The eminent Swiss botanist **Alphonse de Candolle** (1806–1893) responded more critically. Like Galton, de Candolle came from an old and distinguished scientific family, and in fact had been listed along with his father and grandfather among the eminent relatives in *Hereditary Genius*. Unlike Galton, however, he was highly impressed with the importance of environmental and cultural factors in perpetuating successful families like his own.

To test his view, de Candolle collected biographical information on more than three hundred eminent European scientists, which he analyzed statistically in his 1873 book, *History of the Sciences and Scientists over Two Centuries*. Here he conceded that heredity plays a certain role in creating scientific excellence, but also showed clearly that eminent scientists came disproportionately from small to moderate-sized countries with moderate climates, democratic governments, tolerant religious establishments, and thriving commercial interests. Here was concrete evidence for the power of environment, and de Candolle explicitly contrasted his findings with Galton's: "My accounts of the men of science have been gathered in a different manner from those of Mr. Galton. I employed more complete biographical documents . . . [and] thus flatter myself to have penetrated farther into the heart of the question."[14]

A piqued Galton wrote de Candolle complaining of "the injustice you have done to me," but also confessed to being impressed by the depth and originality of the research. "I feel the great service you have done in writing it," he generously concluded, "and shall do what I can to make it known, as it ought to be, in England." De Candolle responded with a conciliatory statement of his own: "If there escaped from me, in the 482 pages of my book, one phrase, one word making it possible to doubt my respect for your impartiality, your character, and your talent for investigation, it could only have been in error and contrary to my intentions." He added that they basically disagreed not about facts, but their interpretation: "I have had the advantage of coming after you, [and while] it was not difficult for me to confirm with new facts the influence of heredity, . . . I never lost sight of the other causes, and the remainder of my researches convinced me that they are generally more important than heredity."[15]

De Candolle's book and letters stimulated Galton to carry out his own further study of scientists, to try to sort out the effects of heredity and environment in their backgrounds. He devised an extensive questionnaire asking for detailed personal information, and distributed it to 192 Fellows of the Royal Society who had gained distinction for their scientific work. This marked the first time the now-ubiquitous **self-questionnaire method** had ever been used to investigate a major psychological issue. The questionnaire items ranged from the social, religious, and political backgrounds of the respondents and their parents to their hair color and the size of their hats. Respondents rated themselves and their relatives on psychological qualities such as "energy of mind," "retentiveness of memory," and "studiousness of disposition." They described their educational experiences, with special emphasis on factors that had led them to science. And they answered the three questions that Galton regarded as the heart of his questionnaire: "Can you trace the origin of your interest in science in general and in your particular branch of it? How far do your scientific tastes appear to have been innate? Were they largely determined by events after you reached manhood, and by what events?"

Galton received completed forms from 104 of his 192 subjects, a majority of whom declared their taste for science as innate. Typical replies: "As far back as I can remember, I loved nature and desired to learn her secrets," and "I was always observing and inquiring, and this disposition was never checked or ridiculed."[16] These responses, naive and unsubstantiated though they might seem to a skeptical environmentalist's eye, nevertheless satisfied Galton that most of the scientists had been *born* with the requisite tastes and aptitudes for their craft. Hence (of course) the predominant causes must have been hereditary.

But some other responses led Galton to make one important concession to de Candolle. Many scientists cited experiences or influences that presumably *strengthened* or *reinforced* their scientific inclinations: Darwin's opportunity to travel on the *Beagle*, for example, or Huxley's youthful apprenticeship to a doctor. Further, a disproportionate share of the eminent scientists were Scottish, and the Scots much more frequently than the others cited their formal education as a positive factor. This seemed evidence for an environmental cause, since Scottish public education was notably broader and less focused on classics than its English counterpart. Thus Galton moderated his hereditarianism slightly, maintaining that inherited tastes and aptitudes were necessary but not sufficient causes of scientific talent, requiring at least a modicum of support from the environment before being fulfilled.

In writing up this study, Galton contributed incidentally but importantly to the language of science. He had long been looking for a pair of convenient terms to denote the separate effects of heredity and environment, and in one early article had written of them as "race" versus "nurture." While analyzing his questionnaire data, however, Galton seems to have recalled a short section of de Candolle's book that criticized many popular uses of the word "nature," and argued that one of its few legitimate usages was as an opposite of "art" or "artifice." Soon thereafter Galton adopted the euphonious catchphrase "nature and nurture," which he called "a convenient jingle of words, for it separates under two distinct heads the innumerable elements of which personality is composed. Nature is all that a man brings with himself into the world; nurture is every influence that affects him after his birth."[17] The phrase caught on, and ever since 1874 biologists and psychologists have used it to differentiate innate developmental factors from environmental ones.

Galton himself used the phrase in the subtitle of his 1874 book describing the questionnaire-study results, *English Men of Science:*

Their Nature and Nurture. There he acknowledged that both nature and nurture had influenced the lives and careers of his subjects, while maintaining that the former had been relatively more important than the latter.

Galton also recognized that nature and nurture can often *interact* with each other in complicated ways, however, and sought some means of sorting them out for separate appraisal. To this end he shortly devised the **twin-study method** — a research technique that remains at the heart of behavior genetics today, and that he introduced in an 1875 article entitled "The History of Twins, as a Criterion of the Relative Powers of Nature and Nurture."

The essence of this method lay in the fact that there are, biologically speaking, two different kinds of twins. Some twin pairs develop from the separate fertilization of two ova by two sperm, while others are produced when a single fertilized ovum splits in half and the two halves develop into separate embryos. The first type, today called **fraternal** or **dizygotic twins**, bear the same genetic similarity to each other as ordinary brothers and sisters, with an average of fifty percent of their genes in common. The others — **identical** or **monozygotic twins** — are genetically identical to each other. Galton — who himself had a pair of identical twins as nephews, and a fraternal pair as an aunt and uncle — decided to conduct a broader survey of different twin pairs.

He solicited detailed case histories from all the twin pairs he could locate, without initial regard for their type. More than a hundred different pairs responded, and he found that their reports fell into two general categories. Some, including his nephews, had gone through life showing marked similarity to each other psychologically as well as physically, and often in spite of having experienced quite different life circumstances. Other pairs, however, grew up to be markedly different from each other, even when they had been deliberately treated as alike by their parents. Galton lacked direct evidence regarding the biological type of these twins, but reasoned that these two categories were exactly to be expected if character and physique had been strongly determined by heredity and less so by environment. Then, genetically identical monozygotic twins *should* develop similarly regardless of differences in their nurture, while fraternal twins should differ as ordinary siblings do, even when treated alike. Thus Galton concluded that his first category must have been composed of primarily monozygotic twins, and his second category of dizygotic types. He confidently asserted, "There is no escape from the conclusion that nature prevails enormously over nurture when the differences in nurture do not exceed what is commonly to be found among persons of the same rank in society and in the same country."[18]

Galton did not here address the possibility that genetically identical twins who start out *looking* alike may consequently be *treated* alike, so their similarities might logically have been produced by nurture as much as nature. Nor did he note that any differences that do occur between identical twins *cannot* be attributed to heredity, since they are identical in that respect. And since *some* differences inevitably arose even between the most highly similar pairs, here was positive proof of an environmental effect of some kind. Thus Galton's twin study introduced an ingenious but still inconclusive approach to the complex issue of nature versus nurture. More elaborate and sophisticated replications of the technique have been performed by later generations of scientists, with highly interesting results. But even so, environmentalists and hereditarians continue to differ about the proper way to interpret twin studies, and the nature-nurture controversy remains almost as unsettled today as when Galton and de Candolle debated it over a century ago.

Eugenics

Almost from the outset of his interest in Darwinian theory, Galton had been possessed by a utopian vision, the ultimate practicability of which depended on the correctness of his hypothesis concerning hereditary ability. He clearly if crudely expressed its central idea in the opening paragraph of *Hereditary Genius*:

As it is easy . . . to obtain by careful selection a permanent breed of dogs or horses gifted with peculiar powers of running, or of doing anything else, so would it be quite practicable to produce a highly-gifted race of men by judicious marriages during several consecutive generations.[19]

A few years later, Galton coined the name **eugenics** for this project of improving the human race through selective breeding.

As we have seen, Galton easily convinced himself (if not every-one else) that human ability is in fact strongly inheritable. This suggested to him that eugenics should be a workable reality. For the second half of his long life, eugenics became Galton's consum-ing passion — quite literally a substitute for the orthodox religious faith he had abandoned after reading Darwin's challenge to the literal interpretation of the Bible. Almost everything he did related in some way to this central vision, and with great imagination and versatility he developed dozens of ideas, many of which had im-plications beyond their original eugenic purposes. Two of the most important for the history of psychology were **intelligence tests** and the concept of **statistical correlation**.

Intelligence Tests To create a eugenic society, Galton believed it necessary to encourage the most highly able young men and women to intermarry and have children at a greater rate than parents of lesser abilities. But how was one to identify these eugenic parents? Ideally, Galton thought they should be men and women like those he had studied in *Hereditary Genius*, whose concrete accomplishments and contributions to society had marked them for eminence. But those kinds of accomplishments usually occurred in middle age or later, and Galton sought a means of identifying potentially eminent people at a younger age, while still within their childbearing prime.

As early as 1865, Galton envisioned the development of com-petitive eugenic examinations to be administered by the state to all young men and women of prime marriageable age. He half-humorously described a future awards ceremony "in which the Senior Trustee of the Endowment Fund would address ten deeply-blushing young men" to congratulate them on having taken the highest places on an examination measuring "those qualities of talent, character, and bodily vigour which are proved, on the whole, to do most honour and best service to our race." Ten young women would also have been selected in a parallel examination measuring "grace, beauty, health, good temper, accomplished housewifery and disengaged affections, in addition to noble qualities of heart and brain." Should these young paragons agree to marry each other, the queen herself would give away the brides at a state wedding, and — of paramount importance — the government would provide ample funds for the care and education of the "extraordinarily talented issue" that would undoubtedly flow from the marriages.[20] In this fanciful scene, we find the first published statement of the idea (although not yet the name) of intelligence tests.

Of course, it was one thing to *imagine* the existence of valid examinations of hereditary ability, and something else again to develop them in reality. Galton devoted intermittent attention to the problem for many years, until at last in 1884 he established his Anthropometric Laboratory for London's International Health Exhibition. As we saw at the beginning of this chapter, he there tried to measure people's hereditary intelligence by means of a series of simple tests of head size, reaction time, and sensory acuity.

In due course, Galton's specific tests were found not to work. High scores on them failed to correlate with meaningful, real-life intellectual accomplishment. The first *successful* intelligence tests had to await the development of altogether different procedures by the French psychologist **Alfred Binet** (1857–1911), based on assumptions different from Galton's. That story shall be told in Chapter 12. For now, it is sufficient to note that Galton originated the *idea* of intelligence testing in a eugenic context, and made it seem an important scientific project worth being taken up by others. From his day onward, the whole issue of intelligence testing has been inextricably connected with genetics, eugenics, and the nature-nurture controversy.

Statistical Correlation and Regression Galton's concern with heredity and eugenics led to another important innovation — this one of a statistical nature — when he sought to express the relative strengths of various hereditary relationships with mathematical precision. Heredity obviously involved variables that *tended* to be associated with one another, although to less than perfect degrees. Tall fathers tend to have tall sons, for example, but only rarely are their heights exactly the same. Between grandfathers and grandsons, the average resemblance is even less, although still greater than chance. Galton sought an exact means of expressing and comparing these cases of partial or imperfect association between variables.

His solution emerged gradually over many years, and began, characteristically, with his measuring, counting, and obtaining some large empirical data bases to work with. He planted peas of varying sizes, and compared the sizes of offspring peas with those of their parents. In his Anthropometric Laboratory, he solicited *families* to come in and be measured on height, weight, and several other physical traits, in addition to the tests described above.

After poring over these sorts of data for countless hours, Galton developed the habit of casting them in the form of **scatter plots** like the one shown in Figure 7-2,[21] which records the heights of 314 adult children and their parents. Before preparing this particular plot, Galton had multiplied all females' heights by 1.08 to render their average equal to males'; he then calculated a "mid-parent's" height for each child as the mean of the father's and corrected mother's heights. Each cell of Galton's scatter plot records the number of cases for that particular combination: the 1 in the upper right-hand cell indicates there was one child between 72 and 73 inches tall with a "mid-parent" between 71 and 72 inches; the 3 diagonally

Children's Heights (Mean = 68.0")

Parents' Heights (Mean = 68.1")	63"	64"	65"	66"	67"	68"	69"	70"	71"	72"	73"
72"						1	2	2	2	1	
71"				2	4	5	5	4	3	1	
70"	1	2	3	5	8	9	9	8	5	3	
69"	2	3	6	10	12	12	2	10	6	3	
68"	3	7	11	13	14	13	10	7	3	1	
67"	3	6	8	11	11	8	6	3	1		
66"	2	3	4	6	4	3	2				
65"											
Mean Height of Parents in Each Column	67.2	67.3	67.4	67.6	67.9	68.2	68.4	68.8	69.1	69.3	

Figure 7-2. *One of Galton's scatter plots.*

adjacent signifies three children between 71 and 72 inches with mid-parents between 70 and 71 inches; and so on.

From scatter plots such as this, Galton discerned a pattern he called **regression toward the mean** — a forbidding-sounding expression meaning simply that extreme scores on one variable tend to be associated with scores closer to the mean on the other. Thus consider the eleven pairs of scores represented in the far left-hand column of Figure 7–2. The children all fall between 63 and 64 inches, so their mean height may be estimated as 63.5 inches; this value is 4.5 inches shorter than the average (68.0 inches) for all 314 children. The figure at the bottom of that column shows that the mid-parents of those eleven children had a mean height of 67.2 inches (calculated by averaging two cases of 65.5 inches, three of 6.5 inches, and so on up the column); this value is only 0.9 inch shorter than the overall parents' mean of 68.1. Thus those parents' heights deviated from the overall mean in the same direction as their children's (both groups were shorter than average), but not as far; the parents' scores showed "regression" toward the population mean.

The pattern repeats throughout. Thus the third column from the

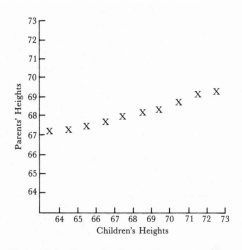

Figure 7–3. *Regression line for data in Figure 7–2.*

right lists thirty-four children between 70 and 71 inches, whose average of 70.5 is 2.5 inches taller than the overall population mean. Their mid-parents' mean height of 68.8 inches, however, exceeds the overall parents' average by only 0.7.

Galton recognized a further mathematical quality of scatter-plotted data: If the means of each of the columns are represented by X's across a graph, they tend to array themselves into an approximately straight line he called a **regression line**. Figure 7–3 shows the regression line plotted from the data on children's and mid-parents' heights in Figure 7–2.

In a great insight, Galton saw that the *steepness* of any regression line will vary directly with the strength of the relationship between the two variables. This becomes clear after considering two "ideal" cases: a perfect relation between the variables, and a completely random relationship between them. The left-hand graph in Figure 7–4 shows the regression line for a hypothetical perfect relationship, which would occur if every child's height turned out to be exactly the same as his or her mid-parent's; the line here would form a perfect diagonal, with a mathematical slope of 1.0. But if children's heights bore absolutely no relation to parental stature, then *all* groups of children — short, average, and tall — would have mid-

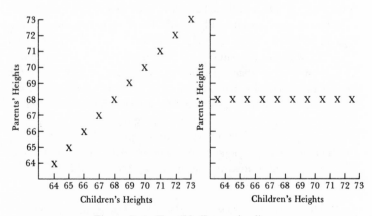

Figure 7-4. *Two "ideal" regression lines.*

233

parents whose average height was close to the mean for the overall parents' group. The regression line in this case would be perfectly horizontal like the right-hand side of Figure 7–4, with a mathematical slope of 0.0.

Galton saw that for positively but imperfectly related variables — such as he expected regularly to find when investigating real-life hereditary relationships — the regression line's slope would always lie somewhere between these values of 0.0 and 1.0 (as it does in Figure 7–3). Moreover, he recognized in 1888 that if all scores were transformed onto a common statistical scale before their regression lines were drawn,* then the mathematical slopes of their lines could be directly and uniformly interpreted as **coefficients of correlation** — numerically precise indices of the strength of the relationships. If the value lay close to 1 — say, 0.8 or 0.9 — it indicated a very strong correlation; if near 0.5 it indicated a moderate degree of association; and if close to 0.0 it showed a weak correlation.

Galton presented these ideas in a short 1888 paper entitled "Co-relations and Their Measurement, Chiefly from Anthropometric Data."[22] The brilliant young mathematician **Karl Pearson** (1857–1936) subsequently took them up and refined them, developing a more convenient formula for computing correlation coefficients, and extending their range to cover *negative* relationships (where high scores on one variable are associated with low scores on the other). "Pearson's r," as this statistic has come to be called, has become one of the most widely used of all statistical tools in psychological, biological, and sociological research. Its application extends far beyond the biological and hereditary relationships originally investigated by Galton to literally *any* situation in which one wonders about the degree of association between two measurable variables. Many modern investigators regard Galton's pioneering discussions of regression and correlation as his greatest gift to science.

Ironically, one of these extended applications of correlation ultimately demonstrated the failure of Galton's own approach to intelligence testing, described in the preceding section. When Pearson

---

*That is, all scores first had to be transformed from inches, pounds, or the like into standardized units of deviation from their group mean such as the "standard deviations" or "probable errors" that will be familiar to students of elementary statistics.

r's were calculated between test scores and real-life measures of intellectual ability such as college grades, they turned out very low. Reaction time and class standing correlated at -0.02 in one study, for example, indicating the former was virtually useless in predicting the latter. Alternative types of tests, producing higher correlations, had to be developed before intelligence testing could be taken seriously as a practical reality.

Other Contributions Over the course of his long life, the versatile and inventive Galton conducted scores of other inquiries that related directly or indirectly to his consuming eugenic passion. Some of these, too, had important consequences.

Galton numbered among the very first serious investigators of **fingerprints**, which he hoped would prove to have an inherited basis. He developed the method of classifying prints (into "loops," "arches," and "whorls") that was first adopted by Scotland Yard and that remains in standard use by police agencies today.

Closer to psychology, Galton also devised questionnaires to study individual differences in **mental imagery**, asking subjects to imagine various scenes and then to describe their images in detail as to brightness and color, distinctness, apparent location, and the like. He found wide individual differences, with some subjects literally "seeing" their images with almost the same distinctness as a real scene, while others (especially scientists, philosophers, and those accustomed to dealing with abstraction) reported only "thoughts" that had no visual properties at all. Galton's questionnaire became a standard instrument for studying mental imagery for many years. His major finding — that normal people vary widely in the frequency, intensity, and vividness with which they imagine things — has been widely replicated.

Another important study focused on **associations**, something obviously created by experience and representing one of Galton's few explicit concessions to the nurture side of the nature-nurture controversy. Galton invented the **word-association experiment**, writing down seventy-five different stimulus words on paper slips, then drawing the slips in random order and recording the first two or three thoughts that came to mind to each stimulus. He went through his list four times, and discovered that many of his associations recurred repeatedly, and dated surprisingly often from events in childhood. He did not find the rich variety of associations he had expected, and commented, "The roadways of our minds are worn into very deep ruts." The task in general seemed "repugnant and laborious," as many of his associations proved to be anxiety arousing or embarrassing. He declined to publish his associations verbatim, noting simply that "they lay bare the foundations of a man's thought with curious distinctness, and exhibit his mental anatomy with more vividness and truth than he would probably care to publish to the world."[23] Although Galton himself never carried these ideas further, the journal in which they appeared in 1879 was read by the young Viennese doctor Sigmund Freud; it is likely Galton's study was one of many different sources of Freud's later development of **free association**, which we shall describe further in Chapter 11.

Many of Galton's other studies were less consequential, but still reflected his curiosity and inventiveness. He developed a system of "composite portraiture," in which facial photographs of family members or members of the same groups (for example, criminals, the insane, or tuberculosis patients) were superimposed upon one another in an attempt to identify and accentuate the features all held in common. He constructed "beauty maps" of the British Isles, according to which the best-looking inhabitants (by Galton's subjective assessment) came from London, the least comely from Aberdeen. He conducted a statistical study of the efficacy of prayer, investigated the effects of influenza on imagination, tried (unsuccessfully) to do arithmetic by using only the sense of smell, and experimented systematically with different techniques of tea making. All of these he pursued with the same enthusiasm and energy he had shown as a young man.

Galton's Influence

Galton's always-lively writings won him a considerable reputation, and in 1909 a knighthood. "A precious bad *knight* I should make now," the eighty-seven-year-old Sir Francis joked at the time: "Even seven years ago it required some engineering to get me on the back of an Egyptian *donkey!* and I have worsened steadily since."[24] But still the honor pleased him.

Indeed, the elderly Galton looked back on just one major life disappointment. Despite the fact that he had married according to the best eugenic principles, to an able woman from a family nearly as distinguished as his own, they had been unable to have children: an ironic caprice of fate that his eugenic science could not have predicted.

But still, Galton had the consolation of seeing his *intellectual* descendants prosper. Few individuals have ever influenced as many different disciplines — from geography, meteorology, and biology through statistics, criminology, and psychology. And he remains one of the most important figures in the history of psychology. Twin studies, questionnaire studies, correlational studies, and investigations of imagery and association remain the lifeblood of many modern psychologists, to say nothing of the vast industry concerned with intelligence testing.

Even Galton's controversies continue unabated and unresolved, as psychologists still debate the nature-nurture question in much the same terms that he debated de Candolle. Psychology's most sensational and widely publicized recent scandal involved the work of Sir **Cyril Burt** (1883–1971), a British psychologist who deliberately represented himself as Galton's intellectual successor. Throughout the 1950s and 1960s, Burt reported a series of studies of identical twins, purportedly separated at birth and reared by completely independent adoptive families. Despite being reared in different environments, these twins were said by Burt to have intelligence test scores that correlated at the level of about $+0.80$ — indicating a much stronger hereditary than environmental determination of intelligence. In fact, Burt's entire study was apparently fraudulent, and his separated twins fictitious. Other twin studies, conducted honestly by more conscientious researchers, have produced interesting but somewhat ambiguous results suggesting prominent effects from both heredity and environment. The nature-nurture controversy with respect to differences in human intelligence remains today very much unresolved.[25]

In the following chapters we shall see further how Galton's ideas joined with those of Darwin in giving psychology a new functional and differential emphasis, especially as the new science developed in America.

Suggested Readings

Reprinted editions have been issued of Francis Galton's *Hereditary Genius* (Gloucester, MA: Peter Smith, 1972) and *English Men of Science* (London: Frank Cass, 1974). Many of his important shorter works, including his studies of twins, anthropometric tests, association, and mental imagery, are reprinted in his *Inquiries into Human Faculty and Its Development* (New York: Dutton, 1907). Galton's highly readable autobiography is entitled *Memories of My Life* (London: Methuen, 1908); for more on his life and work see D. W. Forrest, *Francis Galton: The Life and Work of a Victorian Genius* (London: Elek, 1974). Further discussion of Galton and his influence is included in Raymond E. Fancher, *The Intelligence Men: Makers of the IQ Controversy* (New York: Norton, 1985).

8

William James and Psychology in America

The well-attended Third International Congress of Psychology, held in Munich in 1896, signified that psychology had fully arrived on the world scene as a respectable scientific and academic discipline. Strangely, however, the two men who had been most responsible for the new science's growth — and who had been informally proclaimed the "psychological popes" of the old and the new worlds — both stayed away from the conference.[1] The old-world "pope" was Wilhelm Wundt, whose pioneering labors we have reviewed in Chapter 5; his missing American counterpart was the Harvard professor **William James** (1842–1910). James had taught the first American university courses on the new scientific psychology, and in 1890 had vibrantly summarized the field in an acclaimed textbook, *The Principles of Psychology*. Less of a program builder but more of a popular communicator than Wundt, James helped create an intellectual climate in America highly receptive to the new science. Thanks largely to the efforts of Wundt and James in their home countries, Germany and the United States led the world in the numbers of psychologists and psychological laboratories they had produced.

But ironically, the two psychological popes did not highly esteem each other's work. Wundt found little new or original in James, except for a style that he judged overly personal and informal. "It is literature, it is beautiful, but it is not psychology," he grumbled about James's *Principles*.[2] Part of his dissatisfaction doubtlessly arose from James's treatment of his own work, for after praising the innovative features of Wundtian experimental psychology the American had added acidly that it "could hardly have arisen in a country whose natives could be *bored*. . . . There is little of the grand style about these new prism, pendulum, and chronograph-philosophers. They mean business, not chivalry."[3]

In a private letter to a friend, James wrote even more acerbically:

[Wundt] aims at being a sort of Napoleon of the intellectual world. Unfortunately he will never have a Waterloo, for he is a Napoleon without genius and with no central idea which, if defeated, brings down the whole fabric in ruin. [When his critics] make mincemeat of some one of his views by their criticism, he is meanwhile writing a book on an entirely different subject. Cut him up like a worm, and each fragment crawls; there is no [vital center] in his mental medulla oblongata, so that you can't kill him all at once.[4]

Just possibly, a touch of envy here colored James's outburst about Wundt's great literary productivity. Himself a slow writer, he had labored for twelve years on *Principles of Psychology*.

Obviously, a vast difference in personality style separated the mercurial James from the professorial Wundt, and much of their antagonism arose from this difference. But the difference in personality also correlated with a difference in the substance of the psychology each promoted. And for all of their unique individuality, Wundt and James were also each broadly representative of the different intellectual climates of their respective countries. The psychology that James fostered, and that flourished in America after him, had a character quite different from its continental counterpart. More personal and focused on the individual, and more practical than theoretical in its goals, American psychology still retains much of this distinctive character today.

In this chapter, we shall examine the development of modern American psychology by focusing first on the life and pivotal work of William James, and then turning to three of his most important students and successors.

William James (1842–1910). *Archives of the History of American Psychology, University of Akron.*

James's Early Life

William James was born on 11 January 1842 in New York City, the eldest child in a family very wealthy by virtue of his grandfather's shrewd investment in the building of the Erie Canal. During boyhood and adolescence he moved incessantly with his family throughout America and Europe, as his unconventional father sought but never found the ideal place for bringing up his five children.

The father, Henry James Sr. (1811–1882), had led a materially privileged but spiritually troubled life. After attending Princeton Theological Seminary for two years, he had felt oppressed by the stern Presbyterian doctrines of predetermination taught there and dropped out. Despite his substantial inherited fortune, he had worried acutely about his lack of a meaningful vocation, especially during the years following his marriage to Mary Walsh in 1840. His life reached a dramatic crisis — one that would later be echoed by his eldest son — in 1844. The father vividly remembered his own crisis as follows:

One day, . . . having eaten a comfortable dinner, I remained sitting at the table after the family had disappeared, idly gazing at the embers in the grate, thinking of nothing, and feeling only the exhilaration incident to a good digestion, when suddenly — in a lightning flash, as it were — "fear came upon me, and trembling, which made all my bones to shake." To all appearances it was a perfectly insane and abject terror, without ostensible cause, and only to be accounted for to my perplexed imagination, by some damned shape squatting invisible to me within the precincts of the room, and raying out from his fetid personality influences fatal to life. The thing had not lasted ten seconds before I felt myself a wreck; that is, reduced from a state of vigorous, joyful manhood to one of the most helpless infancy.[5]

Doctors could do nothing to help, and Henry James Sr. remained for two years prone to anxiety attacks and a constant sense that the foundations had been pulled from beneath his existence. Then he learned that the Swedish mystical philosopher Emmanuel Swedenborg (1688–1772) had written about attacks like his own, calling them "vastations." The elder James now read everything he could find by or about Swedenborg, and somehow this brought him the assurance he needed to recover from his breakdown. Moreover, he at last found his vocation, and spent the rest of his life trying to communicate Swedenborgian philosophy to others in rather obscure lectures and books.*

*His obscure literary style hindered sales of his books, and became something of an open joke among family and friends. Following publication of his book entitled *The Secret of Swedenborg*, a friend quipped that he had not only found the secret, but also kept it.

Now Henry Sr. developed another consuming interest: the education of his children. William had been followed in turn by Henry Jr. (the future great novelist), Garth Wilkinson, Robertson, and Alice. Determined they should have the best possible education, the father could never quite decide what that was. Thus he led them on an educational odyssey from private school to private tutor, from one continent to another and back again. Nothing ever worked out quite as he hoped. Throughout these numerous dislocations, only the stimulating intellectual atmosphere of the James home remained as an educational constant. Everyone was encouraged to engage in active discussion, to express opinions freely and to defend them against lively familial opposition. Guests observed with amusement that the children, in the heat of dinner-table discussion, would sometimes leave their seats to gesticulate on the floor, or invoke humorous curses on their father, such as that "his mashed potatoes might always have lumps in them."[6]

Perhaps unsurprisingly, this vagabond and intellectually roistering life-style produced mixed effects. All five children became cosmopolitan and proficient in several languages, and the two oldest boys went on to become famous intellectual figures. The two younger sons seem to have felt intimidated and overshadowed by their elders, however, and despite early promise they grew up unhappily susceptible to neurotic illness and alcoholism. Alice, the youngest child and only daughter, suffered worst of all. Although extremely gifted, she was denied educational opportunity because of her sex. And partly because so many of her contemporary males were killed in the Civil War, she was unable to do what her Victorian father thought women *ought* to do: marry and raise a family of her own. She grew up to become a chronic invalid, plagued by bouts of hysterical prostration and disturbing inclinations toward "knocking off the head of the benignant pater."[7] She produced a fascinating diary before her early death from cancer at age forty-three, and was unquestionably a prime victim of the restrictive sexual attitudes of her time.

Even the ultimately famous oldest sons had problems. Henry Jr., born just fifteen months after William, was old enough to be a companion but young enough to feel always overshadowed. Unable to

243

match the venturesome antics and aggressive wit of his brother, he retreated into a world of books and literature. William himself, the oldest and thus the prime subject of his father's educational experiments, was always "out front" and under constantly vacillating paternal pressure. He wound up having just as much difficulty as his father in finding a vocation.

As a teenager, William showed considerable talent and inclination for drawing and art — a profession Henry Sr. did not find suitable. The father exerted both direct and indirect pressure to deflect this interest, moving the family away from William's art teacher, and hinting that he might even commit suicide if his son persisted in an artistic direction. Finally in 1861, William was sent to Harvard to study chemistry — another field in which he had shown some interest and aptitude. But while Henry Sr. saw science as preferable to art as a career for his son, he also worried that it would lead William to adopt materialism and lose sight of the spiritual values he himself found so important. Unsurprisingly, William absorbed much of his father's ambivalence and indecision.

Once at Harvard's Lawrence Scientific School, William quickly shifted his interest from chemistry to physiology, a science just then making great strides under the mechanistic doctrines of the likes of Müller, Helmholtz, and du Bois-Reymond. Soon afterward, the James family fortune showed its first signs of being finite, and William had to consider ways of eventually earning a living. Thus in 1864 he turned to *applied* physiological study, and enrolled in Harvard's Medical School.

A year later he interrupted medical study to go on a specimen-hunting expedition to the Amazon led by **Louis Agassiz** (1807–1873), the eminent Harvard biologist and America's most outspoken critic of Darwin's recently published *Origin of Species*. James responded to the southward sea journey with seasickness to rival Darwin's on the *Beagle*. He wrote his family, "No one has a right to write about the 'nature of Evil,' or to have any opinion about evil, who has not been at sea."[8] His job in Brazil — the collecting and crating of jellyfish — failed to cheer him up before he was stricken with smallpox. He soon concluded he was not cut out to be a field biologist, and returned home to resume medical study.

Now he suffered from a residual eye weakness from smallpox that made it difficult to read, and from a lower back condition that made it painful to stand. Worse still, he felt oppressed by his family, who had moved to Cambridge and insisted he live with them. Privately he contemplated suicide, but in April of 1867 succeeded in convincing his father that he should go to Germany—both for its mineral spring baths for his back and for the opportunity to perfect his familiarity with scientific German.

James stayed in Germany for a year and a half, while his eyes improved more than his back and enabled him to meet at least his second goal. He read omnivorously in the German physiological literature, attended lectures by du Bois-Reymond, and became even more impressed by the explanatory power of the new mechanistic physiology. He also read a thirty-three-page article by a then little-known Heidelberg physiologist named Wilhelm Wundt, on "Recent Advances in the Field of Physiological Psychology." As we noted in Chapter 5, this led him to report enthusiastically to a friend:

It seems to me that perhaps the time has come for psychology to begin to be a science—some measurements have already been made in the region lying between the physical changes in the nerves and the appearance of consciousness. . . . I am going to study what is already known, and perhaps may be able to do some work at it. Helmholtz and a man named Wundt at Heidelberg are working at it, and I hope I live through this winter to go to them in the summer.[9]

James's frail back precluded travel to Heidelberg, so both his first meeting with Wundt and his antagonism for him were postponed for several years. He returned home and went through the motions of completing his medical degree, outwardly full of enthusiasm but inwardly in despair. The new German mechanistic physiology had powerfully impressed him intellectually, but oppressed him spiritually with its deterministic philosophical implications. The death of a favorite cousin depressed him further, and in the spring of 1870 he suffered a sudden crisis that he later recalled as follows:

Whilst in [a] state of philosophical pessimism and general depression about my prospects, I went one evening into a dressing-room in the twilight to procure some article that was there; when suddenly there fell upon me without any warning, just as if it came out of the darkness, a horrible fear

245

of my own existence. Simultaneously there arose in my mind the image of an epileptic patient whom I had seen in the asylum, a black-haired youth with greenish skin, who used to sit all day on one of the benches, . . . moving nothing but his black eyes and looking absolutely non-human. This image and my fear entered into a species of combination with each other. *That shape am I*, I felt, potentially. Nothing that I possess can defend me against that fate, if the hour for it should strike for me as it struck for him. There was such a horror of him, and such a perception of my own merely momentary discrepancy from him, that it was as if something hitherto solid within my breast gave way entirely, and I became a mass of quivering fear. After this the universe was changed for me altogether.[10]

This crisis remarkably resembled Henry James Sr.'s "vastation" of twenty-six years earlier. Like his father, William had been chronically worried about finding a vocation, and oppressed by a deterministic doctrine. And like his father's, his life too was instantaneously transformed by a sudden awareness of "that pit of insecurity beneath the surface of life" that left him feeling utterly prostrated and unable to work.

And again like his father, William James worked a gradual recovery and found a new purpose in life, partly through the chance exposure to some philosophical writings. On 29 April 1870 he read an essay on free will — precisely the agency that seemed to be denied by mechanistic physiology — by the French philosopher **Charles Renouvier** (1815-1903). The next day he confided in his diary:

I think that yesterday was a crisis in my life. I . . . see no reason why [Renouvier's] definition of free will — "the sustaining of a thought *because I choose to* when I might have other thoughts" — need be the definition of an illusion. At any rate, I will assume for the present — until next year — that it is no illusion. My first act of free will shall be to believe in free will. . . . Hitherto, when I have felt like taking a free initiative, like daring to act originally, . . . suicide seemed the most manly form to put my daring into; now, I will go a step further with my will, not only act with it, but believe as well; believe in my individual reality and creative power.[11]

While James's decision to believe in free will occurred suddenly, a more gradual element in his recovery derived from his reading the British philosopher-psychologist **Alexander Bain** (1818-1903) on the subject of *habit*. In his 1859 book, *The Emotions and the Will*,

Bain had stressed the importance of *voluntary repetition* of morally desirable actions if they are to become habitual and automatic. Only after many repetitions, he argued, do permanent neural connections become established between the sensory impressions created by a given situation and a particular desirable response to it. Thus desirable actions like getting out of bed early in the morning may be very difficult to perform at first, but after they have been assiduously repeated many times they become permanently impressed into the nervous system, and automatic. Bain emphasized the moral danger of allowing exceptions to occur while a habit is being formed, since "every gain on the wrong side undoes the effect of many conquests on the right."[12]

Combining the advice of Renouvier and Bain, William James tried to will himself to think more optimistic and less oppressive thoughts. And with repetition, the initially difficult reactions gradually became habitual. His trial adoption of a belief in free will lasted not just to the end of the year, but to the end of his life. In a curious way, his adoption of this most unmechanistic of beliefs freed him of his intellectual inhibitions, and enabled him to regard the implications of the new mechanistic physiology and psychology even more seriously than before.

Gradually, he found he could entertain mechanistic ideas and take them seriously *scientifically*, without fully accepting them *personally*. In personal life it was useful to think and behave as if he had free will, while as a scientist it was useful to accept mechanistic determinism. Both views were essentially articles of faith, incapable of absolute proof or disproof. In the absence of any absolute criterion for judging their "truth," James decided to evaluate ideas according to their *utility* within specified and limited contexts. Thus since free will seemed a useful concept in personal life, he would accept it as "true" there; determinism, useful scientifically, could be equally "true" when he functioned as a scientist. The evaluation of ideas relativistically, according to their varying usefulness in varying situations, eventually became a hallmark of James's general philosophy, which he appropriately labeled **pragmatism**.

In the immediate aftermath of his crisis, however, James was still far from advancing a coherent philosophy. Although he had completed his medical training and had read widely in the new physio-logical and psychological sciences, he had never held a real job or completed a major independent project. Nearing thirty years of age, he still lived with his parents and remained dependent upon them.

At last in 1872 he received a crucial vocational opportunity when Harvard's president, Charles Eliot, a Cambridge neighbor, invited him to teach half of a newly instituted physiology course. After much deliberation he accepted, and did well enough to be asked to take over the entire course. He was now on his way to becoming one of Harvard's most outstanding and legendary teachers.

James the Teacher

Once James got used to teaching, he effectively conveyed his personal involvement in ideas with infectious zest, and treated his students as intellectual equals engaged in a common quest for knowledge. Unlike many of his authoritarian colleagues, James regularly walked to and from class with his students, constantly engaged in animated conversation. Noting his casual and informal manner, one visitor to his class thought him more like a sportsman than a professor.

One student recalled James's intense absorption in his subject as he lectured: "James would rise with a peculiar suddenness and make bold and rapid strokes for a diagram on the blackboard— I can remember his abstracted air as he wrestled with some idea, standing by his chair with one foot upon it, elbow on knee, hand to chin." Another student remembered a seminar held in James's own home, when he had trouble keeping his small portable blackboard within the full class's vision: "Entirely bent on what he was doing, his efforts ended at last in his standing [the blackboard] on the floor while he lay down at full length, holding it with one hand, drawing with the other, and continuing the flow of his commentary."[13]

Genuinely interested in his students' reactions to his classes, James solicited their written course evaluations many years before that became a common practice in university classrooms. Perhaps his most celebrated teaching episode involved the writer Gertrude Stein, one of his best students while a Radcliffe undergraduate. After looking at James's final exam questions she wrote, "Dear Professor

James, I am sorry but really I do not feel like an examination paper in philosophy today," and left the exam room. James responded, "Dear Miss Stein, I understand perfectly how you feel; I often feel like that myself," and awarded her the highest mark in the class.[14] (Stein's ploy should probably not be tried by students less secure in their professor's esteem that she obviously was.)

Preeminently, James succeeded as a teacher because of his personalized and lively approach to subject matter. No ivory tower professor, he constantly sought to extract from his subjects something useful for living. Having found philosophical and psychological ideas useful in resolving his own problems, he tried to make such ideas seem personally relevant to his students.

James regularly changed the subject matter of his courses as his own interests changed, teaching himself first and then transmitting the new information to his students. Initially hired to teach physiology and anatomy, he soon altered his course's title to "The Relations between Physiology and Psychology." Between 1878 and 1890, as he worked on *The Principles of Psychology*, he dropped traditional physiology altogether to focus exclusively on psychology. And as he became increasingly involved with philosophy after 1890, psychology in turn gradually disappeared from his course offerings.

But while James's tenure as a "psychologist" was temporary and brief, it was extraordinarily influential. In his lectures, articles, and textbooks — particularly *The Principles of Psychology* — he made the new science come alive. Wundt had brought psychology to the university for specialists; James made it a living subject for anyone who chose to read or listen to him.

The Principles of Psychology In 1878, just as James began to teach courses exclusively devoted to psychology, he contracted with the publisher Henry Holt to write a comprehensive textbook of the field. Already familiar with most of the German, French, and English literature on the subject, he confidently promised to finish it in two years. But by 1880 he had scarcely begun, and the project began to seem a dark cloud destined to hover over him indefinitely. Over the next several years he managed to write several journal and magazine articles on psychological subjects, and as the 1880s ended he realized he could shape these into chapters of his textbook. At last, in January of 1890, he sent Holt the first 350 pages of manuscript, with assurance that the remaining four-fifths of the book would soon follow. He thought Holt might wish to begin setting it in type immediately, and seemed surprised when the publisher decided to wait for the rest before proceeding! But this time James was true to his word, and actually completed the long manuscript within the next few months.

By now thoroughly sick of the project — which he characterized to his publisher as "the enormous *rat* which . . . ten years gestation has brought forth" — James showed that he could treat himself and his own work with the same acerbity he had directed at Wundt:

No one could be more disgusted than I at the sight of the book. *No* subject is worth being treated of in 1000 pages! Had I ten years more, I could rewrite it in 500; but as it stands it is this or nothing — a loathsome, distended, tumefied, bloated, dropsical mass, testifying to nothing but two facts: *1st,* that there is no such thing as a *science* of psychology, and *2nd,* that W.J. is an incapable.[15]

Two aspects of this self-critique were partly correct: the book *was* huge, and it did reveal psychology as unsystematic and incomplete ("like physics before Galileo," James remarked in a letter to a friend). But it also revealed James as a master of English prose rather than an "incapable," and once published it quickly became the leading psychology text in English. The book succeeded for the same reasons his teaching succeeded: stress on the personal utility and relevance of psychological ideas, and an unselfconscious frankness and naturalness in discussing them.

James's great text resists easy summarization. In twenty-eight chapters and nearly 1,400 pages, it touched on all of the major topics of the day's psychology, including brain function, habit, the stream of thought, the self, attention, association, memory, sensation, imagination, perception, instinct, the emotions, will, and hypnotism. We will here consider just a few of these subjects, to give the flavor of James's style.

The Stream of Consciousness. James's most famous psychological metaphor occurs in a chapter entitled "The Stream of Thought," where he argues that the contents of human consciousness are better thought of as a *stream* than as a collection of discrete elements or ideas. The Greek philosopher Heraclitus had observed that one can never enter twice into exactly the same stream, for its fluid contents change constantly even while its banks and course remain much the same. Analogously, thought James, one can never have exactly the same sensation, idea, or other experience twice. Every new experience is inevitably molded and framed by all the old experiences that have gone before, and since this background constantly changes and enlarges no two experiences can ever be precisely alike.

Further, James believed thought and a stream share the quality of *continuousness*. Even when gaps occur in consciousness, as from anesthesia, epileptic fits, or sleep, a subjective sense of continuity is maintained. The remembered experiences immediately before and after the periods of unconsciousness — "the broken edges of sentient life," as James put it — seem to "meet and merge over the gap, much as the feelings of space of the opposite margins of the 'blind spot' meet and merge over that objective interruption to the sensitiveness of the eye. Such consciousness as this, whatever it be for the onlooking psychologist, is for itself unbroken. It *feels* unbroken."[16]

James warned that thought's streamlike quality makes it foolish to analyze it introspectively in terms of static "elements," such as particular sensations or feelings. Real thought can never be "frozen" and studied analytically without doing damage to its essential nature:

> Let anyone try to cut a thought across the middle and get a look at its section, and he will see how difficult the introspective observation . . . is. The rush of the thought is always so headlong that it almost always brings us up at the conclusion before we can arrest it. [Introspective analysis] is in fact like seizing a spinning top to catch its motion, or trying to turn up the gas quickly enough to see how the darkness looks.[17]

James privately referred to psychologists like Titchener, who persisted in trying to break consciousness down into static elements, as "barbarians." For him, psychology entailed the study of *dynamic* and constantly changing conscious processes.

Habit. In another famous chapter entitled "Habit," James stressed the enormously important influence of habitual responses for the maintenance of society:

Habit is . . . the enormous fly-wheel of society, its most precious conservative agent. It alone is what keeps us all within the bounds of ordinance,
and saves the children from the envious uprisings of the poor. It alone
prevents the hardest and most repulsive walks of life from being deserted
by those brought up to tread therein. . . . It dooms us all to fight out the
battle of life upon the lines of nurture or our early choice, and to make
the best of a pursuit that disagrees, because there is no other for which
we are fitted, and it is too late to begin again. It keeps different social strata
from mixing. Already at the age of twenty-five you see the professional
mannerism settling down on the young commercial traveller, on the young
minister, on the young counsellor-at-law. You see the little lines of cleavage
running through the character . . . from which the man can by-and-by
no more escape than his coat-sleeve can suddenly fall into a new set of
folds.[18]

After emphasizing the power and inevitability of human habits,
James characteristically proceeded to draw a lesson. Echoing the
ideas of Alexander Bain that had so influenced his own life, he noted
that the laws of habit formation are impartial, and capable of producing morally good or bad actions. And once a good or bad habit
has begun to be established, it is difficult to reverse the course:

Every smallest stroke of virtue or vice leaves its never so little scar. The
drunken Rip Van Winkle, in Jefferson's play, excuses himself for every
fresh dereliction by saying, "I won't count this time!" Well! he may not
count it, and a kind Heaven may not count it; but it is being counted up
none the less. Down among his nerve-cells and fibres the molecules are
counting it, registering and storing it up to be used against him when the
next temptation comes.[19]

James believed his college-aged audience still had just enough
youthful flexibility left to counteract old bad habits and foster new
good ones. Thus he urged them to decide on some desirable behavior, and then practice it deliberately and repeatedly: "Never suffer an exception to occur till the new habit is securely rooted in
your life. . . . Seize the first possible opportunity to act on every
resolution you make. . . . Keep the faculty of effort alive in you
by a little gratuitous exercise every day." A student who does this
need have no anxiety about the upshot of his education: "If he keep
faithfully busy each hour of the working-day, he may safely leave
the final result to itself. He can with perfect certainty count on wak-

ing up some fine morning to find himself one of the competent ones of his generation."[20]

Of course this advice represented exactly the prescription James himself had followed in dealing with his personal crisis of 1870, when he willed himself to think undeterministic, free, and cheerful thoughts.

Emotion. Another chapter entitled "Emotion" also derived directly from James's crisis and its resolution, and introduced one of his most important theoretical contributions to psychology. According to James, an emotion is actually the *consequence* rather than the cause of the bodily changes associated with its expression — a reversal of the commonsense view:

Common sense says, we lose our fortune, are sorry, and weep; we meet a bear, are frightened, and run; we are insulted by a rival, are angry, and strike. The hypothesis here to be defended says this order of sequence is incorrect, that the one mental state is not immediately induced by the other, that the bodily manifestations must first be interposed between, and that the more rational statement is that we feel sorry because we cry, angry because we strike, afraid because we tremble, and not that we cry, strike, or tremble because we are sorry, angry, or fearful, as the case may be.[21]

The Danish physiologist **Carl Lange** (1834–1900) published a similar view at just about the same time as James. To honor both men, the notion that emotions represent the perception of bodily reactions has traditionally been called the **James-Lange theory of emotion**.

As usual, James tried to derive practical lessons from his theorizing, including a technique for dealing with emotional distress:

Whistling to keep up courage is no mere figure of speech. On the other hand, sit all day in a moping posture, sigh, and reply to everything with a dismal voice, and your melancholy lingers. There is no more valuable precept in moral education than this, as all who have experience know: if we wish to conquer undesirable emotional tendencies in ourselves we must assiduously, and in the first instance cold-bloodedly, go through the *outward movements* of those contrary dispositions which we prefer to cultivate. The reward of persistency will infallibly come, in the fading out of sullenness or depression, and the advent of real cheerfulness and kindliness in their stead.[22]

James himself had done precisely this to overcome depression during his youthful crisis. After repeatedly willing himself to think himself free and cheerful, he began actually to feel that way. He had also followed this prescription after his parents' deaths in 1882, willing himself to act more cheerfully than he really felt until his grief gradually passed. The James-Lange theory is now recognized to have limitations, but for all its stiff-upper-lip oversimplicity it can still usefully account for many aspects of emotional experience.

Will. James's personal experience shone clearly through one further chapter, simply entitled "Will." Here he dealt openly with the question that had troubled him during his crisis: whether or not free will exists.

First, he defined an act of will as one accompanied by some subjective sense of mental or attentional *effort*: "The most essential achievement of the will, . . . when it is most 'voluntary,' is to ATTEND to a difficult object and hold it fast before the mind. . . . Effort of attention is thus the essential phenomenon of will."[23] Then he asked whether the subjective sense of effortful attention was a completely mechanistically determined *consequence* of the thought process, or whether it introduced certain non-mechanistic and non-predictable influences of its own. Scientific psychology assumed the former to be true, while personal, subjective experience suggested the latter.

James believed that a true science *had* to postulate complete determinism, because "before . . . indeterminism, science simply *stops*." Modern psychology's most impressive gains had occurred via the assumptions of mechanism and determinism. Thus as long as he was writing as a psychologist and a scientist, James would accept the tenets of determinism and push them as far as possible. "Psychology will be Psychology, and Science Science, as much as ever (as much and no more) in this world, whether free will be true in it or not. . . . We can therefore leave the free-will altogether out of our [psychological] account." He hastened to add, however, that science "must be constantly reminded that her purposes are not the only purposes, and that the order of uniform causation which she has use for, and is therefore right in postulating, may be enveloped in a wider order, on which she has no claims at all."[24] Science and psychology did not and could not contain all the answers for James. Thus when he was not functioning as a psychologist, but as moral philosopher or simply as a feeling, willing, and socially responsive human being, he could and would adopt a belief in free will.

Such was the essence of James's psychology: neither a finished system nor a provider of absolutely certain conclusions, but a collection of vivid and informed personal reflections on all of the major areas of the emerging new science. Students who read James not only learned all of the major facts in the new psychology, but also were challenged to *think about* them in useful and creative ways.

James's Later Career and the Philosophy of Pragmatism

After 1890, James felt increasingly frustrated by the limitations and uncertainties of the science he had so brilliantly elucidated. He complained to a colleague that psychology was "a nasty little subject; . . . all one cares to know lies outside." His son recalled how he occasionally chafed at being personally identified as a "psychologist":

In June, 1903, when he became aware that Harvard was intending to confer an honorary degree upon him, he went about for days before Commencement in a half-serious state of dread, lest, at the fatal moment, he should hear President Eliot's voice naming him "Psychologist, psychical researcher, willer to believe, religious experiencer." He could not say whether the impossible last epithets would be less to his taste than "psychologist."[25]

James here exaggerated his feelings in a typically colorful way, for he still carried on considerable psychological activity. He twice accepted the presidency of the American Psychological Association (in 1894 and 1904), and continued to write on psychology. In 1892 he abridged his textbook into one volume entitled *Psychology: Briefer Course.* Informally called "Jimmy" as opposed to its longer predecessor "James," this too met great success. In 1899 James applied his psychological ideas to pedagogy in *Talks to Teachers,* and three years later explored the relationships between abnormal psychology and religious experience in *Varieties of Religious Experience.* He remained sufficiently interested in psychology to travel to Clark University in 1909, just before his death and at considerable expense to his health, "to see what Freud was like" when the founder of psycho-analysis made his only visit to America.*

But psychology did become less prominent among James's activities after 1890. In 1892 he brought the German psychologist (and Wundt student) **Hugo Münsterberg** (1863–1916) to Harvard to assume major responsibility for scientific psychology, while he turned his own primary attention to other subjects.

One was psychic research, a topic much in the news of the time as several well-publicized "mediums" claimed the ability to communicate with departed spirits. Unlike the skeptical Wundt, who disdained such phenomena as unworthy of serious attention (see pages 155–156), James became a leader of an official organization devoted to the scientific investigation of "spiritistic" phenomena — the American Society for Psychical Research. James openly *hoped* to find convincing positive evidence, but time and again his hard data proved inconclusive or worse. Once a hidden observer detected that Eusapia Paladino, a famous medium in whom James had rested particularly high hopes, produced her "psychic manifestations" through contortionist-like movements of her foot. Her séance came to an ignominious end when the observer seized her foot, and inspired one of James's friends to compose a poem:

> Eeny, meeny, miney mo,
> Catch Eusapia by the toe,
> If she hollers, then you know,
> James's theory is not so.[27]

James took the jibe in good spirit, and shortly before his death confessed that although he had devoted twenty-five years to psychical research,

I am theoretically no "further" than I was at the beginning; and I confess that at times I have been tempted to believe that the Creator has eternally intended this department of nature to remain *baffling*, to prompt out hopes

---

*James had been the first American to call favorable attention to Freud's early work on hysteria, in 1894. At Clark he was still impressed, but with reservations. Freud's ideas "can't fail to throw light on human nature," he wrote to a friend, "but I confess that he made on me personally the impression of a man obsessed with fixed ideas."[26]

and curiosities and suspicions all in equal measure, so that, although ghosts and clairvoyances, and raps and messages from spirits, are always seeming to exist and can never be fully explained away, they also can never be susceptible of full corroboration.[28]

During the final decades of his life, James devoted his greatest attention to philosophy. As a young man he had joined with some Cambridge friends in a "Metaphysical Club" to discuss philosophical questions. There **Charles S. Sanders Peirce** (1839–1914) promoted a view he called **pragmatism**, according to which scientific ideas and knowledge can never be absolutely certain, but only subject to varying degrees of "pragmatic belief." That is, ideas *worked* with varying degrees of effectiveness in adapting to the world. Peirce and the other Metaphysical Club members enthusiastically adopted the new Darwinian world view, according to which no adaptation to the world should be considered perfect or permanent, but always subject to evolution or replacement by a better competitor. Thus Peirce extrapolated this perspective to ideas and knowledge: Just as a biological trait that is adaptive in one environment may prove ineffective or dangerous in another, or just as a once-successful species may be surpassed and overrun by a new and better-adapted one, so may ideas gain or lose their value depending upon their particular "environments" and "competitors."

Of course this attitude meshed nicely with James's personal convictions following his crisis; his decision to believe in free will was pragmatically adaptive and "correct" because it worked. Later, he had implicitly applied the pragmatic criterion to psychological theories in *Principles of Psychology*. Never interested in facts for their own sake, or theories in isolation from their context, he always stressed their usefulness (or lack thereof) in specific contexts.

Toward the end of his life, James expanded on the philosophical implications of this approach in numerous articles and books, including *Will to Believe and Other Essays* (1897), *Pragmatism* (1907), and *A Pluralistic Universe* and *The Meaning of Truth* (both 1909). Although he adopted Peirce's term "pragmatism" to define his philosophy, he extended its approach to include emotional, ethical, and religious ideas as well as scientific theories. Peirce disagreed with this elaboration of his philosophy, and tried vainly to redesignate his own view "pragmaticism," to differentiate it from James's. This led one of James's biographers to declare, "The movement known as pragmatism is largely the result of James's misunderstanding of Peirce."[29] But whatever their origin, James's philosophical writings became very popular, and following his death from heart disease in 1910 no less a philosopher than Bertrand Russell described him as "one of the most eminent, and probably the most widely known, of contemporary philosophers."[30]

Three Eminent Students:
Hall, Calkins, and Thorndike

Despite James's relatively brief and ambivalent tenure as a full-time psychologist, and the unsystematic and incomplete nature of his psychological work, he also left a huge impact on American psychology. His influence differed markedly from that of his fellow "pope" Wundt, however, for rather than building a school or a specific theoretical orientation to psychology, he created a general atmosphere about the subject that made it seem something interesting and worthwhile to pursue. Instead of training "followers" to carry forth with a "Jamesean" psychology, he inspired many different students to develop their own individual approaches. Indeed, because he treated so many subjects as interesting but open, and did not presume to offer more than "pragmatic" solutions to the problems he posed, his writings seem less obsolete than those of his contemporaries and can still be read for pleasure and stimulation today.

Thus it is fitting to illustrate James's influence with sketches of three of his students, who all went on to contribute significantly to the development of American psychology in their own distinctive ways. **G. Stanley Hall** (1844–1924) encountered James at the very beginning of his teaching career. Nearly James's own age, and with an already established agenda of his own, Hall was not so much "taught" by James as assisted by him in the launching of his career. Hall went on to become something James was not—a major "founder" and institution builder for the new science in America. **Mary Whiton Calkins** (1863–1930), by contrast, met James just after *Principles of Psychology* had been published, and got her real introduction to psychology from that work. As one of the first women to seek a career in psychology, Calkins faced appalling discrimination; James provided moral as well as intellectual support as she went on to become a president of the American Psychological Association. **Edward Lee Thorndike** (1874–1947) went to study with James after being inspired by *Principles*. James encouraged Thorndike to start a study of animal learning that subsequently became his Ph.D. thesis at Columbia, and one of the most cited papers in American psychology. After James's death, Thorndike replaced him as the best-known psychologist in the country.

G. Stanley Hall G. (for Granville) Stanley Hall was born near Ashfield, Massachusetts, the son of an educated farmer who had also taught school briefly, and served a term in the Massachusetts state legislature. His deeply religious mother had also been a schoolteacher, and was pleased when Hall entered Union Theological Seminary in New York after graduating from Williams College in 1867. She was less pleased when her son found the secular stimulation of the big city, and the controversial Darwinian theory then so much in the air, more appealing than theology. Hall recalled that after he preached his trial sermon to faculty and students at the seminary, the president did not offer a customary critique and commentary, but knelt and prayed for the salvation of Hall's soul. Realizing his prospects must lie elsewhere, Hall borrowed money for three years of independent study in Germany, where he concentrated on philosophy but also studied physiology with the great mechanist, du Bois-Reymond.

Running out of funds before he could take a degree, Hall returned to the United States in 1871. After losing one position because of his avowed Darwinian sympathies, he finally won a junior appointment teaching philosophy and religion at Antioch College in Yellow Springs, Ohio. While there he read Wundt's newly published *Principles of Physiological Psychology*, and decided the new experimental science of the mind was for him. He left Antioch in 1876 intending to go to Wundt in Leipzig, but en route stopped off at Harvard and was fortuitously offered an instructorship in English. This he accepted, and although he found its duties arduous he also met

William James. Just two years older than Hall and at the beginning of his own teaching career, James encouraged Hall to do an experiment on the role of muscular cues in the perception of space, which could serve as a Harvard Ph.D. dissertation. Hall did so, and although nominally in philosophy his degree actually represented the first American Ph.D. to be awarded in experimental psychology.

In 1878, James's first Ph.D. student carried out his plan to study in Leipzig, and arrived just as Wundt's institute was getting established. Thus Hall became *Wundt's* first American student, although a postgraduate one. He did not stay long, but served as a subject in some of the early Ph.D. research at Leipzig and won Wundt's recommendation for any future openings in the new psychology in America.

Upon Hall's return home in 1880, however, no permanent jobs were available. He went back to Cambridge, and was invited by Harvard's president to deliver a series of Saturday morning lectures on the subject of education. This opportunity proved crucial to Hall in two ways. First, it turned his serious attention for the first time to problems of developmental psychology and pedagogy — interests that would dominate the rest of his professional life. Second, the popular success of his lectures attracted the attention of Daniel Coit Gilman, president of the new Johns Hopkins University in Baltimore.

Established in 1876, Hopkins was the first in a series of new American universities modeled deliberately after the German system, and intended primarily as *graduate* institutions specializing in research training for the Ph.D. With positive recommendations from both Wundt and James, Hall won the new university's first professorship of psychology and pedagogy in 1884. Hopkins also provided a research laboratory for Hall to direct, the first such in the United States. In 1887 Hall raised funds to establish the *American Journal of Psychology*, the first English-language periodical explicitly devoted to the new experimental psychology.

Following these administrative successes, Hall in 1888 was appointed the first president of Clark University in Worcester, Massachusetts — another institution originally devoted exclusively to graduate study. There he remained for the rest of his life, despite

some difficult times that arose partly because of Clark's limited financial resources and partly because of his own high-handed administrative style. He continued to teach psychology and pedagogy, and
throughout the 1890s his institution produced more than half of
all the new American Ph.D.s in psychology.

The entrepreneurial Hall also founded the journal *Pedagogical
Seminary* in 1893, a periodical still published today as the *Journal
of Genetic Psychology*. The previous year he had taken the lead in
organizing a national professional society for psychologists, the
American Psychological Association, and was elected its first president. Starting with just thirty-one members in 1892, the APA has
grown almost exponentially ever since. With more than sixty thousand current members, its annual conventions can be accommodated only in the largest and most hotel-rich of North American
cities.

As American psychology's most important "founder" — of laboratories, departments, journals, and professional societies — Hall resembled Wundt more than James. But in his *research* he lay more
clearly in the functional and practical American tradition that had
been pioneered by James. His most innovative work arose out of
his combined interests in psychology, pedagogy, and evolutionary
theory. In the early 1880s he began a large series of questionnaire
studies of kindergarten-aged children, designed to find out what
they knew and thought about a great variety of things such as their
bodies, games and stories, animals, the sun and stars, and religion.
Hall published his findings in an 1893 work whose title — *The Contents
of Children's Minds on Entering School* — suggests its partly practical goal
of informing teachers of what to expect in dealing with their young
charges.

Subsequently Hall and his students issued questionnaires to older
children, and in 1904 he summarized these results in his most
famous book, *Adolescence: Its Psychology and Its Relation to Physiology,
Anthropology, Sociology, Sex, Crime, Religion and Education*. This book
brought the previously unusual word "adolescence" into popular use,
and fully documented for the first time the emotional turbulence
associated with that phase of the life cycle. The book also reflected
Hall's interest in *developmental* issues — his conviction that children

261

must be regarded as constantly growing and changing individuals, with different kinds of knowledge, emotions, and intellectual characteristics at varying stages of the life cycle.

Hall proposed a Darwinian and "recapitulationist" theory of child development, according to which each individual's intellectual, emotional, and general psychological development parallels the stages traversed by our pre-human ancestors. This idea had been hinted at in Darwin's essay on his infant son, and more explicitly espoused by the German biologist Haeckel (see page 204). Hall carried the idea further still, arguing that a child's progress from crawling on all fours to walking upright, and through successive stages of social, playful, and artistic activity, exactly repeats the evolutionary sequence leading to modern humanity. This strict recapitulationist view is no longer credited today, but Hall's work nonetheless marks the beginning of a general interest in developmental psychology. Clark University remains a major center for that field.

Hall's work on adolescence inevitably involved him with many of the same issues of emotional turbulence and sexuality concurrently being investigated in a different way by the Viennese "psychoanalyst" Sigmund Freud. Among the first to recognize Freud's importance, Hall invited him to speak at Clark University's twentieth anniversary celebrations in 1909. The event—Freud's only visit to America—proved a great success and effectively introduced his ideas to the New World. His lectures were published afterward in Hall's *American Journal of Psychology*, and have remained ever since one of the most popular and effective short introductions to psychoanalytic theory.[31]

Unfortunately, the imperious Hall was often difficult to get along with, and wound up alienating Freud along with many others. Sometimes he even turned against his mentors, as when he published a review of James's *Principles of Psychology* that sarcastically called the James-Lange theory the "sorry because we cry theory," and one of the chief "impediments" to psychology's future progress. In 1912 Hall published a critical account of Wundt's life and work, alleging among other things that the young Wundt had been fired as Helmholtz's assistant because of mathematical incompetence. Wundt labeled Hall's work "a biography of me which is invented from the beginning to the end."[32]

America's first historian of psychology, **E. G Boring** (1886–1968), wrote of Hall and James: "Each appreciated the other's qualities, but they were on different tracks. . . . Hall was a comet, caught for the moment by James's influence, but presently shooting off into space never to return."[33] Yet for all the bitter distance Hall placed between himself and his teachers, he also genuinely promoted their new psychologies. Thanks to the institutions, journals, and organizations that Hall founded, the ideas of Wundt, James, Freud, and countless others found a much larger, more receptive, and better-educated audience in America than would have been the case otherwise.

Mary Whiton Calkins A later and more consistently friendly student of James was Mary Calkins. The eldest child of a Presbyterian minister, Calkins was born in Hartford, Connecticut, grew up in Buffalo, New York, and moved with her family to Newton, Massachusetts, at age seventeen. Her mother had earlier suffered a physical and mental collapse, leaving Mary with much of the responsibility for raising a younger sister and three brothers. She also assumed increasing responsibility for her mother, remaining unmarried and in the parental home for the rest of her life.

Still, she grew up in an intellectually stimulating early environment. Her parents had lived in Germany before Mary's birth, and deliberately spoke only German to each other as their daughter was learning to talk; thus she became fluent in German as well as English. Unusually supportive of education for daughters as well as sons, her father sent seventeen-year-old Mary to study at Smith College in Northampton, Massachusetts, shortly after the family's move to Newton. Recently founded in 1875 as one of America's first women's colleges, Smith provided young Calkins excellent training in English and classics.

After graduation Calkins planned to offer private Greek tutoring in Newton, but was unexpectedly offered a position in the Greek department of nearby Wellesley College — another new women's college founded the same year as Smith. Unlike Smith, however, Wellesley then hired only women for its faculty. The pool of highly trained candidates being small, Wellesley often recruited promising but relatively untrained scholars like Calkins, and supported

263

their further study even while they themselves were teaching under-graduates.

Thus after one year of teaching Greek, Calkins found herself under consideration for the job of introducing *experimental psychology* into Wellesley's curriculum. Her only real qualification was an interest in the subject, for she had taken and enjoyed just one psychology course at Smith — and that had been in the philosophical, speculative tradition. No better-prepared candidate appeared, so in 1890 Calkins was offered an instructorship in psychology, contingent upon her completing a year of advanced study in that field.

But where? Nearby Harvard and Clark offered graduate training in psychology, but admitted only men. Indeed, the number of graduate schools in the entire world willing to admit women could be counted on one's fingers, and they were inconveniently located. She finally contacted Josiah Royce, Harvard's professor of mental philosophy, about the possibility of studying with him at the "Harvard Annex" — an officially unsanctioned program of private courses offered by a few of the Harvard faculty. She greatly impressed Royce, who recommended instead that she attend the regular Harvard seminars offered by himself and William James, who did not teach at the Annex. After interviewing Calkins, James enthusiastically concurred.

But at first Harvard's president Charles Eliot refused to support this plan, arguing that the two sexes ought to be educated separately. Royce told Calkins, "I regard this official view as one of the mysteries which no one may hope to penetrate who is not himself accustomed to the executive point of outlook." James added, "It is flagitious* that you should be kept out. — Enough to make dynamiters of you and all women." Both professors continued to press Eliot, aided by a long petition from Calkins's father noting that what was being asked for was "post-graduate and professional instruction for one who is already a member of a college faculty," so her acceptance would not open the floodgates to other women. Eliot finally relented, and in October of 1890 the Harvard Corporation

---

*This excellent but now little-used word, meaning "shamefully wicked; vile and scandalous," deserves to be revived.

officially allowed Royce and James to admit Calkins to their seminars with the stipulation that "by accepting this privilege Miss Calkins does not become a student of the University entitled to registration."[34]

Thus Calkins began to study with James. And when the other members of the seminar dropped out (for unexplained reasons), Calkins found herself and her teacher "quite literally at either side of a library fire. The *Principles of Psychology* was warm from the press, and my absorbed study of those brilliant, erudite, and provocative volumes, as interpreted by their writer, was my introduction to psychology."[35] She immediately proved to be a pupil who could teach her teacher, for during the first year she wrote a paper on "Association" suggesting an elaboration and modification of James's published treatment of that topic. Saying the paper gave him "exquisite delight," James encouraged her to revise and publish it — which she duly did for her first professional publication in 1892. When he soon after revised his chapter on association for his *Briefer Course*, James referred approvingly to this paper.

In the meantime, Calkins was also receiving unofficial but expert advice on how to equip a psychological laboratory from **Edmund C. Sanford** (1859–1924), a young Johns Hopkins Ph.D. whom Hall had brought with him to Clark the year before. Although another ten years would pass before Clark University officially admitted a female student, Sanford agreed to help Calkins to plan a laboratory for Wellesley. Just then preparing the laboratory manual that for years remained the standard in its field, Sanford was arguably the best-qualified person in the world for that job. And like James he found a valued collaborator as well as a pupil in Calkins, as they worked together on an experimental study of dreams ultimately published in Hall's *American Journal of Psychology*.

After this productive year of study, Calkins returned to Wellesley to teach psychology from her small but well-equipped laboratory. Immediately, however, she felt she needed further graduate study. After considering several possibilities, she applied to carry on at Harvard with James's newly arrived protégé, Hugo Münsterberg. Münsterberg enthusiastically supported her application, and the Harvard Corporation grudgingly conceded her permission "to attend the instruction of professor Münsterberg in his laboratory as a guest, but not as a registered student of the University."[36]

Once again Calkins justified her teacher's confidence, as she originated the **paired associates technique** while conducting an important experimental study of associative learning. Here she presented subjects with stimuli consisting of numerals paired with colors. After varying numbers of presentations she showed the colors alone and tested for recall of their paired numerals. She showed that numerals associated with vivid colors were remembered somewhat better than those with neutral colors, but that the single most important determinant of remembering was simply the frequency of exposure to each pair. This study — far more original and extensive than most Ph.D. theses — appeared in print as a monographic supplement to *Psychological Review* in 1896.

The year before, Calkins had requested and been given an unofficial Ph.D. examination. James described her performance as "much the most brilliant examination for the Ph.D. that we have had at Harvard," and he jibed at his junior colleague with the best previous examination: "Now Santayana, go hang yourself." Münsterberg petitioned the Harvard Corporation to reconsider and admit Calkins to official degree candidacy, calling her superior to all the male students, and "surely one of the strongest professors of psychology in the country."[37] The Corporation peremptorily refused.

Thus Calkins returned to Wellesley in 1895 with more than the substance of a Harvard Ph.D., but without the title. And so she would remain for the rest of her life. In 1902 she was offered a *Radcliffe* Ph.D., Radcliffe College having been founded in 1894 as Harvard's coordinate institution for women. But Calkins declined on the grounds that Radcliffe was an undergraduate school that had not even existed during much of the time she studied in Cambridge, and that the degree would not reflect the fact that she had actually worked at *Harvard*. Rather than acquiesce in deception, she would entirely forgo the degree she had earned.

The degreeless Calkins went on to a predictably distinguished professional career at Wellesley. Besides writing a well-received *Introduction to Psychology* in 1901, she developed and advocated throughout the early 1900s an influential psychology of the **self**.

Calkins saw the self as an active, guiding, and purposive agency present in all acts of consciousness, and requiring to be included in any complete introspective report. Although couched in the terms and procedures of an introspective experimental psychology that are no longer common today, Calkins's self theory anticipated in some ways the influential personality theory later developed by the Harvard psychologist **Gordon W. Allport** (1897–1967). In 1905 Calkins was officially recognized by her colleagues in being elected president of the APA—the first woman to be so honored.

Afterward, she followed the model of her teacher James by gradually giving up psychology in favor of philosophy. Here too she distinguished herself, and in 1918 became the first woman elected president of the American Philosophical Association.

In 1903, Calkins and two other women were identified by a poll of their peers as ranking among the fifty most important American psychologists, worthy of having their names starred in the biographical dictionary *American Men of Science.** In making their outstanding careers, all of these women had had to overcome innumerable discriminatory obstacles because of their sex.

Like Calkins, the other two had great difficulty in getting graduate training. The brilliant young mathematician **Christine Ladd-Franklin** (1847–1930) had grudgingly been allowed to attend graduate classes at Johns Hopkins between 1878 and 1882, but not to register officially or earn a Ph.D. Only in 1926 did Hopkins relent and officially award her the degree she had truly earned forty-four years earlier. In the meantime, she had worked in Helmholtz's laboratory and become an acknowledged expert on color vision. In 1892 she published an important paper proposing that red-green color sensitivity marked a later stage of evolutionary development than blue-yellow or black-white. **Margaret Floy Washburn** (1871–1939) audited James McKeen Cattell's graduate courses at Columbia and won his full respect and support, but university authorities denied her official credit. On Cattell's advice she transferred to Cornell, one of the very few universities that did accept women as offi-

*The very title of this dictionary illustrates attitudes typical of the time. Even though it listed a few women from the beginning, its title was not changed to *American Men and Women of Science* until the 1960s.

cial graduate students. There in 1894 she became the first woman actually to obtain a Ph.D. in psychology, under the nominal supervision of the newly arrived E. B. Titchener.

Despite his willingness to supervise female students, Titchener in another way proved to be a poor friend of women's rights. In 1904 he created a "Society of Experimental Psychologists," to meet annually for informal discussion of research problems. In order to help budding careers, Titchener decreed that "youngsters [will be] taken in on an equality with the men who have arrived." But he arbitrarily excluded all women, of any level of accomplishment, on the grounds that their presence would inhibit the men's freedom to smoke and to engage in "frank criticism and discussions."[38] Ladd-Franklin tried vainly for years to join this august body—which in fact *did* constitute an invaluable communication network—but Titchener kept her out. Washburn and one other woman finally did get elected, but only two years after Titchener's death when the Society was a quarter of a century old. In the meantime Washburn had achieved a professional record equaled by few male members of the Society, writing the country's leading comparative psychology textbook, editing several major psychological journals, and in 1921 being the second woman elected president of the APA.

The pioneering efforts of Calkins, Ladd-Franklin, and Washburn helped somewhat to clear the path to graduate training for the next generation of women. By 1917, thirty-nine women had qualified for membership in the APA (usually by completing Ph.D.s), and made up more than ten percent of the total. But even with reputations and credentials, women were still excluded from good jobs at the major universities. Washburn spent her teaching career at Vassar—like Calkins's Wellesley an excellent women's college, but lacking graduate programs in which students could be supervised in truly advanced research. Most women psychologists had to make do with lower-status and lower-paying jobs than Washburn's, often in teacher training schools. Those who did not remain single suffered further discrimination still. Thus Ladd-Franklin, who married and had two children, was never offered anything better than ill-paying, part-time teaching positions despite her impressive qualifications.

Thanks partly to the hard-won accomplishments of these early psychologists, educational and professional doors have opened more fully — if still incompletely — to succeeding generations of women. When a book comparable to this is written fifty or a hundred years hence, reflecting the contributions of our present psychologists, it will assuredly contain a vastly higher percentage of female pioneeers than this one does.

Edward Lee Thorndike The last in our trio of James's students, Edward Lee Thorndike was the son of a Methodist minister. He grew up in a succession of New England towns where his father was appointed for two- or three-year periods, and at seventeen entered Wesleyan University in Middletown, Connecticut. There he edited the college newspaper and won his class tennis championship, in addition to compiling a brilliant academic record. He disliked his only psychology course, taught from a traditional, philosophically oriented textbook. But in preparing for an optional prize examination (which he subsequently won), he had to read parts of James's recently published *Principles of Psychology*. He liked these so much that he bought both volumes for his personal library — the only books outside of literature he purchased voluntarily during his entire Wesleyan career.

Thorndike next went to Harvard for graduate study in English and French literature, but during his first semester also took one of James's psychology courses. This so fascinated him that he took two more the second semester, and changed his field of concentration to psychology. Deciding to become a teacher of psychology, he now sought the quickest possible route to a Ph.D.

At about this time, the English biologist and comparative psychologist **C. Lloyd Morgan** (1852–1936) visited Harvard and spoke of some experiments he had done on the ability of chickens to distinguish among different-colored corn kernels. Although James and Harvard had no tradition in animal psychology, Thorndike evidently decided a study of learning in chickens would provide a relatively quick Ph.D. dissertation. James, who little understood exactly what he was getting into, accepted Thorndike's proposal. Thorndike recalled:

I kept these animals and conducted the experiments in my room until the landlady's protests were imperative. James tried to get the few square feet required for me in the laboratory. . . . He was refused and with his habitual kindness and devotion to underdogs and eccentric aspects of science, harbored my chickens in the cellar of his own home for the rest of the year.[39]

To the delight of James's children, Thorndike constructed a series of pens inside a larger enclosure which contained his chicken flock. Then he placed individual chickens in the pens, and observed how and how quickly they learned to find the exit to the pen and rejoin the flock. At first, a chicken would typically peep loudly and run around agitatedly, in obvious distress, until finally finding the exit. With successive trials, however, both the signs of distress and the time required to find the exit diminished markedly.

At this point, Thorndike began to think of leaving Harvard. For all of James's charisma and helpfulness, he had not built a strong program in psychology. Münsterberg had left Harvard after a three-year stint in 1895, and although he came back in 1897 his continuing presence could not yet be counted on. James's own main interests were shifting to philosophy, so he taught relatively few courses in psychology. Several other graduate students Thorndike knew had come to Cambridge and been inspired by James, but then gone elsewhere to complete their actual Ph.D.s.

In 1897, prompted further by a distressing personal situation, Thorndike too followed this route. He had proposed marriage to a young woman from a nearby town, and been rejected. Wishing to leave the scene of his emotional distress, Thorndike applied successfully (and with James's blessing) for a graduate fellowship under James McKeen Cattell at Columbia University.

Thorndike moved into a New York apartment along with "the most-educated hens in the world," and briefly led his neighbors to believe he was "an animal trainer, sort of a P. T. Barnum lion-trainer, etc."[40] But Cattell soon proved more successful than James had been in finding laboratory space for the animals at Columbia, and after adding cats to his collection, Thorndike was set to perform his most famous research in a proper institutional setting.

Shifting his prime emphasis from the chickens to the cats, he constructed some fifteen makeshift "puzzle boxes" that an enclosed animal could escape from only by making some specific response: pulling a string, pushing a button or lever, etc. In more difficult boxes, the cats had to make *two* responses in sequence in order to escape—for example, pulling a loop and then sliding a latch. In his experiments proper, he placed hungry cats in the boxes, and observed their behavior as they tried to get out and obtain food.

Like Thorndike's chickens, the cats originally responded with a great deal of random-seeming, "trial-and-error" behavior until accidentally making the correct response. (On the more difficult boxes requiring sequences of specific responses, however, some of the subjects never solved the problem at all.) On successive attempts, the trial-and-error behavior gradually decreased and the animals escaped ever more quickly and smoothly.

In discussing these results in his doctoral dissertation, Thorndike suggested that various specific **stimuli** and **responses** became connected or dissociated from each other according to what he called the **law of effect**. This law asserts that when particular stimulus-response sequences are followed by pleasure, those responses tend to be strengthened or "stamped in" the subject's repertoire; responses followed by annoyance or pain tend to be "stamped out." When a cat first encountered the stimulus of being inside a particular puzzle box, it made many responses that *left* it inside. This presumably produced "annoyance," and reduced the likelihood of those unsuccessful responses being repeated. The successful response, once finally made, presumably led to immediate pleasure with escape, and so became stamped in and rendered more likely to be repeated in the future.

Within sixteen months of arriving at Columbia, Thorndike had completed his study, presented it to the APA and the New York Academy of Sciences, written it up as a successful doctoral dissertation, and published it as a monographic supplement to the *Psychological Review*. He had not only finished quickly, but also made a lasting contribution to the literature on animal intelligence and learning. And to cap the year off, the young woman he had left behind in Massachusetts found that absence made her heart grow fonder. Soon thereafter, Elizabeth Moulton became Thorndike's wife.

Following his Ph.D., Thorndike taught for one year at the Women's College of Western Reserve University in Cleveland, then returned to New York for a position at Columbia's Teachers College. There he remained for the rest of his academic career.

Back in New York, Thorndike promptly collaborated on an important study with his friend **Robert Sessions Woodworth** (1869–1962), a fellow James student at Harvard who had also come to Columbia to finish *his* Ph.D. under Cattell. In 1899 they began to investigate the so-called **transfer of training** — the effect of instruction and exercise in one mental function on performance in another. According to the then-popular "doctrine of formal disciplines," such transfer did occur, providing a rationale for instructing students extensively in subjects like classics: The "discipline" acquired in such study presumably transferred to all other areas of mental function, thus preparing students for almost anything.

Thorndike and Woodworth tested this notion by first training subjects in various tasks such as estimating weights or geometrical areas, and then looking for improvement on other tasks more or less similar to those on which training had occurred. Transfer turned out to be very slight, as the authors reported in a major *Psychological Review* paper of 1901.[41] These results seemed consistent with Thorndike's theory of learning from his dissertation: namely, that learning consists of the stamping in or out of highly *specific* stimulus-response connections. They also helped undermine the doctrine of formal disciplines in education, in favor of more specifically task-oriented educational practices.

For the rest of his long career Thorndike remained concerned with human subjects rather than animals, and his work invariably had an applied, functional orientation. Consistent with his early work, he maintained that "intelligence" was not a single thing but a combination of many specific skills and aptitudes, and he accordingly developed intelligence tests that measured skill on separate functions such as arithmetic, vocabulary, and direction-following rather than "general intelligence." He also believed these components of intelligence to be largely hereditary, and strongly agreed with the eugenic policies of Francis Galton. (For more on intelligence testing see Chapter 12.) Interested in how children could better be taught to spell and read, Thorndike made extensive counts of the frequencies with which twenty thousand different English words were used in various kinds of writing, and constructed dictionaries based on the principle that words should always be defined by using terms simpler and more common than themselves.

All of this work led Thorndike to become identified as a leader of the loosely defined movement known as **functionalism** in American psychology. In contrast to Titchenerian "structuralism," which sought only to define and describe the contents of conscious experience, functionalism focused attention on the utility and purpose of behavior.* Of course this orientation had been anticipated by the utilitarian approach of William James. Other leading functionalists of Thorndike's generation included Woodworth at Columbia, and **James Rowland Angell** (1869–1949), **Harvey Carr** (1873–1954), and **John Dewey** (1859–1952) at the University of Chicago.

Thorndike also wrote several textbooks on educational and general psychology, including a 1905 introductory text that carried a warm and generous introduction by William James. His texts enjoyed such success that in 1924 his author's royalties amounted to five times his professor's salary. For his varied accomplishments, Thorndike was elected APA president in 1912, and in 1917 became one of the first psychologists admitted to the National Academy of Sciences. A poll of psychologists in 1921 ranked Thorndike first among those recommended for starred listing in *American Men of Science*. Thus he came to occupy a position at the head of American psychology comparable to that of James a generation earlier.

Of course Thorndike was not James, and his lasting influence and reputation have been somewhat less. Thorndike's books lack the literary flair of his old teacher's, and do not continue to be published. His theories of learning, education, and hereditary intelligence came to be regarded as oversimplified, and the structuralism-

---

*Titchener likened structuralism and functionalism in psychology to anatomy and physiology, respectively, in biology. He argued — without great effect — that just as the physiologist cannot study organic processes until the structures of individual organs have first been clarified by the anatomist, so the functionalist psychologists would have to wait until he and his fellow structuralists had completed their more fundamental work.

functionalism debate lost urgency as the new movement of "behaviorism" swept the American psychological field in the 1920s. Indeed, Thorndike's name is probably best remembered among psychologists today for his very first publications about trial-and-error learning in cats and the law of effect. These provided a starting point for some of the American behaviorists, whose work we shall discuss in the next chapter.

Suggested Readings

For more on James's life see Gay Wilson Allen, *William James: A Biography* (New York: Collier Books, 1967), and Howard M. Feinstein, *Becoming William James* (Ithaca, NY: Cornell University Press, 1984). Biographical information is interspersed with delightful examples of James's correspondence in Henry James, ed., *The Letters of William James*, 2 vols. (Boston: Atlantic Monthly Press, 1920). James's relationship to other American psychologists is well discussed in Daniel W. Bjork, *The Compromised Scientist: William James in the Development of American Psychology* (New York: Columbia University Press, 1983). James's own *Principles of Psychology, Psychology: Briefer Course,* and *The Varieties of Religious Experience* all remain in print in various editions, and are still well worth reading today.

For biographies of Hall and Thorndike see, respectively, Dorothy Ross, *G. Stanley Hall: The Psychologist as Prophet* (Chicago: University of Chicago Press, 1972), and Geraldine Joncich, *The Sane Positivist: A Biography of Edward L. Thorndike* (Middletown, CT: Wesleyan University Press, 1968). The stories of Calkins and her fellow female pioneers are well told in Elizabeth Scarborough and Laurel Furumoto, *Untold Lives: The First Generation of American Women Psychologists* (New York: Columbia University Press, 1987).

9

Psychology as the Science of Behavior: Ivan Pavlov, John B. Watson, and B. F. Skinner

Around the turn of the twentieth century, the eminent Russian physiologist **Ivan Petrovich Pavlov** (1849–1936) felt troubled. He had just completed a monumental set of studies on the physiology of digestion that would shortly win him a Nobel Prize, and was seeking new scientific challenges. Some incidental observations he had made while studying digestion suggested one possibility, but Pavlov questioned its scientific propriety.

His idea was to study a type of salivary reaction he then called "psychic secretions." His earlier research had dealt with innate and reflexive salivary responses in dogs, such as those which occurred automatically and involuntarily whenever food or a mild acid solution was placed in their mouths. But Pavlov had also noted that after dogs became accustomed to laboratory routine, their mouths watered in anticipation while merely being placed in the apparatus in which their salivation was tested. These "psychic" salivary secretions were obviously *learned*, and the result of experience rather than innate reflexes.

Pavlov had already developed apparatus and procedures that could enable him to study these psychic secretions with the same precision he had achieved for innate salivary reflexes. But he worried about the scientific company he might have to keep in such a venture. Psychic secretions seemed obviously within the domain of psychology, and Pavlov disdained the unreliable and introspection-based procedures used by most of his contemporary academic psychologists. It is "open to question," he wrote, "whether psychology is a natural science, or whether it can be regarded as a science at all."[1] Pavlov thought of himself as a rigorous, completely scientific *physiologist*, and he feared being associated with the soft-minded psychologists.

Finally Pavlov resolved his dilemma after recalling *Reflexes of the Brain*, a book written in 1863 by his compatriot **Ivan M. Sechenov** (1829–1905). Sechenov had tried to account for all behavior — including such higher functions as thinking, willing, and judging — in terms of an expanded reflex concept. The higher functions theoretically occurred when acquired reflexes localized in the brain became interposed between the sensory and motor components of innate reflexes. Descartes had long before proposed a similar idea in *Treatise of Man* (see page 21), but Sechenov stated the case in up-to-date physiological language that provided the hint Pavlov needed. Pavlov now decided that his dogs' psychic secretions could be redefined in the pristine physiological terminology of the reflex, while completely avoiding all embarrassing reference to subjective psychological states.

In Pavlov's new terminology, psychic secretions were renamed as **conditioned** (or **conditional**) **reflexes**, while innate digestive responses were called **unconditioned reflexes**. The relations between the two kinds of reflexes could be studied in the laboratory, and interpreted in terms of brain physiology. Pavlov formally banned psychological terminology from his laboratory, and threatened to fire anyone who discussed experiments in mentalistic terms. He spent the rest of his long life studying conditioned reflexes, secure in his belief he was not a psychologist but a physiologist.

Inevitably, however, other people who did consider themselves psychologists took an interest in Pavlov's work. Prime among these

Ivan Pavlov and co-workers in his laboratory at the Military Medical Academy, 1911. *Tass from Sovfoto.*

was the American **John Broadus Watson** (1878–1956), who, like Pavlov, grew suspicious of the unverifiable and "unscientific" nature of introspective psychology. In 1913 Watson electrified American psychologists by asserting that their proper subject was not the traditional mind and its subjective consciousness, but objective, observable *behavior*. Citing Pavlov's conditioned reflex as a model for objective and non-mentalistic theorizing, he went on to create the influential school known as **behaviorism**. This chapter will tell the story of behaviorism, focusing first on the lives and works of Pavlov and Watson, and concluding with **B. F. Skinner** (b. 1904), the Harvard psychologist who has been the movement's most eloquent and effective spokesman in more recent years.

Pavlov's Early Life and Career

Ivan Pavlov was born on 27 September 1849 in the Russian farming village of Ryazan. Although his father was the village priest and his mother the daughter of a priest, both parents had to earn their subsistence by working the fields all day as peasants. At age ten Ivan suffered a serious fall which required a long convalescence in the care of his godfather, the abbot of a nearby monastery. The busy abbot encouraged Ivan to read, but insisted whenever the enthusiastic boy tried to *talk* about his reading that he first write down his observations and comments. This stratagem not only bought the abbot some time free from interruption, but also started young Pavlov on a lifelong habit of systematic observation and reporting.

This habit proved useful in school, and helped Pavlov to benefit from the liberal educational reforms recently instituted by Czar Alexander II. As a poor but gifted student who had done well in school, he won a government-supported scholarship to the University of St. Petersburg (present-day Leningrad). Pavlov's choice of major subject there followed his fortuitous reading of a popularized book on physiology that contained a diagram of the digestive tract. "How does such a complicated system work," the fascinated Pavlov asked himself, and enrolled in the natural science program.[2] Thus he began a scientific quest that would culminate in his Nobel Prize.

At the university Pavlov absorbed the new mechanistic physiology that was then the rage, and became an exceptionally meticulous researcher and organizer, much sought out as an assistant by the faculty and advanced students. He used assistantships to support himself through graduate medical training, being named director of one internal medicine laboratory while still a student. There he helped many doctoral students get *their* degrees even before he completed his own in 1883.

Even though Pavlov had excellent credentials after graduation, good jobs in research were scarce. He had to make do, and support a wife as well, on a series of subordinate and ill-paying positions until he was past forty. In 1890, however, he finally won appointment as a professor at St. Petersburg's Military-Medical Academy, where at last he was free to create and staff his own laboratory, and to pursue his long-standing ambition: experimental study of the physiology of digestion.

Pavlov's Laboratory Pavlov habitually showed two different faces to the world, depending on whether he was outside or inside his laboratory. Outside, he was sentimental, impractical, and absent-minded — often arousing the wonder and amusement of his friends. He became engaged while still a student, and lavished much of his meager income on extravagant luxuries such as candy, flowers, and theater tickets for his fiancée. Only once did he buy her a practical gift, a new pair of shoes to take on a trip. When she arrived at her destination she found only one shoe in her trunk, accompanied by a letter from Pavlov: "Don't look for your other shoe. I took it as a remembrance of you and have put it on my desk."[3] Following marriage, Pavlov often forgot to pick up his pay, and once when he did remember he immediately loaned it all to an irresponsible acquaintance who could not pay it back. On a trip to New York he carried all of his money in a conspicuous wad protruding from his pocket; when he entered the subway at rush hour, the predictable felony ensued and his American hosts had to take up a collection to replace his funds.

But if sentimentality, impracticality, and financial negligence characterized Pavlov's personal life, those traits never showed in his laboratory. In pursuing his research he overlooked no detail. While he uncomplainingly lived frugally at home, he fought ferociously to ensure his laboratory was well equipped and his experimental animals well fed. Punctual in his arrival at the lab and perfectionistic in his experimental technique, he expected the same from his workers. Once during the Russian Revolution he disciplined a worker who showed up late from having to dodge bullets and street skirmishes on the way to the laboratory.

The most remarkable aspect of Pavlov's laboratory was its organization. Whatever his deficiencies in organizing his private life, he ran a large and efficient scientific enterprise that any administrator might envy. Experiments were performed and replicated systematically by the hundreds, according to a simple but ingenious scheme. New workers in the lab were never assigned to new or independent projects, but were required instead to replicate experiments that had already been done. In a single stroke, the new people learned firsthand about work in progress, and provided Pavlov with a check on the reliability of previous results. If the replications succeeded, those results were confirmed and the new worker was ready to move on to something new; if they failed, another replication by a third party would be ordered to resolve the discrepancy.

When he was an old and famous man, Pavlov wrote the following advice in an article for Soviet youth:

This is the message I would like to give the youth of my country. First of all, be systematic. I repeat, be systematic. Train yourself to be strictly systematic in the acquisition of knowledge. First study the rudiments of science before attempting to reach its heights. Never pass to the next stage until you have thoroughly mastered the one on hand.[4]

Someone who only knew Pavlov nonprofessionally might understandably have been incredulous to hear such advice from someone like him. Those who worked in his laboratory, however, knew that he accurately described the secret of his own success.

The Physiology of Digestion Pavlov spent the first decade in his new laboratory attacking the problem that had originally attracted him to science: the complicated workings of the digestive system. Digestion had long resisted direct physiological study, because the organs involved were both concealed and highly susceptible to surgical trauma. When surgically exposed, the digestive organs of experimental animals ceased to function normally; thus observations of them were of limited scientific value. Pavlov's great contribution was to observe *normal* digestive functions in experimental animals, by imitating an almost incredible "natural experiment" that had occurred earlier in the century.

In 1822, a young French-Canadian trapper named Alexis St. Martin suffered a terrible gunshot wound to his stomach. His doctor, **William Beaumont** (1785–1853), thought the wound would be fatal but patched him up as best he could. Surprisingly, however, St. Martin gradually recovered and returned to normal — except for the remarkable fact that the hole in the wall of his stomach never closed up, but remained as a "window" on whatever happened within. Beaumont seized his opportunity, and persuaded St. Martin to serve as a subject for studies of digestion. Beaumont directly observed the stomach as it digested food, and inserted instruments to collect, measure, and analyze the substances it secreted. Until Pavlov, Beaumont's observations of St. Martin provided the best available knowledge about normal digestive processes.

Pavlov decided to replicate Beaumont's observations, only on a more selective and controlled basis, by surgically creating openings, or **fistulas**, in different parts of the digestive tracts of dogs. Others had tried this before and failed, but Pavlov succeeded for two major reasons. First, he was an unusually skillful surgeon who disliked the sight of blood, and who therefore minimized the surgical trauma experienced by his subjects. Second, he was among the first to appreciate the importance of aseptic surgery. At a time when human patients still died by the multitudes from infections contracted in unsanitary surgical wards, Pavlov went to extreme lengths to assure the antiseptic cleanliness of his animal operations. Even though the digestive tract was a particularly dangerous source of infection, most of Pavlov's animals completely recovered from their operations, while most of his predecessors' animals had died.

Pavlov created fistulas in many different parts of the digestive tract, and then conducted hundreds of experiments in his systematic way. After feeding his animals different substances, for example, he collected, measured, and chemically analyzed the resulting secretions from the different parts of the digestive system. These studies won Pavlov the Nobel Prize for physiology in 1904, and are still cited today in modern textbooks on the physiology of digestion.

Among the gastric responses Pavlov studied was salivation, and he learned very early that a splash of dilute acid on a dog's tongue immediately produced a copious secretion. And then, of course, he incidentally noticed the "psychic secretions" of animals who had become accustomed to the laboratory routine: They would begin to salivate even before the acid was splashed on their tongues, as they went through the preliminary procedures of being placed in their experimental apparatus. Thus began his study of conditioned reflexes.

Conditioned Reflexes

Pavlov publicly introduced his idea of conditioned reflexes in his Nobel Prize address of 1904, and then devoted the remaining thirty-two years of his life to their study. Essentially, his studies involved the systematic manipulation of the four basic components of a conditioned reflex, which he named in his new, non-psychological terminology: the **unconditioned stimulus**, the **unconditioned response**, the **conditioned stimulus**, and the **conditioned response**.

An unconditioned stimulus and unconditioned response together constitute an **unconditioned reflex**, the innate and automatic reaction that must exist prior to any conditioning or learning. Descartes had described one unconditioned reflex, although he did not call it that, when he wrote of the heat from a fire (an unconditioned stimulus) producing the automatic withdrawal of a hand that has been brought too near (the unconditioned response). Pavlov's earlier research had focused on unconditioned gastric reflexes, such as the salivation (unconditioned response) automatically produced when dilute acid was splashed in the mouth (the unconditioned stimulus).

Pavlov noted that a typical conditioned stimulus starts out by being "neutral" and eliciting no strong response at all, but subsequently *acquires* the property of eliciting a response after being paired with an unconditioned stimulus a number of times. For his dogs, the sight of their keeper at mealtime or the experience of being placed in their experimental apparatus became conditioned stimuli regularly followed by the unconditioned stimuli of food or acid in the mouth. Soon, these originally neutral stimuli aroused salivation all by themselves, in new stimulus-response connections that Pavlov called conditioned reflexes.

Although conceptually very simple, conditioned reflexes lent themselves perfectly to the sort of systematic research program that Pavlov was so good at. To start, he could systematically vary the types of stimuli, the numbers of pairings, and the conditions under which they occurred, and observe the strengths of the resulting conditioned reflexes. The following example illustrates one of his earliest but most fundamental experiments.

Here a tone served as the conditioned stimulus, followed immediately by the unconditioned stimulus of dilute acid on the tongue. Pavlov varied the number of pairings of these two stimuli before presenting the tone *without* the acid, to see how many were necessary for conditioning to occur. Dogs received 1, 10, 20, 30, 40, or 50 pairings before the test, with their response magnitudes measured by the number of drops of saliva secreted, and latencies by the number of seconds between the presentation of the tone and the first observable salivation:

Number of Pairings	Response Magnitude	Response Latency
1	0	—
10	6	18
20	20	9
30	60	2
40	62	1
50	59	2

Thus the conditioned reflexes became progressively stronger, with response magnitudes regularly increasing and latencies decreasing, over the first thirty or so pairings; after that, the conditioned reflex's strength leveled off.

Other early experiments varied the time interval between the conditioned and unconditioned stimuli, and showed that the strongest and quickest conditioning occurred when the interval was short. If the conditioned stimulus *followed* the unconditioned stimulus, however — even by a very short interval — no conditioned reflexes were produced at all. Another series of basic studies demonstrated **higher-order conditioning**, where a strong conditioned salivary reflex was first established to one stimulus such as the sound of a bell, which then served as the unconditioned stimulus in a further series of pairings with *another* conditioned stimulus such as a flash of light. Thus the bell was first paired with a mild acidic solution, then the light was paired with the bell, and the animals became conditioned to salivate to the light.

Generalization, Differentiation, and Experimental Neuroses Another important series of experiments showed that conditioned reflexes could be elicited by stimuli similar but not identical to the original conditioned stimulus — a phenomenon Pavlov called **generalization**. Thus when a tone of one pitch served as the conditioned stimulus during training, but the test was made with a slightly higher or lower tone, a conditioned reflex still occurred but with somewhat diminished magnitude. The greater the dissimilarity between the conditioned and test stimuli, the weaker was the generalized response.

If the dissimilar stimulus was then presented repeatedly, but never "reinforced" by a succeeding unconditioned stimulus, a further kind of learning occurred that Pavlov called **differentiation**. For example, a dog was first conditioned to salivate to an image of a circle flashed on a screen. Then, the circular stimulus was randomly alternated with an oblong, elliptical figure of about the same size; each presentation of the circle was followed by a splash of acid on the tongue, while the ellipse was never so reinforced. At first, generalization occurred and the dog salivated copiously to the ellipse; but after repeated trials the response to the ellipse decreased in strength and finally disappeared altogether. A differentiation had occurred.

Some of Pavlov's most surprising results occurred when he tested the limits of his animals' ability to differentiate. In the circle-ellipse differentiation, for example, he started with a very oblong ellipse. When the dog stopped salivating to that, he shifted to another that was slightly less oblong and more circle-like. After the animal successfully differentiated that from the circle, he tried one that was more circular still, and so on, progressively reducing the difference between the stimuli. When the non-reinforced stimulus became almost circular, with its height to width in a 9 to 8 ratio, a sudden and dramatic change came over the dog's behavior. Previously placid and tractable, the animal now made frantic efforts to escape from its apparatus, and *remained* agitated and hard to handle long afterward. In fact, animals forced to confront this ambiguous stimulus for very long remained disturbed for weeks or months after the experiment. When re-tested on some of the easier differentiations that had been easily mastered before the crucial trial, the dogs failed. Likening this behavior to stress-induced breakdowns in human beings, Pavlov called these reactions **experimental neuroses**.

From experiments like this, Pavlov theorized that experimental neuroses were likely to occur whenever animals were confronted by unavoidable *conflicts* between two strong but incompatible conditioned-response tendencies; for example, to salivate or to suppress salivation at the sight of the ambiguous ellipse. And from this basic idea, he deduced a new theory of brain functioning.

Pavlov's Theory of the Brain As a self-identified physiologist, Pavlov tried to account for his conditioning results in terms of a physiological theory. Following Sechenov, he argued that unconditioned reflexes are mediated by connections between sensory and motor nerves in the spinal cord and the lower brain centers. Conditioned reflexes presumably occurred when neural pathways in the *cortex* became part of the circuitry, connecting stimuli with responses in new combinations. Crude evidence for the cortical localization of conditioned reflexes came from animals whose cortexes were surgically ablated after they had acquired some conditioned reflexes. Although these animals could be kept alive for several years with full retention of their *un*conditioned reflexes, they permanently lost all of their old conditioned reflexes and never acquired any new ones.

Consistent with the recent discoveries of cortical localization described in Chapter 3, Pavlov reasoned that different conditioned stimuli must excite different specific locations on the cortex, with the locations for similar stimuli lying closer together than those for dissimilar stimuli. He further speculated that two distinctly different kinds of processes must occur in these locations to produce conditioning — **excitation** presumably leads to the acquisition or generalization of conditioned responses, while **inhibition** causes an already acquired response tendency to be suppressed.

Pavlov suggested that excitatory processes arise in a cortical area when the stimulus represented there is reinforced by the presentation of an unconditioned stimulus. Inhibitory processes arise when such reinforcement fails to occur. Moreover, he argued that excitation and inhibition must **irradiate** or spread out in a wavelike fashion over surrounding locations, with their strength dissipating as they get farther away from their center. Cerebral irradiation had never been actually observed (and still has not been), but Pavlov noted that such a process could theoretically account for the phenomena of generalization, differentiation, and experimental neurosis.

In generalization, the presentation of a similar alternative stimulus presumably arouses a wave of excitation in a cortical center *close to* that for the original conditioned stimulus. As the irradiation spreads, it soon reaches and excites the location of the original stimulus, which has acquired (by conditioning) connections to the salivary response apparatus. Thus a salivary response is initiated, although somewhat diminished in strength because the excitation at the conditioned stimulus's location has been partly dissipated through irradiation.

In differentiation training, the cortical centers representing non-reinforced stimuli presumably begin to send out waves of inhibition instead of excitation. Stimuli immediately surrounding these centers correspondingly *lose* the ability to arouse generalized conditioned reflexes. If *many* surrounding stimuli are systematically non-reinforced, the entire cortex surrounding the center for the true conditioned stimulus becomes a field for inhibition rather than excitation. As one textbook observes: "When a [differentiation] is firmly established, only a small region of the brain corresponding to the conditional stimulus will produce a response. Inhibition lies over the rest of the brain like winter over the empty plains of central Russia, limiting all activity to the lonely stockades.[5]

The winter snow metaphor partly misleads, however, by suggesting that inhibition-irradiated areas of the cortex are inert. To the contrary, Pavlov thought of them as fields of great potential energy, which under the conditions of experimental neurosis can violently influence behavior. Pavlov hypothesized that experimental neurosis occurs whenever a stimulus that cannot be avoided arouses very strong excitation and inhibition at the same time. That is, its cortical location lies exactly on a "boundary" between powerful excitatory and inhibitory fields. When this location is strongly stimulated, the boundary may literally "rupture," so the entire cortical region becomes inundated with an indiscriminate mixture of both excitation and inhibition. These two forces, previously confined within boundaries and producing the precise and regular effects of generalization or differentiation, now intermix wildly and produce the disorganized behavior of experimental neuroses.

While studying experimental neuroses in dogs, Pavlov made a further observation that stimulated his major interest for the final years of his life. He noted striking individual differences in the specific symptoms of his subjects. Those animals that had been naturally very active in temperament before the experiments became excessively so in their neuroses — snapping, chewing, howling, and clawing indiscriminately. Animals with more placid prior dispositions tended to develop more "depressive" types of symptoms, such as excessive lethargy and apathy. Pavlov hypothesized that the naturally active animals had brains with more excitatory than inhibitory energy innately within them, while for the "depressive" animals the proportions were reversed. Thus each animal's particular type of neurosis depended on the excitatory or inhibitory predilections of its brain.

In 1929, the eighty-year-old Pavlov began seriously to contemplate the implications of this theory for *human* psychopathology. He attempted to account for the varieties of psychiatric illness in terms of an excess or deficiency of excitation and inhibition, the weakening of cortical neurons, and other variables he had found to be related to experimental neuroses in dogs. He devised physical therapies for these presumed deficiencies, intended to rest or exercise the brain cells at fault or to restore them to health by the application of chemicals such as bromides. In doing so he established a strong tradition of organically based psychiatric treatment in the Soviet Union that continues today.

Pavlov's Influence Pavlov worked vigorously and full time on his new psychiatric projects until 21 February 1936, when he fell ill after a full day's work. As his symptoms rapidly worsened into pneumonia, Pavlov characteristically made systematic observations of his mental state. On the afternoon of 27 February he told his doctor: "My brain is not working well; obsessive feelings and involuntary movements appear; mortification may be setting in."[6] An hour after making this final scientific observation, the eighty-six-year-old Pavlov died.

By the time of his death, Pavlov was a Soviet national hero with even a new town named after him. The government had recognized his value not just as a prestigious representative of Soviet science, but also as promoter of a properly materialistic theory that could form the foundation of a Marxist psychology. He remains a dominant figure in Soviet psychology today.

By the time of his death, Pavlov's influence had also spread to the United States, where his non-mentalistic approach appealed strongly to a group of young scientists who called themselves **behaviorists**. But unlike Pavlov, who steadfastly insisted he was not a psychologist but a physiologist, the behaviorists changed their definition of psychology so as to accommodate their non-mentalistic orientation. Less concerned than Pavlov about the cortical and neurological underpinnings of conditioning, the behaviorists used techniques like his to establish *behavioral* laws regarding stimuli and responses that could stand independent of physiology. For them, psychology became transformed from the science of consciousness or the mind to the science of behavior. We turn now to the story of the founder of American behaviorism.

Watson's Early Life and Career

John Broadus Watson was born on 9 January 1878 near Greenville, South Carolina, the son of a wayward father and a deeply pious mother. Named after John Broadus, a local fundamentalist minister, and constantly steered in a religious direction by his mother, young Watson nonetheless developed a fierce rebellious streak that became a permanent part of his character. His youthful pugnacity earned him the nickname "Swats," and as a teenager he got arrested for fighting and for firing a gun inside city limits. He recalled that at school "I was lazy, somewhat insubordinate, and . . . never made above a passing grade."[7]

Still, Watson at sixteen gained admission as a sub-freshman to Greenville's Furman University, where his mother hoped he would prepare for a career as a clergyman. He almost did, succeeding in his courses and applying to Princeton Theological Seminary in 1899. He would have gone there were it not for a peculiar but characteristic episode during his senior year. His philosophy and psychology professor, Gordon Moore, had warned that any student handing in a paper with the pages backwards would automatically flunk. Watson had been an honor student all year, but, as he put it, "by some strange streak of luck, I handed in my final paper . . . backwards." Moore kept his word, and Watson had to return for an extra year at Furman instead of enrolling in seminary. As partial recompense, he was graduated from Furman in 1900 with a master's rather than a bachelor's degree.

During that extra year Watson's mother died, so he no longer faced family pressure to become a minister. He now made an "adolescent resolve" to upstage his professor by earning a Ph.D. (which Moore did not hold) and one day inducing the older man

John Broadus Watson (1878–1958). *Archives of the History of American Psychology, University of Akron.*

to come to *him* for training. Moore genuinely appreciated Watson's raw ability and helped him get admitted to the still-undivided philosophy-psychology department at the recently founded University of Chicago. (A dozen years later, Moore actually did apply to study with Watson, but sadly had to abandon the plan because of failing eyesight.[8])

Watson went to Chicago expecting to work with the department's eminent chairman, and leader of American "functional" psychology,

289

John Dewey (1859–1952). Ever the maverick, he found Dewey's approach uncongenial: "I never knew what he was talking about then, and unfortunately for me, I still don't know," Watson recalled in his autobiography. Equally unappealing were the introspective methods required for much of the traditional psychological research conducted in the department: "I hated to serve as a subject. I didn't like the stuffy, artificial instructions given to subjects. I was always uncomfortable and acted unnaturally."[9] A fellow student remembered that Watson never learned to give consistent introspective reports that agreed with everyone else's.[10]

But if the philosophical and introspective aspects of psychology came hard, Watson found an emerging area of *animal* study at Chicago in which he truly excelled. As a country boy comfortable with animals, Watson felt at home in this field. He was particularly attracted by the work of department members **Jacques Loeb** (1859–1924), the staunchly mechanistic biologist who had introduced the concept of "tropism" to account for plant and animal movement, and **Henry H. Donaldson** (1857–1938), a neurologist who studied the nervous system of white rats. Donaldson proved supportive practically as well as intellectually, hiring the financially pressed graduate student to tend his colony of experimental rats. As Watson became intimately familiar with the behavior of these tame creatures, he realized they would make suitable subjects for his own doctoral thesis research. Under the joint supervision of Donaldson and psychologist James Angell, he demonstrated that the increasing complexity in the behavior of developing young rats was strongly correlated with increasing growth of myelin sheaths around the neural fibers in their brains. In 1903, Donaldson loaned Watson $350 to publish his thesis under the rather unbehavioristic-sounding title *Animal Education: The Psychical Development of the White Rat.*

Despite his difficulties with traditional psychology, Watson the animal psychologist had become a departmental star — the youngest Ph.D. yet turned out by the university, with the second-best final examination in his department's history. Success came at a price, however, for Watson had had to hold several jobs to support himself, and overwork contributed to an emotional breakdown. He could not sleep without a light on, and suffered anxiety attacks that dissipated only after taking ten-mile walks. He later hinted that sexual concerns may have been involved, when he reported that his breakdown "in a way prepared me to accept a large part of Freud."[11]

Watson's breakdown coincided with complications in his personal life, following his rejection by one young woman he had fallen in love with, and his subsequent engagement to a nineteen-year-old student named Mary Ickes. Mary's brother Harold — a rising figure in Chicago politics who would later become President Franklin Roosevelt's Secretary of the Interior — saw Watson as unreliable, and violently opposed the match with his sister. Thus Watson and Mary married secretly in December of 1903, but lived apart and did not publicly declare their status until the fall of 1904.[12]

Professionally, Watson's life went more smoothly. As an expert in the newly emerging area of animal psychology, he found himself in demand and received several job offers. He elected to stay at Chicago as an instructor, and four years later was about to become promoted to assistant professor there when he was offered an associate professorship by Johns Hopkins University, at the comfortable salary of $2,500 per year. When he hesitated in hopes Chicago would match the associate professorship, Hopkins increased its offer to a full professorship at $3,500. Although Watson liked Chicago, this was more than he could refuse. He set off for Baltimore at age twenty-nine, to assume a major position at one of America's major universities.

The Founding of Behaviorism At Hopkins, Watson's good luck continued. A year after he arrived, his department chairman was arrested in a bordello and resigned in the ensuing scandal. As the department's only remaining full professor, Watson inherited its leadership as well as the editorship of an important journal, the *Psychological Review*. From his position of power Watson immediately began pressing the university president to separate psychology from philosophy, and to forge new ties between psychology and biology.

For a while, he maintained an uneasy alliance with traditional academic psychology and taught courses along the lines of James and Wundt while conducting his own research on animals. But he increasingly bridled when people asked what his research had to do with "real" psychology — which they took to be the study of conscious experience. "I was interested in my own work and felt it was important," he complained, "yet I could not trace any connection between it and psychology as my questioner understood psychology."[13] With characteristic boldness, Watson decided no longer to accommodate himself to the traditional definition of psychology, but instead to redefine psychology so it afforded his specialty a dominant position.

He started to do so in 1913, with an article entitled "Psychology as the Behaviorist Views It," which he conveniently published in *Psychological Review*. The opening paragraph clearly defined the new "behavioristic" psychology he envisioned:

Psychology as the behaviorist views it is a purely objective natural science. Its theoretical goal is the prediction and control of behavior. Introspection forms no essential part of its methods, nor is the scientific value of its data dependent upon the readiness with which they lend themselves to interpretation in terms of consciousness. The behaviorist, in his attempts to get a unitary scheme of animal response, recognizes no dividing line between man and brute. The behavior of man, with all of its refinement and complexity, forms only a part of the behaviorist's total scheme of investigation.[14]

Here Watson declared independence from traditional psychology in three ways. First, he asserted that a properly behavioristic psychology must be completely objective and rule out *all* subjective data or interpretations in terms of conscious experience. While traditional psychology employed objective observations to complement or supplement introspective data, for Watson they became the sole basis of psychology.

Second, Watson declared that psychology's goal was not to *describe and explain* conscious states, as the traditionalists would have it, but rather to *predict and control* overt behavior. Behavioristic psychology was to be highly practical, much more concerned with concrete effectiveness than with theoretical understanding.

And finally, Watson denied the traditional psychological distinction between humans and other animals. Drawing on Darwin's demonstration of the common ancestry of all animal species, Watson argued that psychological similarities among species were just as important as differences. Studies of the behavior of apes, rats, pigeons, and even flatworms should interest psychologists because of the continuity of life forms.

Watson's Behavioristic Writings

After declaring the general principles of a behavioristic psychology, Watson faced the problem of actually putting them into practice. His first attempt, a 1914 textbook entitled *Behavior: An Introduction to Comparative Psychology*, reprinted "Psychology as the Behaviorist Views It" as its first chapter, and went on to summarize the field of animal psychology. The book was well received as a comprehensive account of that field, and enhanced Watson's reputation as he successfully ran for president of the American Psychological Association. But despite the radical prescriptions of its opening chapter, the book had little to say about human psychology and as a whole hardly seemed revolutionary.

Although Watson had condemned introspection he had not yet been able to replace it, and he candidly admitted as much in the opening of his presidential speech to the American Psychological Association in 1915:

Since the publication two years ago of my somewhat impolite papers against current methods in psychology I have felt it incumbent upon me before making further unpleasant remarks to suggest some method which we might *begin* to use in place of introspection. I have found, as you easily might have predicted, that it is one thing to condemn a long-established method, but quite another thing to suggest anything in its place.[15]

But now Watson saw the beginnings of an answer, since his graduate student **Karl Lashley** (1890–1959) had introduced him to recent Russian writings on the conditioned reflex.* He thus learned about Pavlov's conditioned salivary reflexes, and about the related work of Pavlov's compatriot **Vladimir M. Bechterev** (1857–1927). Bechterev had extended Pavlov's technique to study muscular responses such as the withdrawal of a paw when electric shock was administered as the unconditioned stimulus. He had also tried con-

---

*Lashley went on in his career to become a leading neuropsychologist, and to conduct the studies on cerebral localization of memory reviewed on pages 94–97.

ditioning *human* subjects, an idea that Lashley and Watson pushed further. Thus Lashley had devised a removable tube that could be fitted inside the cheek of human subjects and used to measure their salivations. And Watson had constructed an apparatus that administered mild shock to a human subject's finger or toe and measured the strength of the subsequent withdrawal reflex. After pairing neutral conditioned stimuli with shock, he had been able to obtain and measure conditioned withdrawal responses.

Watson believed the main significance of these studies lay not in the bare fact that people and dogs could both be conditioned to salivate to or withdraw their toes from inherently neutral stimuli, but in their implications for further and broader conditioning experiments. Pavlov as a physiologist had been more interested in the brain than in the behavior of his subjects, and for drawing his speculative physiological inferences one type of response — salivation — had been as good as any other. Watson, however, sought a general principle to account for many different kinds of behavior, and seized upon the conditioned reflex as a *model* for a wide variety of different responses. In particular, he suggested in his presidential address that human *emotions* might profitably be thought of as glandular and muscular reflexes which, like salivation, easily become conditioned. If so, then Pavlovian conditioning offered a properly behavioristic, non-introspective avenue to studying one of the most important and complicated subjects in human psychology.

Conditioned Emotional Reactions In 1917, shortly after Watson's APA address, his plan to extend behavioristic methods into human psychology had to be temporarily shelved when the United States entered World War I. He entered the service as a major in the Signal Corps, where his job was to help select and train aviators. Predictably enough, he chafed at the authoritarian military atmosphere, and let his contempt for his superiors show. They, in turn, recommended "that he be not allowed to serve his country in his scientific capacity, but be sent to the line." Only the war's quick end in 1918 spared him from assignment to a highly dangerous intelligence mission.[16]

Safely returned to Johns Hopkins and civilian life, Watson took up where he had left off, and in 1919 published *Psychology from the Standpoint of a Behaviorist*. While his first book had limited itself to comparative and animal psychology, this one aimed at being a *general* text concentrating on *human* behavior — covering such subjects as thought, language, child development, and emotion. As promised, research on conditioned reflexes played a large part in the book, especially its treatment of emotions.

Watson began by asking what human emotional responses were innate and "unconditioned," and in answer described his observations of human infants who presumably had not yet had time to acquire any conditioned responses. (Infants made excellent behavioristic subjects because they could not talk and contaminate the experiments with subjective or introspective reports.) He had presented a great variety of different stimuli to babies, to see what sorts of reactions they elicited, and he had concluded that there were just three kinds of unconditioned emotional responses, each one produced by a surprisingly small number of stimuli.

First, Watson observed an apparently innate **fear response**, defined behavioristically as "a sudden catching of the breath, clutching randomly with the hands, . . . sudden closing of the eyelids, puckering of the lips, then crying."[17] Only two kinds of stimuli seemed able to produce this reaction in very young infants: a sudden and unexpected loud sound, or the sudden loss of support as when the infant was suddenly dropped (and then caught without any physical harm being done). Infants did *not* react in this or any other dramatic way when confronted with darkness or other stimuli commonly regarded as fearful by older people. (Thus Watson must have concluded that his own fear and inability to sleep in the dark during his emotional breakdown in Chicago had been an acquired rather than an innate emotional reaction.)

Second, Watson observed an emotional reaction in infants he called **rage**, in which "the body stiffens and fairly well-coordinated slashing or striking movements of the hands and arms result; the feet and legs are drawn up and down; the breath is held until the child's face is flushed." Just one kind of stimulus — the physical hindering of movement — produced this reaction in a newborn: "Almost any child from birth can be thrown into a rage if its arms are held

295

tightly to its sides; sometimes even if the elbow joint is clasped tightly between the fingers the response appears; at times just the placing of the head between cotton pads will produce it."[18]

Finally, Watson saw evidence for a third unconditioned emotion in infants that he provisionally called **love**:

The original situation which calls out the observable love response seems to be the stroking or manipulation of some erogenous zone, tickling, shaking, gentle rocking, patting and turning on the stomach across the attendant's knee. The response varies. If the infant is crying, crying ceases, a smile may appear, attempts at gurgling, cooing, and finally, in older children, the extension of the arms, which we should class as the forerunner of the embrace of adults.[19]

Watson believed that these three responses, and the restricted range of stimuli that produced them, made up the entire complement of innate human emotional reactions. He saw everything else, including such supposedly "natural" reactions as fear of the dark and love for one's mother, as the results of Pavlovian-style conditioning: "When an emotionally exciting object stimulates the subject simultaneously with one not emotionally stimulating, the latter may in time (often after one such joint stimulation) arouse the same emotional reaction as the former."[20] All the complications and complexities of adult emotional experience were presumably nothing more than conditioned responses built upon three relatively simple unconditioned emotional reflexes.

When he wrote his textbook in 1919, Watson had no real experimental support for this theory. It seemed plausible, but he had never observed the actual creation of a conditioned emotional reaction. In 1920 he attempted to remedy this deficiency in an experiment conducted with his graduate student **Rosalie Rayner** (1899–1936). Published under the title "Conditioned Emotional Reactions," the Watson-Rayner study of "Little Albert" remains today one of the most famous and controversial in psychological literature. They conditioned "Albert B.," the eleven-month-old son of a worker in the hospital where they conducted the experiment, to fear a white rat — a stimulus that initially evoked his interest and pleasure rather than fear. For their unconditioned stimulus they loudly struck a steel bar with a hammer just behind Albert's head. They described the first trials as follows:

1. White rat suddenly taken from the basket and presented to Albert. He began to reach for the rat with left hand. Just as his hand touched the animal the bar was struck immediately behind his head. The infant jumped violently and fell forward, burying his face in the mattress. He did not cry, however.

2. Just as the right hand touched the rat the bar was again struck. Again the infant jumped violently, fell forward and began to whimper. In order not to disturb the child too seriously no further tests were given for one week.[21]

When Albert first saw the rat the next week, he kept his distance from the animal but did not cry. Then, on five separate occasions, the experimenters deliberately moved the rat close to Albert and clanged the bar behind his head. After this, the rat alone produced a full-fledged fear response: "The instant the rat was shown the baby began to cry. Almost instantly he turned sharply to the left, fell over on his left side, raised himself on all fours and began to crawl away so rapidly that he was caught with difficulty before reaching the edge of the table."[22]

Five days later Albert still responded to the rat with whimpering and withdrawal. Watson and Rayner tested for generalization of the conditioned response by presenting other furry stimuli: a rabbit, a dog, a seal coat, cotton wool, and a Santa Claus mask. Each produced a noticeable but weakened avoidance reaction. Then Watson put his own hair — which was showing streaks of white — near the child, and got a poetically just response: "Albert was completely negative. Two other observers did the same thing. He began immediately to play with their hair."[23]

Later, Watson and Rayner decided for some unstated reason to "freshen" Albert's generalized response to the rabbit and dog, and clanged the bar after presentation of each of those stimuli. The white rat was similarly freshened, and then Albert was presented with all three stimuli in a room different from that in which the conditioning had occurred. Albert actively feared them all in this new setting. After a further month with no trials at all, Albert was retested with the Santa mask, the fur coat, the rat, the rabbit, and the dog. All still produced pronounced fear responses.

And that was the last Watson and Rayner saw of Little Albert! Irresponsibly — at least from the standpoint of today's research ethics — they let him leave the hospital without trying to decondition the fears they had so spectacularly produced. They only added a section to their paper describing what they *would have* done:

Had the opportunity been at hand we should have tried out several methods, some of which we may mention. 1) Constantly confronting the child with those stimuli which called out the responses in hopes that habituation would come in. . . . 2) By trying to "recondition" by showing objects calling out fear responses (visual) and simultaneously stimulating the erogenous zones (tactual). We should first try the lips, then the nipples and as a final resort the sex organs. 3) By trying to "recondition" by feeding the subject candy or other food just as the animal is shown. . . . 4) By building up "constructive" activities around the object by imitation and by putting the hand through motions of manipulation.[24]

Some of these suggested techniques have since been used with varying degrees of success by behavior therapists, but such words must have come as cold comfort to Albert's mother, if she saw them at all. Moreover, Watson and Rayner stated that the fear responses "in the home environment are likely to persist indefinitely, unless an accidental method for removing them is hit upon." And in a concluding tasteless section of their article, they ridiculed the Freudian psychoanalyst who might one day try to treat Albert's phobia:

The Freudians twenty years from now, . . . when they come to analyze Albert's fear of a seal skin coat . . . will probably tease from him a recital of a dream which upon their analysis will show that Albert at three years of age attempted to play with the pubic hair of the mother and was scolded violently for it. If the analyst has sufficiently prepared Albert to accept such a dream . . . he may be fully convinced that the dream was a true revealer of the factors which brought about the fear.[25]

The sensationalistic tone of "Conditioned Emotional Reactions" was soon echoed in events surrounding Watson and Rayner's personal lives. They fell in love, had an affair, and were discovered by Mary Watson. Encouraged by Harold Ickes, who still despised his brother-in-law and had once even hired a private detective to uncover damaging information about him, she divorced him.[26] Although such an event would make little news today, both the Rayners and the Ickeses were socially prominent families, and Baltimore newspapers gave the story full play. Johns Hopkins had just become coeducational and its administration, particularly sensitive to scandal at that time, forced Watson's resignation. He happily married Rayner, but suddenly found himself in need of a new job. A new and entirely different phase of his career was about to begin.

Advertising and Behaviorism Watson moved to New York, where he soon received job offers from the New School of Social Research and the J. Walter Thompson advertising agency—the latter at a salary of $25,000 per year, four times his previous professor's pay. This eased his sense of loss when he chose advertising over academia, and he plunged into his new career with typical vigor. He started by getting practical experience in the field—doing door-to-door surveys in the rural South to determine the market for rubber boots, peddling Yuban coffee in Pittsburgh, and working part time as a clerk in Macy's department store in New York to study consumer attitudes. Then, back in the main office, he helped plan many innovative and successful advertising campaigns. He got Queen Marie of Roumania to endorse the beauty-enhancing qualities of Pond's cold cream, in one of the first uses of celebrity testimonials in advertising. He hired pediatricians to vouch for the infection-fighting properties of Johnson and Johnson's baby powder, and pretty models to suggest that it was fine for women to smoke as long as they brushed their teeth with Pebeco toothpaste.[27] As Watson later put it, "I began to learn that it can be just as thrilling to watch the growth of a sales curve of a new product as to watch the learning curve of animals or man."[28] By 1924 he was a vice-president of the agency.

He still kept a hand in psychology, however, lecturing part time at the New School for Social Research, and in 1924 publishing those lectures under the title *Behaviorism*. Here Watson employed his new communication skills to produce his most engaging and flamboyantly written book; it sold well, and was acclaimed by a *New York Times* review as marking "a new epoch in the intellectual history of man."[29] While that evaluation may have been exaggerated, the book did present the behaviorist viewpoint with completeness, flair, and colorful examples.

For example, Watson's discussion of conditioned emotions was not only illustrated by the case of Albert, but further enlivened by descriptions of children's behavior when their parents fight or make love in their presence. In accounting for personality disturbances as the potentially reversible results of maladaptive conditioning, Watson described a hypothetical dog who might be first conditioned to sleep in an ash can, foul its own bed, salivate constantly, and fear small animals — before being deconditioned of all these symptoms and turned into a blue-ribbon winner at the dog show.

He also turned his behaviorist's eye toward one of the most popular and controversial concepts of psychoanalysis, unconscious thought. In a chapter entitled "Do We Always Think in Words?" Watson suggested that unconscious thought indeed exists, but not as the mysterious metaphysical entity he accused the psychoanalysts of fostering. He started by defining conscious thought as a series of vocal or subvocal verbal responses; that is, the conscious thinker literally talks to him- or herself. Each verbal response presumably serves as a stimulus capable of calling up one or more new responses, so thinking proceeds in a chainlike fashion. All of the newly elicited responses need not be verbal, however; they can also be visceral or kinaesthetic, and can include emotional reactions. These nonverbal reactions can serve as links in the chain of thought, and call up their own verbal or nonverbal responses. Thus they function as important and sometimes emotion-laden parts of the thought process, but since they are nonverbal they are not experienced as "conscious" by the thinker.

In *Behaviorism*, Watson also strongly presented a case for **radical environmentalism**, the view that environmental factors have overwhelmingly greater importance than heredity or constitution in determining behavior. Of course his theory of emotions had suggested that the great variety of human emotional response derives from the conditioning of just three, relatively simple innate reflexes. He now suggested it was much the same for all other aspects of human personality — that innate factors were so quickly modified and developed by conditioning and experience as to become virtually negligible in accounting for individual differences in human adults. "We draw the conclusion," he wrote, "that there is no such thing as an inheritance of *capacity, talent, temperament, mental constitu-*

tion, and *characteristics.* These things . . . depend on training that goes on mainly in the cradle. . . . A certain type of structure, plus early training — *slanting* — accounts for adult performance." He continued, in one of his most famous passages, to emphasize the degree of *control* caretakers could potentially exert over the development of children, if only they systematically applied the principles of conditioning:

Give me a dozen healthy infants, well-formed, and my own specified world to bring them up in and I'll guarantee to take any one at random and train him to become any type of specialist I might select — doctor, lawyer, merchant-chief and yes, even beggar-man and thief, regardless of his talents, penchants, tendencies, abilities, vocations, and race of his ancestors.[30]

If Watson heard the ground rumble beneath his feet as he wrote that passage, it was perhaps the ghost of Francis Galton rolling over in his grave. Of course, Watson could *prove* his radical environmentalist hypothesis no more than Galton had been able to prove its hereditarian counterpart. But the passage clearly and colorfully stated the case for radical environmentalism, and set the scene for the next stage in Watson's psychological career, in which he attempted to prescribe exactly *how* a good behaviorist should go about raising and training well-adjusted children.

Psychological Care of Infant and Child   Following the success of *Behaviorism,* Watson's psychological writings became geared increasingly to the general public, and appeared in popular magazines rather than scholarly journals. Many bore catchy titles, such as "The Weakness of Women," "What about Your Child?" and "Feed Me on Facts," and dealt with practical issues in childrearing. Assisted by his wife, Watson in 1928 published *Psychological Care of Infant and Child,* a how-to book on childrearing that achieved considerable popular success.

Consistent with Watson's radical environmentalism, this book urged parents to take direct and frankly manipulative control of their children's environments, quite contrarily to the permissive "progressive education" advocated by Watson's old teacher and nemesis, John Dewey. Dewey, said Watson, espoused a "doctrine of mystery" according to which "there are hidden springs of activity, hidden possibilities of unfolding within the child which must be waited for until they appear and then be fostered and tended." Watson argued that, in reality, "there is nothing from within to develop."[31] Parents need only to control their children's environments properly, so the most adaptive conditioned reflexes will develop.

Thus the book elaborated Watson's theory of emotions, and offered practical suggestions about how to avoid the creation of inappropriate conditioned emotional reactions. The home should be set up to minimize the occurrence of banging doors and other random loud sounds that would frighten the child and establish inappropriate fear reactions. Clothing should always be loose enough to allow free movement and prevent unnecessary rage. And above all, Watson recommended that children should *never* be stimulated into "love" responses when they ought to be developing self-reliant behavior. Nothing drew his scorn more than the coddling of children, which he saw as the rewarding of ineffective behavior with hugs, kisses, or other signs of solicitude. "When I hear a mother say 'Bless its little heart' when it falls down, stubs its toe, or suffers some other ill," he grumbled, "I usually have to walk a block or two to let off steam." Instead, parents should treat children "as though they were young adults." "Never hug and kiss them, never let them sit on your lap. If you must, kiss them once on the forehead when they say good night. Shake hands with them in the morning. Give them a pat on the head if they have made an extraordinarily good job of a difficult task."[32]

Few child-care experts today would endorse this Spartan approach (which was not universally accepted even in 1928), and most would say that a certain amount of physical affection is necessary. But Watson also explicitly recognized that there is no single ideal way for raising children, and that behavior deemed desirable may vary widely from time to time and from culture to culture. And the book's general point — that parents can exert much more purposeful control over the upbringing of their children than was commonly supposed — probably helped many parents a great deal.

Watson's Legacy Despite the success of Watson's popular writings, such work was never more than a sideline for him as he became increasingly absorbed in the advertising business. And when he revised *Behaviorism* in 1930, it marked the end of his professional psychological career. He still continued to *practice* his behavioristic principles, however, both in advertising and together with his wife in the raising of two sons, born in 1922 and 1924. The boys were assiduously trained to be practical, self-reliant, fearless, and "masculine," with expressions of affection or emotional tenderness strictly curbed.

The outcome of Watson's home childrearing experiment must be interpreted cautiously, because tragedy intervened in 1936 when Rosalie Watson suddenly died of dysentery. Both boys were subsequently sent to boarding school, and the deeply shaken Watson had only sporadic contact with them afterward. After some initial difficulty in boarding school, both sons went on to successful academic and occupational careers — one becoming a psychiatrist and the other an industrial psychologist and vice-president of a major food company. But both were also plagued by severe depression as adults; one attempted suicide before being helped by psychoanalytic therapy, and the other — the psychiatrist — actually did take his own life in 1963. The surviving son, while recognizing his father's virtues, has placed much of the blame on his childrearing practices:

I have some unhappy thoughts about . . . the effects of behavioristic principles on my being raised into an adult. . . . In many ways I adored [my father] as an individual and as a character. He was bright; he was charming; he was masculine, witty, and reflective. But he was also conversely unresponsive, emotionally uncommunicative, unable to express and cope with any feelings of emotion of his own, and determined unwittingly to deprive, I think, my brother and me of any kind of emotional foundation. . . . He was very rigid in carrying out his fundamental philosophies as a behaviorist.[33]

Of course, many other factors including the premature death of their mother could have contributed to the sons' difficulties. But Watson's view of emotional development, like many other aspects of his theory, was unquestionably simplistic. He habitually made his points by exaggeration and overstatement, so his ideas have subsequently had to be toned down.

For example, most would now agree that children are not so easily conditioned into becoming paragons of adjustment and virtue; that emotional development involves far more than the conditioning of just three basic reactions; that language and thought are more than simple chains of verbal, visceral, and kinaesthetic reflexes; and that radical environmentalism underestimates the effects of constitution and heredity. Pavlovian conditioning, while still recognized as an important form of learning, has proved insufficient to account for the more active kinds of ways organisms learn to manipulate and control their environments.

But still, Watson's ideas contained an element of good sense that continues to impress many psychologists. Many still define their science as the study of behavior, and most still insist that their basic data must be observable and "objective," at least to a degree. Prediction and control of behavior remain the major goals of many psychologists, and the study of learning and conditioning in animals as well as human beings is still an important psychological sub-area. Pavlovian conditioning theories have been retained, although complemented by other models of the learning process. In his autobiography, written long after he had left psychology, Watson assessed his contribution by saying, "I still believe as firmly as ever in the general behavioristic position I took in 1912. I think it has influenced psychology."[34] He was not being immodest.

Among those to be most significantly influenced by Watson was a struggling young writer named B. F. Skinner, who first encountered behaviorism at a particularly low point in his literary career, and decided his future lay in psychology rather than literature. Skinner went on to become the most important behaviorist of his day, and we conclude this chapter with his story.

Skinner and Operant Conditioning

Burrhus Frederic Skinner was born on 20 March 1904 in the small railroading town of Susquehanna, Pennsylvania. His father, a self-taught lawyer who never attended college and passed his bar

B. F. Skinner with one of his subjects. *Ken Heyman.*

examination after one year at law school, was a persuasive speaker and author of a well-regarded textbook on workmen's compensation law. Skinner described his mother as "bright and beautiful" — a Susquehanna native like her husband who had been popular, a good singer, and the second-ranked student in her high school class. Concerning her strict notions of propriety, Skinner wrote: "I was taught to fear God, the police, and what people will think. As a result, I usually do what I have to do with no great struggle."[35]

As a boy in Susquehanna, Skinner showed musical, mechanical, and literary aptitudes. He enjoyed opera on the family Victrola, played the piano and saxophone, and earned pocket money throughout high school by playing in a dance band. His mechanical crea-

305

tions included a Rube Goldberg contraption reminding him to keep his room neat: "A special hook in the closet of my room was connected by a string-and-pulley system to a sign hanging above the door to the room. When my pajamas were in place on the hook, the sign was held high above the door and out of the way. When the pajamas were off the hook, the sign hung squarely in the middle of the door frame. It read 'Hang up your pajamas.'"[36]

Skinner published his first literary work at age ten, a poem entitled "That Pessimistic Fellow," in the *Lone Scout* magazine. Unpublished works written during high school included a morality play featuring the characters Greed, Gluttony, Jealousy, and Youth and a melodramatic novel about a young naturalist's love affair with the daughter of a dying trapper. Skinner did well academically, and in 1922 became his family's first college man as a freshman at Hamilton College in Clinton, New York.

At Hamilton, Skinner took some biology courses and a philosophy course taught by a former student of Wundt's, but no psychology. He majored in English and wrote regularly for the college newspaper, literary magazine, and humor magazine — adopting the pen name of Sir Burrhus de Beerus for the last. An inveterate practical joker, he helped spread a false rumor that Charlie Chaplin was going to speak on campus. After a large crowd gathered for the event and was disappointed, Skinner wrote an editorial in the school newspaper declaring, "No man with the slightest regard for his Alma Mater could have done [such a thing]."[37] As a senior, Skinner publicly parodied the speech teacher, subverted the traditional oratory competition by submitting a farcical speech, and decorated the hall for class day exercises with less than complimentary caricatures of the faculty.

But he also showed a more serious side and worked hard to improve his writing skill. The summer before his senior year he attended a writer's workshop whose faculty included the poet Robert Frost. Frost delighted and encouraged Skinner by telling him, "You are worth twice anyone else I have seen in prose this year."[38]

After graduation Skinner moved into his parents' home in Scranton, Pennsylvania, built a study in the attic, and tried to settle in and write professionally. There ensued what he later called his "Dark Year," as he experienced loneliness, depression, and, worst of all, a profound case of writer's block. He read great literature but found little to say about it. He tried to write about writing but that seemed empty. As he later put it, "The truth was, I had no reason to write anything. I had nothing to say, and nothing about my life was making any change in that condition."[39] He considered consulting a psychiatrist, but finally found some distraction along with remuneration by abstracting several thousand legal decisions for Pennsylvania's Anthracite Board of Conciliation.

Gradually, Skinner consoled himself with the thought that even the best of literature could tell only a part of the truth about human nature. He pondered a critic's comment about one of the novelist Thackeray's characters, to the effect that "Thackeray didn't know it, but she drank," and decided that good writers often accurately describe *how* people behave, but offer little insight as to *why* they do so. At this crucial point in his life, he encountered behaviorism.

Skinner read a book in which the philosopher Bertrand Russell, one of his favorite writers, discussed John B. Watson's recently published *Behaviorism* critically but seriously. "I do not fundamentally agree with [Watson's] view," wrote Russell, "but I think it contains much more truth than most people suppose, and I regard it as desirable to develop the behaviourist method to the fullest possible extent."[40] Intrigued, Skinner read Watson as well as the recently translated Pavlov, liked what he read, and began to suspect that behavioristic analyses might just be able to account for many of those "whys" of behavior that were missing in literature.

A symbolic turning point occurred when Skinner read an article by H. G. Wells about Pavlov and the famous British writer George Bernard Shaw. The irascible and colorful Shaw had greatly disliked Pavlov's writings, and had sarcastically described the Russian as a scoundrel and vivisectionist with the habit of boiling babies alive just to see what would happen. Wells expressed admiration for *both* men and posed a hypothetical question: Pavlov and Shaw are drowning on opposite sides of a pier and you have but one life belt to throw in the water; to which side would you throw it? Skinner instantly knew that his own choice would be for Pavlov, and further resolved to go to graduate school and become a behavioristic psychologist. He applied and was accepted at Harvard, for the autumn of 1928.

Although hardly a hotbed of behaviorism, Harvard's psychology department was nevertheless tolerant and stimulating. Skinner found a few fellow graduate students who shared his interests, and faculty who allowed him to go his own way. During the eight years between 1928 and 1936 — first as a graduate student, then as a postdoctoral fellow, and finally as a junior fellow in Harvard's prestigious Society of Fellows — Skinner laid the groundwork for a whole new kind of behavioristic analysis.

Operant Conditioning Skinner's accomplishment followed his invention of an ingeniously simple piece of apparatus now commonly called the **Skinner box**, which became for him what the salivary reflex apparatus had been for Pavlov, and which made possible the study of a different kind of learned behavior he called **operant conditioning**. Skinner has told the story of how he came to invent this box in a delightfully tongue-in-cheek article, "A Case History in Scientific Method."

According to this account, four "unformalized principles of scientific practice" led to success. First, his box was the end result of a long series of partly completed experiments that had been abandoned in midcourse; thus his first principle: "When you run into something interesting, drop everything else and study it." Second, the box was highly automated and required little work by the experimenter once an animal subject was placed inside; hence "Some ways of doing research are easier than others." Further, some of his most interesting results occurred accidentally or when the apparatus malfunctioned, illustrating principles three and four: "Apparatus sometimes breaks down," and "Some people are lucky."[41]

Besides following these unformalized principles, Skinner was also inspired by a major guiding idea. He had admired the precision Pavlov brought to the study of conditioned reflexes, and he appreciated Watson's attempts to extend the concept of conditioned reflexes into explanations of emotions. But still, something seemed lacking: "I could not . . . move without a jolt from salivary reflexes to the important business of the organism in everyday life."[42] Learning in everyday life involves more than the passive acquisition of reflexive reactions to stimuli that are essentially inflicted upon the organism from the outside; normal organisms also learn to actively manipulate, control, and "operate upon" their environments. Thorndike's chickens and cats had demonstrated this type of learning when they escaped confinement in his famous experiment of 1898 (see pages 269–271). Skinner devised his box to enable him to study actively acquired learning even more systematically.

His box, illustrated in Figure 9-1,[43] was essentially a white rat's cage with a lever-bar mounted on one wall near a food tray, and connected to a mechanism that dropped a food pellet into the tray when the bar was pressed. Each press of the bar also caused a pen mechanism touching a constantly moving roll of paper to rise by a small fixed amount, so that a permanent, **cumulative record** of all of the bar presses could be kept. Figure 9-2 illustrates one typical cumulative record, of an animal who made its first response after being in the box about fourteen minutes, its second at about twenty-five minutes, and who then began to respond at an increasingly rapid rate. Such cumulative records resembled mathematical curves whose steepness reflected the rates of responding. When rates were low there were few pen elevations and the record remained flat, as in the left-hand portion of Figure 9-2; higher rates produced curves with steeper slopes, as on the right.

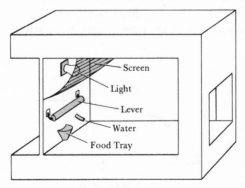

Figure 9-1. *The Skinner box.*

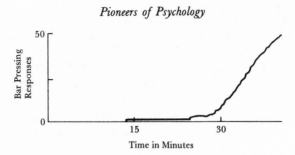

Figure 9-2. *A typical cumulative record.*

Figure 9-2 typifies the cumulative records Skinner obtained with hungry but untrained rats when first placed in the box. At first, bar-pressing responses occurred infrequently and "accidentally," as the animal explored its new environment. After the first few presses were **reinforced** with food, however, the rate increased dramatically and continued high as long as the rat remained hungry.

In further experiments, Skinner varied the **contingencies of reinforcement**—that is, the specific conditions under which the responses were reinforced or not with food pellets. One experiment occurred by chance (illustrating Skinner's third and fourth unformalized principles), when the food dispenser jammed after an animal had already been regularly reinforced and established in a steady response rate. The ensuing cumulative record showed an **extinction curve** like that illustrated in Figure 9-3. At first, the animal responded at a very high rate, partly because it was no longer pausing between responses to eat, and partly because of an

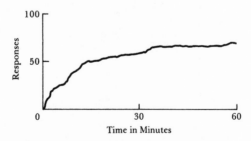

Figure 9-3. *Extinction of an operant response.*

310

Time in Minutes

Figure 9–4. *Fixed-interval conditioning (vertical slashes represent reinforced responses).*

"emotional" or "frustrated" activation of the response. After a few minutes, however, the rate slowed down except for a series of progressively diminishing, wavelike "bursts" of response. And finally the curve flattened out almost completely, indicating that the response was almost never repeated — that is, that it had been "extinguished." Except for the wavelike bursts, the overall shape of the cumulative record approximated a regular, negatively accelerating mathematical curve.

Other experiments varied the contingencies of reinforcement by providing food pellets only intermittently, according to several different **reinforcement schedules**. On a **fixed-interval reinforcement schedule**, for example, reinforcement only came on the first response following a predetermined period of time, regardless of how many responses had been made in the interim. After an acquisition period in which cumulative records generally resembled those for regular reinforcement, the records assumed a characteristic and highly regular scallop shape, illustrated in Figure 9–4 for a three-minute interval schedule. After each reinforced response (designated by a vertical slash), the response rate decreased for a minute or two and then increased sharply as the end of the interval approached. Such a response pattern maximized the total reinforcement for the animal by assuring a response would occur immediately after the end of each interval; it also minimized the effort expended, since responses were seldom "wasted" during the non-reinforced periods immediately following each reinforcement.

On a **fixed-ratio reinforcement schedule**, reinforcement always followed a preset *number* of responses — after every fourth response, or every tenth, or any other number Skinner decided upon. Although it took longer for response rates to stabilize under these conditions, eventually they leveled off at about the same steady slope as for regular reinforcement. Skinner found he could speed things up by increasing his ratios gradually, starting off by reinforcing every second response, then every fourth, and so on — doubling the ratio each time the response rate stabilized. In one experiment, a rat so conditioned pressed industriously at the bar when only every 192nd response was reinforced. Obviously, under the proper conditions organisms could be induced to work harder and harder for progressively diminishing rewards — a principle perhaps already familiar to unscrupulous employers in human society.

Skinner also experimented with **variable-interval** and **variable-ratio reinforcement schedules**, in which the times or numbers of responses between reinforcements were continually varied randomly. These schedules resembled the irregular pattern of payoffs dispensed by slot machines in gambling casinos. As the casino owners well know, such schedules can produce very high rates of response that are remarkably resistant to extinction. After being placed on such schedules, Skinner's animals responded for much longer after reinforcement was cut off altogether than they would have if the original schedule had been regular. It was as if the irregular reinforcement nurtured a constant hope that the "next" response would be rewarded. Rat and casino player alike became hooked, and responded well past the point of diminishing returns.

Thus Skinner saw the rat's bar-pressing behavior as conveniently representing a whole range of learned behaviors by animals and humans in the real world which, in his words, "operate on the environment" to produce various ends. When he published these results in his first book, *The Behavior of Organisms* (1938), he established operant conditioning as a kind of learning distinctly different from the Pavlovian conditioned reflex, but equally as important. He here referred to the general Pavlovian type of learning as

respondent conditioning, and contrasted it with operant conditioning on several dimensions. Respondent conditioning creates completely new connections between stimuli and responses, for example, while operant conditioning strengthens or weakens response tendencies that already exist in the organism's behavioral repertoire. In respondent conditioning the response is *elicited* by the conditioned stimulus, whereas in operant conditioning it must be *emitted* by the subject even before conditioning can take place. In respondent conditioning both conditioned and unconditioned stimuli may be precisely defined, while in operant conditioning one can never say with any certainty which stimuli give rise to the response. And the *strength* of respondent conditioning is typically measured in terms of response magnitude or latency, while that of operant conditioning is measured by response rate. In sum, Skinner had demonstrated a controlled and properly behavioristic method for studying a whole new range of learned responses.

Behavior Shaping and Programmed Instruction   After laying the foundations for the study of operant conditioning at Harvard, Skinner taught at the University of Minnesota and the University of Indiana for twelve years before returning permanently to Harvard in 1948. Over the years he attracted many followers who sought to apply the techniques and findings of operant conditioning to a wide variety of experimental and practical situations, and who created a separate division of the American Psychological Association devoted to "The Experimental Analysis of Behavior." Skinner himself became increasingly concerned with the practical applications and philosophical implications of operant conditioning.

In the 1940s, for example, he extended operant-conditioning techniques to behaviors considerably more complex than bar pressing. He hypothesized that complex behaviors could be thought of as *chains* of simple ones, and then developed methods for building up complex sequences of simple responses in animals. First, he needed a reinforcer that could be easily administered to animal subjects without interfering with the flow of their behavior. Thus he started out by using *respondent* conditioning to pair the sound of clicks from a toy clicker with a strong **primary reinforcer** such as food. After a while, the clicks by themselves became effective **secondary rein-forcers**, as demonstrated by the fact that animals would maintain high rates of responding in a Skinner box when reinforced only by clicks unaccompanied by food.

Skinner now used this secondary reinforcer to progressively "shape up" increasingly complicated or difficult chains of responses. When he wanted to train a pigeon to peck a certain small spot on the wall, for example, he began by clicking each time it made a partial turn in the spot's direction. Soon the animal was constantly oriented in the right direction, and Skinner now withheld reinforcement until it extended its head toward the spot. Once this response was estab-lished, reinforcement was withheld until a peck occurred. And after this highly specific response was emitted and reinforced the first time, repetitions followed much more quickly. By patient shaping like this, Skinner trained pigeons to perform some spectacular feats, such as rolling a ball back and forth to each other across a table in a rudimentary game of Ping-Pong.

Skinner saw no reason why the same basic techniques he used to teach pigeons to play Ping-Pong could not serve as models for *human* education. Inspired by a visit to his daughter's fourth-grade class in 1953, he launched the development of **programmed instruction** — an educational technique where complicated subjects such as mathe-matics are broken down into simple, stepwise components that may be presented to students in order of increasing difficulty. The be-ginning student answers an easy question about the simplest com-ponent, and immediately learns if the response was right or wrong. If right, that knowledge presumably serves as a secondary reinforcer, so the correct response is strengthened. In a carefully designed pro-gram, this correct response should also provide the basis for respond-ing correctly to the next, slightly more difficult question — and so on. When incorrect answers occur, they are followed by reviews and supplementary instructions providing the small amount of new information necessary for success on the next try. Thus, Skinner argued that students may gradually be "shaped" into becoming pro-ficient mathematicians, just as his pigeons were shaped into becom-ing Ping-Pong players.

Today, operant teaching programs have actually been developed for many subjects, and at difficulty levels from preschool through graduate school. And while they may not have become an educational panacea capable of replacing the traditional student-teacher relationship, they have nevertheless proved to be valuable additions to the teacher's resources.

Philosophical Implications of Operant Conditioning As a former man-of-letters, Skinner constantly thought about the philosophical as well as the practical implications of his theory. He concluded very early that if **negative reinforcers** are considered along with positive ones — that is, the environmental consequences an organism will work to avoid or to escape from, as well as those it will work to obtain — then virtually *all* behavior must be controlled by the contingencies of reinforcement. Thus the notion of behavioral freedom or free will must be an illusion. Skinner argued that when we *believe* we are acting freely, we are merely free of negative reinforcement or its threat, and are fully determined instead by the pursuit of things that have reinforced us positively in the past. When we feel other people are behaving "freely," we are simply unaware of their complete reinforcement histories, and of the contingencies that shape their behavior.

Skinner dramatized these ideas in his 1948 utopian novel, *Walden Two*, which described an ideal society in which negative reinforcement has been completely abandoned as a means of social control. Children are here reared only to seek the positive reinforcement that has been made consequent upon their showing socialized and civilized behavior. Inevitably — so the novel claims — they grow up to be cooperative, intelligent, sociable, and happy. The society's justification and rationale are summarized in the following dialogue between Frazier, the novel's hero, and a skeptical visitor named Castle:

"Mr. Castle, when a science of behavior has once been achieved, there's no alternative to a planned society. We can't leave mankind to an accidental or biased control. But by using the principle of positive reinforcement — carefully avoiding force or the threat of force — we can preserve a personal sense of freedom. . . ."

"But you haven't denied that you are in complete control," said Castle. "You are still the long-range dictator."

"As you will," said Frazier, . . . "When once you have grasped the principle of positive reinforcement, you can enjoy a sense of unlimited power. It's enough to satisfy the thirstiest tyrant."

"There you are, then," said Castle. "That's my case."

"But it's a limited sort of despotism," Frazier went on. "And I don't think anyone should worry about it. The despot must wield his power for the good of others. If he takes any step which reduces the sum total of human happiness, his power is reduced by a like amount. What better check against a malevolent despotism could you ask for?"[44]

Unsurprisingly enough, *Walden Two* aroused considerable controversy, and many readers condemned its happy but controlled society as totalitarian. Others responded more positively to Skinner's vision, and a few even tried to create real communities based on his principles. As usually happens with utopian attempts, however, these groups lacked the resources or influence to provide a real test of the underlying principles.

In the meantime, Skinner continued to speak out provocatively about the desirability of social control based on positive reinforcement. His best-selling 1971 book, *Beyond Freedom and Dignity*, argued that the assumption of "autonomous man," upon which so many of Western society's institutions are based, both is false and has many deleterious consequences. According to this assumption, we "credit" people more for doing good deeds "of their own free will" than for doing them because they have to. But the only real difference, argues Skinner, is that in the first case we do not know the contingencies that produced the behavior, and in the second we do. And the dark and obverse side of this position is that if people are to be "credited" for unexplained good behavior, then they must be *blamed and punished* for their "freely" produced bad behavior. The assumption that people are free *requires* that punishment or its threat be constantly employed as negative reinforcers. Skinner summarizes: "Under punitive contingencies a person appears to be free to behave well and to deserve credit when he does so. Nonpunitive contingencies generate the same good behavior, but a person cannot be said to be free, and the contingencies deserve credit when he behaves well."[45]

But since the autonomy of autonomous man is only apparent,

the winning of personal "credit" seems to Skinner very small recompense for the constant exposure to punishment. Further, his experiments had suggested that positive reinforcement is more effective than negative in producing lasting conditioning effects. Thus he believes we should abandon our illusory belief in behavioral freedom, forthrightly accept the inevitability of control, and deliberately start to design real environments like Walden Two in which behavior will be shaped toward socially desirable ends by exclusive means of positive reinforcement.

Skinner's theory does not directly bear on the classic political question of exactly *who* should design the environments and seize the control, but he has argued that once the power of operant conditioning becomes well known, *someone* will surely do so. And since he believes psychologists are likely to have attitudes just as enlightened (or more so) as other groups, he has urged them not to be shy about participating in the project.

These assertions about the ubiquity of environmental control, and the desirability of openly seizing it, have made Skinner at once the most famous and the most controversial of recent American psychologists. He was listed in *The 100 Most Important People in the World*, and shown in a 1975 survey to be the best-known scientist in the United States. But recognition has not always implied approval, and Skinner has frightened or enraged some people with his pronouncements. He himself was made aware of his darker reputation one evening after attending a particularly pleasing concert. The musicians were young and their music delightful — precisely the sort of thing he envisions as part of the good life in a Walden Two — and as he left Skinner praised the young conductor who had done so well. His companion, who knew the conductor, remarked, "You know, he thinks you are a terrible person. Teaching machines, . . . a fascist."[46]

Unpleasant and unfounded rumors also circulated about Skinner's personal and family life. When his younger daughter was an infant, he designed a temperature-controlled, glass-enclosed crib for her which he first playfully called an "Heir Conditioner" and later patented and marketed (not terribly successfully) as the "Aircrib." This device's sole purpose was to provide a comfortable and safe environment for infants, and it compared favorably on both scores to traditional cribs or playpens. Yet inaccurate stories began to circulate that Skinner had raised his children like rats "in a box," and that they had suffered grievously as a result. Perhaps conflating Skinner's children with Watson's, some rumors had it that they became mentally ill or committed suicide. In fact, one of Skinner's daughters became a successful professor of educational psychology, and the other an artist whose work has been exhibited at London's Royal Academy.

Unpleasant and unfair publicity was perhaps the inevitable price for Skinner's raising and taking a stand on difficult questions. There has also been a more principled and knowledgeable reaction against some aspects of Skinner's ideas and behaviorism in general, which we shall refer to in later chapters. But in recompense for all of the attacks, legitimate or otherwise, Skinner has the satisfaction of knowing that many psychologists, educators, and other workers continue daily to apply his ideas in their research and practice.

Suggested Readings

On Pavlov's life, see B. P. Babkin, *Pavlov: A Biography* (Chicago: University of Chicago Press, 1949), and Elizabeth and Martin Sherwood, *Ivan Pavlov* (Geneva: Heron Books, 1970). Pavlov's own most important works on conditioned reflexes are found in his *Lectures on Conditioned Reflexes* (New York: Liveright, 1928) and *Conditioned Reflexes: An Investigation of the Activity of the Cerebral Cortex* (New York: Dover, 1960).

Watson's short but lively autobiography appears in the third volume of Carl Murchison, ed., *A History of Psychology in Autobiography* (Worcester, MA: Clark University Press, 1936). A thorough and scholarly account of his life and work is Kerry W. Buckley's *Behaviorism and the Professionalization of American Psychology: A Study of John Broadus Watson, 1878–1958* (Ann Arbor, MI: University Microfilms International, 1982). Any of Watson's writings cited in the notes are to be recommended, although his reprinted *Behaviorism* (New York: Norton, 1970) is particularly readable and synoptic.

Skinner's short autobiography appears in Volume 5 of *History of*

Psychology in Autobiography, edited by E. G. Boring and Gardner Lindzey (New York: Appleton-Century-Crofts, 1967). He amplifies this material in the three volumes of his full autobiography: *Particulars of My Life* (1976), *The Shaping of a Behaviorist* (1979), and *A Matter of Consequences* (1983), all published in New York by Knopf. Skinner describes his early studies with the Skinner box in *The Behavior of Organisms: An Experimental Analysis* (New York: Appleton-Century-Crofts, 1938); later developments are taken up in *Science and Human Behavior* (New York: Macmillan, 1953). For the social-philosophical implications of his theories see his novel *Walden Two* (New York: Macmillan, 1962), and *Beyond Freedom and Dignity* (New York: Bantam/Vintage, 1971). Norman Guttman provides an apt assessment of Skinner's influence in "On Skinner and Hull: A Reminiscence and Projection," *American Psychologist* (*32*:321–328, 1977).

10

Early Hypnotists and the Psychology of Social Influence

In the fall of 1775, the Prince-Elector of Bavaria appointed a commission to investigate the activities of **Johann Joseph Gassner** (1727–1779), a priest who claimed to cure many illnesses through a simple technique of exorcism. First, he would ensure that his patient believed in the divinity of Jesus Christ, and was undertaking the act of exorcism willingly. Then, in the name of Christ, Gassner would command any demons present in the patient's body to produce their symptoms forthwith, and in great intensity. If nothing happened he declared the patient physically ill and sent him to an ordinary doctor. But if the symptoms did appear — and often they did, as the patient convulsed, twitched, or cried out in pain — Gassner concluded that demons really were at work, and proceeded to "tame" them by commanding them to move about in the body and produce different symptoms. These suggestions too were often effective, as paralyses and pains appeared in different parts of the body, accompanied by groans, cries, and other expressions of extreme emotion. And finally, after having established control of the demons in this way, Gassner would command them to depart from the body altogether, leaving the patient cured.

Many patients reported improvement after Gassner's exorcisms, but his activity created controversy both within and without the Church. Although exorcism was an accepted ritual, many church-men thought Gassner carried it too far and used it too indiscrimi-nately; unsurprisingly, many doctors felt he infringed on medical territory. He also had his avid defenders, however, and the ensu-ing controversy culminated in the investigative commission.

The commission called the Viennese physician **Franz Anton Mesmer** (1734–1815) as a prime witness, because of reports that he could cure patients in ways somewhat similar to Gassner's, only invoking the naturalistic force of *magnetism* as his therapeutic agent instead of supernaturalistic exorcism. Mesmer duplicated many of Gassner's effects for the commission, commanding patients' symptoms to move about their bodies and even disappear — but he explained these effects as the result of a strong magnetic fluid concentrated within his own body. Thus he provided a naturalistic and apparently "scientific" explanation for results like Gassner's. Partly thanks to Mesmer's testimony, Gassner was banished to a country parish and forbidden to practice further exorcisms. He died in obscurity a few years later.

Mesmer's own fame was just beginning, although his role as rep-resentative of enlightened "science" was both temporary and ironic. This paradoxical figure had truly made some important discoveries about the phenomenon we now call **hypnotism**, and had tried to explain them in a scientific way. But his flamboyant methods, gran-diose claims, and not-quite-straightforward manner soon ran *him* afoul of the scientific establishment. In 1784 Mesmer himself became the subject of a royal commission's inquiry, and fared no better than Gassner had. His story, however, constitutes the first episode in the modern history of hypnosis.

Mesmer and "Animal Magnetism"

Little is known of Mesmer's life up until 1766, when he received a doctorate in medicine from the University of Vienna at the age of thirty-two. He listed several other degrees after his name on the title page of his dissertation, but searches of university archives throughout Europe have failed to confirm that he actually earned them. His dissertation itself, "On the Influence of the Planets," was largely plagiarized from an English follower of Isaac Newton, and argued that planetary gravitational influences directly affect biological organisms on earth. Although that idea seems uncomfortably astrological today, it had a certain plausibility in the wake of Newton's discovery of the law of universal gravitation, which held that planets and stars can influence one another's orbits from great distances. One of Mesmer's few unplagiarized passages postulated a force he called **animal gravitation** as the agent of the planets' presumed biological influence.[1]

Mesmer's scholarly indiscretions with his dissertation went undetected in his lifetime, and did not hinder his career. After graduation he married a very wealthy widow ten years his senior, and became a social lion. A skilled amateur musician, he befriended several musical celebrities including Leopold Mozart and his prodigy son, Wolfgang Amadeus. Mesmer commissioned the opera *Bastien and Bastienne* from twelve-year-old Wolfgang in 1768 and staged its premiere performance in a theater he had built in his own large and luxurious gardens. When Benjamin Franklin invented the glass harmonica—a musical instrument played by rubbing damp fingers against a rotating glass drum, and producing a sound like that of a wet finger rubbed around the rim of a wine glass—Mesmer obtained one and became a virtuoso performer; his young friend Mozart later wrote a glass harmonica concerto especially for him.

Mesmer practiced medicine rather sporadically, but possessed a genuine curiosity to keep abreast of current scientific developments. When a local Jesuit priest named Maximillian Hell became enthusiastic about the subject of magnetism, Mesmer frequently talked with him about it. Magnetism seemed to them one of a group of several invisible and mysterious "fluids" with potentially marvelous scientific consequences; others included the recently discovered electricity, gravitation, and the gases that could make balloons miraculously rise to the sky.

These conversations proved crucial in 1773, when Mesmer began to treat Francisca Oesterlin, a young relative of his wife's suffering from periodic attacks of what Mesmer called "hysterical fever," with "convulsions, spasms of vomiting, inflammation of the intestines, inability to make water, agonizing toothache and earache, despondency, insane hallucinations, cataleptic trance, fainting, temporary blindness, feelings of suffocation, attacks of paralysis lasting for days, and other terrible symptoms."[2] At first Mesmer likened the periodicity of these attacks to the tides, caused by the gravitation of the moon. Then he remembered Father Hell and magnetism, and decided to test the therapeutic properties of *this* new force. He had Fraulein Oesterlin swallow a medicine containing iron, and then applied magnets specially designed by Father Hell to various parts of her body. Soon she said she felt a force flowing with her, then entered a "crisis state" with twitching, convulsions, and intense pain in the location of each of her symptoms. When the crisis subsided, symptoms disappeared for six hours. Mesmer repeated the treatment several times, and the cure seemed complete. Leopold Mozart had seen the patient at her emaciated sickest, and when he reencountered her six years later reported, "On my honor, I hardly recognized her, she is so large and fat. She has [married and has] three children, two girls and a boy."[3]

Mesmer repeated the therapy with other patients, only now, with clear ideas of what to expect, he directly and indirectly *suggested* to them that they would fall into crisis states upon application of the magnets. Many patients reacted as he expected. Then he tried the treatment *without* magnets, merely passing his hands over patients' bodies while asserting they would fall into crisis. This too worked, but instead of concluding that magnetism had nothing to do with his cures, Mesmer hypothesized that his own body must be a strong source of **animal magnetism** just as therapeutically effective as a real magnet. He speculated further that every person's body was filled and surrounded by a magnetic force field that sometimes became dis-aligned and weakened, creating the symptoms of illness. The application of a strong, external magnetic source presumably realigned and restrengthened the field in much the same way a strong magnet can magnetize a nail, thus removing the symptoms.

Such was Mesmer's theory when he appeared before the Gassner commission. He testified that Gassner cured people because he was, like himself, a person naturally strong in animal magnetism; in fact,

Mesmer modestly allowed that Gassner might have been even *more* magnetic than himself. Here, in crude form, was one origin of the persistent but mistaken belief that the secret of hypnotic phenomena lies in a mysterious power of the hypnotist, rather than the receptivity of the subject.

Back in Vienna, Mesmer soon became embroiled in two nasty controversies of his own. When he publicized magnetic therapy, his old friend Father Hell claimed priority for the idea. Mesmer responded ungenerously and somewhat disingenuously, claiming to have known about the therapeutic power of magnets for years, else why would he have regularly prescribed medicines with iron in them? Further, he claimed to have already posited a force of animal magnetism in his doctoral dissertation — although actually he had postulated animal *gravitation* instead. After a flurry of pamphlets and counterpamphlets, Father Hell's claims were largely dismissed.

A second controversy, with more serious consequences for Mesmer, followed his treatment of Maria-Theresia Paradis, a teenaged piano prodigy who had been blind since the age of three. (Some have said that Mesmer ran into trouble somewhere between Hell and Paradise, although the joke makes sense only in English because *Hell* in Mesmer's native German means not the underworld but "clear," "bright," or "shining.") Mesmer claimed to have restored the girl's sight by magnetism, until her parents prematurely removed her from his care and she became blind again. Her parents, supported by orthodox physicians, called Mesmer a charlatan and charged him with improper conduct. Mesmer's partisans retorted that the parents were upset only because Maria-Theresia's celebrity value decreased when she gained normal vision. Today we cannot disentangle the truth about this case, although quite possibly she suffered from a psychogenic blindness that Mesmer really did alleviate temporarily. But whatever the truth, he found it expedient to flee Vienna for Paris.

In its unstable state on the eve of the French Revolution, Parisian society was just then particularly prone to fads or "crazes." And if anything was suited to become a craze it was animal magnetism, effectively promoted by the colorful Mesmer. Even though he spoke a heavily accented French that few fully understood, and charged enormous fees that few could afford, he soon attracted more clients than he could handle individually. Thus he devised his famous **baquet** (the French word for "tub") as a means of mass-producing magnetic cures.

The use of a tub may seem quaint today, but in the 1780s it made plausible scientific sense to store an invisible magnetic "fluid" in some sort of receptacle. The so-called "Leyden jar," which presumably stored charges of *electrical* fluid and which was in fact an effective early battery, served as one model for Mesmer. And lighter-than-air balloons — the only phenomenon to rival animal magnetism as a scientific craze in prerevolutionary France — also worked their wonders by containing and storing an invisible but powerful fluid substance. Thus when Mesmer placed magnetized iron filings and water in the bottom of covered wooden tubs or *baquets*, he and his contemporaries could sincerely believe that they became filled with a therapeutic magnetic fluid.

Mesmer inserted metal handles into his *baquet*, and placed it in the middle of a dimly lit treatment room. Patients entered in groups and sat around the *baquet* grasping the handles while Mesmer, in an adjoining room, played ethereal music on his glass harmonica to help set the mood. After a suitable state of anticipation had been established in the patients — most of whom already had a good idea of what to expect before they came — Mesmer emerged dressed in a flowing, lilac-colored robe and began pointing his finger or an iron rod at the afflicted parts of the patients' bodies. Invariably one or two patients passed into a crisis state and served as models for the others. Soon the room was full of convulsing, crisis-ridden patients, the most violent of whom were carried by Mesmer and his assistants to a clearly marked *Chambre de Crises* ("Crisis Room") for individual attention. Not all patients experienced a complete crisis, but even some of these partial responders found their symptoms improved after the séance was over.

By treating his patients in groups, Mesmer increased not only his profits but also the strength of response of many patients, because of a phenomenon social psychologists have since called **social contagion**. The early responders effectively showed the others what

A scene around Mesmer's *baquet. Courtesy Bibliothèque Nationale.*

they were supposed to do, and as more and more members of the group entered crisis the pressure to go along with the crowd increased in the holdouts. As a net result, more people entered crisis, and entered it more strongly, than would have been the case had they been magnetized individually by Mesmer.

Despite his popular and commercial success, Mesmer desperately but unsuccessfully sought recognition from orthodox medical and scientific authorities. He suffered two particularly galling misadventures in 1784. First, he joined the royal court and much of Paris's social elite at a gala concert by a celebrated blind musician from

Vienna — none other than Maria-Theresia Paradis. An eyewitness later recalled: "All eyes turned toward Mesmer who had been unwise enough to come to the concert. He was well aware of being the center of attention and suffered one of the worst humiliations of his life."[4] Gossip about his earlier experience with the girl, and his obvious failure to cure her permanently, immediately began to circulate.

Even more disastrously, Mesmer's practice came under scrutiny by a blue-ribbon scientific commission appointed by the king himself, and chaired by the American ambassador and eminent investigator of electricity, Benjamin Franklin. Other famous commissioners included the great chemist Antoine Lavoisier and the physician Joseph Guillotin (who shortly promoted the use of the "humane" execution device that now bears his name, and to which Lavoisier and countless others would lose their heads during the French Revolution). When the commissioners submitted themselves to magnetic induction they proved insusceptible, but they discovered that "good" subjects fell into crisis when presented with something they merely *believed* was magnetized but really was not. The commissioners reported that they "unanimously concluded, on the question of the existence and the utility of [animal] magnetism, that there is no proof of its existence, that this fluid without existence is consequently without utility."[5] They did not deny that patients were sometimes affected, but this they attributed to the influence of suggestion or "imagination" rather than a physical force. And while that concession may seem significant today, at the time it was generally interpreted to mean that the effects had been simulated, a sham. Essentially, the commission branded animal magnetism as bogus science, and discouraged legitimate scientists and doctors from taking it seriously. For many years thereafter, the serious study of hypnotic phenomena became relegated to scientific amateurs.

Of these, however, there was no dearth. While at the zenith of his fashionability Mesmer had founded a series of mystical, quasi-religious, and expensive schools called "Societies of Harmony," where wealthy students were taught how to magnetize patients. And while Mesmer himself disappeared into relative obscurity after 1784, his nonprofessional but enthusiastic students kept the practice of magnetism alive. One of these aristocratic students — **Amand Marie Jacques de Chastenet**, the **Marquis de Puységur** (1751–1825) — made a particularly important discovery that propelled the study of hypnotism into a new phase.

Puységur's "Artificial Somnambulism" and Faria's "Lucid Sleep"

Puységur's important discovery sprang from his discomfort about the convulsive and often violent nature of the mesmeric crisis state. One day he must have implicitly conveyed this attitude while magnetizing one of his male servants, for instead of becoming crisis-ridden the young man entered a peaceful, sleeplike trance. Unlike a truly sleeping person, however, he continued to respond to Puységur's voice, answering questions and even performing complicated activities when told to. Upon command he talked about his work, pretended to shoot for a prize, and danced happily to imagined music. Then he "awoke" with no recollection of these events, although upon being remagnetized and resuming the trance he promptly remembered them.

Puységur found he could reproduce this state in other patients, and bypass the crisis altogether, simply by suggesting it clearly in the course of induction. First he referred to the new state as a **perfect crisis**, and later as **artificial somnambulism** (because of its apparent similarity to sleepwalking). Other magnetizers quickly copied Puységur's induction techniques.

In artificially somnambulistic subjects, Puységur and his colleagues soon discovered most of the common hypnotic effects as they are known today. They learned that a drastically enhanced **suggestibility** characterized the state; all they had to do was assert that something was so, and many subjects would behave as if it were in fact true. Paralyses and pains appeared and moved about the subjects' bodies upon suggestion; parts of the body were anesthetized so subjects could easily tolerate pinpricks, burns, and other normally painful stimuli without signs of distress; and a wide variety of authentic-seeming emotional expressions could be produced upon command.

Like Puységur's servant, many other subjects also "forgot" the trance experiences upon awakening but remembered them when remagnetized. This effect, called **posthypnotic amnesia** today, was enhanced if the subjects were *told* while in the trance that they would forget everything upon awakening. Puységur also demonstrated what we now call **posthypnotic suggestion**, where subjects in trance are told they will perform a certain act after awakening—for example, scratch their left ear when the hypnotist coughs—but will forget that they had been instructed to. Many subjects comply with such suggestions, and when asked why, they fabricate some plausible but incorrect explanation—for example, they might say that they had a sudden itch. A century after Puységur, these posthypnotic effects would serve Freud and other proponents of "dynamic psychology" as prime examples of unconscious thought and motivation.

While most of Puységur's observations of artificial somnambulism have stood the test of time, he also held two beliefs that have not been justified by further research, although they remain part of the popular mythology about hypnotism. First, he believed that somnambulistic subjects could do things they would find completely impossible normally. It is known today that hypnotized subjects will sometimes do things they *think* are impossible in the waking state, such as make their bodies so rigid that they can remain suspended in air with only one support beneath the head and another under the heels. In fact, most people can easily do this when "normal," although it *sounds* difficult and many would fear to try it. Hypnosis may sometimes make people more relaxed and confident about their ability to do something, and thus *indirectly* improve their performance. But it cannot miraculously add to a person's normal abilities or strengths.

Puységur also believed that subjects could *not* be magnetized against their will, or made to do things in a trance contrary to their moral scruples. In fact, this is usually but not invariably so. Modern stage hypnotists often hypnotize "defiant" subjects—people who loudly proclaim they can never be hypnotized, and challenge the hypnotist to try—simply by issuing firm commands that they shall *not* fall asleep when told to. Such people sometimes fall immediately into a trance state and respond positively to further suggestions.

Whether or not they have been hypnotized "against their will" depends on how one defines "will."

On the question of violating moral scruples, defendants in some criminal trials have pleaded innocent on grounds they acted under the influence of hypnotists. Although such persons may have had deep underlying aggressive tendencies, at least some juries have been convinced they would never have committed their crimes without the hypnotic influence. In these cases — which include the celebrated "Charles Manson case" in which actress Sharon Tate and six other people were brutally murdered by a group of young people allegedly under Manson's hypnotic influence — the actual perpetrators of the crimes received much lighter sentences than the hypnotic masterminds.

On reflection, of course, we ought not expect to find safeguards in hypnosis that do not apply in other, more "ordinary" situations of interpersonal influence. And certainly many nonhypnotic situations exist in which people are induced to do things contrary to their normal wishes or morals. Soldiers regularly face dangers they would rather avoid and commit acts of aggression they would condemn in civilian life, because they have received orders from a superior. Successful teachers and athletic coaches often induce people to reach beyond themselves and do things they individually might not want to do. The classic studies of **obedience** by the American social psychologist **Stanley Milgram** (1933–1985) showed that most subjects in a psychological experiment would administer supposedly dangerous electrical shocks to fellow subjects, after being authoritatively told to do so by a high-status experimenter.[6] And political leaders often achieve greatness precisely because they convince large numbers of citizens to do things that — for good or ill — they would avoid if left to themselves. Thus hypnosis represents just one of many social-influence situations in which people may be led to do things against their "will" or moral conviction.

Despite his errors, the amateur Puységur advanced the scientific cause of animal magnetism, or "mesmerism" as it also was popularly called, by discovering a wide range of intriguing and reproducible phenomena that could be studied outside the overheated and distracting settings of Mesmer's *baquets*. Another amateur, the abbé

José Custodio di Faria (1756–1819), made a different but equally important contribution in the early 1800s. A Portuguese priest who had lived in India before settling in Paris, Faria addressed the venerable question of why all people did not respond equally well to the magnetists' induction procedures.

Even Mesmer had recognized wide individual differences in his patients' responses, and the Franklin Commission had been warned in advance not to expect full crises in many of the cases they investigated. For a theory that placed most of its emphasis on the power presumably wielded by the magnetist, this concession represented something of an embarrassment. Why should only a portion of the population respond to a force of theoretically universal influence? Indeed, the failure to answer this question satisfactorily had contributed to the Franklin Commission's dismissal of the theory of animal magnetism.

Faria fully agreed with the commission's verdict on magnetic theory, writing, "I am not able to conceive how the human species can be so bizarre that it has to search out the cause of [mesmerism] in a *baquet*, in some external force, in a magnetic fluid."[7] But he disagreed with the commission's consequent dismissal of all mesmeric phenomena as the result of an ill-defined and somewhat disreputable "imagination." Faria believed that something real did in fact happen in mesmeric séances, although of a totally nonmagnetic nature, and only in some of the subjects.

To prove these points, Faria demonstrated that trance states could be induced without recourse to magnetic paraphernalia or terminology. Sometimes he asked seated subjects to fixate their gaze on his hand as he slowly moved it toward their face, while commanding them to sleep. Other times he simply had them close their eyes and concentrate on his voice as he authoritatively instructed them, "Sleep." About one person in five responded to these procedures by falling into a deep trance state virtually identical to Puységur's artificial somnambulism, but which Faria named **lucid sleep**. To remove them from the state, Faria simply instructed them to wake up. These are essentially the procedures still followed by most hypnotists today.

Faria further showed that virtually anyone, even a child, could successfully induce lucid sleep in appropriately predisposed subjects. Thus the "secret" of mesmeric phenomena lay not in the magnetic or other mysterious powers of the operator, but in the predispositions and susceptibilities of the *subjects*. Faria referred to trance-predisposed subjects as *"époptes"* (a term he coined from a Greek root meaning "the led" or "the overseen"), and argued that their susceptibility arose from a thinness of the blood—a physiological explanation. This particular theory proved wrong, but in switching the emphasis from the hypnotizer to the hypnotized, and in attempting to pinpoint the characteristics that render some people more hypnotizable than others, Faria began a major research tradition that continues today.

Unfortunately, Faria's very real contributions received scant attention from his contemporaries, partly because of his nonprofessional status and partly because he spoke poor French (although that particular handicap had never bothered the much more flamboyant Mesmer). Further, he was humiliated when an actor simulated lucid sleep at a public demonstration, and Faria failed to detect the deception. Thus after Faria's death in 1819 his ideas passed into obscurity, and hypnotic practice remained in the hands of scientifically unrespectable "magnetizers" and "mesmerists" who continued to speak of their activities in terms of magnetism and other occult fluids supposedly concentrated in their own persons. When Faria's ideas were finally rediscovered, and many mesmeric phenomena were at last given a semblance of respectability and a new, more scientific-sounding name, a full generation had passed and the scene had switched from France to Great Britain.

The Founding of "Hypnotism"

Traveling mesmerists commonly produced artificial anesthesias in their public performances. Magnetized subjects would be told that parts of their bodies had lost feeling, and then they would show no distress when normally painful stimuli were applied to the anesthetized locations. These performances raised doubt because most subjects were hired assistants to the magnetizers, but they eventually aroused the serious attention of a few legitimate physicians and surgeons. Chemical anesthetics were unknown until the mid-1800s, so surgical patients of the time inevitably experienced excruciating pain, and had literally to be strapped to the operating table for restraint. Surgeons made their reputations by speed rather than delicacy, and prolonged operations were impossible. And although conservative medical opinion held that pain was *necessary* for a successful operation, a few pioneering doctors sought some means of lessening the misery of surgery.

John Elliotson (1791–1868), a physician at London's University College Hospital, was accustomed to the ridicule of his colleagues for embracing new ideas. Among the first to use the newly invented stethoscope for listening to the sounds of the heart, he had been told by a superior "You will learn nothing by it, and, if you do, you cannot treat the disease any better." The instrument itself — now perhaps the most universally used of all medical tools — was castigated as "hocus pocus," a useless "piece of wood," and "just the thing for Elliotson to rave about."

All this was mere rehearsal for what happened in 1837 after Elliotson observed a stage mesmerist, was intrigued by what he saw, and made plans to investigate the anesthetic properties of mesmerism in his hospital. Upon learning of these plans, the university council passed a resolution instructing the hospital board "to take such steps as they shall deem most advisable to prevent the practice of mesmerism or animal magnetism in future within the Hospital."[8] Elliotson resigned his position in protest, and never got the opportunity to test mesmeric anesthesia on patients. He did use mesmerism for other medical purposes, however, and in 1843 he founded a new journal, the *Zöist*, to carry articles on "cerebral physiology and mesmerism, and their applications for human welfare."[9] But he remained an outsider, characterized by Britain's leading medical journal in 1846 as "a professional pariah" whose work undermined legitimate medicine and constituted "a black infamy degrading the arms of [University] College."[10] His journal lasted only until 1856 and never attracted much attention from the medical establishment. But still, it marked the start of a formal information exchange for scientists interested in mesmerism.

Meanwhile, a few other physicians had actually begun to test mesmerism as an anesthetic. In 1842 the English surgeon W. S. Ward performed a leg amputation and reported to the Royal Medical Society that his mesmerized patient experienced no pain. One eminent physiologist typified the Society's response when he charged that the patient had been some sort of imposter. Another authority contended that even if Ward's account were true, which he doubted, "still the fact is unworthy of consideration, because pain is a wise provision of nature, and patients ought to suffer pain while their surgeons are operating; they are all the better for it and recover better." The Society's best response, according to this worthy, would be to expunge all record of Ward's report from the minutes, as if it had never occurred at all.[11]

The more extensive experiments of **James Esdaile** (1808–1859), a Scottish physician practicing in India, proved only slightly more difficult to dismiss. Esdaile trained his assistants to magnetize patients before their operations, and became the first person to employ mesmeric anesthesia on a large scale and tabulate his results. He performed more than three hundred such operations in the late 1840s, many of them for the removal of scrotal tumors. Among his mesmerized patients, the mortality rate for this dangerous operation dropped from its normal fifty percent to five percent. Unfortunately, however, these impressive results were widely dismissed on the racist grounds that highly suspect "native" patients had been used, magnetized by equally suspect "native" assistants. The patients actually *liked* to be operated on, it was said, and merely acted to help Esdaile.[12]

Historically, mesmerism ranks among the first successful anesthetics to be systematically employed in Western surgery. And despite its initial dismissal by the establishment, it was gaining ground and would probably have been generally accepted were it not for the independent discovery of effective *chemical* anesthetics. In 1844, the American dentist Horace Wells extracted teeth painlessly from patients put to sleep by nitrous oxide. Within three years the blessings of ether and chloroform were discovered by doctors. These chemical anesthetics seemed much more understandable than mesmerism to mechanistically trained doctors, and had the further real advantage of being more reliable and universally applicable. Thus, after a brief flurry of excitement, the idea of mesmeric anesthesia faded into the background, and this apparently promising avenue to scientific respectability became closed off.

The Scottish physician **James Braid** (1795–1860) finally steered mesmerism close to the British scientific mainstream. After skeptically observing a stage mesmerist perform, Braid had been surprised and impressed when the mesmerist allowed him and a medical colleague to examine the entranced subject. The subject's insensitivity to pain seemed genuine, and his pupils remained dilated after his eyelids were forced open. Braid concluded mesmerism was something real, and that he would study it on his own.

He made few new or original discoveries when he did so, but he confirmed the results of earlier fringe figures, particularly Puységur and Faria. In carefully controlled experiments, he demonstrated the full range of mesmeric effects, and highlighted the susceptibility of the subject as opposed to the power of the operator. Also following Faria, he saw the trance state as akin to the state of sleep, and in 1843 coined the new term **neurypnology** — a contraction from the Greek roots *neuro* for "nervous" and *hypnos* for "sleep" — to cover the full range of mesmeric phenomena. He later altered this simply to **hypnotism**, and thus gave mesmerism the new and more respectable-sounding name that has remained in general use ever since.

Unlike the iconoclast Elliotson, Braid maintained ties to the medical establishment and published his studies in standard scientific form and in standard journals. Although he discovered little that was new, he took mesmerism out of the disreputable medical netherworld in which it had traditionally been practiced and brought it, as hypnosis, into the scientist's laboratory. Braid thus helped pave the way for the full scientific legitimation of hypnosis, which occurred back in France during the final quarter of the nineteenth century. This scientific rehabilitation occurred in the context of a lively controversy about the nature of hypnosis between two competing "schools," one centered in the provincial city of Nancy and the other in the capital, Paris.

335

The Nancy-Salpêtrière Controversy

The so-called **Nancy school** of hypnosis developed around the unlikely figure of a modest country doctor named **Auguste Ambroise Liébeault** (1823–1904). As a medical student he had been fascinated by an old book on animal magnetism he chanced upon. After establishing a successful orthodox practice just outside Nancy, he decided to experiment with hypnotic therapies and offered his patients an unusual bargain: They could be treated hypnotically for free, or by standard methods for the standard fees. At first only a few dared try the still-disreputable hypnosis, but its success and popularity soon grew great enough to endanger his livelihood. "Good Father Liébeault," as he came to be known, finally had to adopt a voluntary system in which he charged no fixed fees, but gratefully accepted whatever his numerous hypnotic patients offered to pay.

He used a simple, straightforward treatment method, telling each patient to stare deeply into his eyes while he repeatedly gave instructions to sleep. As soon as the patient fell into a light sleeplike state, Liébeault asserted that the symptoms would soon disappear. Often they did, showing once again the extent to which physical complaints can be manipulated by psychological and suggestive factors.

In the mid-1860s Liébeault's practice became larger than he could handle, so he temporarily retired to write *On Sleep and Its Analogous States, Considered Especially from the Point of View of the Action of the Mind on the Body*. This rather obscurely written book argued that the hypnotic state resembles normal sleep, except that the subject remains in a constant conscious *rapport* with the hypnotist throughout. A commercial as well as literary disaster, the book reportedly sold just one copy in the ten years following publication. Liébeault returned to practice, and would probably have died with no more than a local reputation had he not attracted the attention of **Hippolyte Bernheim** (1840–1919), a younger doctor from the city of Nancy.

An internist originally specializing in typhoid fever and heart disease, Bernheim heard improbable-sounding stories about the success of Good Father Liébeault and visited the hypnotic clinic to see it for himself in 1882. Instead of finding the farce he expected,

Bernheim was impressed and returned repeatedly to learn the older doctor's methods for himself. Soon he abandoned orthodox internal medicine to become a full-time hypnotherapist, treating hundreds of different patients and carefully analyzing their varying responses to hypnosis.

Following Faria and Braid's dictum that the most important hypnotic factors lay in the subject rather than the hypnotist, Bernheim compared the characteristics of strong versus weak responders to hypnosis and concluded that his more successful cases tended to come from the lower as opposed to the upper social classes. He speculated that lower-class patients may have been more conditioned toward strict obedience than their wealthier counterparts, and that this may have predisposed them to greater hypnotic susceptibility. In his 1886 book, *De la Suggestion et de ses Applications à la Thérapeutique* (literally, *On Suggestion and Its Therapeutic Applications*, but translated into English as *Suggestive Therapeutics*), Bernheim argued that human beings vary on a general trait of **suggestibility**, defined as "the aptitude to transform an idea into an act."[13] Strongly hypnotizable individuals presumably ranked high on this general tendency. Bernheim further argued that suggestible patients could be successfully treated by straightforward persuasion techniques as well as by hypnosis. If only patients could be made to *believe* they would be cured, often they really would.

Considerably more effective at writing and communicating than Liébeault, Bernheim elaborated these ideas in several books and articles which came to be identified as the main statements of the Nancy school. Essentially, they argued that hypnotic susceptibility was a trait closely related to a characteristic of general suggestibility, which varied considerably within the normal population.

As Bernheim was formulating this view in Nancy, a radically different theory of the hypnotizable personality was concurrently proposed in Paris by **Jean-Martin Charcot** (1825–1893), the powerful director of Paris's enormous Salpêtrière Hospital and one of the most eminent figures in European medicine. This "Napoleon of the Neuroses" had observed similarities between hypnosis and the illness called **hysteria**, and declared that hypnotizability and hysteria were aspects of the same underlying abnormal neurological condi-

tion. Thus he disputed the Nancy contention that hypnotic susceptibility was a normal characteristic. Adherents of the Nancy and
Salpêtrière positions vigorously debated with one another for several
years, in a well-publicized controversy that returned hypnotism to
the forefront of French public consciousness.

The son of a carriage builder, Charcot had chosen medicine over
art as a career after considerable deliberation. As a relatively im-
poverished medical student, he had been required to spend time
working in Paris's vast Salpêtrière Hospital, a "city within a city"
housing several thousand indigent and ill women in more than forty
buildings on its 125-acre site. Although *not* considered a plum or
fashionable assignment, the Salpêtrière struck young Charcot as
a potential treasure trove of cases for neurological research. He
resolved to make his fortune first, and then return to the Salpêtrière
as senior physician.

Thus as a young man he became the private physician and traveling companion of a wealthy banker, and then used his contacts to
establish a flourishing private practice. Like Mesmer, he married
a wealthy widow who furthered his entrée into Parisian society. And
with his financial security assured, Charcot made good his earlier
vow and returned to the Salpêtrière as senior physician in 1862.

He quickly expanded the research and teaching facilities of the
hospital, and conducted or directed much important research on
epilepsy, multiple sclerosis, poliomyelitis, and other neurological
diseases. A master showman, he gave brilliant clinical lectures in
which he imitated the symptoms of various neurological diseases,
engaged patients in dramatic dialogue, and had them wear hats
with long feathers whose different vibrations illustrated different
kinds of tremors. By the 1880s his lectures had become major cultural events, attracting large audiences of writers, philosophers, and
even famous actresses as well as doctors. The French government
officially recognized Charcot's achievements in 1882 by creating a
new post especially for him, as professor of neuropathology at the
Salpêtrière.

An autocratic and imperious personality, Charcot commanded
the rigorous devotion of many disciples who worked with him in
close daily collaboration. Unsurprisingly, a few subordinates chafed

under his discipline and sarcastically referred to his circle as *"la charcoterie"* (a play on the French word *charcuterie*, for a pork butcher's shop).[14] One disenchanted colleague, who knew Charcot well enough to be familiar with his medical history, sent him anonymous letters forecasting his imminent demise from a heart condition.

But whatever their personal reactions might have been, almost everyone admired Charcot's clinical brilliance. Recalling his artistic inclinations, Charcot described himself as a *"visuel,"* a person who *saw* things rather than thought them, and who imposed order on his clinical observations only after long periods of careful watching. Sigmund Freud, who as a young doctor spent the winter of 1885–1886 studying with Charcot, described the master's technique as follows:

He used to look again and again at the things he did not understand, to deepen his impression of them day by day, till suddenly an understanding of them dawned on him. In his mind's eye the apparent chaos presented by the continual repetition of the same symptoms then gave way to order: the new [diagnostic] pictures emerged, characterized by the constant combination of certain groups of symptoms.

Freud illustrated Charcot's preference for observation as opposed to theory by relating what happened when a fellow student at the Salpêtrière dared to protest that a clinical interpretation of Charcot's contradicted the Young-Helmholtz theory of color vision. Charcot responded in words that Freud savored for the rest of his life: *"La théorie, c'est bon, mais ça n'empeche pas d'exister"* (roughly, "Theory is fine, but it doesn't prevent things from existing").[15]

Charcot believed that many neurological diseases occurred either in a pure and complete form, which he referred to as the **type** for each particular illness, or, more commonly, in a partial or incomplete **forme fruste** (literally, *blurred form*). His research strategy was to minutely observe large numbers of patients with a particular disease until he could single out a small number as representing its *type*. Then he would study these "pure" cases intensively, in the belief they could reveal the essence of the problem.

The disease of epilepsy provided a model for this approach, subclassified into "grand mal" and "petit mal" forms representing the *type* and *forme fruste*, respectively. A grand mal epileptic seizure entailed three sequential stages: first an aura, a characteristic sensation or feeling that signals the onset of an attack; second a "tonic phase" in which the large muscles of the body go rigid, and the patient loses consciousness and falls (hence the ancient designation of epilepsy as "the falling sickness"); and third a "clonic phase" in which the body convulses spasmodically. Here, presumably, was the pure form of epilepsy, in contrast to petit mal seizures in which patients merely experienced inexplicable "spells" or brief fainting sensations.

Beginning in the 1870s, Charcot used this method to study a group of patients traditionally housed in the same Salpêtrière wards as epileptics, but experiencing a more bewildering variety of symptoms. These patients, suffering from **hysteria**, sometimes experienced "fits" of violent emotion, paralysis, anesthesia, convulsion, and memory loss that partially mimicked epileptic seizures or other neurological symptoms. Hysterics showed no obvious organic lesions, however, and their symptoms had several other features uncharacteristic of ordinary neurological disease. For example, some hysterical paralyses and anesthesias occurred only in sharply delineated body areas such as the part of the hand and wrist normally covered by a glove. Anatomically, this made no sense because the nerves of the hand and arm fall in no such pattern; afflictions resulting from ordinary nerve damage would not have such sharp boundaries. In general, hysterics suffered from symptoms that *resembled* ordinary neuropathology but did not quite follow the accepted and understood rules of neurology.

The name "hysteria" dated from the ancient Greeks, who first described and named the condition. They believed it to be an exclusively feminine disease, caused by the physical "wandering" of the uterus (the Greek word for which was *hystera*) from the abdomen to other parts of the body where it caused symptoms to occur. As therapy, they often prescribed a foul-smelling substance to be rubbed on the afflicted area and a sweet-smelling one for the abdomen, to entice the uterus back to its proper place. Sometimes this treatment seemed to help.

The great Greco-Roman physician **Galen** (*c.* A.D. 130–200) recognized that the uterus itself could not wander, and refined the theory by suggesting that that organ instead gave off pathogenic fluids or vapors that collected in the symptom sites. He prescribed smelling salts to disperse and dilute the pathological vapors, and sometimes this treatment too was followed by improvement.

When Charcot began to study hysteria seventeen centuries later, most medical thinking about hysteria had not radically improved. The prevailing medical opinion dismissed hysteria as simple malingering; symptoms which violated the accepted rules of neuroanatomy strained the credulity of many mechanistically oriented doctors, who felt patients were merely simulating their illnesses. Those physicians who did take the condition seriously still overwhelmingly believed hysteria to be exclusively feminine, and caused by some sort of abnormality of the reproductive system.

Charcot challenged both of these common views. He thought hysterical symptoms caused too much genuine distress to be merely faked. And further, he had examined several *men* outside the Salpêtrière who showed identical symptoms. Since hysteria could occur in men (although apparently less often than in women), it clearly could not be a disease of the feminine reproductive system. To determine the real problem, he applied his observational procedures to large numbers of hysterical patients, and eventually identified a few as representing the *type* for the condition. In Charcot's language, these patients suffered from **la grande hystérie**, or "major hysteria."

Intensive examination of these few patients convinced Charcot that their symptoms could be produced or alleviated by pressing on particular body locations, or "hysterogenic zones."* And when major hysterical attacks occurred, they came in a regular, four-stage progression. An "epileptoid stage," with symptoms similar to the onset of a grand mal epileptic seizure, came first. This was followed, in order, by a "large movement stage" where the patient performed seemingly automatic and sometimes violent acts; a "hallucinatory stage" in which imaginary sensations and feelings seemed subjectively real to the patient; and a final "delirious stage." The major-

---

*More than coincidentally, one of the most frequent hysterogenic zones isolated by Charcot was in the abdominal region of his female patients, near the uterus. Old theories lingered on in subtle ways, even for innovators like Charcot.

ity of hysterical patients who failed to display this spectacular and perfectly regular sequence of symptoms were said to have *petite hystérie*, or "minor hysteria."

Charcot's patients with *grande hystérie* were regularly featured at his public lectures, and became genuine celebrities at the hospital. They reveled in their role, and competed with each other for attention. Sometimes, it was reported, one might even mischievously sabotage a rival's demonstration by pushing her hysterogenic zone, to turn her symptoms off just before the public demonstrations.

Borrowing from a theory of "morbid heredity" then very popular in France, Charcot speculated that the root cause of hysteria lay in a hereditary, progressive, and generalized degeneracy of the nervous system, which interferes with the ability to integrate and interconnect memories and ideas in the normal way. Thus individual memories and emotional reactions that normally would cluster together become "dissociated," and are experienced by hysterics in isolation from one another.

As Charcot became increasingly committed to this view of hysteria, he was struck by the fact that hypnotized subjects seemed to have much in common with hysterical patients. Highly responsive hypnotic subjects could experience paralyses, anesthesias, and amnesias, and they often performed consciously inexplicable acts (posthypnotic suggestions) just as hysterical patients did. Hypnosis and hysteria both produced physical and mental anomalies that made little sense anatomically and that seemed beyond the conscious control of the subject or patient. Moreover, some of Charcot's prize patients with *grande hystérie* turned out to be highly hypnotizable, and in fact demonstrated their cycles of symptoms even more perfectly when hypnotized.

From this coincidence, Charcot concluded that hypnotic effects and hysterical symptoms had identical causes, and that hypnotic susceptibility in fact represented a *symptom* of hysteria: Only people with pathological nervous systems should experience such dissociated effects. Now deciding that hypnosis deserved further study as an aspect of hysteria, Charcot reasoned that the best cases to examine closely would be the best cases of hysteria. Thus his major hysterics did double duty, serving also as prime exemplars of hypnotic susceptibility in Salpêtrière research.

342

Charcot's assistants did most of the actual hypnotizing in this research, and one of their most important subjects was **Blanche Wittmann**, an attractive young woman whose spectacular performance of the stages of *grande hystérie* and haughty attitude toward other patients had earned her the nickname "Queen of the Hysterics."[16]

When hypnotized, Wit and the other compliant Salpêtrière subjects characteristically passed through three stages: **catalepsy**, where they became muscularly relaxed, motionless, and generally insensitive to external stimulation; **lethargy**, where the body muscles were generally flaccid, but sporadically activated into strong contractions and movements; and **somnambulism**, where complex automatic movements and actions occurred upon suggestion. The final stage strongly resembled the deep somnambulistic trances of earlier magnetic and hypnotic subjects. Charcot recognized that many hypnotic subjects did not follow the three-stage progression, but wrote them off according to his well-worn diagnostic formula of *types* and *formes frustes*. The three-stage subjects, he argued, manifested a "pure" state of **grand hypnotisme**, while the other, more common

Charcot lecturing on Blanche Wittmann. *The National Library of Medicine, Bethesda, Maryland.*

subjects represented only incomplete, *formes frustes* of the hypnotized state.

In 1882, Charcot presented his theory of *grand hypnotisme* to the French Academy of Sciences. The subject of hypnotism had been in official disgrace in France ever since the Franklin Commission, and the Academy had twice since then rejected reports on it. But Charcot's immense prestige ensured he would be carefully heard, and his neurologically oriented theory appealed to the conservative, mechanistic biases of the scientific establishment. Thus his presentation met enthusiastic approval; Charcot finally reversed the legacy of Mesmer and succeeded in getting hypnotism accepted as a legitimate subject of study by an official French scientific organization.

Just as Charcot made his triumphant presentation to the Academy in Paris, however, the seeds for dispute were being sown in Nancy by Bernheim, who was beginning his own serious study of hypnotism. Unlike Charcot, Bernheim did his own hypnotizing, and on hundreds of subjects as opposed to the select handful at the Salpêtrière. And as we have seen, he concluded that hypnotic susceptibility was a variable but *normal* characteristic, present in many people who were not major hysterics. In his patients, states of catalepsy and lethargy had *not* inevitably preceded somnambulism. Thus he attacked Charcot's theory, charging that *grand hypnotisme* was an artifact of the highly peculiar Salpêtrière setting. Charcot and his disciples reacted angrily, and dispute filled the French scientific literature throughout the 1880s.

In this disagreement between an obscure doctor from the provinces against a grand figure from the capital, most scientific observers naturally leaned at first toward the Salpêtrière side. But gradually, weaknesses in the Salpêtrière position became clear to objective observers.

Serious questioning began in the mid-1880s, after Charcot's young assistants **Alfred Binet** (1857–1911) and **Charles Féré** (1852–1907) reported some surprising experiments with Blanche Wittmann. Harkening back to Mesmer, they reintroduced the magnet into hypnotic sessions. With Wit in the somnambulistic stage, they induced paralyses or other effects on one side of her body, and then reversed the polarity of a large magnet they held in front of her.

Wit's effects immediately transferred to the other side. The hypnotists similarly reversed emotional states: After telling the hypnotized Wit that she felt very sad, for example, they transformed her piteous sobs into gay laughter with a simple flick of their magnet. In all seriousness, they suggested that here was an experimental technique for discovering pairs of "complementary emotions" analogous to the "complementary colors" already discovered by researchers of color vision. While admitting that some of their results seemed implausible, they assured their readers that the effects had been "entirely unexpected" and had "issued from nature herself, . . . showing an inflexible logic."[17]

But the logic of these experiments seemed suspicious to **Joseph Delboeuf** (1831–1896), a respected Belgian physiologist who five years earlier had publicly rebuked the young Binet for rushing into print with an ill-researched article on psychophysics. Delboeuf had a side interest in hypnosis, and in the early stages of the Nancy-Salpêtrière controversy accepted Charcot's theory of *grand hypnotisme*. But when he saw the impetuous Binet's name on this Salpêtrière study with improbable results, he began to doubt. "One fine morning I could contain myself no longer," he wrote, and he went to Paris to observe the Salpêtrière scene for himself.[18] He later offered a vivid portrait of what he found:

I will never forget those delicious hours. M. Féré and Binet are both young, both tall; M. Féré more reflective, it seems to me, and more accessible to objections raised; M. Binet more adventurous and more affirmative; the former with serious physiognomy, and a clear and profound gaze, the latter with fine features and a mischievous expression. Between them sat . . . the placid and "appetizing" Alsacienne Wit . . . not only wearing a complacent look, but finding visible pleasure in getting ready to do anything that should be asked of her; then myself, the old scholar, head full of reflections and questions, but never having had at hand this kind of experimental offering, a veritable human guinea pig.

When the young hypnotists began their demonstration for Delboeuf, he observed that Wit was extraordinarily responsive to the slightest hints. Féré dealt with her "as if playing upon a piano. . . . A light touch on any muscle — or even pointing to it without touching — made Wit . . . contract any muscle, even in her ear."[19] The celebrated magnet was large and wielded openly before Wit; Binet and Féré also spoke openly about her expected responses as if she were not there. When Delboeuf asked why they did not use an electromagnet whose polarity could be reversed surreptitiously, and take other measures to disguise their expectations from Wit, he was told that such was unnecessary because Wit was oblivious to such cues while in the somnambulistic stage of *grand hypnotisme*.

Delboeuf suspected otherwise, and returned to Belgium to replicate the Salpêtrière experiments on his own — only with adequate precautions against transmitting prior expectations to his subjects. He concluded that not only magnetic effects but also the entire enactments of *grand hypnotisme* were artifacts: the results of patients with great investment in their roles as prize subjects responding to implicit or explicit suggestions from their examiners. Delboeuf became a strong and influential supporter of the Nancy school, and the tide began to turn in their direction.

By 1891 even the Salpêtrière protagonists admitted they had been wrong. Binet learned a particularly valuable lesson from the experience, for he left the hospital and went on to become the most proficient experimental psychologist in France. In his later experiments he took great pains not to influence his subjects artificially, and he referred bitterly to unintentional suggestion as the "cholera of psychology."[20] We shall return to Binet and his more positive contributions in Chapter 12.

Charcot, too, admitted his errors on hypnotism, and privately predicted that his theories of hysteria would not long survive him. Soon after, in 1893, the warnings of his anonymous tormentor came true and he succumbed to a heart attack. Charcot's prediction was also correct, for people with different theories took over the Salpêtrière and by 1899 all that remained of *grande hystérie* were a few former patients who would reenact its four stages for the payment of a fee.

Yet for all his mistakes, Charcot made many positive contributions. Quite apart from his early neurological achievements in orthodox neurology, he was among the first to explore interactions between emotional and physical factors. He raised the important subjects of hysteria and hypnosis out of scientific obscurity. He trained many important students including Sigmund Freud and Alfred Binet, both of whom remembered Charcot with respect as a master clinician who had identified important problems for them. Problem *finders* can be just as important as problem *solvers*, and Charcot filled that role admirably. Largely because of his influence, hysteria, hypnosis, suggestion, and psychopathology all became topics of considerable general interest in *fin de siècle* France.

Another subject of considerable public interest at the time was the behavior of *crowds*. Since the Revolution, France had experienced more than a century of periodic social upheavals marked by "crazes" and examples of "mob hysteria." Inevitably, given the prominence of the Nancy-Salpêtrière controversy in public consciousness, some began to speculate about similarities and connections between the irrational behavior of hypnotized or hysterical subjects and that of people in crowds. Among the most influential of these was the energetic and controversial **Gustave Le Bon** (1841–1931), whose writings incidentally helped set the patterns and problems for newly emerging disciplines of sociology and social psychology.

Le Bon and the Psychology of Crowds

Born into a wealthy family, Gustave Le Bon had the income and the leisure to indulge a wide variety of interests over the course of his long life. He earned a medical degree but never practiced seriously, devoting his young adulthood instead to extensive travel in little-known regions of central Europe, north Africa, and Asia. Impressed by differences in character among the peoples he visited, he wrote a half-dozen ethnographic books about them. By today's standards his ethnography was crude and highly racist, depicting non-European groups as low on the evolutionary scale.

In the 1890s, Le Bon blended his racial attitudes with a conservative political ideology and a familiarity with the new literature on hypnosis to produce two influential books on group behavior. Neither *The Psychology of Peoples* (1894) nor *The Crowd* (1895) treated its subject with subtlety or scholarly depth, and Le Bon made no attempt to mask prejudices that seem highly offensive today. But the books explicitly raised several issues that have continued to engage social psychologists ever since.

Le Bon asserted that the most fundamental social responses of any person derive from *unconscious* ideas and motives. Posthypnotic suggestions and amnesias dramatically highlighted such unconscious processes, but Le Bon believed they pervaded many nonhypnotic situations as well. Indeed, his experience at training horses had convinced him that the most effective motivating ideas in *any* situation were unconscious. He argued that a horse was never satisfactorily trained until the specific "ideas" of the proper responses had become completely automatic and unconscious. The horse's experience presumably paralleled that of human beings, who focus a great deal of conscious attention on their behavior while *learning* a new task, but who perform it unconsciously and automatically after they have learned it really well. According to Le Bon, the best-learned (and therefore most effective) motivating ideas always operate at such an unconscious level, in horse and person alike.

Turning to *groups* of people, Le Bon argued that the most fundamental differences between nations or cultures derive from their different unconscious ideas and predispositions. Certain characteristic ideas within each group get so deeply assimilated in the course of development as to become ingrained, unconscious, and beyond the reach of normal rational deliberation. Le Bon pessimistically added that these unconscious national predispositions make genuine international harmony impossible. Although national leaders might be able to understand and rationally discuss each other's *conscious* ideas and motives, the more important unconscious ones must remain inaccessible. Thus he saw international strife and warfare as inevitable.

In *The Crowd*, Le Bon argued that individuals' already modest degree of conscious control over their behavior becomes even further diminished when they congregate in groups. He asserted that people in crowds tend to abandon both individuality and rationality, while assuming a kind of collective mind that can impel them to do things they would never dream of while alone. Unconscious racial ideas common to all members of the crowd presumably here become especially dominant:

General qualities of character, governed by forces of which we are unconscious, and possessed by the majority of the normal individuals of a race in much the same degree—it is precisely these qualities, I say, that in crowds become common property. . . . The heterogeneous is swamped by the homogeneous, and the unconscious qualities gain the upper hand.[21]

In elaborating upon the characteristics of crowds, Le Bon had something of a hidden agenda. A staunch political conservative, he deeply feared the consequences of mass uprisings in French society, which since the Revolution had usually (although not always) had left-wing goals. Accordingly, Le Bon attempted to discredit the motives and actions of typical crowds by describing them in generally negative terms. He depicted a crowd as always intellectually inferior to an isolated individual, and further marked by characteristics such as "impulsiveness, irritability, incapacity to reason, the absence of judgment and of the critical spirit, the exaggeration of the sentiments, and others besides—which are almost always observed in beings belonging to inferior forms of evolution—in women, savages, and children, for instance."[22] (Le Bon was no more a supporter of women's rights than of racial equality.)

Le Bon conceded that individuals in crowds sometimes perform heroic or noble acts, especially in warfare, that isolated individuals would be too timid to attempt. This too presumably happened because of the greater impulsiveness and thoughtlessness of crowds. "Were peoples only to be credited with the great actions performed in cold blood," he wrote, "the annals of the world would register but few of them."[23] Le Bon also felt, however, that these occasional positive and heroic products of the group mind were more than counterbalanced by responses of a destructive nature.

In trying to explain *why* crowds behave as they do, Le Bon posited three factors. First, he argued that people in a crowd sense both the power of their numbers and the anonymity of their individual selves. Their power enables them to do things that would be impossible for individuals, and their presumed anonymity helps them to disregard conventional assumptions of personal responsibility for their actions.

Second, Le Bon cited the effect of **social contagion**—the fact that when people observe others behaving in a certain way they become more inclined to follow suit. This effect had been well known since the days of Mesmer's *baquet*, and Le Bon explicitly referred to it and his third factor — enhanced **suggestibility** — as essentially "hypnotic" phenomena. In discussing these factors, Le Bon made the hypothetical connection between crowd responses and hypnosis explicit:

The most careful observations seem to prove that an individual immerged for some length of time in a crowd in action soon finds himself . . . in a special state, which much resembles the state of fascination in which the hypnotised individual finds himself in the hands of the hypnotiser. The activity of the brain being paralysed in the case of the hypnotised subject, the latter becomes the slave of all the unconscious activities in his spinal cord, which the hypnotiser directs as well. . . .

Such also is approximately the state of the individual forming part of a psychological crowd. He is no longer conscious of his acts. In his case, as in the case of the hypnotised subject, at the same time that certain faculties are destroyed, others may be brought to a high degree of exaltation. Under the influence of suggestion, he will undertake the accomplishment of certain acts with irresistible impetuosity. This impetuosity is the more irresistible in crowds than in that of the [single] hypnotic subject, from the fact that, the suggestion being the same for all the individuals of the crowd, it gains in strength by reciprocity.[24]

Note that even though the Nancy-Salpêtrière controversy had already been conclusively resolved in Nancy's favor when Le Bon wrote this, he found it convenient to emphasize aspects of both positions. He adopted Bernheim's language of suggestibility, while still associating the general state of hypnosis with enfeebled or pathological neurological functioning like Charcot. The connection between hypnosis and psychopathology died hard.

A further important chapter of *The Crowd* discussed the qualities of crowd *leadership*. According to Le Bon, the most effective (and dangerous) crowd leader is unreflective, single-minded, irrational, and fanatical — one who "has himself been hypnotized by an idea, whose apostle he has since become. It has taken possession of him to such a degree that everything outside it vanishes, and that every contrary opinion appears to him an error or a superstition." Further:

The leaders we speak of are more often men of action than thinkers. They are not gifted with keen foresight, nor could they be, as this quality usually conduces to doubt and inactivity. They are especially recruited from the ranks of those morbidly nervous, excitable, half-deranged persons who are bordering on madness. . . . The intensity of their faith gives great power of suggestion to their words. The multitude is always ready to listen to the strong-willed man, who knows how to impose himself upon it. Men gathered in a crowd lose all force of will, and turn instinctively to the person who possesses the quality they lack.[25]

According to Le Bon, effective leaders augment their personal magnetism by applying three simple techniques in communicating with their followers. First is **affirmation**. The effective leader always concisely accentuates the positive about his cause, denying opportunity for doubt and avoiding complicated reasoning. Simple slogans and credos which may be shouted in unison, and which are easy to remember and direct in their appeals to action and belief, are the stock in trade of a crowd leader.

The second technique is **repetition**. Effective leaders ensure that their simple affirmations and slogans get repeated over and over again, until finally they join the ranks of their followers' supremely powerful unconscious ideas. Le Bon illustrated this point with a homely example from everyday life:

The influence of repetition on crowds is comprehensible when the power is seen which it exercises on the most enlightened minds. This power is due to the fact that the repeated statement is embedded in the long-run in those profound regions of our unconscious selves in which the motives for our actions are forged. At the end of a certain time we have forgotten who is the author of the repeated assertion, and we finish by believing it. To this circumstance is due the astonishing power of advertisements. When we have read a hundred, a thousand times that X's chocolate is best, we imagine we have heard it said in many quarters, and we end by acquiring the certitude that such is the fact.[26]

Finally, Le Bon noted that effective leaders consciously take advantage of **social contagion**, by ensuring that at least a few enthusiastic supporters of their causes are planted in their audiences beforehand. These people can start a favorable "current of opinion" which spreads through the crowd by contagion. Although Le Bon described these techniques nearly a century ago, they will still seem highly familiar to anyone who has observed or participated in a modern political campaign.

Of course, the principles of affirmation and repetition had long been familiar to hypnotists, who typically repeated positive statements such as "Sleep!" or "Your eyelids are getting heavier and heavier" while inducing hypnosis. And ever since Mesmer's *baquet*, they had been aware of the value of contagion. So Le Bon once again borrowed concepts directly from the hypnotic situation when analyzing the principles of crowd leadership.

Despite its biased, unscholarly, and often sensationalistic tone, Le Bon's work addressed a large number of fundamental social psychological issues, and helped begin a tradition that persisted in the work of his more respectable successors for many years. As noted, he linked group phenomena not only with hypnotism in general but also with the *psychopathological* connotations originated by the Charcot school. For better or for worse, Le Bon helped forge a connection between social psychology and abnormal psychology. For many years the leading social psychological journal in the United States was called the *Journal of Abnormal and Social Psychology*, and only gradually did that conjunction of subjects come to be seen as arbitrary and not always appropriate.

And still today, many of the major research areas in social psychology bear on social-influence processes that originally arose in the general hypnotic situation. Consider, for example, such typical social psychology textbook headings as "persuasion and persuasibility," "attitude change," "suggestibility," "leadership," "obedience," "conformity," and "social facilitation." All of these currently important subjects address the general issue of how one person can influence the thought, feeling, or behavior of another, or how an individual is influenced by being part of a group. As such, they place modern social psychologists in a research tradition that extends directly back to Mesmer and animal magnetism.

Suggested Readings

For Mesmer's biography see Vincent Buranelli, *The Wizard from Vienna* (New York: Coward, McCann and Geoghegan, 1975), and for an excellent account of his movement's role in prerevolutionary France see Robert Darnton, *Mesmerism and the End of the Enlightenment in France* (Cambridge, MA: Harvard University Press, 1968). Useful general histories of hypnosis are Chapter 2 of Henri F. Ellenberger, *The Discovery of the Unconscious* (New York: Basic Books, 1970); Frank Pattie's "A Brief History of Hypnotism" in Jesse E. Gordon, ed., *Handbook of Clinical and Experimental Hypnosis* (New York: Macmillan, 1967); Chapter 1 of Peter W. Sheehan and Campbell W. Perry, *Methodologies of Hypnosis: A Critical Appraisal of Contemporary Paradigms of Hypnosis* (Hillsdale, NJ: Erlbaum, 1976); and Chapter 9 of Gregory Zilboorg, *A History of Medical Psychology* (New York: Norton, 1967).

Biographical material on Charcot appears in Chapter 2 of Ellenberger, cited above, and in George F. Drinka, *The Birth of Neurosis: Myth, Malady and the Victorians* (New York: Simon and Schuster, 1984). Sigmund Freud's reminiscences of Charcot appear in his 1893 obituary, "Charcot," reprinted in Volume III of *The Standard Edition of the Complete Psychological Works of Sigmund Freud* (London: Hogarth, 1962). Mark S. Micale's "The Salpêtrière in the Age of Charcot: An Institutional Perspective on Medical History in the Late Nineteenth Century," in *Journal of Contemporary History* (*20*:703–731, 1985), presents a vivid picture of the setting for Charcot's work.

Gustave Le Bon's always readable if sometimes outrageous *The Crowd* is available in paperback editions. For discussion of the context and importance of Le Bon's work see Gordon W. Allport's "The Historical Background of Modern Social Psychology," in Volume 1 of Gardner Lindzey and Elliott Aronson, eds., *The Handbook of Social Psychology* (New York: Addison Wesley, 1968), and Erika Apfelbaum and Gregory R. McGuire's "Models of Suggestive Influence and the Disqualification of the Social Crowd," in Carl F. Graumann and Serge Moscovici, eds., *Changing Conceptions of Crowd Mind and Behavior* (New York: Springer-Verlag, 1986).

11

Mind in Conflict: The Psychoanalytic Psychology of Sigmund Freud

---

"But Doctor, I'm not asleep, you know; I can't be hypnotized." Those words, half apologetic yet half taunting, rang in the ears of Sigmund Freud one afternoon in 1892. The young Viennese doctor felt sure he could cure this patient of her troublesome symptoms if only he could hypnotize her. And yet, in spite of his repeated assertions—"You are feeling drowsy; your eyelids are heavier and heavier; soon you will be fast asleep!"—the patient remained disconcertingly awake.[1]

Freud's patient suffered from **hysteria**, a condition that irritated or baffled most of his colleagues since its assorted symptoms had no discernible physical basis. Paralyses, tremors, losses of feeling and memory—these and many other problems usually associated with injury to the nervous system plagued hysterical patients, yet neurological examinations revealed no physical injuries. Perhaps understandably, most of Freud's fellow doctors dismissed hysterical patients as malingerers or fakers, simply trying to avoid their responsibilities through imaginary illnesses.

But Freud thought otherwise. He had studied with Jean Charcot, the great French neurologist who taught — as we saw in Chapter 10 — that hysterical symptoms were real, and worthy of serious attention. And Freud had visited the "Nancy school" in France, whose members had been partially successful in treating hysteria by hypnotizing patients, then simply and directly suggesting that their symptoms would disappear. Sometimes, though not always, they did. Freud had returned to confirm the partial success of direct hypnosis with some of his own hysterical patients.

More promising still, in Freud's view, was a technique using hypnosis *indirectly*, developed by his older friend **Josef Breuer** (1842–1925) while treating just one remarkable hysterical patient named **Bertha Pappenheim** (1859–1936). While nursing her terminally ill father, the young woman developed a series of debilitating hysterical symptoms. Breuer, a prominent physician who did not normally treat hysterics, made an exception for his family friends the Pappenheims. Gradually, and working together virtually as collaborators, doctor and patient devised a **cathartic method** that removed her symptoms.

In this treatment, Breuer hypnotized Pappenheim and then asked her to try to recall the first time she had experienced a physical sensation like one of her symptoms. Often, the hypnosis facilitated her recall of a previously "forgotten" but highly emotion-laden memory associated with the symptom. Upon remembering such an incident, she would give vent to its previously suppressed emotion. Following this emotional "catharsis" the symptom would disappear. For example, a severe and involuntary squinting of the eyes was traced under hypnosis to an occasion when she had sat by her dying and comatose father's bed, much upset and with tears in her eyes. Her father had suddenly awakened and asked for the time. Trying to hide her distress, Pappenheim had had to squint to see her watch and reply. Afterward, memory for the incident disappeared but the squint remained as a permanent symptom. Upon remembering the scene under hypnosis, however, she finally expressed the long-suppressed emotion, and the symptom disappeared. Other symptoms were treated similarly.

As the treatment progressed, however, Pappenheim became increasingly and openly attached to Breuer emotionally — a development that disturbed the proper doctor greatly, and his wife even more so. At the earliest possible moment he terminated treatment, and could never be persuaded to accept another hysterical patient.* But he did tell his young friend Freud about the case, and years later Freud remembered it when he began treating his own patients with hysteria. He tried the cathartic method himself, and found it worked far better than direct hypnosis, or any other technique he knew about. He treated several cases successfully, and then persuaded Breuer to collaborate in writing a book. Their *Studies on Hysteria* (1895) is recognized today as the first great classic of the new field that came to be called **psychoanalysis**.

Here, Freud and Breuer described several of their cases (including Bertha Pappenheim, disguised under the pseudonym "Anna O.") and offered the startling general hypothesis that *"hysterics suffer mainly from reminiscences."*[2] They did not mean ordinary reminiscences, but memories of emotionally charged experiences that have been somehow "forgotten" and placed beyond the reach of ordinary consciousness, to become disease-producing, **pathogenic ideas**. Without access to normal consciousness, the emotional energy accompanying pathogenic ideas cannot be gradually expressed and dissipated in the normal way, but instead remains bottled up or "strangulated." Stimuli that would normally arouse the memory now activate the strangulated emotional energy instead, which "discharges" into the musculature to produce a hysterical symptom. Thus, Freud and Breuer referred to many hysterical symptoms as **conversions** (of emotional into physical energy). With hypnotic assistance, however, patients could regain conscious access to their pathogenic ideas, and thus to the normal expression of their strangulated emotional energy. The causes of their symptoms could thus be removed.

Unfortunately, however, this promising cathartic method of treatment worked only with people who could be deeply hypnotized — and Freud had found to his chagrin that many patients could not be. Instead of falling into a sleeplike state where their memories

---

*Pappenheim eventually recovered from her infatuation with Breuer as well as her hysteria. After moving to Frankfurt, she became one of Germany's first social workers and an early feminist leader. Her achievements led to her commemoration on a 1954 West German postage stamp, in the "Helpers of Humanity" series.

became exceptionally fluent, they remained puzzled, anxious, or even defiant: "But Doctor, I'm not asleep, you know; I can't be hypnotized."

Freud's efforts to solve this problem led to an expanded and revolutionary theory — not just of hysteria, but of human nature in general. His remarkable solution did not emerge suddenly, however, nor was it simply the result of his own isolated genius. Developing over a period of several years, it integrated and synthesized a great many ideas Freud had been exposed to in a rich educational and personal background. We now turn to that background, as a preface to the theory that emerged.

Freud's Early Life

Sigmund Freud was born on 6 May 1856 in Freiberg, Moravia (the present-day town of Přibor, Czechoslovakia). His family moved to Vienna in 1860, where Freud remained until the Nazi menace forced him to London in 1938, for the final year of his life. Freud's father, twenty years older than his mother, had had two sons by a previous wife, and one of these had a son of his own just before Sigmund was born. Sigmund himself was the first of eight children borne by his mother. Thus he grew up as the oldest child in his immediate household, but with half-brothers as old as his mother, and a nephew older than himself. This unusual family constellation may have particularly sensitized Freud to the vagaries of family relationships, which he emphasized in his later theories.

As the oldest child in his immediate family, Sigmund became the unchallenged leader of his siblings. An outstanding student, he was granted a room of his own for study, and ample book-buying funds — both considerable luxuries given his father's modest income as a wool merchant. Freud justified these indulgences by developing independent talents — teaching himself Spanish so he could read *Don Quixote* in the original, for example — while still remaining at the top of his class at *Gymnasium* (secondary school). His early interests in history and the humanities seemed to be drawing him toward a career in law, until a chance encounter with an inspiring essay on "Nature" aroused his scientific ambitions during his last year

Sigmund Freud (1856–1939). *The National Library of Medicine, Bethesda, Maryland.*

at *Gymnasium*. Almost on the spur of the moment, the seventeen-year-old Freud enrolled in the University of Vienna's medical school in 1873.

There, he encountered several outstanding teachers, beginning with the philosopher and "act psychologist" **Franz Brentano** (1838–1917). In 1874, Brentano published an important book entitled *Psychology from an Empirical Standpoint*, which argued that the proper units of psychological analysis are *acts* of consciousness, rather than static sensations or feelings. Brentano further taught that any adequate psychological theory must be "dynamic," or capable of accounting for the influence of ever-changing *motivational* factors on thought. He also distinguished sharply between the "objective reality" of physical objects and the "subjective reality" of private thought, and he skeptically but seriously examined the literature on unconscious thought. Brentano thus introduced the young Freud to several issues that would preoccupy him throughout his career. Freud took five elective courses with Brentano in his first two years of medical school, and planned to take a philosophy degree with him after completing medical training. Soon, however, an even more influential teacher led him to change his mind.

Ernst Brücke (1819–1892), director of the university's Physiological Institute, became for Freud the figure "who carried more weight with me than anyone else in my whole life." Together with Hermann Helmholtz, Émile du Bois-Reymond, and other students of Johannes Müller, Brücke had been a founder of the enormously productive "new physiology" which rejected vitalism and sought mechanistic explanations for all organic phenomena. Tremendously impressed by Brücke and his mechanistic physiology, Freud began devoting all his spare time to volunteer research at the Institute — even delaying progress toward his medical degree so he could do so. He worked well, and by 1880 had published four articles on neuroanatomy, and looked forward to a career in that field.

Paying research positions were scarce, however, and Freud was a Jew in an anti-Semitic society that often discriminated in making university appointments. Still financially dependent upon his father in 1882, Freud fell in love with Martha Bernays and suddenly appreciated the necessity of earning money if he were ever to marry and support a family of his own. Somewhat reluctantly, he faced reality and began the several years of practical training at Vienna's General Hospital that would qualify him for a private medical practice.

At the hospital, Freud naturally gravitated toward specialties connected with neurophysiology, and concentrated his study under the famous brain anatomist **Theodor Meynert** (1833–1893). Freud became a prize pupil, particularly skilled in the diagnosis of localized brain injuries. In 1885, he won Meynert's support for a traveling grant to study in Paris with the celebrated Charcot. There he impressed the French master as he had Meynert, and won permission to translate Charcot's writings into German. Thus when he returned

to Vienna the following year, the thirty-year-old Freud had im-
peccable credentials, and felt able at last to marry and to begin a
private practice in the treatment of neurological diseases.

His return was marred, however, when he lectured to the Vienna
Medical Society about his study with Charcot and reported favorably on the Frenchman's theory of hysteria—a subject that had been
incidental to his interests when he went to Paris. Meynert objected
to the theory, particularly the part suggesting that men as well as
women could be hysterics. Freud felt that from this time forward
he lost favor with the Viennese medical establishment, and became
an "outsider." (Several years later, Freud reportedly had a deathbed
reconciliation with Meynert, who then confessed that he himself
had been a male hysteric, and that his opposition had originated
in his desire to hide the fact.)

Freud soon found he could not make a living by treating just
ordinary neurological cases, even though he bolstered his reputation by writing well-received books on cerebral palsy and aphasia.
He decided to augment his income by accepting patients with hysteria, and since he was among the very few Viennese doctors with
the background and willingness to take their symptoms seriously,
many came to him for help. Thus, almost by default, Freud arrived
at his position at the beginning of this chapter, seeking a universally applicable substitute for hypnosis in the cathartic treatment
of hysteria.

The Discovery of Free Association   Freud took a first step toward solving his problem by recalling an incident from his visit to the Nancy
clinic. A recently hypnotized subject had shown a typical posthypnotic amnesia until Bernheim, the hypnotist, placed a hand on his
forehead and said, "Now you can remember." The subject immediately recalled his entire hypnotic experience in minute detail.
Freud wondered if a similar technique might not help his patients
overcome their nonhypnotic amnesias for pathogenic ideas.

Accordingly, he devised a **pressure technique**, where patients
lay on a couch with their eyes closed as for hypnosis, but remained
normally awake. Freud then asked them to recall their earliest experiences of their symptoms, until their memories inevitably failed

before getting to the crucial pathogenic ideas. Freud then simply pressed their foreheads with his hand, and confidently assured them that further memories would follow. Often they did, and the chain of reminiscences could be continued. After repeated applications of pressure, some apparently genuine pathogenic ideas emerged, followed by emotional catharsis and symptom relief.

At first, Freud applied pressure frequently, whenever it seemed to him that memories were flowing in an unpromising direction. But he soon learned how hard it was to distinguish unpromising from promising directions. Once, for example, a patient responded to pressure by reporting flickers and starlike flashes of light. At first Freud assumed these were merely phosphenes (the sensations of light that normally occur whenever the eyeball is pressed) and was about to try again when the patient suddenly said the images were assuming geometrical shapes — crosses, circles, triangles, etc. — that resembled Sanskrit writing. Now intrigued, Freud asked what the figures made the patient think about. The crosses symbolized "pain," she reported, and a circle represented "perfection." Then she emotionally described and "catharted" her own feelings of pain and imperfection — feelings that had been recently intensified by reading an article in a spiritualist magazine, translated from the Sanskrit. Thus she arrived at genuine pathogenic material, but through a roundabout train of interconnected associations. From experiences like this, Freud learned to heed *everything* his patients reported as potentially significant, even if it seemed unimportant at first.

Further, Freud gradually learned he did not have to apply physical pressure at all in order to stimulate the memory. He only had to encourage his patients to let their thoughts run free, and to honestly and fully report whatever came to mind — even if it seemed irrelevant, stupid, embarrassing, obnoxious, or otherwise anxiety arousing. Though more difficult to follow than it sounds at first, this new practice of **free association** soon became Freud's standard method of treatment, used even with his hypnotizable patients. He believed it led reliably to pathogenic ideas, and also attuned him to several subtle but important psychological phenomena that had been masked by his previous reliance on hypnosis. When he used the old way, any peculiarity or failure in the treatment was easily explained away as a deficiency of *hypnosis*, such as the shallowness of the trance. But now, Freud focused more attention on the patient's associations per se, and on the relationship between patient and himself. With this new focus, Freud discerned several new and interesting features of hysterical illness.

First, he found that the pathogenic ideas recalled under free association lacked the one-to-one relationship with particular symptoms that had seemed to be the rule in patients like Bertha Pappenheim. Instead, a whole *series* of pathogenic ideas were often revealed behind an individual hysterical symptom. A patient with hysterical hand tremors, for example, associated three different emotion-laden memories with her symptom: of being strapped on her hand as a childhood punishment, of once being badly frightened while playing the piano, and of being required to massage her father's back. The only common feature to these memories was that they all involved her hands; yet with the recall of each, and the expression of the emotion connected with it, her symptom's intensity decreased. In Freud's new terminology, her symptom had not been simply determined by one pathogenic memory, but **overdetermined** by three of them at the same time. He came to believe that most hysterical symptoms were similarly overdetermined.

Patients' attempts to recover memories through free association led Freud to another, even more important idea. He increasingly became convinced that unconscious pathogenic ideas had not been simply "forgotten" in the way unimportant details are. Instead, the memories seemed to have been willfully and actively, although perhaps also unconsciously, **repressed** by his patients.

As evidence for this hypothesis, Freud observed that patients invariably "resisted" the free-association process somewhere along the line, in many different ways. Frustratingly often, they interrupted their associations suddenly and at crucial points, just as important and emotion-laden memories seemed about to be recalled. Occasionally in such instances, patients would directly admit with obvious signs of anxiety or embarrassment that what had come to mind was too ridiculous or obnoxious to be expressed. More often, however, their resistance was indirect and unconscious. Their minds suddenly and mysteriously went blank, for example, or they subtly changed the subject, or decided to question Freud's medical credentials and the justification for his unorthodox treatment methods. From the regularity of such direct and indirect resistances, Freud concluded his patients did not *want* to recall some of their pathogenic ideas, although often they remained completely unaware of the fact.

This unconscious resistance suggested to Freud that his patients held very complex attitudes toward their illnesses. On the one hand, they genuinely suffered from their symptoms, and wanted to co-operate with the doctor in getting rid of them. But on the other, their unconscious resistances undermined the progress of their therapy. Seemingly, a conscious part of each patient wanted to face the music and be cured, while another unconscious part feared that the emotional pain of a successful treatment would be too much to bear, and tried to sabotage the process. In short, Freud detected **intrapsychic conflict** in his patients, with different aspects of each personality clamoring for mutually exclusive goals. Later, he would come to see intrapsychic conflict as extending far beyond hysteria, and pervading virtually all human activity.

A further hypothesis emerged because many of the most strongly resisted memories and ideas turned out to involve *sexual* experiences from childhood. More and more patients reluctantly recalled scenes of early sexual mistreatment, often by parents or other close relatives. The patient with the hand tremor, for example, eventually recalled that her father had sexually assaulted her following the back massage. After several such reports, Freud speculated that repressed sexual experiences may have been *necessary* for hysteria to begin, constituting the most important pathogenic ideas that in some way began the entire repressive pattern.

In 1896, Freud boldly published this **seduction theory** of hysteria in a medical journal article. *All* hysterics, he confidently asserted, must have undergone sexual mistreatment as children. Freud did not then believe children were capable of genuinely "sexual" experience, however, because at that point in his career he accepted the common view that the sexual impulse arises only after puberty. Thus children presumably did not immediately experience their seductions as sexual. But with puberty and the arousal of the sexual drive, the *memories* of those experiences presumably became sexualized "after the fact." This reversal of the normal process, with memories becoming *increasingly* emotionally charged over time, was perhaps what made them subject to repression. So now, instead of consciously remembering their seductions and experiencing new and uncomfortable emotions with the memories, the patients would unconsciously produce hysterical conversion symptoms as a substitute. Symptoms would thus function as **defenses** against psychologically dangerous pathogenic ideas, appearing in consciousness as the lesser of two evils — unpleasant perhaps, but still less anxiety arousing than the pathogenic ideas themselves.

Perhaps understandably, Freud's seduction theory met a poor reception from many medical colleagues, who regarded him as something of a crank and stopped referring patients to him. Still worse, Freud himself soon began to believe that his patients' childhood seductions had been imaginary rather than real. Despite the sincerity with which the scenes were recalled and reported, in too many cases the stories did not stand up to other independent evidence.* "I no longer believe in my *neurotica* [theory of the neuroses]," Freud ruefully confessed to a friend in 1897.[3]

But if these free associations were not real memories, what were they? Freud was haunted by this question for many months. He could not believe his entire approach to hysteria was wrong: His therapy often helped, and it still made sense to regard symptoms as defenses against pathogenic ideas of *some* kind, even if they were not actual memories. Sexuality must have been important in *some* way, or else why would so many patients report scenes of childhood seduction in their free associations? The seduction theory was obviously wrong in detail, yet promising in its general direction. Eventually, Freud corrected and reconstructed his theory of hysteria in

*Freud's own sincerity in abandoning the seduction theory has been questioned by Jeffrey M. Masson in his provocatively entitled book *The Assault on Truth: Freud's Suppression of the Seduction Theory* (New York: Farrar, Straus and Giroux, 1984). Masson here charges that Freud merely caved in to the medical establishment by disavowing an unpopular point of view. Masson's charge seems unfounded however, since Freud seldom hesitated to stand up for *other* unpopular ideas throughout his life. And as the following account will show, he shortly developed a more reasonable alternative to the seduction theory.

a surprising new way. But to do so, he had first to investigate a new and superficially unrelated subject: the meaning and nature of **dreams**.

The Interpretation of Dreams

Freud became scientifically interested in dreams for several different reasons. For one, patients occasionally brought up dream material in the course of their free associations. For another, Meynert had taught that there were similarities between dreams and certain psychopathological conditions, a line of thought that Freud had elaborated on in some unpublished theoretical speculation of his own in 1895. And perhaps most important of all, Freud himself was a "good" dreamer, frequently remembering and being fascinated by his own dreams. In this combination of circumstances, Freud began subjecting dreams to analysis by free association — something he could do himself just as well as his patients. When he did so, he found that the free associations suggested a surprising new explanation for these common but often perplexing nighttime experiences. In 1900 Freud reported his findings in *The Interpretation of Dreams*, a long book commonly regarded as the most important of all his works.

Here, Freud distinguished between the consciously experienced content of the dream, which he called the **manifest content**, and a hidden or **latent content**, which originally inspired the dream but which emerged in consciousness only after free association. The manifest content, typically marked by disjointed chronology and fantastic images, often seemed unintelligible to the dreamer and failed to "make sense" in terms of his or her normal waking experience. But the latent content — those ideas and memories called up after extensive free association to the manifest content — seemed to have the greatest personal significance for the dreamer. Moreover, dreamers often *resisted* the uncovering of this latent content, much as hysterical patients resisted the recollection of their pathogenic ideas.

Freud's associations to his own "Dream of Irma's Injection" exemplified his general findings. He had dreamed of a social gathering where "Irma," one of his real-life patients, had fallen ill and was given an injection of the chemical propyl by one of his medical colleagues. Then Freud vividly hallucinated the letters and numbers comprising the formula for trimethylamin, yet another chemical substance. This strange manifest content made little immediate sense to Freud, for neither propyl nor trimethylamin was a real medicine, and a propyl injection would in fact have probably been dangerous.

But free association led to several ideas that did make sense. For one, Freud thought with relief that at least it was not he himself who had administered the ridiculous injection, so his colleague would have to bear responsibility for any unfavorable outcome. Further, he remembered that in real life Irma's nose had been operated on by his best friend, who had neglected to remove all the surgical packing. The patient, legally under Freud's care, had nearly died. Though Freud had made excuses for his friend, and had been unwilling to blame him for negligence, he now had to admit to feelings of anger and reproach. Finally, he remembered a recent conversation with this same friend about the chemistry of sex, in which the substance trimethylamin had been mentioned. This led to the thought that Irma's illness must have been sexual in nature.

This fragmentary analysis illustrates several essential relations between latent and manifest content, which Freud came to believe held true generally. He argued that every dream originates with a series of latent thoughts or ideas, which the sleeping mind *transforms* into manifest content by means of three processes he referred to collectively as the **dream work**.

First, the latent content contains thoughts more anxiety or conflict arousing than those of the manifest content, so Freud concluded that the manifest content *symbolizes* the latent content, although in a relatively "safe" way with images less distressing than the unvarnished latent content. In his language, a process of **displacement** occurs, with the psychic energy of the highly charged latent content being deflected or displaced to the related but emotionally more neutral ideas of the manifest content. Displacement thus serves a "defensive" function, enabling the dreamer to experience images less disturbing than the thoughts that originally inspired them.

In the second process of the dream work, several different latent thoughts may be symbolized by a single image or element of the manifest content. In Freud's analysis above, for example, trains of thought involving both sexuality and Freud's troublesome relationship with his friend were associated with the single image of "trimethylamin." Freud called this process **condensation**, on the logic that two or more latent thoughts sometimes "condense" onto a single manifest dream image.

Third, Freud observed that the manifest content typically represents latent *ideas* by means of concretely experienced *sensations*, or hallucinations. Dreams are not subjectively experienced as mere thoughts, but as real sights, sounds, feelings, etc. Thus Freud argued that the latent dream thoughts receive **concrete representation** in the subjectively real sensations of the manifest content.

The Primary and Secondary Processes The sharp-eyed reader may have noted that the three aspects of the dream work closely resembled processes Freud had already postulated to underlie hysteria. In hysteria, several emotion-laden and resistance-arousing pathogenic ideas could presumably be indirectly and "defensively" symbolized by a single and highly concrete physical sensation — namely, the overdetermined symptom. The unconscious "meaning" of a symptom — that is, its originating pathogenic ideas — could only be determined by free association, just like the latent content that gave meaning to dreams. Thus Freud saw both dreams and hysterical symptoms as resulting from similar unconscious symbolic processes.

Freud further reflected that these processes were the direct opposites of the mental activities normally associated with "logical" or "scientific" thinking. There, one uses terms that refer to concepts explicitly, rather than allusively and indirectly. One also uses concepts with precisely limited rather than surplus meanings, and progresses from concrete particulars to abstract generalizations in forming ideas, rather than the reverse. Moreover, in logical or scientific deliberation the various steps are available to consciousness, and subject to some degree of voluntary control. In dream or symptom creation, by contrast, all acts of displacement, overdetermination-condensation, and concrete representation occur unconsciously, and the dream or symptom finally appears involuntarily and "from out of the blue," so far as the dreamer or patient is concerned.

Accordingly, Freud hypothesized two ideal and diametrically opposed modes of mental activity—one unconscious and associated with dream and symptom formation, the other conscious and responsible for rational thought. Since he believed infants are born with the capacity for dreams but have to *learn* how to think rationally, he labeled the unconscious mode of thought the **primary process**, and the conscious mode the **secondary process**. Thus Freud saw adults' dreams and hysterical symptoms as instances where "mature," secondary-process thinking is abandoned in favor of the developmentally earlier primary process; that is, where a **regression** to earlier and more primitive ways of thinking has occurred.

Freud later came to believe that primary-process thought was not restricted to maladaptive or "abnormal" states such as dreaming and hysteria, but could also play a *positive* role in creative and artistic thinking. He noted that artists and poets use symbols to make points indirectly by allusion (displacement); produce works that may be interpretable on several different levels of meaning (overdetermination-condensation); and often symbolize abstract ideas by means of concrete scenes and images (concrete representation). Moreover, creative people often report that their inspirations occur to them involuntarily and from out of the blue—just the way dreams and hysterical symptoms intrude themselves into consciousness. In these cases, the "regression" to primary-process modes of thinking serves a good and adaptive purpose.

With all of these ideas, Freud did not "discover" the unconscious. He knew from his study with Brentano that many predecessors—going back at least to Leibniz with his "minute perceptions" (see pages 67–69)—had already postulated the existence of unconscious psychological activity. But Freud broke new ground by hypothesizing specific *rules* for the unconscious, describing it as a *lawful* phenomenon. Thus his conceptualization of the primary process as an unconscious mode of thought characterized by displacement, overdetermination-condensation, and concrete representation was an important milestone in the history of dynamic psychology.

The Wish-Fulfillment Hypothesis On a more immediately practical level, Freud's growing appreciation of the primary process in dreams helped him solve his dilemma regarding hysteria and the seduction theory. For a number of reasons — including some theoretical deductions as well as experiments with free association — Freud had concluded that all dreams represent the **fulfillments of wishes**. As he and his patients analyzed their dreams by free association, it seemed in virtually every case that the latent content included significant though often conflict-laden *wishes*, even when the manifest content seemed the opposite of a wish fulfillment. In such cases, the disagreeable manifest content helped deflect attention from the embarrassing or anxiety-laden nature of the latent content, thus assisting the defensive process of displacement.

For example, one patient who prided herself on being a superb hostess dreamed that she had had to cancel an important dinner party because of lack of food in her house. In the manifest dream and upon awakening she felt great disappointment, and she challenged Freud to demonstrate how her dream could possibly represent the fulfillment of a wish. Free association, however, revealed that the newly married patient had been worried about her husband's attention to another woman, and he had reassured her by remarking that the potential rival was too thin for his taste. On the day before the dream, Freud's patient had met this woman, who had said in a complimentary way that she hoped to be invited soon for dinner, since the patient always served such excellent meals that she stuffed herself. Thus the dream expressed the wish that the other woman would remain in a slender, unthreatening condition.

Another patient dreamed of the death of her favorite nephew — the very opposite of a wish fulfillment. But her free associations included recollections of a former suitor to whom she still felt strongly attracted, and whom she had last seen at the real funeral of her nephew's older brother. Thus her dream expressed a latent wish for a chance to see this desirable man again.

With this view of dreams, Freud found himself in an interesting logical position. Manifest dreams and hysterical symptoms seemed strikingly similar to each other structurally. Both symbolized unconscious and anxiety-arousing ideas indirectly by allusion (displacement); both could represent several unconscious ideas simultaneously with single images or symptoms (condensation or overdetermination); both gave concrete representation to ideas through subjectively real sensory or physical experiences; and both were created unconsciously and involuntarily. They only differed strikingly in their presumed causes, with dreams being stimulated by latent *wishes*, symptoms by apparent sexual *memories*.

But here, of course, was precisely where the seduction theory erred! The sexual experiences so regularly "remembered" by Freud's patients had never actually occurred. Freud now saw a possible explanation. Perhaps dreams and symptoms were similar in their origins as well as in their structure, and the seduction scenes reported by hysterical patients indirectly reflected sexual *wishes* rather than actual experiences. Such wishes would run counter to the civilized and consciously adopted values of his patients, who would deny and repress them. But perhaps the wishes were still real, and demanded at least partial and symbolic expression through the unconscious primary process. This idea, shocking as it seemed at first, gained unexpected reinforcement when Freud seriously examined *his own* free associations during a personally very difficult time in the late 1890s.

Self-Analysis and the
Theory of Childhood Sexuality

After hypothesizing that hysterics' pathogenic ideas really represented disguised sexual wishes, Freud had to do some hard thinking about the nature of human motivation. It now seemed that his patients, while outwardly completely proper and morally virtuous, secretly and unconsciously harbored sexual ideas and fantasies that respectable society would never tolerate. Furthermore, the ideas dated so far back into his patients' histories as to suggest they originated in *childhood*. As noted earlier, Freud at first shared the common belief that the normal human sexual instinct arises only after puberty. Thus he may have been tempted to hypothesize that hysteria resulted from an abnormally precocious sexuality; that is, that hysterics were people with a pathological sexual instinct that arose prematurely, and necessitated the extreme defensive reactions of conversion and dissociation.

Plausible as such an idea might have seemed at first, Freud soon had to reject it for some intensely personal and painful reasons. In autumn of 1896 his father died at the age of eighty-one, after a lingering illness. Though he had been expecting the death for some time, Freud was disconcertingly shaken by the event — "as if I had been torn up by the roots," he wrote to a friend.[4] For months he felt severely depressed, anxious, and unable to work — until finally he decided to regard *himself* as a patient and subject his own dreams and symptoms to systematic free association. He found some disturbing things in his self-analysis, things that led him to regard his hysterical patients in a new and even more sympathetic light.

The interpretation of a vivid childhood dream, parts of which had recurred during his adult crisis, loomed large in Freud's self-analysis. In this dream, "I saw my beloved mother, with a peculiarly peaceful, sleeping expression on her features, being carried into the room by two (or three) people with birds' beaks and laid upon the bed."[5] Free association revealed a welter of significant but disturbing latent thoughts, associated with this highly condensed manifest content. First, Freud saw that the dream was about death. The beaked figures resembled pictures of Egyptian *funerary* gods Freud had seen in the family Bible, and the expression on his mother's face was exactly like the one he had actually seen on his *dying grandfather*, shortly before the original dream. This image combining his mother and dying grandfather led to the thought of a dying *father*, and Freud recognized with a shock that one of his dream's latent wishes must have been for the death of his father. In childhood, he apparently had harbored unconscious hostile wishes toward his consciously loved father.

Equally disturbing *sexual* associations soon followed. Freud recalled that the German slang term for sexual intercourse (*vögeln*) derived from the word for "bird" (*Vogel*). Further, he had first learned that slang term from an older boy named *Phillip*, and the family

Bible with the beaked figures was an edition known as *Philippson's Bible*. Thus notions of sexuality were strongly associated with the image of his sleeping mother, and Freud felt forced to conclude that even as a child he had had "sexual" wishes regarding her.

Freud thus interpreted his childhood dream as surreptitiously expressing two repugnant but still deeply felt wishes: for his father's death, and for his mother's sexual attentions. "Death" and "sexuality" had presumably not meant exactly the same things to him as a boy that they did as an adult — with death implying simply *absence*, and sexuality meaning *any* kind of sensual, physical gratification — but Freud believed these were logical precursors to the adult concepts. And now he interpreted his peculiarly intense adult reaction to his father's death as the result of the fulfillment of his conflict-laden childhood wish. The "civilized" and conscious side of his personality had understandably rejected this wish, creating severe internal conflict and the eruption of his symptoms. Freud's followers have observed that it took great courage to uncover and acknowledge such distressing truths about himself, and number his self-analysis among the most important achievements of his life.

Soon, however, Freud came to believe he was not alone in having held repugnant childhood wishes. Indeed, he concluded that virtually *anyone* who honestly subjected himself or herself to analysis by free association would discover traces of similar wishes. Analyses of popular myths and legends as well as the dreams of "normal" people seemed to corroborate Freud's findings with hysterical patients and himself: The infantile desire to possess the opposite-sexed parent for one's exclusive sensual pleasure, and to be rid of the same-sexed parent as the major rival for such attentions, seemed an inevitable consequence of growing up in a typical Western family. *Oedipus Rex*, the classic Greek tragedy by Sophocles, portrays a story where these events occur: The hero, Oedipus, unwittingly kills his father and marries his mother. Thus Freud named this apparently universal constellation of unconscious wishes the **Oedipus complex**.

Further observations convinced Freud that these "Oedipal" wishes and fantasies were accompanied by other disturbing residues from childhood. "Perverted" or "disgusting" free associations involving the mouth or anus also regularly emerged, and Freud concluded that these too represented childhood wishes — wishes regarded with horror and repressed by the conscious, adult side of the personality, but that continued to press unconsciously for expression via the primary process. By 1905, Freud had had sufficient experience with these kinds of ideas to propose a radically new theory of both childhood and sexuality, in a book entitled *Three Essays on the Theory of Sexuality*.

Stages of Childhood Sexuality   At the turn of the century, childhood was usually viewed as a period of innocence and purity, terminated and corrupted with the physiological developments of puberty. The "normal" sexual instinct was thought to be absent in children, arising only with puberty. And when the instinct finally did appear, it was assumed to be highly specific, impelling the individual toward the single goal of propagating the species through genital heterosexual intercourse.

Freud's new theory contradicted this popular view on all counts. From the apparent universality of Oedipal fantasies, he inferred that sexuality profoundly influenced every child's mental life. Further, the sexuality of childhood seemed much broader than the "normal" adult kind, involving many kinds of activities considered deviant or perverted from the adult perspective. Accordingly, Freud postulated a *generalized* form of human sexual drive, present from birth onward, and potentially capable of gratification in many different ways. Its goal was physical or sensual pleasure of *any* kind, with "normal" genital stimulation being only one variety.

According to this new theory, the human infant is born in a state Freud called **polymorphous perversity**, capable of taking sexual (that is, sensuous) pleasure from the gentle stimulation of any part of the body. In the course of normal development, however, certain parts of the body inevitably get singled out as **erogenous zones** by being regularly and frequently stimulated in a pleasant way. In earliest infancy, the mouth or **oral zone** predominates as the locus of this broadened form of sexual gratification. When toilet training begins and children start to find pleasure in the voluntary control of their bodily functions, the **anal zone** assumes particular importance. Only later, after children have developed fuller control over their bodies, does stimulation of the **genital zone** become a major source of sexual pleasure.

Freud argued that social factors within the family strongly interact with these developments, as many pleasure-producing activities arouse parental anxiety or disapproval and the child learns that only a relatively small number of gratifications are socially acceptable. Gradually, expressions of the originally undifferentiated sexual drive become channeled into socially acceptable forms, and by late adolescence they typically assume a heterosexual-genital orientation. Thus for Freud the "normal" expression of sexuality is not a preordained consequence of an inalterably fixed instinct, but only the most common end result of a long process of social and psychological development. Only after consciously abandoning most of their childhood forms of sexuality do individuals become "civilized" and sexually "normal." In sum, Freud argued that the traditional picture had things exactly backwards: Children are not innocents who become corrupted sexually by the evils of the world; instead, they are born with primitive, undisciplined, and "perverted" tendencies that they must learn to curb as they mature and become civilized.

Freud further theorized that the conflict between unruly childhood sexuality and the forces of socialization typically becomes particularly acute at about the age of five. By then, the three erogenous zones have usually been discovered, and the opposite-sexed parent has been singled out as the most desirable source of sensual gratification with the same-sexed parent as the major rival. Thus the Oedipus complex emerges. Oedipal wishes produce great inner conflict, however, because the child recognizes the same-sexed parent as larger, stronger, and potentially dangerous. If that parent *knew* what the child was thinking, he or she might reciprocate the negative wishes, with disastrous results. Thus the Oedipal wishes themselves become dangerous, because they threaten to cast the child into a dangerous and hopeless battle. Here is the child's motive to repress the Oedipal wishes, to force them into unconsciousness so they no longer emerge to arouse anxiety. Most other aspects of childhood sexuality, associated as they are with Oedipal wishes, disappear from consciousness along with them.

Freud argued that the child at this point enters a **latency stage**, which lasts until the physical maturation of puberty reawakens the sexual drive with renewed force. During latency, the positive side of the child's feelings toward the same-sexed parent dominates consciousness, facilitating a positive identification with a socially approved role model. Freud emphasized that these positive feelings had always existed alongside the negative ones, even during the height of the Oedipal complex. He believed that people's deepest feelings toward the important people in their lives are never completely positive *or* negative, but always combine both attitudes in a state he called **ambivalence**. During latency, however, the negative feelings toward the Oedipal rival become repressed, along with childhood sexuality. Thus freed from the preoccupations and anxieties generated by the sexual drive, the child enters a psychologically tranquil period ideally suited for the kinds of learning tasks typically imposed by schools and other socializing institutions outside the immediate family.

Freud took pains to add, however, that the Oedipus complex and childhood sexuality are never *destroyed*, but merely *repressed*. They always persist beneath the surface of consciousness, seeking whatever indirect and disguised forms of expression they can find. Dreams provide one natural and usually benign outlet, hysterical symptoms a more extreme and maladaptive one. And as we shall see later, Freud came to see much of everyday behavior as an attempt to resolve conflicts engendered by the omnipresent but largely submerged sexual drive.

Psychoanalytic Psychotherapy

Even as Freud theorized about normal people's dreams and the psychology of children, he continued to earn his living as a psychotherapist for disturbed adults. And like his general theories, his therapeutic technique changed and developed over the years.

At first, Freud saw his therapeutic task as simple and straightforward. All he had to do, it seemed, was encourage free association until the repressed pathogenic ideas became conscious and the symptoms became unnecessary. But Freud gradually learned that his patients' unconscious resistances to the treatment could be devilishly subtle and insidious, and that he often had to be content with modest improvement rather than complete "cures" of his patients. Sometimes treatments that began promisingly ended disastrously, as in the instructive case of "Dora."

The Case of Dora Eighteen-year-old Dora suffered from mild hysteria, and was brought to Freud by her father after threatening suicide. Intelligent and verbal, she took quickly to free association and seemed to understand Freud's early interpretations of her associations in terms of infantile sexuality. After just a few sessions, Freud wrote confidently to a friend that "the case has opened smoothly to my collection of picklocks."[6]

Dora's conflicts arose from her relationships with her parents and their close friends, a couple Freud called "Herr and Frau K." Dora's personable father was often ill and in need of nursing, a service more often provided by Frau K. than by Dora's mother, whom she described as a drab and unaffectionate woman obsessed by housecleaning. As Dora entered adolescence, she recognized that Frau K. had become her father's mistress as well as his nurse. Herr K. apparently made no fuss about his wife's liaison with his friend, but contented himself with amorous adventures with his servants. As Dora grew into an attractive young woman, however, he also turned his attention toward her. He presented her with an expensive jewel-case, and once tried to kiss her—an act Dora said disgusted her because of the strong smell of cigar smoke on his breath.

This sordid situation reached a climax shortly before Dora saw Freud, when her family and the K.s shared a vacation house. Herr K. complained that he got nothing from his wife, and propositioned Dora directly. Dora indignantly refused but said nothing to her parents. Then every night for two weeks she had the same vivid nightmare, after which she insisted on accompanying her father on a business trip away from the vacation house. On the trip she told her father about Herr K. and her nightmare ceased, although she began to experience hysterical symptoms. After they worsened and she threatened suicide, Dora's father brought her to Freud.

Once in analysis with Freud, Dora's dream recurred. Freud

naturally asked her to describe it and free-associate to it. The manifest content was the following:

A house was on fire. My father was standing beside my bed and woke me up. I dressed myself quickly. Mother wanted to stop and save her jewel-case; but father said: "I refuse to let myself and my two children be burnt for the sake of your jewel-case." We hurried downstairs, and as soon as I was outside I woke up.[7]

Dora's fluent free associations to this dream lent Freud his initial optimism about the case. Herr K. was obviously involved through associations to the jewel-case and the fire, which recalled the smell of tobacco smoke from his breath. Dora remembered that she had always dressed quickly in the vacation house, as in the dream, because her bed was in an exposed hall and she feared being seen in partial undress by Herr K. The fire also seemed to symbolize the sexual stirrings that Dora admitted she was beginning to feel. She finally acknowledged a certain attraction to Herr K., along with her fear and repugnance.

Freud was not surprised when Dora also produced associations to childhood sexuality. The fire led to thoughts of water, which in turn recalled childhood memories of bedwetting and masturbation. After Dora remarked that her father used to wake her up at night and take her to the bathroom to prevent the bedwetting, Freud felt sure he understood the major latent wish expressed by the dream.

He believed the dream had substituted Dora's original Oedipal attraction to her father for her current, conflict-laden attraction for Herr K. He summarized: "She summoned up an infantile attraction for her father so that it might protect her against her present affection for a stranger."[8] The wish expressed by the dream was to run away with her father, and to be protected by him from the disturbing impulses of her maturing sexuality, just as she had been protected by him from her bedwetting as a child. When Dora went with her father on the business trip, she fulfilled that wish in reality and the dream consequently ceased to recur.

Dora seemed to accept this interpretation, lending Freud added confidence that she would soon have full insight into her problems and be cured. Shortly afterward, however, she stunned him by announcing that she had had enough of his treatment and would return no more, even though many of her problems remained unresolved. She kept her word and never returned.

In retrospect, Freud realized that he had been totally insensitive to one whole dimension of the case, and that he had failed to carry his interpretation of the dream as far as he should have. For while he had explained why the dream had originally occurred at the vacation house, he had not asked why it recurred in the middle of treatment. Its reappearance, he now believed, signified not only Dora's previous complicated feelings toward *Herr K.*, but also her current ambivalence toward *Freud himself.* He too was a heavy cigar smoker, and he had frequently used the expression "There can be no smoke without fire" in the course of the treatment. And while he was not a philanderer like Herr K., he did openly discuss highly charged sexual topics with Dora. Thus her dream was once again useful in expressing complex feelings about her emotional entanglement with a "stranger" and her wish to flee to the relative safety of her father — only this time the stranger was Freud instead of Herr K. And just as Dora fulfilled the first wish by fleeing from Herr K., so she now fled from Freud.

This experience with Dora, reinforced by similar if less dramatic exchanges with other patients, convinced Freud that therapy sessions were inevitably complicated by what he called **transference** feelings. That is, patients tended to transfer onto him, as the therapist, motives and attributes of the important people from their past lives who were implicated in their neurotic symptoms. Regardless of what Freud was "really" or "objectively" like, his patients would react to him *as if* he were like their mothers, fathers, or other emotion-charged figures such as Herr K. All too easily, as with Dora, transference feelings could become part of the resistance and hinder therapeutic progress. In short, Freud learned that he and his patients would have to pay just as much attention to the transference relationships between themselves as to the symptoms per se, if therapy was to proceed as it should.

Now, individual symptoms seemed less important to Freud, since he saw them as relatively superficial manifestations of underlying emotional conflicts, each one capable of expressing itself in many different ways including dreams, transference, and a variety of different specific symptoms. Thus symptoms were not independent entities. The disappearance of any particular symptom signified little because the conflict that had caused it might promptly reexpress itself in another, equally maladaptive substitute. Any enduring "cure" thus required the uncovering and analysis of the entire complex of underlying conflicts — a process likely to take months or even years to complete.

To judge when an analysis approached successful completion, Freud now attended more to the transference relationship than to the symptoms. Both symptoms and transference reflected the same underlying conflicts, but the transference lay closer at hand for constant scrutiny. When Freud could feel that a patient was beginning to respond to him more as he really was, and less as if he were a shadowy figure from the past, he judged that the long analytic process was finally nearing completion.

Thus in the end, Freud did not provide the quick and specific cures for hysterical symptoms he had originally hoped for. Instead, he provided *psychoanalysis* — a long and often difficult process of self-examination that offered symptom relief almost as an incidental consequence of increased insight into one's unconscious mental life.

Metapsychology and the Ego's Defense Mechanisms

From the very beginning of his career, Freud sought to place his clinical discoveries within a broader theoretical context, to ask about the *general* features of the human mind that enabled it to produce symptoms, dreams, and transferences along with the great variety of everyday and "normal" mental phenomena. He referred to these attempts to develop a general model of the mind as his **metapsychology**.

Freud's earliest metapsychological theorizing relied heavily on his neurophysiological background. Consistent with Brücke's and Meynert's training, Freud attempted to hypothesize neurological structures and mechanisms capable of producing dreams and hysterical symptoms, as well as normal secondary-process thought. He wrote out his ideas in 1895 in a long draft manuscript never intended for publication, but found by his editors after his death and published under the title *Project for a Scientific Psychology*. This un-completed and sometimes obscure manuscript has proven extraor-dinarily interesting to Freud scholars for the light it sheds on Freud's developing but not yet mature theory. Among the subjects to receive their first treatment there were the opposition between primary and secondary processes, the wish-fulfillment theory of dreams, and the concept of an "ego" as the directive, executive agency in the mature human psyche.[9]

But while the *Project* was unquestionably a valuable undertaking for Freud, he soon came to feel that its neurophysiological frame-work imposed unnecessary constraints on his theorizing. The nervous system was too poorly understood to allow him to specify detailed neural mechanisms for all of the psychological phenomena that in-terested him. Thus Freud decided to avoid neurological technicali-ties by expressing his metapsychology in completely psychological terms. He would try to keep his concepts *consistent with* available neurological knowledge, and he would hope that future neurological discoveries by others would suggest precise mechanisms to account for them. As he wrote in 1900:

I shall entirely disregard the fact that the mental apparatus with which we are . . . concerned is also known to us in the form of an anatomical prepara-tion, and I shall carefully avoid the temptation to determine psychical local-ity in any anatomical fashion. I shall remain upon psychological ground.[10]

Freud's most famous descriptions of "psychical localities" appeared in a short 1923 book entitled *The Ego and the Id*. Here he extrapo-lated from his clinical experience and argued that the human mind is constantly beset by three different kinds of demands that inevi-tably *conflict* with one another, and that the mind's major function is to resolve those conflicts as best it can.

The first class of demands arises from within the body itself, in biologically based urges for nourishment, warmth, sexual gratifica-tion (in the broadened Freudian sense of the term), and the like. Freud referred collectively to these internal, biologically based de-mands as the **instincts**. A second group of demands is imposed by external reality; in order to survive, a person must learn to manipu-late the environment to avoid physical dangers and to obtain the objects necessary for gratifying the instincts. From his earliest metapsychological writings onward, Freud had emphasized situations where instinctual and reality-based demands conflicted with each other, especially where instinctual gratifications had been delayed, modified, or abandoned because of the constraints of the real world.

By 1923, Freud had further come to believe that *moral* demands impinge on the mind independently of the instincts and external reality, because of the obvious fact that one's conscience often conflicts with both wishes and reality. People often refrain from gratifying their impulses because they think it would be *wrong*, even if there is nothing in physical reality to prevent them from doing so. People sometimes ignore the dangers of physical reality and risk their lives in the service of a moral ideal. Since moral demands could motivate people in directions contrary to both the instincts and the demands of physical reality, Freud believed that any complete model of the human psyche would have to make an important and separate place for them.

Accordingly, Freud's 1923 model posited separate systems to process and represent the three kinds of psychic demands. First, he postulated the **id** as the repository of unconscious but powerful impulses and energies from the instincts. Then he hypothesized a **perception-consciousness system** — habitually abbreviated simply as **pcpt.-cs.** — that conveys information about external reality to the mind. This system not only produces immediate consciousness of whatever is being perceived, but also leaves behind *memories* that remain open to future consciousness in a part of the psyche Freud described as "preconscious." Moral demands, arising independently of instincts and external reality alike, presumably originated from a separate agency completely within the psyche which Freud called the **superego**.

Thus the id, the external-perception system, and the superego all introduce their differing and inevitably conflicting demands into the psyche, which must sort them out and achieve some sort of compromise among them. Specific responses must be devised and executed that will permit some degree of instinctual gratification, but that will not endanger the organism from physical reality or violate the dictates of conscience. Freud's hypothetical psychic agency for affecting these compromises was the **ego**.

While recognizing that graphical representations of abstract concepts may not appeal to everyone, Freud drew an "unassuming sketch" of his psychic structures which is reproduced here as Figure 11–1.[11] The id lies open to the instincts from the body at the bottom of the diagram, while pcpt.-cs. is perched like an eye on the top, oriented to the external world. The superego is contained within the psyche to one side. Squarely in the middle, where it must mediate among all of the conflicting parties, is the ego.

Consistent with its central location in Freud's diagram, the ego attracted much of Freud's theoretical attention during the latter part of his career. He came to see virtually everything a person does as the result of some sort of compromise among conflicting demands, and hence a product of the ego.

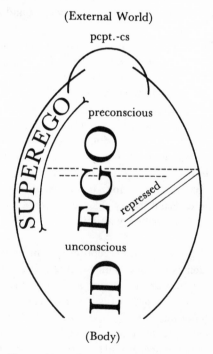

Figure 11–1. *Freud's diagram of the psyche.*

Some of the ego's compromises favor one kind of demand over the others, and some are more adaptive than others. Hysterical symptoms represent relatively maladaptive compromises where considerations of external reality are largely ignored and where the wishful pressures of the id are confronted mainly by the superego; thus the id impulses receive disguised rather than overt expression. Dreams are similar, although not so maladaptive because they occur in a sleeping state where the consequences of ignoring reality are not so severe. These relatively dramatic kinds of compromises, of course, had been the starting points for Freud's analysis of intrapsychic conflict.

Increasingly, however, Freud saw everyday life as dominated by other, less dramatic ego compromises he called **defense mechanisms**. Assisted by his daughter **Anna Freud** (1895–1982), who had herself become a skillful theoretician as well as a pioneer in the psychoanalysis of children, he distinguished and defined a number of specific defense mechanisms that we shall only sample here, for illustrative purposes.

The common defense mechanism of **displacement** is said to occur whenever someone redirects an impulse toward a substitute target that resembles the original in some way, but is "safer." A classic example is the man who suffers in silence the taunts of his boss, then "displaces" his anger at home by yelling at his wife and kicking his dog. Oedipal sexual impulses are presumably displaced when people fall in love with partners who resemble their opposite-sexed parents in some significant way—an extremely common occurrence, according to Freud.

The defense mechanism of **projection** occurs when one does not directly acknowledge one's own unacceptable impulses, but reverses the onus by attributing them to someone else instead. If you become angry at someone but have a superego that interprets hostile feelings as wrong, you may project your anger and see your target as angry and hostile toward *you* instead. Now, of course, you may act aggressively toward your target, but interpret your action as self-defense or retaliation rather than unprovoked hostility. A venerable psychologist's joke about the inkblot test illustrates the projection of sexuality: A patient repeatedly sees and reports sexual images in the ambiguous shapes of the inkblots, and the examiner says that he is obsessed by sex. The patient replies indignantly, "What do you mean? *You're* the one who's showing the dirty pictures!"

In **intellectualization**, some impulse- and emotion-charged subject is directly approached, but in a strictly intellectual manner that avoids emotional involvement. An adolescent beset by sexual urges may read up in the technical literature on sexuality, for example, while avoiding any direct sexual entanglements. Academics and professors are said to intellectualize frequently, becoming technical experts in subjects associated with their personal emotional conflicts.

Some other defense mechanisms affect the *memory* of gratifications after they have been allowed to occur. In **denial**, for example, a person believes and behaves as if an instinct-driven event had never occurred. Upon hearing an adult approaching, two furiously fighting children may suddenly begin behaving quietly and sociably; after the adult departs they continue to be friends, successfully denying the aggression they had been openly expressing shortly before. More sophisticated than simple denial is **rationalization**, where people act because of one motive but explain the behavior (to themselves as well as to others) on the basis of another, more acceptable one. Thus a father may get a certain amount of satisfaction from spanking his child, but argue and believe afterward that the spanking had been completely for the child's own good.

Similar to the defense mechanisms, although usually placed in a separate category because of their unambiguous adaptiveness and social desirability, are the ego compromises Freud called **sublimation** and **love**. Sublimation theoretically occurs when the primal energy from an instinct becomes channeled and "tamed" by superego and reality demands, so as to produce a creative and socially valuable result. An artist may create a work about sexuality and aggression, for example, much as a dreamer creates a manifest dream about the instinct-laden latent dream thoughts. Artists, however, "work over" their images and symbols by secondary-process thought so that their final products are more polished and communicative than ordinary dreams. Freud believed that all effective artists, scientists, social reformers, and other creative people are originally motivated by primitive instinctual energies, but that their egos manage to "sublimate" those energies, redirecting them in socially useful directions.

For Freud, "love" occurs when the well-being of another person becomes as important a goal as one's own; thus the gratification of the loved person can be a satisfying substitute for gratification of the self. Moreover, love relationships can be mutual, so one receives gratification and concern in return. Sexual and affectional needs may also be met in truly loving relationships, so instinct, reality, and conscience are all satisfied at once.

But while Freud saw love and sublimation as the best of the compromises available to the ego, they also had limitations that increasingly preoccupied him toward the end of his life. In a somber work entitled *Civilization and Its Discontents* he observed that love poses problems because of the possibility of losing the loved person through desertion, death, or other separation. Few human experiences are more catastrophic than the loss of a loved person, and those who have once lost at love may be reluctant to try it again as the answer to the human dilemma. Effective sublimation often requires a degree of skill (such as artistic ability) beyond the reach of ordinary people, and the gratification it provides is mild and several steps removed from its original instinctual goal. Freud feared that most people could never be fully satisfied by such attenuated gratifications. Finally, Freud observed the catastrophe of World War I and the incipient rise of Hitler in Germany, and worried that modern "civilization" was developing in such a way as to increase opportunities for expression of the instincts of aggression and death, while decreasing them for sexuality and love. Organized acts of murder and carnage were increasingly promoted by society and praised in the name of patriotism and morality. If the trend continued, Freud thought humanity's future would be bleak.

In sum, Freud saw irreconcilable conflict as the essence of the human condition. His theory of the mind led to the rather sobering conclusion that the best a person can hope for is to make decent compromises among the conflicting demands of life. If one has developed a strong and resourceful ego, either naturally or through a process like psychoanalysis, and if one is fortunate enough to live in a society that provides ample opportunities for sublimation and love, the chances of doing this are enhanced. But even so, there can be no guarantees.

The Freudian Legacy

Some of the pessimism expressed in Freud's later works undoubtedly sprang from his increasingly difficult personal situation. In 1923 his favorite grandson died of tuberculosis, causing Freud to shed tears publicly for the only recorded time in his life, and enhancing his sense of the fragility of relations with loved ones. That same year Freud himself developed cancer of the jaw, and underwent the first in a long series of painful and disfiguring operations that darkened the last sixteen years of his life. Hitler's rise made Vienna increasingly dangerous for Jews throughout the 1930s, and Freud and his immediate family finally fled to London in June of 1938. His four elderly sisters were denied exit visas and stayed behind, shortly to perish in the Nazi gas chambers. Perhaps fortunately, Freud himself never learned of this, for he succumbed to his long illness on 23 September 1939, as Europe lay on the very brink of World War II.

Freud left an extraordinary intellectual legacy, and has remained constantly in the public eye for the half century since his death. Books defending or attacking him and his theories continue to pour from the presses today, and new biographies continue to fascinate the public as his unpublished papers and correspondence become available to scholars.[12] And for present-day psychotherapists and psychologists, Freudian theory remains a major source of both inspiration and contention.

During his lifetime, Freud inspired a large band of followers to create the International Psycho-Analytic Association as the official organization for carrying on and developing his practices and theories. The Association continues today, and many psychoanalysts earn their living by practicing therapy much as Freud did.

Another significant group of therapists and theorists continue to accept *part* of Freud's theory, or acknowledge Freud as the starting point for their own somewhat different approaches. **Erik Erikson** (b. 1902), for example, has proposed a series of psycho*social* stages to parallel the child's typical development through the psycho*sexual* periods originally hypothesized by Freud, and has extended the developmental analysis to include later stages of the life cycle. The **object relations school** — originating in the close analysis of infants' earliest relationships with their mothers by **Melanie Klein** (1882–1960) and further developed by the British psychoanalysts **W. R. D. Fairbairn** (1889–1964) and **D. W. Winnicott** (1896–1971) — places less emphasis than Freud did on the role of the instincts and more on the details of relationships with love objects.

Several other influential theorists started out as Freud's followers, but later formally broke with him and his group for various reasons to create their own "neo-Freudian" schools. For example, **Alfred Adler** (1870–1937), **Carl Gustav Jung** (1875–1961), and **Karen Horney** (1885–1952) all believed Freud had overemphasized sexuality in his theory and proposed their own alternative systems emphasizing various social or cultural factors. Still others who were originally *trained* in Freudian techniques subsequently reacted against them. Thus **Carl Rogers** (1902–1986) came to feel that the classical Freudian psychoanalyst assumed an unwarranted air of omniscience in dealing with patients and developed a more nondirective **client-centered therapy** as an alternative. And **Joseph Wolpe** (b. 1915) disagreed with the Freudian emphasis on underlying conflicts as opposed to individual symptoms and developed several techniques of **behavior therapy** to provide quick and symptom-specific relief.

As these sketchy descriptions suggest, the current psychotherapeutic scene is highly diverse, with only a minority of practitioners using the same techniques as Freud. Yet one generalization is possible: Most modern therapists use techniques that were developed either by Freud and his followers or by dissidents in explicit reaction against his theories. Freud remains a dominating figure, for or against whom virtually all therapists feel compelled to take a stand.

Freud's influence has been equally pervasive among academic psychologists in the field of personality research. In their studies of personality types, sleep and dreams, sexuality and sex differences, aggression, creativity, and the influence of childrearing practices on personality development, these psychologists pursue topics that were pioneered by Freud. Like the psychotherapists, they may often disagree with his theories, but they are nonetheless compelled to take them seriously.

Of course, Freud's influence has not been limited to professional psychotherapists and psychologists. Just after Freud's death, the poet W. H. Auden summarized his general legacy in the following often-quoted lines:

> If often he was wrong and at times absurd,
> To us he is no more a person now
> But a whole climate of opinion
> Under whom we conduct our differing lives.[13]

Although always controversial, Freud struck a responsive chord with his basic image of human beings as creatures in conflict, beset by irreconcilable and often unconscious demands from within as well as without. His ideas about repression, the importance of early experience and sexuality, and the inaccessibility of much of human nature to ordinary conscious introspection have become part of the standard Western intellectual currency.

Suggested Readings

The standard biography of Sigmund Freud is Ernest Jones's *The Life and Work of Sigmund Freud*, 3 vols. (New York: Basic Books, 1953–1957); a more recent work, benefiting from the extensive Freud scholarship published after Jones's biography, is Peter Gay's *Freud: A Life for Our Time* (New York: Norton, 1988).

Anyone interested by the ideas presented in this chapter deserves the pleasure of reading Freud's own writing. His complete psychological works have been superbly translated, edited, and fully documented in twenty-four volumes by James Strachey in *The Standard Edition of the Complete Psychological Works of Sigmund Freud* (London: Hogarth, 1953–1974). Freud's most important individual works have also been published separately in numerous paperback volumes; it is worth making sure one obtains those that have been taken from the *Standard Edition*. Freud's own general introductions to his theory, written for nonspecialists, were *Introductory Lectures on Psycho-*

analysis and *An Outline of Psychoanalysis*. Readers desiring a more detailed presentation of his theory are advised to examine his major works in the order in which they were written. One good sequence is *Studies on Hysteria* (1895); *The Interpretation of Dreams* (1900); *Three Essays on the Theory of Sexuality* (1905); *The Ego and the Id* (1923); and *Civilization and Its Discontents* (1930).

Several secondary introductions to Freud are available in paperback. I will disavow modesty and particularly recommend my own *Psychoanalytic Psychology: The Development of Freud's Thought* (New York: Norton, 1973).

12

The Developing Mind: Alfred Binet, Jean Piaget, and the Study of Human Intelligence

In the late 1880s, the beleaguered young psychologist **Alfred Binet** (1857–1911) found instruction as well as welcome diversion by observing the behavior of his two little daughters, Madeleine and Alice. As an outspoken disciple of Jean Charcot and supporter of the fanciful theory of *grand hypnotisme* described in Chapter 10, Binet found himself under increasing professional attack at work. But at home he was enchanted by the growing abilities of his girls, and as an inveterate experimenter he could not resist trying out several new psychological tests he had read about. These home experiments yielded data for three scientific publications, and produced some important new attitudes in Binet about the nature and measurement of intelligence.[1]

Some of the tests measured reaction time and sensory acuity, following the recent model of Francis Galton's Anthropometric Laboratory. As shown in Chapter 7, Galton hypothesized that innate and hereditary intelligence would be associated with powerful and efficient nervous systems. His tests were intended primarily for young adults, but Binet tried them on his much younger daughters and was surprised at what he found.

When they attended to the task of reaction time, the girls responded just as quickly as normal adults. They did not always pay attention, however, and so had slower *average* reaction times than adults. But Binet thought this signified a difference between children and adults in *attention*, not in underlying neurological reactivity or sensitivity. Further, on tests of sensory acuity requiring the discrimination of variously sized angles or the matching of colors, three-year-old Alice did almost as well as normal adults and five-year-old Madeleine scored slightly *better*.

Tests that did show major differences between children and adults required skills largely untapped by Galton's measures. Binet's daughters could not *name* the colors printed on strips of paper as quickly as adults, for example, even though they could discriminate and match the same colors by sight just as well. And when asked to define simple everyday objects, the children did not offer formal "definitions" as adults would, but responded by describing immediate actions or purposes. For example, a knife "is to cut meat," a box "is to put candies in," and a snail was, simply and emphatically, "Squash it!"[2]

At this point in his career, Binet was not concerned with measuring degrees of intelligence as Galton and some others had been. But the experiments left him with a permanent distrust of Galton's whole general approach to testing. When young children with manifestly undeveloped intellects could approach or match the performance of adults, such measures hardly seemed promising discriminators of intelligence *between* adults or anyone else. Much more promising, it seemed, would be tests involving "higher" and more complex functions such as language and abstract reasoning. A decade and a half later, when Binet finally did turn his attention to the specific problems of developing an intelligence test, these attitudes would bear fruit and enable him to succeed where Galton and many others had failed.

Binet was not the only pioneer investigator of intelligence to learn from his children. Some thirty years after Binet's first experiments with Madeleine and Alice, the Swiss psychologist **Jean Piaget**

(1896–1980) systematically observed the behavior of his daughter Jacqueline and her cousin Gérard, in looking for lost objects. A chance observation of thirteen-month-old Gérard at play with a ball started things off. First the ball rolled under an armchair where Gérard could still see it; he crawled after it and retrieved it. Later the ball disappeared from his sight under a fringed sofa on the other side of the room. After just a cursory glance at the sofa, Gérard crossed the room to the *armchair* and searched for the lost ball in the place he had found it the time before.

From this "irrational" reaction, Piaget inferred that the baby Gérard lacked an adult's sense of the ball as a distinct "object," independent and separate from himself and his perception of it. Thus as Piaget's daughter Jacqueline passed through infancy, he carefully studied her developing grasp of what he called the **object concept**. During her earliest months, she acted as if objects ceased to exist as soon as they left her immediate sensory awareness. For example, when Piaget placed a toy in front of her she reached to get it, but immediately stopped when he blocked her view of it with his hand or a screen. When he placed a cloth over the toy, in full view, she made no attempt to remove the cloth and recover the toy. By eleven months she would search actively and successfully for such hidden objects, while still showing a limitation reminiscent of Gérard: When Piaget placed a toy parrot under bedcovers to Jacqueline's immediate left, she promptly retrieved it; but when he next ostentatiously hid it under covers on her right, she looked for it where she had been successful before, on the left. At twenty-one months, however, she was fully proficient at locating hidden objects, as Piaget documented in the following report:

I put a coin in my hand, then put my hand under a coverlet. I withdraw my hand closed; Jacqueline opens it [and finds nothing], then searches under the coverlet until she finds the object. I take back the coin at once, put it in my hand and then slip my closed hand under a cushion situated on the other side (on her left and no longer on her right); Jacqueline immediately searches for the object under the cushion.[3]

Now Jacqueline could conceive of objects as entities in their own right, having an existence apart from her own immediate experience of them. And only now, Piaget reasoned, could she logically be

392

expected to attach *names* to stable and meaningful object-concepts, and to begin the sort of verbal discourse and thought that characterizes mature intelligence. This reinforced his hypothesis, already established on other grounds, that the mind or "intelligence" of a child is *not* simply a miniature replica of the adult's, but something that grows and develops through a series of stages that originally bear little obvious similarity to the finished result.

Binet's and Piaget's observations of their children constituted small but important parts of their overall investigations, which established the fact that a full understanding of the adult mind requires prior understanding of the child's. In moving now to the fuller stories of these two psychologist-fathers, we shall see the foundations of two different but equally influential approaches to the study of human intelligence.

Binet's Early Life and Career

Alfred Binet's wealthy parents separated soon after his birth on 11 July 1857 in Nice, France. He was raised in Nice and Paris mainly by his amateur artist mother, although his physician father figured in at least one crucial childhood experience. To cure Alfred's timidity, Dr. Binet forced him to touch a cadaver. The "treatment" served only to increase the boy's anxieties, and its memory haunted him thereafter.

After a creditable if unspectacular secondary school career, Binet took a degree in law but decided against practice. Then he tried medical school, where the horrors of the operating theater evidently exacerbated emotional scars from his childhood trauma. He suffered a severe breakdown and withdrew without a degree. At twenty-two — dispirited, emotionally exhausted, and vocationless — he began passing time by reading extensively in Paris's great library, the Bibliothèque Nationale. Apparently by accident, he discovered books on the new experimental psychology, became fascinated, and realized that he had at last found his vocation.

He plunged untutored into this new field, with more enthusiasm than discretion. He read a few studies of the "two-point threshold," showing that when two points are simultaneously pressed against

Alfred Binet (1857–1911). *Archives of the History of American Psychology, University of Akron.*

the skin, they must be separated by some minimum distance that varies both with individuals and with the parts of the body stimulated if they are to be correctly perceived as two rather than one. After experimenting briefly on himself and some friends, he wrote an article proposing a "new" theory of this phenomenon, which appeared in 1880 as Binet's first scientific publication. His pleasure at seeing his work in print quickly changed to embarrassment, as the Belgian physiologist **Joseph Delboeuf** (1831–1896) published a critical reply: Binet's experiments had flaws, and the "new" theory had already been published years before by Delboeuf himself.

Undaunted, Binet next became enthusiastic about the associationistic psychology of John Stuart Mill, one of Locke's most important successors in stressing the importance of experience and education in shaping human character. In a second published article, Binet made the extreme claim that "the operations of the intelligence are nothing but diverse forms of the laws of association: all psychological phenomena revert to these forms, be they apparently simple, or recognized as complex."[4] Although associationism clearly had merits (and Binet's appreciation of them would eventually help him to succeed where the arch-hereditarian Galton had failed in devising a workable intelligence test), this statement went much too far. Work in "dynamic psychology" had already clearly demonstrated that ideas can become *dis*associated or *dis*connected from each other, and that a given stimulus can lead to totally different trains of association under different motivational conditions. Laws of association could not easily account for these phenomena, and Binet was fortunate to escape a second public rebuke.

Evidently finding this out on his own, Binet next sought training in the new dynamic psychology from one of its most famous proponents. The eminent Jean Charcot, just then developing his theories of *grand hystérie* and *grand hypnotisme* at Paris's Salpêtrière Hospital, accepted the enthusiastic and independently wealthy young Binet as an unpaid assistant and trainee. Binet remained with Charcot for nearly eight years, becoming one of the most prolific researchers of the "Salpêtrière school." He published three books and more than twenty papers on varied topics ranging from mental imagery to sexual "fetishism" (a term he originated, to denote cases in which patients invest inappropriate objects or body parts with sexual significance).

Binet's most spectacular work at the Salpêtrière involved the hypnotic reactions of Charcot's prized "major hysterics." He and his colleague Charles Féré produced astonishing results in deeply hypnotized subjects merely by reversing the polarity of a horseshoe magnet in their presence: Symptoms moved from one side of the body to the other, for example, and emotions turned into their opposites. As recounted in Chapter 10 (pages 344–346), these implausible results aroused the skepticism of Binet's old nemesis Delboeuf, who visited the Salpêtrière and saw the young experimenters' carelessness in openly expressing their expectations to the hypnotized subject. Delboeuf's consequent exposé helped turn the tide of informed opinion against Charcot's entire theory of *grand hypnotisme* in favor of the less flamboyant Nancy school.

At first, Binet tried to defend himself and Charcot by arguing that Delboeuf and the Nancy school could not reproduce the Salpêtrière findings only because they lacked access to the crucial cases of "major hysteria" — found more easily in the big city than in the provinces. Delboeuf responded sarcastically:

> What has the school of the Salpêtrière replied to [my] deductions, so strongly upheld by facts? That my subjects and those of Nancy were only "commonplace *somnambules*," that Paris alone had access to "profound hypnotism," while we — we had only "*le petit hypnotisme*," a hypnotism of the provinces! It would be difficult to find in the history of the sciences another [such] example of an aberration perpetuating itself . . . by pure overweening pride.[5]

Finally in 1891 Binet himself recognized the terrible truth that he had placed too much faith in Charcot's name and prestige and had accepted the master's theories too uncritically. Humbled, he admitted publicly that his earlier hypnotic studies "present a great many loopholes for error. . . . One of the chief and constant causes of mistakes, we know, is found in suggestion — that is to say, in the influence the operator exerts by his words, gestures, attitudes, even by his silences, on the subtle and alert intelligence of the person he has put in the somnambulistic state."[6] From this school of hard knocks, Binet learned an invaluable lesson about how psychological experiments ought *not* to be conducted. Never again would he trust unauthenticated authority or go out on a limb for a position he had not tested thoroughly himself.

Further, just as the hypnosis debacle was coming to a climax, Binet began his series of experiments at home with his daughters. Besides suggesting to him the weakness of the Galtonian approach to mental testing, his observations of Madeleine and Alice reinforced one *positive* lesson from Charcot and the Salpêtrière. In conducting intensive studies of relatively few cases, Charcot had inevitably emphasized the essential *individuality* of all subjects in psychological study. Binet found ample further evidence of individuality in his two daughters.

A proud and doting father, he saw both his girls as bright and able. But from earliest childhood onward they *showed* their intelligence in characteristically different ways—the elder Madeleine always proceeding cautiously and deliberately, while the younger Alice behaved with greater enthusiasm and imagination. Thus in learning to walk, Madeleine held on to a chair or table for support, and "risked abandoning that support only when she had visually selected another object a short distance away which would offer new support; she directed herself very slowly towards the second object, . . . with great seriousness and in perfect silence." Alice, by contrast, was "a laughing and turbulent child" who "never anticipated which object could furnish support, because she advanced without the slightest hesitation to the middle of an empty part of the room. She cried out, she gestured, she was very amusing to watch; she advanced staggering like a drunken man, and could not take four or five steps without falling."[7]

Such stylistic differences recurred in countless other situations, leading Binet to characterize the sensible and down-to-earth Madeleine as "the observer" (*"l'observateur"*), and the ever more impulsive and fanciful Alice as "the imaginer" (*"l'imaginitif"*). And for the rest of his career Binet would also respect the great individuality of every person's intelligence, lending his mature psychology a particular sensibleness and power.

Individual Psychology By 1891, the thirty-four-year-old Binet had learned enough positive and negative lessons at the Salpêtrière and at home to become a first-rate experimental psychologist. He lacked only a position, for he understandably did not wish to remain at the Salpêtrière after his humiliation, and other institutions—just as understandably—did not beat down his door with offers.

Finally in late 1891 Binet had a chance meeting in a railroad station with Henri Beaunis, a physiologist and the director of the newly created Laboratory for Physiological Psychology at the Sorbonne in Paris. Beaunis had favored the Nancy school against Binet and

Charcot in the hypnosis controversy, and must have seemed an unlikely ally. Nevertheless, Binet summoned his courage and offered
to work without pay in the new laboratory. With a meager budget,
Beaunis perhaps felt he had little to lose. In any case, he appointed
Binet as his unpaid assistant and got a wonderful bargain. Binet
soon gained recognition as France's leading experimental psychologist, and succeeded Beaunis as director of the laboratory in 1894.
The following year he founded *L'Année Psychologique*, the first French
journal explicitly devoted to experimental psychology. He remained
at the Sorbonne, always without pay, until the end of his life.

Prominent among the multitude of topics Binet studied from
his Sorbonne base was **suggestibility** — the phenomenon that had
ruined his hypnotic experiments and that he now acidly called the
"cholera of psychology." He began by developing a simple test of
memory for schoolchildren, in which subjects were briefly shown
a single straight line and asked to remember its length before being
asked to choose its match from a pair of unequal lines. After establishing average accuracy levels on this task under "neutral" conditions, Binet tried to manipulate responses by suggestion. Sometimes
he established "preconceived ideas" by making the top (or bottom)
line of the pair correct for several consecutive trials and then deliberately switching. Other times he instructed subjects previously
identified as "leaders" to make their choices publicly, before the
others made theirs.* In still other experiments he made leading
comments, such as "Are you *sure*? Mightn't it be the *other* line?" All
of these manipulations had an effect, somewhat greater on younger
subjects than older ones, and with substantial individual differences.
Binet observed that these results raised serious doubts about the
veracity of children's testimony in judicial proceedings, particularly
when elicited by "leading questions" from lawyers.

Binet summarized these experimental results statistically, giving
average numbers of correct and incorrect responses for groups of
subjects under the various conditions. But as he did so he also recalled the lesson of individuality he had learned from Charcot and

---

*Students of social psychology will recognize that these experiments closely antici-
pated the classic studies of conformity conducted by Solomon Asch in the 1950s.

his daughters. "Mere numbers cannot bring out . . . the intimate essence of the experiment," he warned. He felt uneasy about expressing "all the oscillations of thought in a simple, *brutal* number, which can have only a deceptive precision. . . . It is necessary to complete this number by a description of all the little facts that complete the physiognomy of the experiment."[8]

Binet also now looked zealously for signs of suggestibility in *himself* whenever he conducted an experiment. When he found it he reported it, as in a study from the late 1890s involving head measurements from several hundred subjects. Following Galton, he had hypothesized a positive relationship between head circumference and mental ability. To his chagrin, however, he found that when he *expected* heads to be small, his measurements averaged some three millimeters less than when he reexamined the same heads under more neutral expectations. This discrepancy exceeded the disappointingly small *real* difference he found between the average head circumferences of schoolchildren classified by their teachers as either very bright or very dull. Besides illustrating the experimental dangers of suggestibility, these findings further convinced Binet of the inadequacy of the Galtonian theory of mental testing.

In other work during the 1890s, Binet conducted in-depth case studies of unusually talented people, including several of France's most famous authors and two "lightning calculators" — men who could quickly and accurately perform complicated mathematical operations entirely in their heads. He learned from these studies that sharers of the same special ability often go about it in entirely different ways. One calculator always *saw* the numbers in his imagination as he worked, for example, while the other always *heard* them instead. Some authors worked best during intense, intermittent periods of "spontaneous inspiration," while others — with equally good results — wrote methodically and systematically every day. Thus different people used different intellectual strategies to arrive at similar extraordinary results.

So impressed was Binet by this fact of individuality that he and his younger colleague **Victor Henri** (1872–1940) launched a program called **Individual Psychology** in 1895. They sought a series of short tests, administerable to one person in less than two hours, that could provide information comparable in richness, complexity, and comprehensiveness to that obtained from the many hours of observations and interviews traditionally devoted to individual case studies. Ideally, a short summary of these test results would serve as an adequate substitute for the sort of extended case reports Binet had written of his extraordinary subjects.

In trying to develop such tests, Binet continued to experiment with his daughters Madeleine and Alice. Throughout their adolescence they served as subjects on scores of tasks designed to test their memory, judgment, imagination, and general personality. Some of these tasks required word associations, the interpretation of inkblots, or the telling of stories about "neutral" stimuli; thus Binet anticipated several "projective tests" that would much later come into vogue with clinical psychologists. Binet summarized the results of twenty such tests in his 1903 book, *L'Étude Expérimentale de l'Intelligence* (*The Experimental Study of Intelligence*) — regarded by some psychologists as Binet's most creative work. This book repeatedly showed how the two girls had continued to manifest their "intelligence" in characteristically different ways — Madeleine as the down-to-earth "observer," and Alice as the "imaginer." Consider, for example, the two teenaged girls' contrasting responses when their father asked them to write something about a chestnut tree leaf:

Madeleine: "The leaf [was] gathered in the autumn, because the folioles are all almost yellow except for two, and one is half green and yellow. . . . The folioles are not of the same size; out of the 7, 4 are much smaller than the three others. The chestnut tree is a dicotyledon, as one can tell by looking at the leaf, which has ramified nervures."

Alice: "This . . . has just fallen languidly in the autumn wind. . . . Poor leaf, destined now to fly along the streets, then to rot, heaped up with the others. It is dead today, and it was alive yesterday! Yesterday, hanging from the branch it awaited the fatal flow of wind that would carry it off, like a dying person who awaits his final agony. But the leaf did not sense its danger, and it fell softly in the sun."[9]

But while Binet's attempts to realize the goals of Individual Psychology produced some interesting isolated results, he concluded in 1904 that the program as a whole had failed. No short combination of tests had emerged that could satisfactorily substitute for an extended case study. Binet ruefully concluded: "It is premature to look for tests permitting a diagnosis during a very limited time (one or two hours), and . . . much to the contrary, it is necessary to study individual psychology without limiting the time — especially by studying outstanding personalities."[10] The most significant concrete results of Individual Psychology remained his extended case studies of his daughters, and of a few prominent literary figures.

But while technically unsuccessful, Binet's testing experiments in Individual Psychology helped pave the way for his most famous achievement. He had gained valuable experience by trying out innumerable tests of varied functions such as memory, imagination, comprehension, attention, suggestibility, and the aesthetic and moral senses. He had confirmed his belief that only relatively direct tests of the higher, complex mental functions measured significant intellectual differences. When he began in 1905 to seek a test of "intelligence" in a narrower and more specific context than he had been concerned with before, these experiences helped him to succeed where Galton and his other predecessors had failed.

The Binet Intelligence Scales

During the first years of the twentieth century, Binet and many others became increasingly interested in the problem of mental *subnormality*. The recent passage of universal education laws in France had brought a new public visibility to mentally handicapped children. Previously, most such children had either dropped out of school at an early age or never attended at all. Now they were required by law to attend school — and since they usually could not keep up with an ordinary curriculum, they required special attention and special schools.

In 1904, Binet joined a government commission charged with investigating the state of the mentally subnormal in France, and soon concluded that accurate *diagnosis* of subnormality posed the most pressing problems. "It will never be a mark of distinction to have passed through a special school," he remarked, "and those who do not merit it must be spared the record."[11] Thus with **Théodore Simon** (1873-1961), a young physician who had come to study

psychology with him in 1899, Binet set out to develop a test to identify children whose mental handicap rendered them permanently
unable to benefit from an ordinary education.

The 1905 Tests Binet and Simon started out with few theoretical
predispositions regarding the "intelligence" whose deficiency they
hoped to measure. Thus they proceeded empirically, identifying
groups of children who had been unequivocally diagnosed as subnormal or normal by their teachers or doctors, and then testing them
on many different specific measures. They avoided tests that relied
heavily on reading, writing, and other clearly school-related skills,
so as not to confuse lack of intelligence with mere lack of school-
ing. But they did not hesitate to try items that assumed a basic
familiarity with everyday French life and culture—many of which
Binet had already used in his earlier studies of his daughters and
other children.

At first Binet and Simon were frustrated, because while the
normal and subnormal groups showed differences in average performance on most items, no item came close to being a perfect dis-
criminator. That is, at least some of the normal children failed on
every test and/or some subnormal children passed. But soon a key
insight dawned—one that seemed perfectly obvious once recognized,
but that had eluded previous workers in the field. *Age* had to be
considered: Normal and subnormal children might both learn to
pass the same tests, but normal children invariably did so at a
younger age. Binet and Simon summarized: "It was almost always
possible to equate [subnormal children] with normal children very
much younger."[12] Following this insight, it has become customary
to describe the subnormal population as "mentally retarded."

Their idea enabled Binet and Simon in 1905 to construct the first
test of intelligence that actually worked, comprising thirty separate
items of increasing difficulty. The first item simply tested whether
subjects could follow a lighted match with their eyes, demonstrating
the elementary capacity for *attention* that is prerequisite for all intelligent behavior. Next, subjects had to grasp a small object placed
in their hand, to unwrap and eat a piece of candy, to shake hands
with the examiner, and to comply with a few simple spoken or ges-

tured requests. Normal children could do all of these things by the age of two, but the most profoundly retarded of any age could *never* do some of them. Intermediate problems, passable by normal five- or six-year-olds but by none of the moderately retarded, required them to state the differences between pairs of objects such as "paper and cardboard" and "a fly and a butterfly" and to memorize and repeat sentences such as "I get up in the morning, dine at noon, and go to bed at night." The more difficult items, which in effect defined the upper borderline of subnormality, required subjects to find rhymes for the French word *obéissance*; to construct a sentence containing the three given words "Paris," "river," and "fortune"; and to figure in their heads what time it would be if the hands of a clock were reversed (for example, twenty past six would become half past four). Most normal children of eleven or twelve could pass these, but few genuinely subnormal individuals of any age could.

The 1908 and 1911 Scales The Binet-Simon test of 1905 marked a turning point in the history of psychology, for it truly made useful discriminations among lower degrees of intelligence. But it focused primarily on the very retarded and the very young, while many of the most difficult educational decisions involved older children close to the borderline of "normality." Accordingly, Binet and Simon extended and refined their pool of items, producing revised intelligence tests in 1908 and 1911. On these, each item was specifically designated according to the age at which a sample of normal children had first been able to pass it. Thus each item at the six-year level had been passed by a minority of normal five-year-olds, about half of the six-year-olds, and a majority of older children. The 1908 revision contained fifty-eight items located at age levels between three and thirteen; its 1911 counterpart had five questions for each age between five and fifteen, and five more in an "adult" category. Here are a few examples:

At the *three-year level*, children had to name common objects in a picture, correctly repeat a six-syllable sentence, and point to their eyes, noses, or mouths upon request. At *six*, they were expected to state the difference between morning and evening, and count thirteen coins. At *ten*, they normally could reproduce several line

drawings from memory; answer questions involving social judgment such as why people should be judged by their acts rather than
their words; and detect and describe the logical absurdities in statements such as: "The body of an unfortunate girl was found cut into
18 pieces; it is thought that she killed herself." Items at the *fifteen-
year level* asked subjects to recall correctly seven digits, and to deal
with problems such as: "My neighbor has been receiving strange
visitors. He has received in turn a doctor, a lawyer, and then a
priest. What is taking place?"

With age-standardized items such as these, Binet had a genuine
"scale" of intelligence, capable of providing a single score or **intellectual level** for each child who took it. Questions were always asked
in ascending order of difficulty, until five in a row were missed.
Then the examiner took the highest year for which all five items
had been successfully passed as the base, and added one-fifth of
a year for each subsequent correct answer to compute the child's
intellectual level. For example, a child who answered all of the questions at the age-seven level, four at age-eight, and two at age-nine
would be assigned an overall intellectual level of 8.2 years.

In diagnosing mental subnormality, Binet compared each child's
tested intellectual level with his or her actual age. He collected statistics suggesting that children whose intellectual levels trailed their
ages by less than two years could usually manage in the regular
school system, while those who showed greater discrepancies (about
seven percent of the population) usually had trouble. Accordingly,
he proposed a rule of thumb that children with intellectual levels
more than two years behind their actual ages be seriously considered
for special education.

Even as he suggested this rule, however, Binet also counseled
caution. He still denied the ability of "brutal" numbers adequately
to summarize any complex quality, and emphasized that different
children could achieve identical intellectual levels by correctly answering widely varying patterns of specific questions. He also recognized that no score could be valid for a child poorly motivated to
take the test, or who had been reared in a culture other than that
of the sample of children he had used to standardize his questions.
And the early proponent of Mill's associationism still emphatically

believed that the "intelligence" measured by his test was not a fixed quantity, but something that grows naturally with time, and that — at least for retarded children and within limits — may be increased by training. He developed a program he called **mental orthopedics**, with exercises like the games of "Statue," in which children had to freeze in position upon hearing a signal, and "Concentration," where they had to remember several objects that were briefly removed from a box and then rehidden. Children whose deficits stemmed from an inability to sit still and to concentrate often benefited from these exercises, increasing not only their "intellectual levels" as measured by Binet's tests, but also their intelligent behavior in real life.

The Rise of Intelligence Testing

At the height of his powers when he developed mental orthopedics and his revised intelligence scales, Binet had little time to enjoy his accomplishments. His wife suffered from an ill-defined malady that inhibited social life, and Binet himself seemed susceptible to gloomy thoughts, reflected in a series of plays he co-authored with André de Lorde, a popular dramatist known as the "Price of Terror." Protagonists in these plays included a released psychiatric patient who murders his brother, a deranged father who kills his infant son after being denied admission to an asylum, and another father who performs ghoulish experiments trying to restore his dead daughter to life.[13] And all too soon the ultimate tragedy occurred in real life, as Binet himself suffered a stroke and died in 1911, at the early age of fifty-four.

As his most enduring legacy, Binet left behind the basic technology that still underlies modern intelligence tests. Although some psychologists still hope ultimately to find measures of innate intelligence that are "culture free" and closely tied to direct neurophysiological functions, all of the most practically useful tests developed to date still rely on items basically like Binet's — questions directly entailing a variety of higher and complex functions such as memory, reasoning, verbal facility, and practical judgment. But while Binet might feel comfortable about the item content of most modern intelligence tests, he probably would have reservations about some *other* developments in their interpretation and use—developments that began to occur almost immediately after his death.

One concerned the general conception of "intelligence" presumably measured by the items. Binet himself had adopted a flexible and pragmatic definition of intelligence, seeing it as a rather loose collection of separate capacities for memory, attention, reasoning, and the like, all tied together by a faculty he simply called "judgment" or "good sense." A rival view, the theory of **general intelligence**, or "**g**," was effectively promoted by the English psychologist **Charles Spearman** (1863–1945) soon after Binet's death.

Spearman first observed and emphasized a fact that has been repeatedly confirmed ever since—namely, that when correlation coefficients (see pages 230–235) are computed between them, all of the various items and submeasures used on intelligence tests tend to be positively and hierarchically intercorrelated with each other. People who do well on vocabulary tests, for example, tend also to score high on arithmetic problems, the detection of similarities, the assembling of painted blocks into specified patterns, the memory for digits, or any of the other items. Further, while all of the subtests tend to intercorrelate positively, some of them achieve generally *higher* levels of correlation than others. Subtests involving abstract reasoning (such as similarities), for example, intercorrelate more strongly than do measures of rote memory with other items across the board.

To explain these findings, Spearman theorized that all intellectual tasks must entail the exercise of a single common "factor" he called "general intelligence" and abbreviated as "g." He further proposed that each individual type of item required an ability specific to itself, an "s" factor; his theory is accordingly called the **two-factor theory of intelligence**. Writing metaphorically, Spearman went on to liken each person's "g" capacity to an overall supply of mental energy or power, capable of driving any number of specific neurological "engines" required for performing different specific tasks (and thus constituting the material basis for the individual "s" factors). Thus a person's performance on any task was theoretically a joint function of the overall energy or "g" available, as well as the efficiency of the particular "s" engine involved. The hierarchical nature of the correlations suggested that some tasks, such as abstract reasoning, depended relatively much on "g" and relatively little on "s"; for rote learning the proportions were reversed. But even tasks relatively "unsaturated" with "g" — like rote learning — required *some* degree of mental energy. Thus for Spearman the single most important fact to know about any person's intelligence was his or her general intelligence level, or overall mental power.

Although not the only possible explanation for the observed hierarchies of positive intercorrelations, Spearman's theory has held considerable support from its inception. Suggesting that "intelligence" is not so much a loose collection of varying functions and aptitudes as a network of engines all driven by a common energy source, it has fostered attitudes toward testing very different from Binet's. While Binet believed different intelligence levels could be represented only approximately and inadequately by numbers, Spearman's theory suggested that a single figure representing each person's "g" level, or overall "mental horsepower," would be the most important thing to know about that person's intelligence.

A means of calculating such single numbers from Binet's intelligence tests was proposed in 1912 by the German psychologist **William Stern** (1871–1938), with his concept of the **intelligence quotient**. Stern had worried over experimental findings showing that the discrepancy between a child's real or "chronological age" and the tested intellectual level or "mental age" (as Binet's term was usually translated) often increased over time. When re-tested after exactly one year, children whose scores were below par the first time usually gained less than one year in mental age, while those who had been above average gained more than a year. Thus Binet's suggestion to adopt a two-year discrepancy between chronological and mental age as diagnostic of subnormality seemed suspect, because it implied different standards for different age groups. Many children's discrepancies inevitably grew from less than two at an early age to more than two later on, making diagnoses of subnormality relatively more frequent at later ages.

To remedy this inequality, Stern suggested taking not the absolute discrepancy between mental and chronological age as the measure of retardation, but rather the *ratio* of mental age to chronological age — a fraction Stern called the "intelligence quotient." Thus a five-year-old with a mental age of four would have an intelligence quotient of 4 divided by 5, or 0.80; to achieve the same quotient, a ten-year-old would have to get a mental age of eight, two years rather than one behind the chronological age.

While perhaps simplifying the problem of diagnosis, Stern's innovation had one effect that Binet would certainly have deplored. As a final, summary score of test results, the intelligence quotient was much further removed from the actual "physiognomy of the experiment" than the simple mental age or intellectual level. Binet had complained because the same mental age could be produced by different patterns of specific answers; now the problem was compounded because the same intelligence quotients could be produced by different combinations of mental and chronological ages.

For many psychologists, however, this simplification of results carried a major benefit. The intelligence quotient was potentially interpretable as an index of a unitary, quantifiable intellectual power like Spearman's "g." All that remained was to demonstrate that *high* quotients were indicative of *superior* intellectual power. In 1920 this was not a foregone conclusion. Binet himself had experimented briefly on children with advanced mental ages, been disappointed with the results, and concluded that "the most valuable applications of our scale will not be for the normal subject, but instead for the inferior degrees of intelligence."[14] That is, he saw his tests as primarily useful in detecting the *lack* of intelligence in subnormal children, and doubted their usefulness in measuring *positive* intelligence.

The first major attempt to demonstrate otherwise occurred during World War I, when tests adapted for group administration were given to nearly two million U.S. Army recruits. The results were used not only to screen out mental defectives, but also to select high-scoring individuals for advanced training. But while this program represented a spectacular organizational accomplishment for psychologists, and helped place intelligence testing "on the map" of public consciousness, the war ended before the tests' validity in predicting positive performance could be accurately or fully evaluated. In fact, there were many glaring deficiencies and inequalities in the way the testing program was run.[15]

First to argue *persuasively* for the usefulness of Binet tests in diagnosing superior intelligence was **Lewis M. Terman** (1877–1956), a Stanford University psychologist who had worked on the army program. Terman in 1916 had introduced "The Stanford Revision of the Binet-Simon Scale," an extensive reworking of Binet's test adapted for American subjects and standardized on a considerably larger sample of children. The "Stanford-Binet" quickly became the most widely used individual intelligence test in North America. When introducing this test, Terman had endorsed Stern's intelligence quotient concept, and further suggested that the fraction be multiplied by 100 to eliminate decimals, with the result being abbreviated as the **IQ**. Ever since, an exactly average level of intelligence has been denoted by an IQ of 100.

Terman's major interest, however, lay in children with IQs *higher* than average. Perhaps partly because he had himself been a precocious student who passed through school much faster than most, he suspected that "advanced" children in general tended to grow up as unusually capable adults. To test his hypothesis, he followed two complementary strategies. First, he and his graduate student Catherine Cox examined the childhood biographies of more than three hundred eminent historical "geniuses."[16] Although data were often scanty, virtually every case showed *some* evidence of childhood accomplishment in advance of one's years — often quite spectacular accomplishment. (Included in Terman-Cox's list of documented child prodigies were several pioneers from earlier chapters of the present book, including Descartes, Leibniz, Kant, Darwin, and Galton.) Terman and Cox accordingly argued that *if* Binet-type intelligence tests had been available in the past, most people who turned out intellectually great in adulthood would also have achieved high IQs as children.

Terman's second attempt to relate childhood precocity to adult achievement followed a complementary strategy, and led to his most extensive and famous research program. In the early 1920s his students tested more than 250,000 California schoolchildren, to identify a group of 1,528 "gifted children" with IQs above 140. He then proceeded to investigate all aspects of these children's lives at regular intervals as they grew up. Terman's successors still continue to study the survivors of this group, now well into their seventies.[17]

And how did they fare? Statistically speaking, the answer is that they did very well indeed. Compared to a random sample, a high proportion entered the professions, with many earning national or international reputations. More than thirty became eminent enough to be listed in *Who's Who*. Taken as a whole, the group attained more education, earned more money, and in general led healthier and apparently happier lives than the national average.

At the same time, the study showed that high IQ alone does not guarantee success, for a significant minority failed to lead objectively successful lives. Moreover, the group contained surprisingly few individuals successful in the creative arts (as opposed to the professions), and none who have won the Nobel Prize or become celebrated "geniuses." In countless other studies since Terman's, IQ scores in the general population have been found to correlate moderately but far from absolutely with variables such as academic grades, years of education finally completed, and salary levels in adulthood. Thus, in general, high IQs have turned out to be good but far from perfect predictors of intellectual success. In spite of the widespread tendency to equate high IQs with "genius," the evidence suggests that the tests still work relatively better for their original purpose — the diagnosis of retardation.

Still, Terman and other advocates made IQ scores into common intellectual currency, and a vast testing industry developed. New tests were subsequently designed for adults, calculating IQ scores not by the traditional mental age to chronological age ratio, but according to the distributions of result within each age group. Thus a twenty-five-year-old and a sixty-year-old, each with an IQ of 100, stand at the exact average of people in their age groups. IQs of 80, 110, and 135 always stand respectively at about the 9th, 74th, and 99th percentiles for the age group in question.

In sum, modifications of Binet's testing procedures became applied to all segments of the population, with results summarized by a single score for each subject. Inevitably, these scores were also interpreted by some — particularly those who accepted Spearman's conception of intelligence as dominated by a biologically given general factor — as Galton's long-sought measure of *hereditary* natural ability. Others have disputed this contention, seeing IQ as a variable primarily determined by environment and education, rather than heredity. Indeed there remains great controversy today over the exact meaning of IQ scores. Were he alive today, Binet himself would undoubtedly regret all of the fuss about these issues, but be pleased to see that his testing techniques have retained their usefulness for individual educational and clinical diagnoses.

One further development would probably please him as well. In 1920, the young Swiss psychologist Jean Piaget came to work in one of Binet's old laboratories, under the direction of his colleague Simon. Using a clinical interview method much like that endorsed by Binet, Piaget arrived at a new conception of exactly *how* children's intelligence normally develops with age. Concerned with qualitative rather than quantitative intellectual developments, Piaget revolutionized the field of child psychology.

Piaget's Early Life and Career

Jean Piaget was born on 9 August 1896 in Neuchâtel, Switzerland, the son of an academic who wrote prolifically about medieval literature and local history. Piaget recalled his mother as intelligent and kindly, but also prone to emotional disorders that often made the domestic atmosphere uncomfortably tumultuous. To cope with the tumult, he said he identified with his father and buried himself in serious intellectual work. Even as a child he wrote prodigiously, and he continued throughout his life to publish at a rate not far short of Wundt's. When asked as an adult how he could write so much, Piaget frankly replied, "Fundamentally I am a worrier whom only work can relieve."[18]

Piaget's boyhood works included a pamphlet describing his invention of a combination wagon-locomotive, and a small handwritten book entitled *Our Birds*. His ornithological knowledge was real, for at age ten his essay describing a partly albino sparrow appeared in a local journal of natural history — his first scientific publication. Shortly thereafter, young Piaget became a volunteer assistant to the director of Neuchâtel's natural history museum, a man who specialized in malacology, the study of mollusks. Piaget learned this field too, and between the ages of fifteen and nineteen published twenty-one malacological papers in assorted international journals.

Few readers knew his age, and one offered him a curator's job in Geneva that Piaget had to decline because he still had two years of high school remaining.

This background in scientific observation and methodology helped Piaget get through an emotionally difficult late adolescence, plagued by religious doubts and what he called "the demon of philosophy." His godfather helped him resolve his crisis by suggesting that philosophical and even theological concerns could be brought into connection with biology:

I recall one evening of profound revelation. The identification of God with life itself was an idea that stirred me almost to ecstasy because it now enabled me to see in biology the explanation of all things and of the mind itself. . . . The problem of knowing (properly called the epistemological problem) suddenly appeared to me in an entirely new perspective and as an absorbing topic of study. It made me decide to consecrate my life to the biological explanation of knowledge.[19]

Piaget now immersed himself in philosophical works that tried to integrate biology and epistemology, especially the "creative evolution" of **Henri Bergson** (1859–1941). Bergson saw the universe as divided into two fundamental substances: living and inert matter, with the living matter evolving constantly so as to better apprehend and operate freely within the inert matter with which it must contend. But while impressed by Bergson's general notion of mind as progressively adapting to and "understanding" external reality, Piaget felt dissatisfied by the lack of solid experimental support provided for the argument. "At that moment," he recalled, "I discovered a need that could be satisfied only by psychology."[20] At that point, Piaget had little notion of what formal psychology was, but his interests had conspired to create his life's ambition: the construction of an empirically and experimentally based theory explaining how people come increasingly to know about their world. His goal here resembled John Locke's in the *Essay Concerning Human Understanding*, but in conceptualizing the human mind as a biologically given, organic, and evolving entity, Piaget would also follow in the tradition of Locke's great rival Leibniz.

Before pursuing his great goal, however, Piaget was forced by ill health to spend his twentieth year recuperating in the mountains.

Jean Piaget. *Yves De Braine from Black Star.*

During this time he read a little psychology, but concentrated mainly on writing a philosophical novel entitled *Recherche* (literally, *"Search"* or *"Quest"*). Although far from a masterpiece, this was published in 1917. Returning from the mountains, he enrolled in the doctoral program at his home University of Neuchâtel, where psychology was not offered. Instead, Piaget took courses in biology, geology, chemistry, and mathematics, while writing a thesis on local mollusks. He received his Ph.D. in natural history at age twenty-two. Only now did the internationally known malacologist, published novelist, and amateur philosopher seek training in psychology.

At first he went to Zurich, where he studied briefly with Freud's erstwhile follower Carl Jung, and learned something about abnormal psychology. Then, seeking something more experimental, he went to Paris and the Sorbonne, where he met by chance Binet's collaborator Théodore Simon. Simon had moved to Rouen following Binet's death, but remained the nominal director of Binet's old pedagogical laboratory in Paris. Just then, he wished to use the laboratory to standardize the French translations of a series of reasoning tests recently developed by Cyril Burt, the most enthusiastic English proponent of the Binet-Simon approach to testing.* Impressed by Piaget, Simon offered him the job of supervising this project. Piaget held reservations about the project and the entire "psychometric" approach to studying intelligence, but the opportunity to be his own master in a good-sized laboratory seemed too good to refuse. He accepted, and soon found that the seemingly pedestrian task of standardizing children's intelligence tests could lead to unexpected and exciting findings. He summarized his early discoveries as follows:

> I noticed that though Burt's tests certainly had their diagnostic merits, based on the number of successes and failures, it was much more interesting to try to find the *reasons* for the failures. Thus I engaged my subjects in conversations patterned after psychiatric questioning, with the aim of discovering something about the reasoning processes underlying their right, but especially their wrong answers. I noticed with amazement that the simplest reasoning task involving the inclusion of a part in the whole . . . presented for normal children up to the age of eleven or twelve difficulties unsuspected by the adult.[21]

Thus by careful questioning of individual children, Piaget attempted to cut through the simple, "brutal" numbers that normally stood as intelligence test scores, in order to reveal the children's actual underlying thought processes. Had he been alive, Binet certainly would have applauded even though Piaget's findings pointed to a view of intelligence different from his own.

Binet's testing approach assumed that intelligence grows with age in primarily a *quantitative* sense. Employing similar types of items for many different age levels, it showed that older children could

---

*Much later in his career, Burt would publish the apparently fraudulent set of separated-twin studies described on page 237, purporting to demonstrate the strong heritability of intelligence.

perform more tasks more quickly than younger children of comparable intellectual rank — suggesting that intelligence increases with age in much the same way that height and weight do. Piaget, by focusing on the reasoning processes underlying incorrect answers, concluded that this represents only one aspect of intellectual development. He found evidence that older children do not just think "faster" or "more" than younger ones; they also think in entirely different ways, employing cognitive abilities and structures that enable them to understand some problems and concepts completely beyond the grasp of younger children. In short, intelligence develops *qualitatively* with age, as well as quantitatively.

Piaget now saw that the systematic study and description of qualitative developments in maturing children's intelligence could provide an approach to the epistemological problem that interested him so much. By learning how children understand the world, and how their thought processes gradually mature and become more like adults', he could come to grips with the nature of human knowledge itself. Moreover, his new view of intelligence showed promising analogies to the biology he thought fundamental to any world view. Just as a physically growing embryo gradually develops new organs and structures out of rudimentary predecessors, and these new structures make possible the performance of totally new functions, so the intellect presumably develops in gradual stages that allow the emergence of totally new ways of thought. To emphasize this presumed link between the biological and the intellectual, Piaget coined the name **genetic epistemology** for his ensuing program to study the development of children's intelligence. (He used the term "genetic" here to denote "developmental," not to suggest that intelligence was necessarily hereditary or determined by the genes.)

Piaget spent the rest of his life tirelessly pursuing this project, moving to Geneva to become director of research at the J. J. Rousseau Institute in 1921. He remained affiliated with the Institute until his death in 1980. Although at first he worked in relative obscurity, he gradually attracted students from around the world, and produced hundreds of studies in genetic epistemology that reshaped the way psychologists think about both childhood and intelligence.

Genetic Epistemology

Piaget's voluminous publications describe children of different ages working at simple but ingeniously devised tasks in widely diverse areas including rattle play, language use, moral judgment, the conception of numbers, space perception, algebra, the description of dreams and fantasies, and cognition in general. Within each area, he found evidence of sequential **stages of development** — systematic and qualitative differences between the ways younger and older children conceptualized and attacked the tasks. This vast corpus of work cannot be summarized briefly, but its general nature may be illustrated by some of his specific findings regarding the stages of general cognitive development.

Piaget's studies suggested the existence of four major stages between infancy and late adolescence, which he called, in sequence, the **sensory-motor stage**, the **preoperational stage**, the **stage of concrete operations**, and the **stage of formal operations**. Each successive stage introduces new cognitive structures and strategies permitting the solution of previously insoluble problems; thus the stages may be defined in terms of tasks that children in them can and cannot do.

Piaget's conception of the first, sensory-motor stage — which he saw as extending from birth to approximately two years of age — derived from observations of his own nephews and children like those described in the introduction to this chapter. "I learned in the most direct way," he recalled, "how intellectual operations are prepared by sensory-motor action, even before the appearance of language."[22] As the term implies, a child's "intelligence" during this stage presumably involves elementary sensory and motor activities, and has nothing to do with abstract thought in the adult sense. Before one can think about objects in any abstract way, one must first learn how they strike the senses and how they can be manipulated — the general goal of the sensory-motor period.

More specifically, the sensory-motor child must achieve the sense of what Piaget called **object constancy** — the knowledge that objects have continuing existences even when outside immediate sensory awareness. His observations of Gérard and Jacqueline, described in the chapter's introduction, illustrate various stages in the development of object constancy. Piaget noted that it arises gradually, as infants gain increasing mastery over their bodies and learn to manipulate objects and their appearances. As they do so, they take great delight in games such as peekaboo, where the repetitive disappearance and reappearance of familiar faces and objects holds particular fascination. And only after children learn to make many objects disappear and reappear through their own efforts — by reversing or alternating the behaviors that produce appearance or disappearance — do they acquire the sense of a stable universe containing continually existing objects independent of themselves. Only now, after objects are recognized as permanent, does it become possible to *name* them, signifying their continuing independent existences by words to represent them.

Once these rudiments of language have been acquired, enabling children to express and symbolize the continuing existence of specific objects in the world, they are equipped for the second, "preoperational stage" which lasts approximately from age two through five. Although preoperational children can recognize that objects continue to exist even when they cannot immediately see or act upon them, they strikingly fail to understand that certain *properties* of objects — such as their quantity or volume — remain the same regardless of transformations of their specific appearance. Consider the following example. A child receives two lumps of clay, and instructions to remove small bits from the larger one until both seem exactly the same size. Then the experimenter breaks up one of the equal lumps into many pieces and places them in a pile, asking the child which now has more clay, the remaining large lump or the new pile? Virtually all preoperational children will now be deceived by the different appearances of the two choices, and see one as having more clay than the other. Most will note that the pile takes up more space and *looks* bigger, and so choose it; a minority will emphasize the smallness of the pieces in the pile, and choose the single large lump.

Similarly, a preoperational child may be misled by the appearances of equal quantities of liquids. Shown two identical glasses of orange juice, most preoperational children will judge that one of the contents miraculously becomes "more" than the other when poured into a taller and thinner glass, because the liquid rises higher in the new container. A few children say it becomes less because the column is thinner, but in either case a misjudgment is made because of the differences in appearance. In Piaget's terms, preoperational children fail to appreciate the **conservation of quantity** — that the overall amounts of substances remain the same even as they assume different shapes and configurations.

Besides showing that young children may be tricked into thinking they have more or less of particular foods or beverages just by altering their presentation, these simple experiments beautifully illustrate Piaget's main point. Older children and adults think about abstract properties such as quantity or amount in altogether different ways from young children. Not just "better" with numbers, or capable of handling larger quantities, they make judgments of quantity on an altogether different basis. Younger children judge according to the way things immediately look. Older children have learned that by reversing behaviors in these new contexts they can re-form a pile of clay pieces into its originally sized lump, or re-pour the tall thin column of juice into its original shape in the original glass. They mentally transcend the immediate appearance of things, and recognize that the same quantity may manifest itself in many different guises.

At age seven or so most children begin to enter Piaget's "stage of concrete operations." Now they successfully solve most conservation problems, but remain tied to the immediately given situation in still other ways. They cannot completely solve some kinds of conceptual and reasoning problems until entering the "stage of formal operations," which typically begins to emerge around the age of eleven. One of Piaget's experimental tasks required the systematic manipulation of chemicals, and nicely illustrated the differences between these last two stages.

Here subjects received four flasks numbered 1 through 4, and a smaller container labeled "g" (not to be confused with Spearman's "g" for general intelligence), each filled with an identical-looking transparent liquid. The experimenter explained that by adding a few drops of g to the correct *combination* of liquids from Flasks 1 through 4, a chemical reaction could be produced turning the entire mixture yellow. Subjects then were invited to experiment with the liquids and discover the correct combination.

In actuality, g was potassium iodide, a chemical that produces a yellow precipitate when mixed with oxygenated water in an acid solution. Flasks 1 and 3 held dilute sulfuric acid and oxygenated water, respectively, so the combination of g + 1 + 3 yielded the desired result. Flask 2 contained plain water, which had no effect on the reaction; but Flask 4 held thiosulfate, a chemical base that neutralizes sulfuric acid. Thus g + 1 + 2 + 3 also produced the color, but g + 1 + 2 + 3 + 4 did not.

Piaget found that both concretely and formally operational children could solve this problem, but they typically went about doing so in very different ways, and with vastly different consequences. The younger, concretely operational children usually proceeded by trial and error, trying random mixtures until finally hitting upon one that worked. As far as they were concerned, the task was then finished. Formally operational children, by contrast, could see at once that there were only a limited number of *possible* combinations, and that these could be investigated systematically and completely — yielding the maximum possible amount of information from their experiments. Thus some started out by adding g to each of the four liquids by itself, discovering that no single chemical produced yellow with g. Then they tried each of the six possible combinations of *two* chemicals with g (1 + 2, 1 + 3, 1 + 4, 2 + 3, 2 + 4, and 3 + 4), until discovering the one that worked.

Even after finding an answer, however, formally operational children often continued to experiment with the five remaining untested combinations: the four possible combinations of three (1 + 2 + 3, 1 + 2 + 4, 1 + 3 + 4, and 2 + 3 + 4), and all four mixed together. Following this complete set of trials, they could generalize about the nature of the chemicals — recognizing that the contents of Flask 4 could counteract the crucial 1 + 3 combination, while adding Flask 2 made no difference. In being able to conceptualize all of the possible combinations at the outset, and then to test them systematically, the formally operational children were able to extract the maximum amount of information from their experiments.

From innumerable observations like these, Piaget demonstrated that rational, adult, "scientific" thinking and the knowledge that proceeds from it represent the end points of extensive developmental processes. At the beginning of life, human thinking remains tied to the sensory and bodily experiences of the immediate present. Only gradually does it come to deal with imagined rather than immediately experienced concepts: first the memories of objects when they are no longer physically present, then abstract properties such as quantity which may remain constant throughout a variety of transformations of specific form, and finally the matrices of combinatorial possibilities in problems like the chemistry experiment.

In summarizing the implications of his work in 1970, Piaget emphasized the *active* nature of these developmental processes:

I find myself opposed to the view of knowledge as a passive copy of reality. . . . I believe that knowing an object means acting upon it, constructing systems of transformations that can be carried out on or with this object. Knowing reality means constructing systems of transformations that correspond, more or less adequately, to reality. The transformational structures of which knowledge consists are not copies of the transformations in reality; they are simply possible isomorphic models among which experience can enable us to choose. Knowledge, then, is a system of transformations that become progressively [more] adequate.[23]

Piaget thus stands as a recent representative and integrator of several venerable strands in the history of mental philosophy. Like Locke, he sought to understand the nature and limits of human knowledge. But like Descartes he saw the rational mind as an active rather than passive participant in the creation of that knowledge, and like Leibniz he stressed the organic and biological nature of that active mind. And in seeing knowledge as a series of "transformations" of external reality produced by the mind, involving developing conceptions of space, number, causality, and the like, Piaget partook strongly of the tradition of Kant.

Piaget's pioneering work has stimulated countless contemporary developmental psychologists, who continue to study different aspects of the child's mind as it develops from infancy through maturity. Besides having considerable theoretical interest, this work has inevitably also been of great practical interest to educators. Piaget himself, while admitting that he was no pedagogue, argued that schools could improve their teaching by always providing pupils with problems and challenges appropriate to their stages of intellectual development. Thus it is foolish to try to instruct preoperational children in the formal, hypothetico-deductive reasoning processes of mature scientists, for example, but it is possible and desirable to help such children develop conservation of quantity by giving them many opportunities to manipulate and transform the shapes and appearances of varying substances. Piaget advised: "It is a matter of presenting to children situations which offer new problems, problems that follow [developmentally] on one another. You need a mixture of direction and freedom."[24]

Educators have naturally been interested in the question of how far children's development and learning can be *accelerated* by such practices. Piaget himself saw intellectual development as tied to biological and social development as well. Therefore, while intellectual growth in a child may presumably be nurtured and facilitated like physical growth, it cannot be accelerated beyond certain natural and biologically given limits. The exact nature of those limits, the extent to which children may be speeded through the developmental stages, and the desirability of doing so all remain important and unresolved issues.

Thus like so many of his predecessors among psychology's pioneers, Jean Piaget produced knowledge that at once holds practical implications, and raises issues about human experience and conduct that have a continuing fascination in their own right.

Suggested Readings

The best English-language study of Binet's life and work is Theta H. Wolf, *Alfred Binet* (Chicago: University of Chicago Press, 1973). Binet and Simon's articles introducing their intelligence tests of 1905, 1908, and 1911 appear in English translation in A. Binet and T. Simon, *The Development of Intelligence in Children (The Binet-Simon Scale)*, reprint edition (New York: Arno Press, 1973). For a fuller story of Binet and his successors in the intelligence-testing field, see Raymond E. Fancher, *The Intelligence Men: Makers of the IQ Controversy* (New York: Norton, 1985).

Piaget's autobiography appears in Richard I. Evans, *Jean Piaget: The Man and His Ideas* (New York: Dutton, 1973), along with transcripts of an informative interview and Piaget's general article entitled "Genetic Epistemology." John Flavell's *The Developmental Psychology of Jean Piaget* (New York: Van Nostrand, 1963) and Herbert Ginsburg and Sylvia Opper's *Piaget's Theory of Intellectual Development*, 3rd edition (Englewood Cliffs, NJ: Prentice-Hall, 1988), provide good overviews of his work. Piaget's observations of object constancy in his nephew and daughter are included in his book *The Construction of Reality in the Child* (New York: Basic Books, 1954). Many of his most important observations of later intellectual development appear in Jean Piaget and Barbel Inhelder, *The Growth of Logical Thinking from Childhood to Adolescence* (New York: Basic Books, 1958).

Afterword
Tomorrow's Pioneers

When a book of this type comes to be written fifty or a hundred years from now, many of today's psychologists will then be regarded as major pioneers. It is beyond the scope of this book to speculate on specifically who they will be, but some general predictions about them may safely be made, based on our study of the already established pioneers.

First, tomorrow's pioneers will undoubtedly be a highly diversified group of men and women, representing an extremely broad range of interests and abilities, Psychology has never been dominated by a single towering figure like Newton in physics or Darwin in biology, whose thought has given direction to virtually everyone else's work. Instead, psychology has been defined by a large group of individuals whose major interests touched on widely varying adjoining fields including philosophy, mathematics, politics, medicine, anatomy and physiology, linguistics, genetics, anthropology, and sociology.

Modern psychology clearly reflects the diversity of its originators. The American Psychological Association, the largest professional and scientific organization for psychologists, currently encompasses more than forty official divisions, each one devoted to a separate specialty interest. These include such varied fields as experimental psychology; physiological and comparative psychology; evaluation, measurement, and statistics; developmental psychology; personality and social psychology; the psychological study of social issues;

psychology and the arts; clinical psychology; industrial and organizational psychology; educational psychology; theoretical and philosophical psychology; psychotherapy; psychological hypnosis; humanistic psychology; and clinical neoropsychology. Further, individual psychologists routinely collaborate with experts from other fields in varied interdisciplinary ventures denoted by names such as "neuroscience," "sociobiology," and "psychohistory." Tomorrow's pioneers of psychology will be drawn from this richly varied and multidisciplinary setting, thus continuing their predecessors' traditions for diversity.

They will also share another quality that Wilhelm Wundt ascribed to himself and all other intellectual leaders when he declared, "We are all epigones."[1] The unusual term he used here derives from the Greek *epigonos*, for "born after," and literally means "descendants" or "successors." The word carries further interesting connotations, however, originating in ancient Greek mythology. According to legend, seven heroes tried to capture the city of Thebes, shortly after the tragic reign of King Oedipus. They fought valiantly but unsuccessfully, with six of the seven losing their lives. Years later their sons—called collectively "the Epigoni"—took up the task and captured the city, thus becoming the founders of a new Theban government. But while successful, their actions lacked the heroic quality of the original "seven against Thebes." Thus the term "epigone" has taken on a sort of double-edged meaning: On the one hand it connotes descendants or followers who bring their forebears' projects to fulfillment, while on the other it implies that their behavior is neither quite so original nor pursued quite so heroically as that of their predecessors. According to the *Oxford English Dictionary*, the term is sometimes taken to mean "the less distinguished successors of an illustrious generation."

Thus when Wundt made his statement, the "father" of modern academic and experimental psychology modestly acknowledged his own reliance upon foundations established by his illustrious predecessors. Several of those foundations have been described in the early chapters of this book: the mental philosophies of Descartes, Leibniz, and Kant, for example, as well as the experimental techniques originated by Donders, Fechner, and Helmholtz.

Wundt's assertion that we are *all* epigones—no matter how novel or even "revolutionary" the implications of our ideas—is fully supported by case studies of other major historical figures. Even the great Isaac Newton—a man not normally noted for modesty—admitted his dependence on predecessors with the help of a now-famous metaphor: "If I have seen further [than others], it is by standing upon the shoulders of giants."[2] We have seen in this book how Darwin's epoch-making theory of evolution built on the ideas of many others including Lyell, Malthus, and his own grandfather; and how Freud's psychoanalysis synthesized many earlier concepts ranging from Leibniz's "minute perceptions" to Charcot's "major hysteria." Pavlov's conditioned reflex theory derived immediately from Sechenov and more remotely from Descartes's conception of the reflex. And despite Descartes's position at the beginning of this book, it should be emphasized that he, too, was an epigone with innumerable important and influential precursors. His selection as the opening figure was largely arbitrary, since any book of limited and selective scope necessarily has to start *somewhere*. The historical survey *could* have begun much earlier, and Descartes's thought too could have been shown to be the culmination of many long traditions that preceded him.

Beyond doubt, tomorrow's pioneers will also be epigones like their predecessors, even as they break new intellectual ground in innovative ways. Consider the field of **cognitive psychology**, whose dramatic rise over the past forty years has been one of the major developments in recent psychology, and which is believed by many psychologists to represent the wave of the future. Both the "newness" and the "revolutionary" nature of this field have been highlighted in the title of Howard Gardner's admirably lucid survey written in 1985: *The Mind's New Science: A History of the Cognitive Revolution.*[3] Gardner shows how both terms are appropriate, in that cognitive psychologists apply tools and techniques developed only recently in the computer age, to the investigation of questions involving human knowledge, thought, and consciousness that had been ruled out of bounds by the previously dominant behavioristic ethos. Yet Gardner also shows that those questions have been basic to the Western intellectual tradition since the time of the ancient Greeks.

Thus when the new cognitivists look further back than the behaviorists against whom they immediately rebelled, they find ample historical company. If the likes of Descartes, Locke, Leibniz, and Kant could miraculously reappear in a modern cognitive laboratory, they would need some time to familiarize themselves with the techniques of the ongoing research. But they would feel immediately at home in the general debates about the *interpretation* of that research, for they helped shape the very nature of those debates.

I hope this book has shown that other pioneers of psychology would feel equally at home with the other important general debates that go on today—whether about the nature of the brain and nervous system, the respective roles of nature and nurture, the influence of unconscious factors, the measurement of intelligence, or the best way to practice psychotherapy, to name just a few. Thus tomorrow's pioneers—however diverse, innovative, and influential their contributions to these debates will turn out to be—are unquestionably participating in traditions that go far into the past, and that shall extend indefinitely into the future.

Notes

Chapter 1. René Descartes and the
Foundations of Modern Psychology

1. René Descartes, *Discourse on Method,* in *Discourse on Method and Meditations,* ed. and trans. L. J. Lafleur (New York: Library of Liberal Arts, 1960), pp. 7-8.

2. Ibid., p. 5.

3. Julian Jaynes, "The Problem of Animate Motion in the Seventeenth Century," in Mary Henle, Julian Jaynes, and John J. Sullivan, eds., *Historical Conceptions of Psychology* (New York: Springer, 1973), pp. 166-179.

4. Descartes, *Discourse,* p. 9.

5. Quoted in Jack R. Vrooman, *René Descartes: A Biography* (New York: G. P. Putnam's Sons, 1970), p. 23.

6. Ibid., pp. 49-50.

7. Charles Singer, *A Short History of Scientific Ideas to 1900* (London: Oxford University Press, 1962), p. 226.

8. Descartes, *Discourse,* p. 10.

9. Ibid., p. 15.

10. René Descartes, *Treatise of Man,* trans. Thomas Steele Hall (Cambridge, MA: Harvard University Press, 1972), p. 113.

11. Ibid., p. 21.

12. Jaynes, "Problem of Animate Motion," p. 171.

13. Descartes, *Treatise of Man,* p. 106.

14. Quoted in John Morris, *Descartes Dictionary* (New York: Philosophical Library, 1971), p. 15.

15. Descartes, *Discourse,* p. 24.

16. Ibid., p. 25.

17. René Descartes, *Passions of the Soul,* excerpted in Norman Smith, ed. and trans., *Descartes: Philosophical Writings* (New York: Modern Library, 1958), pp. 265-296, see pp. 275-276.

18. Adapted from Descartes, *Treatise of Man,* p. 84.

19. Descartes, *Passions of the Soul,* pp. 283-284.

Chapter 2. Philosophers of Mind:
John Locke and Gottfried Leibniz

1. Quotations reported in Maurice Cranston, *John Locke: A Biography* (London: Longmans, 1957), p. 417.

2. Ibid., pp. 76, 90.

3. Ibid., p. 100.

4. John Locke, *An Essay Concerning Human Understanding*, 5th edition, reprinted in two volumes (London: Dent, 1965/1706), Vol. I, p. xxxii.

5. Maurice Cranston, *Locke* (London: Longmans, Green & Co., 1961), p. 17.

6. Cranston, *John Locke*, p. 482.

7. Locke, *Essay*, 1, p. xxxv.

8. Ibid., p. 81.

9. Ibid., p. 77.

10. Ibid., p. 114.

11. Maurice von Senden, *Space and Sight: The Perception of Space and Shape in the Congenitally Blind before and after Operation* (New York: Free Press, 1960); Richard Gregory, *Eye and Brain* (New York: McGraw-Hill, 1973), pp. 193–198.

12. Locke, *Essay*, II, p. 133.

13. Ibid., I, p. 108.

14. Ibid., p. 336.

15. Quoted in D. B. Klein, *A History of Scientific Psychology: Its Origins and Philosophical Backgrounds* (New York: Basic Books, 1970), p. 456.

16. G. MacDonald Ross, *Leibniz* (New York: Oxford University Press, 1984), p. 26.

17. Ibid.

18. Quotations in Mary W. Calkins, *The Persistent Problems of Philosophy* (New York: Macmillan, 1907), p. 76.

19. G. W. Leibniz, *New Essays on Human Understanding*, translated and edited by Peter Remnant and Jonathan Bennett (Cambridge: Cambridge University Press, 1982), p. 48.

20. Ibid., p. 50.

21. Ibid., p. 52 (emphais added).

22. Ibid., p. 51.

23. Ibid., p. 53.

24. Ibid., p. 54.

25. Ibid., pp. 54–55.

26. Ibid., p. 56.

27. Ibid., p. 166.

Chapter 3. Physiologists of Mind:
Brain Scientists from Gall to Penfield

1. Quoted in Robert M. Young, *Mind, Brain and Adaptation in the Nineteenth Century* (Oxford: Clarendon Press, 1970), p. 10.

2. Quoted in Richard J. Herrnstein and Edwin G. Boring, eds., *A Source Book in the History of Psychology* (Cambridge, MA: Harvard University Press), p. 212.

3. Diagram adapted from John D. Davies, *Phrenology: Fad and Science* (New Haven, CT: Yale University Press, 1955), p. 6.

4. Quoted in J. M. D. Olmsted, "Pierre Flourens," in E. A. Underwood, ed., *Science, Medicine, and History* (New York: Oxford University Press, 1953), Vol. 2, pp. 290–302, see p. 296.

5. Ibid., p. 293.

6. Quoted in Young, *Mind, Brain and Adaptation*, p. 61.

7. Walther Riese, "Auto-observation of Aphasia Reported by an Eminent Nineteenth Century Medical Scientist," *Bulletin of the Institute of the History of Medicine* (*28*:237–242, 1954), p. 241.

8. Ibid., p. 237.

9. Quoted in Byron Stookey, "A Note on the Early History of Cerebral Localization," *Bulletin of the New York Academy of Medicine* (*30*:559–578, 1954), p. 571.

10. Quoted in Howard Gardner, *The Shattered Mind* (New York: Knopf, 1975), p. 68.

11. Adapted from Karl S. Lashley, *Brain Mechanisms and Intelligence* (Chicago: University of Chicago Press, 1929), p. 74.

12. Ibid., pp. 24–25.

13. Quoted in Keith Oatley, *Brain Mechanisms and Mind* (London: Thames and Hudson, 1972), p. 145.

14. Roberts Bartholow, "Experimental Investigations into the Functions of the Human Brain," *The American Journal of the Medical Sciences* (*67*:305–313, 1874), quotations from pp. 309, 311, 312.

15. Quoted in Peter Nathan, *The Nervous System* (Harmondsworth, UK: Penguin Books, 1969), p. 241.

16. Ibid., p. 239.

17. Wilder Penfield and Lamar Roberts, *Speech and Brain-Mechanisms* (Princeton: Princeton University Press, 1959), pp. 45–47.

18. Wilder Penfield, *The Mystery of the Mind* (Princeton: Princeton University Press, 1975), p. 80.

429

Chapter 4. The Sensing and Perceiving Mind:
Immanuel Kant, Hermann Helmholtz, and Gustav Fechner

1. Quoted in J. Bronowski and Bruce Mazlish, *The Western Intellectual Tradition* (New York: Harper and Row, 1960), p. 474.

2. Other major critical works by Kant included *Prolegomena to Any Future Metaphysics* (1783), *Critique of Practical Reason* (1788), *Groundwork of the Metaphysics of Morals* (1790), and *Critique of Judgement* (1790).

3. Quoted in Siegfried Bernfeld, "Freud's Scientific Beginnings," *American Imago* (6:163–196, 1949), p. 171.

4. Quoted in Leo Koenigsberger, *Hermann von Helmholtz*, trans. Frances A. Welby (New York: Dover, 1965), pp. 64, 73.

5. Ibid., p. 90.

6. See Gordon L. Walls, "The G. Palmer Story (Or, What It's Like, Sometimes, to Be a Scientist)," *Journal of the History of Medicine* (11:66–96, 1956).

7. Hermann von Helmholtz, "Recent Progress in the Theory of Vision," in Russell Kahl, ed., *Selected Writings of Hermann von Helmholtz* (Middletown, CT: Wesleyan University Press, 1971), p. 192.

8. Quoted in Nicolas Pastore, "Re-evaluation of Boring on Kantian Influence, Nineteenth Century Nativism, Gestalt Psychology and Helmholtz," *Journal of the History of the Behavorial Sciences* (10:375–390, 1975), p. 387.

9. Hermann von Helmholtz, "The Facts of Perception," in Kahl, ed., *Selected Writings of Helmholtz*, p. 381.

10. Quoted in Kahl, Introduction to *Selected Writings of Helmholtz*, p. xii.

11. See William R. Woodward, "Fechner's Panpsychism: A Scientific Solution to the Mind-Body Problem," *Journal of the History of the Behavioral Sciences* (8:367–386, 1972), p. 367.

12. "Ernst Heinrich Weber (1795–1878) on Weber's Law, 1834," in Richard J. Herrnstein and Edwin G. Boring, eds., *A Source Book in the History of Psychology* (Cambridge, MA: Harvard University Press, 1965), pp. 64–66, see p. 64 (emphasis added).

Chapter 5. Wilhelm Wundt and
the Establishment of Experimental Psychology

1. Figure 5–1 from Wilhelm Wundt, "Die Geschwindigkeit des Gedankens," *Gartenlaube* (1892: 263–265), p. 264.

2. Erwin A. Esper, *A History of Psychology* (Philadelphia: Saunders, 1964), p. vi.

3. Wilhelm Wundt, "Neuere Leistungen auf dem Gebeite der physiologischen Psychologie," *Vierteljahrsschrift für Psychiatrie in ihren Beziehungen zur Morphologie und Pathologie des Central-Nerven-Systems, der physiologischen Psychologie, Statistik und gerichtlichen Medicin (1*:23–56, 1867).

4. Letter from William James to Thomas W. Ward, November 1867, in Henry James, ed., *The Letters of William James*, 2 vols. (Boston: Atlantic Monthly Press, 1920), Vol. 1, pp. 118–119.

5. Quoted from "Selected Texts from the Writings of Wilhelm Wundt," translated and edited by Solomon Diamond in R. W. Rieber, ed., *Wilhelm Wundt and the Making of a Scientific Psychology* (New York: Plenum Press, 1980), 155–177, see pp. 157, 158.

6. Quoted in S. Diamond, "Wundt before Leipzig," in R. W. Rieber, *Wilhelm Wundt*, pp. 3–70, see p. 59.

7. William James, "Review of Wundt's *Principles of Physiological Psychology*," reprinted in W. G. Bringmann and Ryan D. Tweney, eds., *Wundt Studies: A Centennial Collection* (Toronto, Canada: C. J. Hogrefe, 1980), pp. 114–120, see pp. 116, 120. The review originally appeared unsigned in *North American Review (121*:195–201, 1875).

8. The article appeared in English translation as Wilhelm Wundt, "Spiritualism as a Scientific Question," *Popular Science Monthly (15*:577–593, 1879).

9. Quotes taken from Marilyn E. Marshall and Russell A. Wendt, "Wilhelm Wundt, Spiritism, and the Assumptions of Science," in Bringmann and Tweney, *Wundt Studies*, pp. 158–175, see pp. 169–171.

10. James McKeen Cattell, "The Psychological Laboratory at Leipsic," *Mind (13*:37–51, 1888), p. 38.

11. James McKeen Cattell, "The Time Taken Up by Cerebral Operations," *Mind (11*:220–242, 377–392, 524–538, 1886), Figure 5–2 from pp. 223, 225.

12. Ibid., p. 387.

13. Ibid., p. 534.

14. Quoted in Arthur L. Blumenthal, *Language and Psychology: Historical Aspects of Linguistics* (New York: Academic Press, 1975), p. 21.

15. Quoted in Thomas H. Leahey, *A History of Psychology: Main Currents in Psychological Thought*, 2nd edition (Englewood Cliffs, NJ: Prentice-Hall, 1987), pp. 189–190.

16. Ibid., p. 197.

Chapter 6. Charles Darwin and the Theory of Evolution

1. Charles Darwin, *The Autobiography of Charles Darwin* (New York: Norton, 1969), pp. 27, 28.

2. Ibid., pp. 47, 48.

3. Ibid., p. 60.

4. Frederick Burkhardt and Sydney Smith, eds., *The Correspondence of Charles Darwin*, Vol. 1 (Cambridge: Cambridge University Press, 1985), p. 160, Note 1, and p. 181, Note 4.

5. Darwin, *Autobiography*, p. 62.

6. Henslow to Darwin, 24 August 1831, in Burkhardt, *Correspondence*, pp. 128–129.

7. Darwin, *Autobiography*, p. 72.

8. Frederick Watkins to Darwin, 18 September 1831, in Burkhardt, *Correspondence*, p. 159.

9. Darwin to R. W. Darwin, 7 February 1831, ibid., p. 201.

10. Quoted in Alan Moorehead, *Darwin and the Beagle* (Harmondsworth, UK: Penguin Books, 1971), p. 47.

11. Ibid., p. 86.

12. Charles Darwin, *The Voyage of the Beagle* (New York: Bantam Books, 1972), p. 335.

13. Quoted in Moorehead, *Darwin and the Beagle*, p. 247.

14. These notebooks still exist and have now been published, offering an extraordinary inside look into the thought processes of one of the world's greatest scientists. See Paul H. Barrett et al., eds., *Charles Darwin's Notebooks, 1836–1844: Geology, Transmutation of Species, Metaphysical Enquiries* (Ithaca, NY: Cornell University Press, 1987).

15. Quoted from P. H. Gosse in Lynn Barber, *The Heyday of Natural History* (London: Jonathan Cape, 1960), p. 247.

16. Quoted in Howard E. Gruber, *Darwin on Man* (London: Wildwood House, 1974), pp. 234–235.

17. Quoted in Ronald W. Clark, *The Survival of Charles Darwin: A Biography of a Man and an Idea* (New York: Random House, 1984), p. 76.

18. Darwin, *Autobiography*, p. 123.

19. Quoted in Clark, *Survival of Darwin*, p. 84.

20. Ibid., p. 109.

21. T. H. Huxley to Charles Darwin, 23 November 1859, in Francis Darwin, ed., *The Life and Letters of Charles Darwin* (New York: Appleton, 1887), Vol. II, p. 27.

22. Quoted in Clark, *Survival of Darwin*, pp. 142–143. Clark also gives some slightly differing versions of the Oxford confrontation.

23. Charles Darwin, *On the Origin of Species by Means of Natural Selection, or the Preservation of Favoured Races in the Struggle for Life* (London: Murray, 1859), p. 488.

24. Charles Darwin, *The Descent of Man, and Selection in Relation to Sex*, 2nd edition (London: Murray, 1879), p.6.

25. Ibid., p. 66 (emphasis added).

26. Ibid., p. 126.

27. Charles Darwin, *The Expression of the Emotions in Man and Animals* (Chicago: University of Chicago Press, 1965; originally published 1872), p. 360.

28. Charles Darwin, "A Biographical Sketch of an Infant," *Mind: Quarterly Review of Psychology and Philosophy* (2:285–294, 1877), p. 285.

29. Ibid., p. 292.

30. Ibid., p. 294.

31. Darwin, *Autobiography*, pp. 108–109.

Chapter 7. The Measurement of Mind:
Francis Galton and the Psychology of Individual Differences

1. Francis Galton, *Inquiries into Human Faculty and Its Development* (New York: Dutton, 1907), pp. 19–20.

2. Francis Galton, *Memories of My Life* (London: Methuen, 1908), p. 35.

3. Ibid., pp. 27, 37.

4. Quoted in Karl Pearson, *The Life, Letters and Labours of Francis Galton*, 3 vols. in 4 (Cambridge, England: The University Press, 1914–1930), Vol. 1, p. 164.

5. Galton, *Memories*, p. 79.

6. The complete phrenologist's report is preserved in File 81 of the Galton Papers, housed in the Archives of the Library at University College London. Portions of it have been published in D. W. Forrest, *Francis Galton: The Life and Work of a Victorian Genius* (London: Elek, 1974), p. 37, and in Raymond E. Fancher, *The Intelligence Men: Makers of the IQ Controversy* (New York: Norton, 1985), p. 24.

7. Francis Galton to Darwin Galton, 23 February 1851, quoted in Pearson, *Life of Galton*, Vol. 1, p. 232.

8. Ibid., p. 240.

9. Ibid., Vol. 2, Plate XVIII.

10. Francis Galton, *Hereditary Genius* (Gloucester, MA: Peter Smith, 1972; originally published 1869), p. 45.

11. Ibid., p. 80.

12. Ibid., pp. 81–82.

13. Darwin to Galton, 3 December 1869, quoted in Galton, *Memories*, p. 290; Charles Darwin, *The Descent of Man, and Selection in Relation to Sex*, 2nd edition (London: Murray, 1879), p. 28.

14. Translated from Alphonse de Candolle, *Histoire des Sciences et des Savants depuis Deux Siècles* (Geneva: Georg, 1873), pp. 93–94.

15. de Candolle to Galton, 2 January 1873, in Pearson, *Life of Galton*, Vol. 2, p. 137.

16. Francis Galton, *English Men of Science: Their Nature and Nurture* (London: Frank Cass, 1970; originally published 1874), pp. 148–150.

17. Ibid., p. 12.

18. Francis Galton, *Inquiries into Human Faculty and its Development* (New York: Dutton, 1907), p. 172. This volume reprints Galton's original 1875 article on twins, along with several of his other shorter writings.

19. Galton, *Hereditary Genius*, p. 45.

20. Francis Galton, "Hereditary Talent and Character," *Macmillan's Magazine* (*12*:157–166, 318–327, 1865), p. 165.

21. Adapted from data in Pearson, *Life of Galton*, Vol. 3a, p. 14.

22. Francis Galton, "Co-relations and Their Measurement, Chiefly from Anthropometric Data," *Proceedings of the Royal Society* (*45*:135–145, 1888).

23. Galton, *Inquiries*, pp. 138, 145.

24. Quoted in Forrest, *Francis Galton*, p. 281.

25. For the full story of Burt's fraud, and the current state of separated-twin research, see Fancher, *The Intelligence Men*, Chapter 5.

Chapter 8. William James and Psychology in America

1. Kurt Danziger, "On the Threshold of the New Psychology: Situating Wundt and James," in Wolfgang G. Bringmann and Ryan D. Tweney, eds., *Wundt Studies: A Centennial Collection* (Toronto: Hogrefe, 1980), pp. 363–379, see p. 363.

2. Quoted in Arthur L. Blumenthal, *Language and Psychology: Historical Aspects of Psycholinguistics* (New York: Wiley, 1970), p. 238.

3. William James, *The Principles of Psychology*, 2 vols. (New York: Dover, 1950; originally published 1890), Vol. 1, pp. 192–193.

4. William James to Carl Stumpf, 6 February 1887, in Henry James, ed., *The Letters of William James*, 2 vols. (Boston: Atlantic Monthly Press, 1920), Vol. 1, p. 263.

5. Quoted in F. O. Mattheissen, ed., *The James Family: Including Selections from the Writings of Henry James Senior, William, Henry & Alice James* (New York: Knopf, 1961), p. 161.

6. Gay Wilson Allen, *William James: A Biography* (New York: Collier Books, 1967), p. 67.

7. Quoted in Jean Strouse, *Alice James: A Biography* (New York: Bantam Books, 1980), p. 128.

8. James, *Letters*, I, p. 58.

9. William James to Thomas W. Ward, *c.* November 1867, ibid., pp. 118-119.

10. William James, *The Varieties of Religious Experience: A Study in Human Nature* (New York: Penguin, 1982; originally published 1902), p. 160. James here attributed the passage to an anonymous French correspondent, but it has since been identified as autobiographical. See Mattheissen, *The James Family*, pp. 216-217.

11. James, *Letters*, I, pp. 147-148.

12. Quoted in Howard M. Feinstein, "The 'Crisis' of William James: A Revisionist View," *The Psychohistory Review* (*10*:71-80, 1981), p. 74.

13. James, *Letters*, II, p.16.

14. Allen, *William James*, p. 305.

15. James to Henry Holt, 9 May 1890, in James, *Letters*, I, pp. 293-294.

16. James, *Principles of Psychology*, I, pp. 237-238.

17. Ibid., p. 244.

18. Ibid., p. 121.

19. Ibid., p. 127.

20. Ibid., pp. 123-127.

21. Ibid., II, pp. 449-450.

22. Ibid., p. 463.

23. Ibid., pp. 561-562.

24. Ibid., p. 576.

25. James, *Letters*, II, pp. 2-3.

26. James to Theodore Flournoy, 28 September 1909, ibid., pp. 327-328.

27. Poem by Josiah Royce, quoted in Allen, *William James*, p. 471.

28. Quoted in Ruth Brandon, *The Spiritualists* (Buffalo, NY: Prometheus Books, 1984), pp. 245-246.

29. Quoted in Howard M. Feinstein, *Becoming William James* (Ithaca, NY: Cornell University Press, 1984), p. 301.

30. Quoted in Allen, *William James*, p. 494.

31. Sigmund Freud, "The Origin and Development of Psychoanalysis," *American Journal of Psychology* (*21*:181-218, 1910). The lectures have also been widely reprinted under the title *Five Lectures on Psycho-Analysis*, edited and re-translated from Freud's original German by James Strachey.

32. Quoted in Norma J. Bringmann and Wolfgang G. Bringmann, "Wilhelm Wundt and His First American Student," in Bringmann and Tweney, eds., *Wundt Studies*, pp. 176-192, see p. 178.

33. Edwin G. Boring, *A History of Experimental Psychology*, 2nd edition (New York: Appleton-Century-Crofts, 1957), p. 519.

34. Elizabeth Scarborough and Laurel Furumoto, *Untold Lives: The First Generation of American Women Psychologists* (New York: Columbia University Press, 1987), pp. 29-35.

35. Mary Whiton Calkins, Autobiography in Carl Murchison, ed., *A History of Psychology in Autobiography*, Vol. 1 (Worcester, MA: Clark University Press, 1930), pp. 31-62, see p. 31.

36. Scarborough and Furumoto, *Untold Lives*, p. 42.

37. Ibid., pp. 44-46.

38. Ibid., p. 117.

39. Edward Lee Thorndike, Autobiography in Carl Murchison, ed., *A History of Psychology in Autobiography*, Vol. 3 (Worcester, MA: Clark University Press, 1936), pp. 263-270, see p. 264.

40. Geraldine Joncich, *The Sane Positivist: A Biography of Edward L. Thorndike* (Middletown, CT: Wesleyan University Press, 1968), pp. 105-106.

41. E. L. Thorndike and R. S. Woodworth, "The Influence of Improvement in One Mental Function upon the Efficiency of Other Functions," *Psychological Review* (*8*:247-261, 1901).

Chapter 9. Psychology as the Science of Behavior:
Ivan Pavlov, John B. Watson, and B. F. Skinner

1. Ivan P. Pavlov, *Conditioned Reflexes: An Investigation of the Physiological Activity of the Cerebral Cortex* (New York: Dover, 1960), p. 3.

2. B. P. Babkin, *Pavlov: A Biography* (Chicago: University of Chicago Press, 1949), p. 214.

3. Ibid., p. 37.

4. Ibid., p. 110.

5. George A. Miller, *Psychology: The Science of Mental Life* (New York: Harper and Row, 1962), p. 189.

6. Quoted by W. Horsley Gantt, Introduction to I. P. Pavlov, *Conditioned Reflexes and Psychiatry* (New York: International Publishers, 1941), p. 35.

7. John Broadus Watson, Autobiography in Carl Murchison, ed., *A History of Psychology in Autobiography*, Vol. 3 (Worcester, MA: Clark University Press, 1936), pp. 271–281, see p. 271; also see Kerry W. Buckley, *Behaviorism and the Professionalization of American Psychology: A Study of John Broadus Watson, 1878–1958* (Ann Arbor, MI: University Microfilms International, 1982), pp. 1–3.

8. Watson, Autobiography, p. 272.

9. Ibid., pp. 274, 276.

10. Walter Van Dyke Bingham, Autobiography in E. G. Boring, H. S. Langfeld, H. Werner, and R. M. Yerkes, eds., *A History of Psychology in Autobiography*, Vol. 4 (Worcester, MA: Clark University Press, 1952), pp. 1–26, see p. 7.

11. Watson, Autobiography, p. 274.

12. Buckley, *A Study of Watson*, pp. 67ff.

13. John B. Watson, "Psychology as the Behaviorist Views It," *Psychological Review* (*20*:158–177, 1913), p. 159.

14. Ibid., p. 158.

15. John B. Watson, "The Place of the Conditioned Reflex in Psychology," *Psychological Review* (*23*:89–116, 1916), p. 89.

16. Watson, Autobiography, p. 278.

17. John B. Watson, *Psychology from the Standpoint of a Behaviorist* (Philadelphia: Lippincott, 1919), p. 200.

18. Ibid.

19. Ibid., p. 201.

20. Ibid., p. 214.

21. John B. Watson and Rosalie Rayner, "Conditioned Emotional Reactions," *Journal of Experimental Psychology* (*3*:1–14, 1920), p. 4.

22. Ibid., p. 5.

23. Ibid., p. 7.

24. Ibid., pp. 12–13.

25. Ibid., pp. 12, 14.

26. Buckley, *A Study of Watson*, pp. 178ff.

27. Ibid., Chapter 9.

28. Watson, Autobiography, p. 280.

29. Quoted in Richard J. Herrnstein, Introduction to John B. Watson, *Behavior: An Introduction to Comparative Psychology* (New York: Holt, Rinehart and Winston, 1967), p. xxii.

30. John B. Watson, *Behaviorism* (New York: Norton, 1970), pp. 94, 104.

31. John B. Watson, *Psychological Care of Infant and Child* (New York: Norton, 1928), pp. 40–41.

32. Ibid., pp. 81–82.

33. Quoted in Mufid James Hannush, "John B. Watson Remembered: An Interview with James B. Watson," *Journal of the History of the Behavioral Sciences* (*23*:137–152, 1987), p. 137.

34. Watson, Autobiography, p. 281.

35. B. F. Skinner, Autobiography in G. E. Boring and Gardner Lindzey, eds., *A History of Psychology in Autobiography*, Vol. 5 (New York: Appleton-Century-Crofts, 1967), pp. 387–413, see p. 407.

36. Ibid., p. 396.

37. B. F. Skinner, *Particulars of My Life* (New York: Knopf, 1976), p. 237.

38. Ibid., p. 249.

39. Ibid., p. 264.

40. Quoted in ibid., p. 298.

41. B. F. Skinner, "A Case History in Scientific Method," in Sigmund Koch, ed., *Psychology: A Study of a Science*, Vol. II (New York: McGraw-Hill, 1959).

42. Ibid., p. 362.

43. Adapted from F. S. Keller and W. N. Schoenfeld, *Principles of Psychology* (New York: Appleton-Century-Crofts, 1950), p. 45.

44. B. F. Skinner, *Walden Two* (New York: Macmillan, 1962), p. 264.

45. B. F. Skinner, *Beyond Freedom and Dignity* (New York: Bantam/Vintage, 1971), p. 76.

46. Skinner, Autobiography, p. 412.

Chapter 10. Early Hypnotists and the Psychology of Social Influence

1. Frank Pattie, "A Brief History of Hypnotism," in Jesse E. Gordon, ed., *Handbook of Clinical and Experimental Hypnosis* (New York: Macmillan, 1967), p. 13.

2. Quoted in Vincent Buranelli, *The Wizard from Vienna* (New York: Coward, McCann and Geoghegan, 1975), p. 59.

3. Ibid., p. 67.

4. Henri F. Ellenberger, *The Discovery of the Unconscious* (New York: Basic Books, 1970), p. 67.

5. Pattie, "Brief History," p. 21.

6. Stanley Milgram, *Obedience to Authority: An Experimental View* (New York: Harper and Row, 1974).

7. Quoted in Peter W. Sheehan and Campbell W. Perry, *Methodologies of Hypnosis: A Critical Appraisal of Contemporary Paradigms of Hypnosis* (New York: Erlbaum, 1976), p. 21.

8. Gregory Zilboorg, *A History of Medical Psychology*, (New York: Norton, 1967), p. 352.

9. Edwin G. Boring, *A History of Experimental Psychology*, 2nd edition (New York: Appleton-Century-Crofts, 1950), p. 121.

10. Zilboorg, *History of Medical Psychology*, p.352.

11. Ibid., pp. 352-353.

12. Boring, *History of Experimental Psychology*, pp. 123-124.

13. Ellenberger, *Discovery of the Unconscious*, p. 87.

14. Mark S. Micale, "The Salpêtrière in the Age of Charcot: An Institutional Perspective on Medical History in the Late Nineteenth Century," *Journal of Contemporary History* (*20*:703-731, 1985), p. 709.

15. Sigmund Freud, "Charcot," in James Strachey, ed., *The Standard Edition of the Complete Psychological Works of Sigmund Freud*, 24 vols. (London: Hogarth, 1953-1974), Vol. 3, pp. 9-23, see pp. 12, 13.

16. The reproduced painting is "Une Leçon Clinique à la Salpêtrière," by André Brouillet (1887).

17. Alfred Binet and Charles Féré, "La Polarisation Psychique," *Revue Philosophique* (*19*:369-402, 1885), p. 375.

18. Quoted in Theta Wolf, "Alfred Binet: A Time of Crisis," *American Psychologist* (*19*:762-771, 1964), p. 764.

19. Quoted in Theta Wolf, *Alfred Binet* (Chicago: University of Chicago Press, 1973), p. 50.

20. Ibid., p. 156.

21. Gustave Le Bon, *The Crowd* (New York: Viking, 1960), p. 29.

22. Ibid., pp. 35-36.

23. Ibid., p. 34.

24. Ibid., pp. 31-32.

25. Ibid., pp. 118-119.

26. Ibid., p. 125.

Chapter 11. Mind in Conflict:
The Psychoanalytic Psychology of Sigmund Freud

1. Sigmund Freud and Joseph Breuer, *Studies on Hysteria*, in James Strachey, ed., *The Standard Edition of the Complete Psychological Works of Sigmund Freud*, 24 vols. (London: Hogarth, 1953-1974), Vol. 2, p. 108.

2. Ibid., p. 7.

3. Letter from Sigmund Freud to Wilhelm Fliess dated 21 September 1897, published in Freud, "Extracts from the Fliess Papers," *Standard Edition*, Vol. 1, p. 259.

4. Sigmund Freud, *The Origins of Psycho-Analysis* (New York: Basic Books, 1954), p. 170.

5. Sigmund Freud, *The Interpretation of Dreams*, in *Standard Edition*, Vol. 4, p. 583.

6. Freud, *Origins of Phycho-Analysis*, p. 325.

7. Sigmund Freud, "Fragment of an Analysis of a Case of Hysteria," in *Standard Edition*, Vol. 7, p. 64.

8. Ibid., p. 86.

9. For more on the importance of *Project for a Scientific Psychology* see Raymond E. Fancher, *Psychoanalytic Psychology: The Development of Freud's Thought* (New York: Norton, 1973), especially Chapter 3.

10. Sigmund Freud, *Interpretation of Dreams*, in *Standard Edition*, Vol. 5, p. 536.

11. Adapted from Sigmund Freud, *New Introductory Lectures on Psycho-Analysis*, in *Standard Edition*, Vol. 22, p. 78.

12. See, for example, Peter Gay, *Freud: A Life for Our Times* (New York: Norton, 1988); Ernest Gellner, *The Psychoanalytic Movement* (London: Palladin, 1985); Jeffrey M. Masson, *The Assault on Truth: Freud's Suppression of the Seduction Theory* (New York: Farrar, Strauss and Giroux, 1984); and William J. McGrath, *Freud's Discovery of Psychoanalysis: The Politics of Hysteria* (Ithaca, NY: Cornell University Press, 1986).

13. W. H. Auden, "In Memory of Sigmund Freud," in *Collected Poems* (New York: Random House, 1976), pp. 215–216.

Chapter 12. The Developing Mind:
Alfred Binet, Jean Piaget, and the Study of Human Intelligence

1. The papers appeared in French in 1890, and may be found in English translation in R. H. Pollack and M. W. Brenner, eds., *The Experimental Psychology of Alfred Binet: Selected Papers* (New York: Springer, 1969), under the titles "The Perception of Lengths and Numbers in Some Small Children" (pp. 79–92); "Children's Perceptions" (pp. 93–126); and "Studies of Movements of Some Young Children" (pp. 156–167).

2. Binet, "Children's Perceptions," p. 120.

3. Jean Piaget, *The Construction of Reality in the Child* (New York: Basic Books, 1954), p. 79.

4. Translated from Alfred Binet, "Le Raissonnement dans les Perceptions," *Revue Philosophique* (*15*:408–432, 1883), p. 412.

5. Quoted in Theta H. Wolf, *Alfred Binet* (Chicago: University of Chicago Press, 1973), p. 61.

6. Alfred Binet, *Alterations of Personality*, in D. W. Robinson, ed., *Significant Contributions to the History of Psychology*, Series C, Vol. 5 (Washington, D.C.: University Publications of America, 1977; originally published 1891), p. 76.

7. Binet, "Studies of Movements of Children," p. 157.

8. Translated from Alfred Binet, *La Suggestibilité* (Paris: Schleicher, 1900); pp. 119–120 (emphasis added).

9. Translated from Alfred Binet, *L'Étude Expérimentale de l'Intelligence* (Paris: Schleicher, 1903), pp. 218–219.

10. Quoted in Wolf, *Alfred Binet*, p. 140.

11. Translated from Alfred Binet and Théodore Simon, "Sur la Necessité d'Établir un Diagnostic Scientifique des États Inférieurs de l'Intelligence," *L'Année Psychologique* (*11*:161–190, 1905), p. 164.

12. Translated from Alfred Binet and Théodore Simon, "Applications des Méthodes Nouvelles au Diagnostic du Niveau Intellectuel chez les Enfants Normaux et Anormaux d'Hospice et d'École Primaire," *L'Année Psychologique* (*11*:245–336, 1905), pp. 320–321.

13. See Theta H. Wolf, "A New Perspective on Alfred Binet: Dramatist of *Le Théâtre de l'Horreur*," *The Psychological Record* (*32*:397–407, 1982).

14. Alfred Binet and Thédore Simon, "Le Développement de l'Intelligence chez les Enfants," *L'Année Psychologique* (*14*:1–94, 1908), p. 85.

15. For accounts of the army testing see Daniel J. Kevles, "Testing the Army's Intelligence: Psychologists and the Military in World War I," *Journal of American History* (*55*:565–581, 1968), and Franz Samelson, "World War I Intelligence Testing and the Development of Psychology," *Journal of the History of the Behavioral Sciences* (*13*:274–282, 1977). Stephen Jay Gould's *The Mismeasure of Man* (New York: Norton, 1981) presents a scathing description of many of the deficiencies and inefficiencies in the actual conduct of the army testing.

16. Lewis M. Terman, "The Intelligence Quotient of Francis Galton in Childhood," *American Journal of Psychology* (*28*:209–215, 1917), and Catherine Cox, *The Early Mental Traits of Three Hundred Geniuses* (Stanford, CA: Stanford University Press, 1926).

17. See Daniel Goleman, "1,528 Little Geniuses and How They Grew," *Psychology Today* (*13*:28–43, February 1980).

18. Jean Piaget, "An Autobiography," in Richard I. Evans, *Jean Piaget: The Man and His Ideas* (New York: Dutton, 1973), pp. 105–143, see p. 138*n*.

19. Ibid, p. 111.

20. Ibid.

21. Ibid., pp. 118–119 (emphasis added).

22. Ibid., p. 128.

23. Jean Piaget, *Genetic Epistemology* (New York: Norton, 1970), p. 15.

24. Quoted in Evans, *Jean Piaget*, p. 53.

Afterword: Tomorrow's Pioneers

1. Quoted in D. B. Klein, *A History of Scientific Psychology* (New York: Basic Books, 1970), p. 878.

2. For an engaging discussion of Newton's saying see Robert K. Merton, *On the Shoulders of Giants: A Shandean Postscript* (New York: Free Press, 1965).

3. Howard Gardner, *The Mind's New Science: A History of the Cognitive Revolution* (New York: Basic Books, 1985).

INDEX

443

Index

Assayer, The (Galileo), 14
association, 265
  directed, 175-76
  free, 236, 360-64, 365
  paired technique of, 266
  word, tests of, 235-36
associationism, 51-52, 395, 404-5
astigmatism, 121
astronomy, 6, 11
  transit reading variations in, 149-50
atomism:
  as opposed by Gestalt psychologists, 168-75
  of Titchener, 168-70, 174-75
Aubertin, Ernest, 86-87, 88
Auden, W. H., 388
auras, in epilepsy, 99-100
axons, 73*n*

Bain, Alexander, 246-47, 252
Bartholow, Roberts, 98-99
Bastien and Bastienne (Mozart), 322
Beagle, H. M. S., 76*n*, 181, 182, 184, 186, 226, 244
  voyage of, 187-91, *188*
Beaumont, William, 280
Beaunis, Henri, 397-98
Bechterev, Vladimir M., 293-94
Beeckman, Isaac, 10-11
Behavior (Watson), 293
behaviorism, 94, 274, 275-319
  child care and, 301-2, 303-4
  creation of, 277, 291-93
  Descartes's influence on, 32, 276, 282
  education and, 314-15
  Locke's influence on, 52-53
  radical environmentalism and, 300-301, 304
  terminology of, 282-84
  see also operant conditioning; Pavlov, Ivan Petrovich; reflexes; reinforcement; Skinner, B. F.; Watson, John B.
Behaviorism (Watson), 299, 300, 301, 303, 307
Behavior of Organisms, The (Skinner), 312
behavior therapy, 387

Bell, Charles, 108
Bergson, Henri, 412
Berkeley, George, 51-52, 69
Bernays, Martha, 359
Bernheim, Hippolyte, 336-37, 344, 350, 360
Bessel, Friedrich Wilhelm, 149
Beyond Freedom and Dignity (Skinner), 316
Bible, literal interpretation of, 187, 196, 219
binary arithmetic, 56
Binet, Alfred, 393-401, *394*
  death of, 405
  early life and career of, 393-401
  hypnosis studies of, 344-47, 395
  individual psychology and, 397-401
  intelligence tests of, 230, 390-91, 401-5, 407
  legacy of, 405-6, 410-11
Binet, Alice, 390, 391, 396-97, 400-401
Binet, Madeleine, 390, 391, 396-97, 400-401
"Biographical Sketch of an Infant, A" (Darwin), 199, 202-4, 262
birds, evolution of, 199
blind spot, 121
blushing, 202
Boineburg, Baron Johann Christian von, 55, 58
Boring, E. G., 263
Bouillaud, Jean Baptiste, 86
Boyle, Robert, 39, 40, 42, 45
Boyle's law of gases, 39
Braid, James, 335, 337
brain, 72-104, *89*
  ablation of, 80-84, 87, 90, 95, 97, 285
  Aristotle's view of, 72-73, 89
  Broca's area of, 88, 90, 92, 93, 94
  Descartes's physiology of, 19-20, 27-28, 32, 73, 84
  equipotentially of, 96
  Flourens's ablation experiments on, 80-84, 87, 95
  frontal lobes of, 91
  Gall's work on, 74-75, 95
  halves of, 74, 90
  hologram theory of, 97-98

Index

Index

geology, catastrophism vs. uniformitarianism in, 187–88, 190
George I, King of England, 59, 61
Gesamtvorstellung (general ideas), 165–
66
Gestalt psychology:
atomism opposed by, 168–75
definition of, 170–71
founding of, 171
principle of organization of, 174
Gibson, Eleanor, 129
Gilman, Daniel Colt, 260
glass harmonica, 322, 325
God:
in Aristotelian cosmology, 6
Descartes on, 25–26
in Leibniz's philosophy, 63, 64
ground and figure, 173
Guillotin, Joseph, 327
Gulliver's Travels (Swift), 85

habit:
Bain on, 246–47, 252
James on, 246–47, 251–53
Haeckel, Ernst, 204n, 262
Hall, G. Stanley, 259–63
children's studies of, 261–62
early life and career of, 259–60
Freud and, 262, 263
James and, 258, 260, 261, 262,
263
recapitulationist theory of, 204n,
262
Wundt and, 259, 260, 261, 262,
263
Handbook of Physiological Optics
(Helmholtz), 118–19
Hartley, David, 52
Harvey, William, 18
Hell, Maximillian, 322, 323, 324
Helmholtz, Hermann, 110, 111–29,
143, 144, 267, 359
early life of, 111–12
education of, 112–14
hearing studies of, 118
mechanism of, 113, 118, 164, 244
military service of, 114, 115
nerve impulse experiments of, 116–
18
ophthalmoscope invented by, 115–
16

other achievements of, 128
on perception and sensation, 118–
19, 125–27, 129, 133, 134–35,
150, 152–53
place of, in psychology, 128–29,
140
vision studies of, 118–27, 196
Henri, Victor, 399
Henslow, John Stevens, Darwin and,
185–86, 189, 191
Heraclitus, 251
Hereditary Genius (Galton), 220, 223,
229
heredity:
of intelligence, 219–20, 222–24,
272–74, 300–301
see also nature-nurture question
*History of the Sciences and Scientists over
Two Centuries* (de Candolle),
224
"History of Twins, as a Criterion of
the Relative Powers of Nature
and Nurture, The" (Galton),
227
Hitler, Adolf, 385, 386
Hitzig, Eduard, 89–90, 98
Hobbes, Thomas, 50–51
hologram theory of brain, 97–98
Holt, Henry, 249, 250
Hooker, Joseph, 197
Horney, Karen, 387
Hume, David, 52, 105
Huxley, Thomas Henry, 226
Darwin supported by, 198
Huygens, Christian, 45, 56
hypnotism, 70, 320–53
early medical interest in, 332–35
first use of term, 335
hysteria and, 337–38, 342, 354
limits of, 329–30
Nancy-Salpêtrière controversy of,
336, 344–46, 350, 395, 396,
397
posthypnotic amnesia and, 329
posthypnotic suggestion and, 329
receptivity of subject and, 324,
329, 331–32, 335, 337, 350
stage, 329, 332, 335
see also animal magnetism; Faria,
José Custodio di; Mesmer, Franz
Anton; Puységer, Marquis de

449

Index